Seventh Edition

Unit Method of Clothing Construction

Seventh Edition

Unit Method of Clothing Construction

Phyllis Brackelsberg & Ruth Marshall
Iowa Association of Family and Consumer Sciences

WAVELAND
PRESS, INC.
Long Grove, Illinois

For information about this book, contact:
Waveland Press, Inc.
4180 IL Route 83, Suite 101
Long Grove, IL 60047-9580
(847) 634-0081
info@waveland.com
www.waveland.com

Illustrated by Leanne Glasnapp
Harriet Allen
Donna Danielson

10-digit ISBN 1-57766-054-4
13-digit ISBN 978-1-57766-054-5

Printed in the United States of America

11 10 9 8 7 6

CONTENTS

PREFACE

The *Unit Method of Clothing Construction* is a comprehensive reference and textbook for students, educators, and other professionals. The current edition has been revised extensively with new information and over 500 new illustrations. It is unique in that it includes information on sewing with the conventional lockstitch sewing machine and the serger or overlock machine. New chapters include "Components of Fit," "Bands, Plackets, Casing, and Yokes," "Special Fabrics," and "Working with Knitted Fabrics." Some of the new techniques added include: working with ribbings, bindings, and casings; five methods for making front placket bands; shoulder pads; tailored and dart sleeve plackets; and waistbands using commercial waistband interfacing tapes. The chapter on "Components of Fit" includes: factors affecting fit, characteristics of good fit, signs of poor fit, and recommended fitting sequence during construction.

This text covers all of the basic information needed by the beginning sewer. In addition, many construction alternatives for a procedure are presented to allow the sewer to select the method appropriate for the fabric used, skill level of the sewer, time available, and end use. The discussion of these methods provides the background necessary for selecting alternate procedures when working on specialty fabrics or when generating a construction plan for original garment designs. The principles discussed and techniques presented are applicable to garments for men, women, and children.

The *Unit Method of Clothing Construction* is sponsored by the Iowa Association of Family and Consumers Sciences. The royalties from the sale of this book are used for graduate scholarships in home economics programs at Iowa's three state universities. The IHEA is appreciative of the many hours of work given by the authors, Phyllis Brackelsberg and Ruth Marshall; by the illustrator, Leanne Glasnapp; and by the reviewers; Evelyn Shibles and Carolyn Kundel.

Sara Kadolph
President
Iowa Association of Family and
Consumer Sciences

Unit Method of Clothing Construction

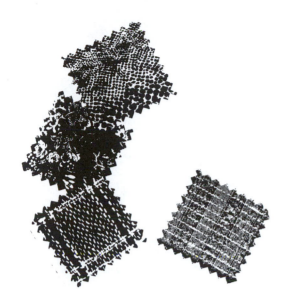

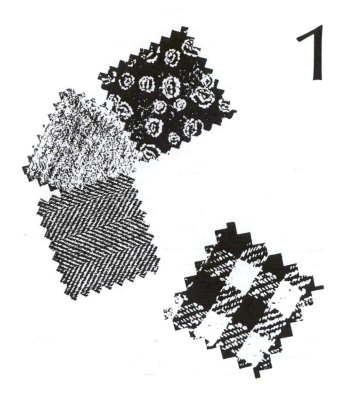

1 An Introduction to Unit Construction

The unit method of clothing construction is an organized way to assemble a garment. Units consist of the individual parts of the garment; new units are formed as these parts are joined.

Unit method suggests that the sewer complete as much work as possible on one unit before joining that unit with other parts of the garment. For example, in unit construction, cuffs and bands are attached to the set-in sleeve before the sleeve is set into the garment.

Unit method offers the following advantages:

—Time spent constructing a garment is minimized.

—Since parts of the garment that belong together are kept together, the sewer will spend less time hunting needed pieces.

—Sections of the garment will be handled less.

—The sewer can make good use of time by working on those units that require the time available.

Techniques for Unit Construction

Unit method of clothing construction makes use of both closed or open (flat construction) techniques. The garments in Figures. 1.1 and 1.2 illustrate the difference in the two techniques.

The shirt in Fig. 1.1 is constructed using the closed technique. The steps in completing the garment include:

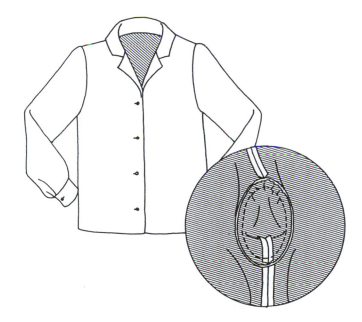

Fig. 1.1   Shirt with standard set-in sleeve illustrating the closed construction technique

1. Sew shoulder seams
2. Complete collar unit
3. Attach collar to garment

3

4. Complete sleeve unit
   a. Finish placket opening
   b. Attach cuff or band
5. Sew garment side seams
6. Attach sleeve to garment
7. Make buttonholes
8. Hem garment

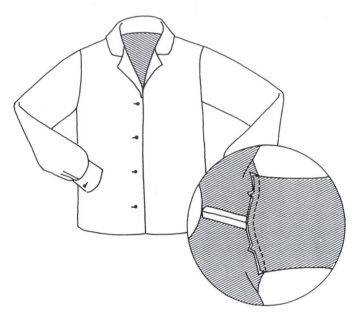

Fig. 1.2   Shirt with shirt-style sleeve illustrating the open construction technique

The shirt in Figure 1.2 illustrates open or flat construction techniques. The steps are the same as the closed technique through step 3.

1. Sew shoulder seams
2. Complete collar unit

3. Attach collar to garment
4. Complete placket opening on sleeve
5. Attach sleeves to garment at armscye
6. Sew underarm seams
7. Attach cuff or band
8. Make buttonholes
9. Hem garment

The open technique is used in most ready-to-wear garments, more often in men's wear than women's wear. It has been used less commonly for personally sewn garments, although advocates of quick techniques often suggest it as an alternative to closed construction techniques. For example, in open construction the band is attached to the sleeve before the underarm seam is sewn, a technique that may be quicker to do but that can result in mismatched edges. The sewer needs to evaluate this method for the desired results before deciding to adopt it.

Closed construction uses as its base the rule that lengthwise closings and seams are completed before crosswise seams. In closed construction, the sleeve band or cuff is attached to the sleeve after the underarm seam of the sleeve has been stitched.

The design of the garment will, in many cases, dictate the method of construction to use. However, in other instances, the sewer has the choice of open or closed construction, a choice that will be based on personal skill, the end use of the garment, and the desired effect.

Both techniques described use the open method through step 3 when the collar is attached to the garment. Having the garment flat for this procedure makes this task easier than trying to do it after the side seams have been stitched.

Before starting a garment, the efficient sewer will study the pattern guide sheet and make modifications in it to accommodate some of the suggestions made in this book. One such change might be to organize the construction process by units.

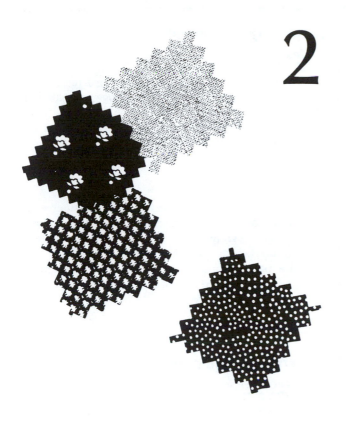

2 Sewing and Patternwork Equipment

A quick look in the notions section of any fabric department or store will reveal a myriad of sewing and patternwork equipment. The equipment needed by a sewer depends on the amount and type of sewing to be done. Some of the basic items needed for cutting, marking, measuring, and patternwork are described in this chapter.

Cutting Equipment

Pinking or Scalloping Shears

Pinking and scalloping shears come in various sizes and provide a decorative edge finish for fabrics that have little, if any, tendency to ravel. These shears are not recommended for use on most woven fabrics, and they are *not* used to cut out a garment.

Rotary Cutting Wheel

The rotary cutter is used with a special mat to protect the cutting surface from damage. Similar to a pizza cutter, this device works well for cutting suedes and leathers and, with care, it can be used for many firmly woven fabrics. Persons who have difficulty with the use of scissors and shears may find the rotary cutter an appropriate substitute.

Scissors

Scissors have handles of the same size, and the blades are usually less than 6 inches (15 cm) in length. A pair of scissors with 3–4 inch (7.5–10 cm) blades is convenient for cutting threads, trimming seams, and cutting buttonholes.

Shears

With one handle larger than the other, shears are more satisfactory for cutting fabric than scissors, whose handles are identical in size. The blades of shears are 5–12 inches (12.5–30.5 cm) in length, with those in the 7–8 inch (18–20.5 cm) range being practical for most apparel fabrics. The handles of shears can be bent or straight; bent-handled shears work well for cutting fabric because the blades operate parallel to the table. Shears are available for both the right-handed and the left-handed sewer.

Shears made of high-quality steel hold a sharp cutting edge. The blades should move easily and cut smoothly along the entire length of the blade. They should have sharp points that come together. These points are important for clipping, notching, and cutting buttonholes. Electric shears are available; some are battery operated, while others must be plugged into an electric outlet for operation.

There are many different weights of shears. The lighter-weight shears can be used successfully for general cutting on medium- to lightweight fabrics, but the points are not strong enough to be used for clipping and notching on most fabrics. The heavier shears are more versatile in that they can be used on all weights of fabric. The points are sturdy enough to be used for small details such as clipping, notching, and cutting buttonholes.

Marking Equipment
Fabric Marking Pen

The ink used in marking pens is water soluble. In most cases, these pens can be used safely to mark on either the right or wrong side of washable fabrics, but the sewer will want to check the marking on a scrap of fabric before using the pen on a garment. Some pens have the added feature of disappearing markings, where the ink will be invisible after a specified period of time, usually a few hours. Such a pen would be helpful in marking features such as buttonholes but not for construction details requiring a longer period of use. Markings made by the fabric marking pen should be removed before pressing, as the heat from the iron may make it more difficult to remove the markings after pressing.

Marking Pencil

Chalk marking pencils come in a variety of colors and often have a brush eraser on one end. Points of these pencils need to be kept sharp for accurate marking.

Tailor's Chalk

Chalk comes in a variety of colors and in two forms, thin square pieces and pencils. Edges of the chalk pieces and the pencils both can be sharpened to provide accurate markings. Wax-type chalk works well on wool, but it is not recommended for synthetic fabrics because it has a tendency to leave a stain after the garment is pressed.

Dressmaker's Carbon Paper

Dressmaker's carbon paper is available in white and several colors and is used with the tracing wheel to transfer pattern markings to the garment pieces.

Tracing Wheel

A tracing wheel is used with dressmaker's carbon paper to transfer pattern markings to the fabric. The wheel may be smooth or serrated. The serrated wheel has a tendency to damage some fabrics; the smooth wheel is recommended for knitted fabrics. The tracing wheel can be used without carbon paper when doing patternwork, including pattern alterations. (See Chapter 5.)

Measuring Equipment
Seam Gauge

For marking or for measuring short distances, a 4–6 inch (10–15 cm) adjustable seam gauge is helpful. It should be clearly marked and have an adjustable metal or plastic tab that slides easily but remains set at the desired place.

Tape Measure

A tape measure is used to take body measurements, to measure a pattern to determine needed alterations, and to align the grainline on the pattern with the straight grain of the fabric. It needs to be 60 inches (152 cm) long, be made of a nonstretchable material, have metal tips, and be numbered so that it can be read from either end. Tape measures are available in both English and metric measures.

Patternwork Equipment
Curved Stick

The curved stick, also called the hip curve, is shaped similar to the hip curve on the body and is helpful in drawing that or any area with a similar shape.

Flexible Curve

The flexible curve can be shaped into whatever configuration is needed for redrawing a pattern curve. It can be used also to compare a person's body contour to that of the pattern.

French Curve

The French curve is a clear plastic device used when redrawing curved lines or when tracing curved lines from the pattern to the fabric.

L-Square

The L-square, with one arm at a 90 degree angle to the other, provides a guide when marking perpendicular lines on a pattern or when placing a pattern on fabric straight of grain.

Ruler

A see-through ruler, 12–18 inches (30.5–45.7 cm) in length, is a must for doing pattern alterations and pattern designing. Rulers that have grid markings in both the lengthwise and crosswise directions are especially good for doing patternwork.

Yardstick or Meterstick

Measuring sticks aid in marking long, straight lines. They also can be used as an alternative to a commercial hem marker. Metal sticks and L-squares generally outlast wooden ones and are not apt to warp.

Sewing Accessories

Beeswax

Beeswax strengthens the thread and reduces its tendency to tangle and knot during hand sewing. Beeswax is available in a plastic holder with grooves to guide the thread through the wax before the thread is used.

Glue Stick

The glue stick comes in a tube and is used to hold two pieces of fabric together for sewing.

Hem Marker

An adjustable hem marker is an accurate guide for marking hems because it can be adjusted so that pins are inserted in the fabric at the exact fold line of the hem. A yardstick may be used if an adjustable hem marker is not available. Self-operated hem markers leave a chalk marking when a bulb is squeezed by the sewer.

Needles

Needles are available for both hand and machine sewing. The type selected depends primarily on the fabric type and weight.

Hand Sewing Needles

The needles most commonly used for hand sewing are "sharps" and "crewels" in sizes 8 to 10, the larger the number the shorter and finer the needle. Crewel or embroidery needles have longer eyes and may be easier to thread than sharps. Sharps and crewels should have sharp, straight points. Ballpoint needles, with a rounded point, are made especially for use with knitted fabrics.

Sewing Machine Needles

Sewing machine needles come in three basic types: sharp, ballpoint, and universal ballpoint. Sharp-pointed needles are designed to pierce woven fabrics. Ballpoint needles have a rounded point and are designed for use on knitted fabrics. The ballpoint will push the yarns aside, rather than pierce them. Universal ballpoint needles, designed with a special taper, can be used for either knits or wovens.

The United States and Europe use different num-bering systems for sizes of sewing machine needles. United States numbers range from 9 to 18, with the smaller numbers referring to finer needles and the larger numbers to larger or coarser needles. The European numbers range from 60 to 120, with needles increasing in size as the number increases. When working on a very fine fabric, the sewer would want to choose a size 9 or 60 needle; for a heavy, coarse fabric, the sewer would want at least a 16 or 100 needle. A larger needle is also desirable when topstitching with the heavier topstitching thread or with two strands of the regular sewing thread.

Special purpose needles are available for sewing fabrics such as leathers, vinyl, and denim and for tasks such as topstitching. Multiple needles are available for sewing two or three parallel rows of stitching at a time. With a double or triple needle attached to one shank, these needles are especially good for decorative topstitching. They require the use of the zigzag presser foot and throat plate.

The top end of a machine needle is rounded on one side and flat on the other. When inserting a needle into the machine the *rounded* side should face the direction from which the needle is threaded. Dull, bent, or damaged needles should be replaced immediately, as they will damage the fabric. If the needle snags a yarn in the fabric or if it sounds like it is "pounding" the material while sewing, it has been damaged and should be replaced.

Pins

Fine pins with sharp points are used when cutting and constructing garments from woven fabrics. Ballpoint pins are available for use on knits. Silk pins or dressmaker pins, size 15 or 16, are medium length, slender, and rustproof. Only rustproof pins should be used for sewing; those that are not rustproof may leave marks in the fabric. Longer pins can be purchased for use with heavier fabrics. Pins with large heads are available and may be easier for some sewers to handle, but they have a tendency to be thick and may be hard to use on some fabrics.

Pincushion

A pincushion is useful for keeping a supply of pins close to the work; one that can be worn on the wrist is considered a convenience by many sewers. Magnetic pincushions are available in the notions department of many fabric stores.

Seam Ripper

The seam ripper is used to remove unwanted stitches, either hand or machine. Care must be taken when using a seam ripper so as not to damage the fabric.

Seam Sealant

Seam sealant is a clear liquid that can be placed on edges of fabric to prevent raveling during the construction process. It is not durable enough to withstand many machine washings, so it should not be used as a permanent edge finish.

Thimble

A thimble is an aid for hand sewing. The thimble should be made of a hard, lightweight material (metal or plastic) in a size to fit the middle finger of the sewing hand.

Weights

Weights are used instead of pins when cutting patterns from fabrics that leave puncture marks, such as suedes and leathers. Weights are available in the notions section of the fabric store. Such objects as eating utensils (knives are especially effective) and canned goods may be used in place of the commercial weights.

3 Selecting and Using a Commercial Pattern

A personally sewn garment requires that the sewer select a commercial pattern and fabric. In addition, notions such as thread, buttons, zippers, and trims will be required. Many garments need a shaping or support fabric, such as an interfacing or a lining. This chapter will discuss the selection of the pattern; Chapter 4 will discuss choosing fabrics and notions.

The Pattern

Pattern companies produce a variety of patterns in a number of categories. These are shown in pattern catalogs where patterns are sold. Some companies have a range of styles for men, women, and children; others specialize in one type of pattern (e. g., for knitted fabrics only). Patterns are presented in the catalogs by sections for easy reference.

When selecting a pattern, a number of factors should be considered, including the sewing experience and ability of the sewer, personality and figure of the wearer, and garment end use. Patterns with few pieces and simple design details should be selected by inexperienced sewers. Some companies label these patterns as "Level I" or "Very Easy." Many pattern alterations and fitting problems can be eliminated, or at least minimized, by selecting patterns having extra fullness or ease in areas where figure irregularities are present.

Conventional patterns identified as "recommended for knits" can be used with either woven or knitted fabrics. The sewer may need to take a larger seam allowance when using this pattern with a stretchy knit since the pattern also can be used on woven fabrics. Patterns that are designated "for knits only" have less ease for fitting and should be used with stretchable knits only. The extra room needed for movement is provided by the stretch in the knitted fabric rather than being built into the design of the pattern. Many patterns designated "for knits only" have a guide on the back of the pattern envelope showing how much the fabric should stretch to be suitable for the pattern. For proper fit and appearance of the finished garment, this guide needs to be followed carefully. Some patterns designed for knitted fabrics make use of a seam allowance that is less than the standard 5/8 inch (1.6 cm).

Some pattern companies offer patterns that provide for easy fitting. Others produce patterns for use with specific sewing equipment such as the overlock or serger sewing machine.

The Pattern Envelope

Pattern pieces are folded and placed, along with a construction guide, in an envelope that contains a wealth of information. On the front of the envelope will be such things as the company name, pattern number, price, pattern size(s), and pictures of the different views available from this pattern. The latter is especially important because the view selected will determine the amount of fabric to be purchased.

The back of the pattern envelope provides some additional information for the sewer. A written garment description, which some pattern companies provide, may clarify details of the garment that are not evident from the drawing or photograph on the front of the envelope. This information, along with a sketch of the garment back and an indication of the number of pattern pieces, will provide a clue as to the difficulty of the pattern. As a general rule, the difficulty of a pattern increases as the number of pattern pieces increases. The back of the pattern envelope also contains finished garment measurements such as the width of pant legs or skirt hems.

Other information found on the back of the pattern envelope includes suggested fabrics, yardage requirements, and notions. Yardage requirements generally are given in both English and metric measures and are determined by the pattern size chosen, the view of the pattern being constructed, the width of the fabric, and whether the fabric has a nap. More fabric often is needed when napped fabric is chosen as pattern pieces must all be cut in the same direction. (See Chapter 4 for a discussion of napped fabrics.)

The sewer needs to study the back of the pattern envelope carefully before purchasing the pattern. Knowing the information on the pattern envelope helps the sewer to be efficient in purchasing all the needed fabrics and notions at one time, thus saving time and energy once the assembly process has begun. Patterns, once purchased, rarely can be returned to a store for exchange or refund.

Figure Types and Sizes of Patterns

Choosing a pattern involves selecting both a figure type and a pattern size. Both are based on *actual body measurements* and may or may not be consistent with ready-to-wear sizes. Patterns are available for women and girls, men and boys, and children. The latter category includes patterns for infants, toddlers, and children through size 14; designs for both boys and girls are available in each of the children's size categories.

Some pattern companies offer patterns proportioned for the taller-than-average and the shorter-than-average figure. There usually are fewer design offerings within these categories than for those found in the standard figure types.

Patterns for Women and Girls

Patterns for women and girls are proportioned to fit various figure types. They are designed for a *size, not an age*, and are available in misses', miss petite, junior, junior petite, young junior/teen, girls', women's, and half-size. The differences in body proportions for the figure types for girls' and women's patterns are shown in Figure 3.1.

Fig. 3.1   Difference in girls' and women's figure types

Misses' patterns are for the average female figure; therefore, the largest selection of patterns is found in this category.

Miss petite is designed for shorter misses' figures.

Girls' patterns are for the small, developing figure and have small bustline darts or ease in the underarm seam. These patterns are relatively short from shoulder to waistline.

Young junior/teen patterns fit the developing figure with a high bustline, and the patterns are shorter from shoulder to waist than misses' patterns.

Junior patterns are for the figure that is shorter waisted and has a higher bustline than the one that fits a misses' pattern.

Junior petite patterns are for the small, mature figure, shorter waisted than misses' but with the average bust-line position.

Women's patterns are designed for the larger figure with an average bust position.

Half-size patterns fit the short-waisted figure with a lower bustline. These patterns also are larger in the waist and hips than misses' patterns.

Patterns for Men and Boys

Men's and boys' patterns also are sized according to body types and are designed for a *body build, not an age*. They are available in men's, teen-boys', and boys' sizes; the differences in the body types are shown in Figure 3.2.

Men's patterns are for the adult male of average build with neck and shoulders fully developed.

Teen-boys' patterns are for the young male figure, smaller in the shoulders and narrower in the hips when compared to a man's figure.

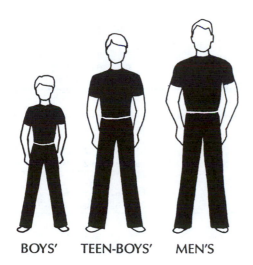

BOYS'   TEEN-BOYS'   MEN'S

Fig. 3.2   Differences in boys' and men's figure types

Boys' patterns are for the growing boy whose figure is starting to mature.

Determining Figure Type and Size of Pattern

The appropriate figure type needs to be determined *before* the pattern size is selected. The figure type and size of pattern needed are determined by comparing a person's actual body measurements with charts similar to those found in Figures 3.1 and 3.2 and in most pattern books. Figure type is based on back waist length, body proportion, and height. After the figure type has been determined, the correct pattern size is selected.

When determining the pattern size, the sewer uses actual body measurements and compares those to a pattern measurement chart (See Tables 3.1 and 3.2). If a person's body measurements do not correspond exactly to those in the chart, then the size which comes closest should be chosen and appropriate alterations made. Pattern sizes may vary depending on the type of garment being made. For example, a person may need a different size pattern for a garment that fits the upper half of the body than for one that fits the lower half.

The most difficult alterations to make are in the upper chest area; therefore, a pattern should be chosen to fit that area whenever possible. If a difference of 2 inches (5 cm) or more exists between the high bust and the full bust measurements, a woman should purchase the pattern that conforms most nearly to the high bust measurement and make the needed alterations in the bust area. For women with larger bust curves the garment selected by the high bust measurement will fit better through the shoulder and armhole areas than if the pattern had been selected by the full bust measurement.

Most women's patterns are made for the figure with a B-cup bust. Adjustments will need to be made for the woman whose cup size varies from the standard used by the pattern industry. Some patterns are printed with adjustments for different cup sizes which makes it easier to alter the bust area.

Many patterns are printed for more than one size; these may be convenient for the person who requires different sizes from one part of the body to another. The pattern guide sheet will provide directions for using the alternate sizes in the various areas. Care must be taken when cutting to preserve the design lines of the garment when moving from one size to another within the pattern. The multiple-sized patterns have cutting lines but no stitching lines marked on the pattern. When measuring the pattern to check for needed pattern alterations, one must first mark the stitching line so measurements will not include the seam allowance. The seam allowance marking is also important when making pattern alterations on these patterns if the change is to go to but not through a stitching line. (See Chapter 5 for a discussion on pattern alterations.)

TABLE 3.1
Standardized Pattern Measurement Chart for Women*

Inches

Misses'

Size	6	8	10	12	14	16	18	20
Bust	30½	31½	32½	34	36	38	40	42
Waist	23	24	25	26½	28	30	32	34
Hip	32½	33½	34½	36	38	40	42	44
Back Waist Length	15½	15¾	16	16¼	16½	16¾	17	17¼

Miss Petite

Size	6mp	8mp	10mp	12mp	14mp	16mp
Bust	30½	31½	32½	34	36	38
Waist	23½	24½	25½	27	28½	30½
Hip	32½	33½	34½	36	38	40
Back Waist Length	14½	14¾	15	15¼	15½	15¾

Junior

Size	5	7	9	11	13	15
Bust	30	31	32	33½	35	37
Waist	22½	23½	24½	25½	27	29
Hip	32	33	34	35½	37	39
Back Waist Length	15	15¼	15½	15¾	16	16¼

Junior Petite

Size	3jp	5jp	7jp	9jp	11jp	13jp
Bust	30	31	32	33	34	35
Waist	22	23	24	25	26	27
Hip	31	32	33	34	35	36
Back Waist Length	14	14¼	14½	14¾	15	15¼

Young Junior/Teen

Size	5/6	7/8	9/10	11/12	13/14	15/16
Bust	28	29	30½	32	33½	35
Waist	22	23	24	25	26	27
Hip	31	32	33½	35	36½	38
Back Waist Length	13½	14	14½	15	15⅜	15¾

Girls'

Size	7	8	10	12	14
Breast	26	27	28½	30	32
Waist	23	23½	24½	25½	26½
Hip	27	28	30	32	34
Back Waist Length	11½	12	12¾	13½	14¼
Approx. Heights	50	52	56	58½	61

Women's

Size	38	40	42	44	46	48	50
Bust	42	44	46	48	50	52	54
Waist	35	37	39	41½	44	46½	49
Hip	44	46	48	50	52	54	56
Back Waist Length	17¼	17⅜	17½	17⅝	17¾	17⅞	18

Half-Size

Size	10½	12½	14½	16½	18½	20½	22½	24½
Bust	33	35	37	39	41	43	45	47
Waist	27	29	31	33	35	37½	40	42½
Hip	35	37	39	41	43	45½	48	50½
Back Waist Length	15	15¼	15½	15¾	15⅞	16	16⅛	16¼

Centimeters

Misses'

Size	6	8	10	12	14	16	18	20
Bust	78	80	83	87	92	97	102	107
Waist	58	61	64	67	71	76	81	87
Hip	83	85	88	92	97	102	107	112
Back Waist Length	39.5	40	40.5	41.5	42	42.5	43	44

Miss Petite

Size	6mp	8mp	10mp	12mp	14mp	16mp
Bust	78	80	83	87	92	97
Waist	60	62	65	69	73	78
Hip	83	85	88	92	97	102
Back Waist Length	37	37.5	38	39	39.5	40

Junior

Size	5	7	9	11	13	15
Bust	76	79	81	85	89	94
Waist	57	60	62	65	69	74
Hip	81	84	87	90	94	99
Back Waist Length	38	39	39.5	40	40.5	41.5

Junior Petite

Size	3jp	5jp	7jp	9jp	11jp	13jp
Bust	76	79	81	84	87	89
Waist	56	58	61	64	66	69
Hip	79	81	84	87	89	92
Back Waist Length	35.5	39	37	37.5	38	39

Young Junior/Teen

Size	5/6	7/8	9/10	11/12	13/14	15/16
Bust	71	74	78	81	85	89
Waist	56	58	61	64	66	69
Hip	79	81	85	89	93	97
Back Waist Length	34.5	35.5	37	38	39	40

Girls'

Size	7	8	10	12	14
Breast	66	69	73	76	81
Waist	58	60	62	65	67
Hip	69	71	76	81	87
Back Waist Length	29.5	31	32.5	34.5	36
Approx. Heights	127	132	142	149	155

Women's

Size	38	40	42	44	46	48	50
Bust	107	112	117	122	127	132	137
Waist	89	94	99	105	112	118	124
Hip	112	117	122	127	132	137	142
Back Waist Length	44	44	44.5	45	45	45.5	46

Half-Size

Size	10½	12½	14½	16½	18½	20½	22½	24½
Bust	84	89	94	99	104	109	114	119
Waist	69	74	79	84	89	96	102	108
Hip	89	94	99	104	109	116	122	128
Back Waist Length	38	39	39.5	40	40.5	40.5	41	41.5

SKIRTS, PANTS, AND SHORTS

Inches

Misses'

Waist	23	24	25	26½	28	30	32	34
Hip	32½	33½	34½	36	38	40	42	44

Junior

Waist	22½	23½	24½	25½	27	29
Hip	32	33	34	35½	37	39

Junior Petite

Waist	22	23	24	25	26	27
Hip	31	32	33	34	35	36

Young Junior/Teen

Waist	22	23	24	25	26	27
Hip	31	32	33½	35	36½	38

Women's

Waist	35	37	39	41½	44	46½	49
Hip	44	46	48	50	52	54	56

Centimeters

Misses'

Waist	58	61	64	67	71	76	81	87
Hip	83	85	88	92	97	102	107	112

Junior

Waist	57	60	62	65	69	74
Hip	81	84	87	90	94	99

Junior Petite

Waist	56	58	61	64	66	69
Hip	79	81	84	87	89	92

Young Junior/Teen

Waist	56	58	61	64	66	69
Hip	79	81	85	89	93	97

Women's

Waist	89	94	99	105	112	118	124
Hip	112	117	122	127	132	137	142

*Approved by the Measurement Standard Committee of the Pattern Fashion Industry.

TABLE 3.2
Standardized Pattern Measurement Chart for Men*

	Inches								Centimeters							
Men's																
Size	**34**	**36**	**38**	**40**	**42**	**44**	**46**	**48**	**34**	**36**	**38**	**40**	**42**	**44**	**46**	**48**
Chest	34	36	38	40	42	44	46	48	87	92	97	102	107	112	117	122
Waist	28	30	32	34	36	39	42	44	71	76	81	87	92	99	107	112
Hip (seat)	35	37	39	41	43	45	47	49	89	94	99	104	109	114	119	124
Neckband	14	14½	15	15½	16	16½	17	17½	35.5	37	38	39.5	40.5	42	43	44.5
Shirt sleeve	32	32	33	33	34	34	35	35	81	81	84	84	87	87	89	89
Teen-Boys'																
Size	**14**		**16**		**18**		**20**		**14**		**16**		**18**		**20**	
Chest	32		33½		35		36½		81		85		89		93	
Waist	27		28		29		30		69		71		74		76	
Hip (seat)	32½		34		35½		37		83		87		90		94	
Neckband	13½		14		14½		15		34.5		35.5		37		38	
Boys'																
Size	**7**		**8**		**10**		**12**		**7**		**8**		**10**		**12**	
Chest	26		27		28		30		66		69		71		76	
Waist	23		24		25		26		58		61		64		66	
Hip (seat)	27		28		29½		31		69		71		75		79	
Neckband	11¾		12		12½		13		30		31		32		33	

*Approved by the Measurement Standard Committee of the Pattern Fashion Industry.

Patterns for skirts, pants, and shorts are sized according to waist and hip measurements. The waist measurement is used to determine the pattern size for skirts and pants that have fullness through the hips. The hip measurement is used to determine the size for fitted skirts, pants, and shorts.

Mens' shirt patterns are purchased by chest and/or neck size, mens' jacket patterns by chest size.

While pattern sizes are based on actual body measurements, the paper pattern will contain additional room, or ease, in certain parts to provide for movement and comfort. The amount of *comfort or wearing ease* varies from one pattern company to another, from one type of pattern to another, and from one area of the body to another. Minimum amounts of ease required in certain areas of a garment are listed in Tables 3.3 and 3.4. Those patterns designed "for knits only" will have a minimum of comfort ease allotted. Many patterns also contain *design or style ease*, which is additional fullness added to a pattern through the use of design features such as tucks, gathers, pleats, or flare.

Taking Body Measurements

Body measurements are used not only to help determine the correct size pattern to buy but also to decide pattern alterations to make. Therefore, one must be extremely careful to take accurate body measurements and, thus, avoid costly errors.

All body measurements are taken over the type of undergarments to be worn with the garment. Areas to be measured for taking upper body measurements are numbered and illustrated in Figures 3.3 and 3.4; locations for taking lower body measurements are illustrated in Figure 3.5. The numbers correspond to the outlined instructions that follow and to the numbers in Tables 3.3 and 3.4.

Body measurements are taken with the tape measure snug but not tight. The person doing the measuring needs to hold the tape measure in such a way that the fingers are not included in the measurement.

As the measurements are taken, they can be recorded in Tables 3.3 or 3.4. Place the actual body measurements in column 1; those used to determine the pattern size and figure type are so labeled. To these measurements add the minimum ease allowances found in column 2. Adding columns 1 and 2 produces column 3, the minimum required. The pattern measurements recorded in column 4 are taken from the actual paper pattern pieces, not including seam allowances, darts, tucks, or gathers. Record the differences between columns 3 and 4 in column 5; these indicate the needed alterations. The amount of ease needed in a garment will vary by personal preference, the type of fabric used, and the design of the garment. Less ease is required for knitted fabrics than for most woven fabrics. More ease will be needed if there is design or style ease added to the design in addition to the comfort ease. More discussion on the use of this chart for doing pattern alterations is found in Chapter 5.

To insure accuracy, another person's help is needed when taking body measurements. Before taking any measurements, certain body points need to be located. A washable pen or soft lead pencil can be used to mark these locations on the body.

1. The natural waistline can be located by tieing a

TABLE 3.3
Measurement Chart for Women

	(1) Body measure- ment	(2) Ease to be added	(3) Minimum required (1 + 2)	(4) Pattern measure- ment	(5) Alteration (Compare 3 + 4)
Upper Body					
1. High bust		This measurement is compared to the full bust measurement for the purpose of selecting pattern size.			
2. Full bust*		3–5″ (7.5–12.5 cm)			
3. Center front bodice length		¼–½″ (6–13 mm)			
4. Center of shoulder to bust tip					
5. Center back bodice length*		¼–½″ (6–13 mm)			
6. Back shoulder width		½–1″ (1.3–2.5 cm)			
a. Center back neck to back shoulder width level					
7. Shoulder seam length					
Sleeves					
8. Upper arm circumference		2–3″ (5–7.5 cm)			
9. Arm length a. Shoulder to elbow					
b. Shoulder to wrist					
10. Wrist circumference		½–1″ (1.3–2.5 cm)			
Lower Body					
11. Waist*		1″ (2.5 cm)			
12. Full hip (seat)*		2–3″ (5–7.5 cm)			
a. Waist to full hips					
13. Upper leg circumference		2″ or more (5 cm or more)			
14. Pants outseam (side seam)					
15. Crotch depth		½–1″ (1.3–2.5 cm)			
16. Crotch length		½–1″ (1.3–2.5 cm)			
17. Skirt length					
18. High hip, 3″ (7.5 cm) below waist		1–1½″ (2.5–3.8 cm)			
19. Thigh—full body circumference		2–3″ (5–7.5 cm)			
a. Waist to full thigh circumference					

*Basic measurements for pattern selection.

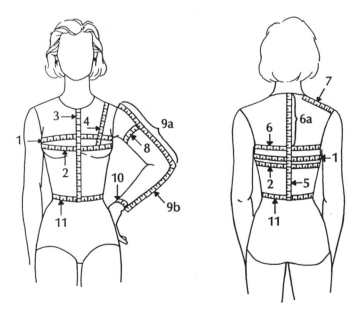

Fig. 3.3 Location for taking upper body measurements for women

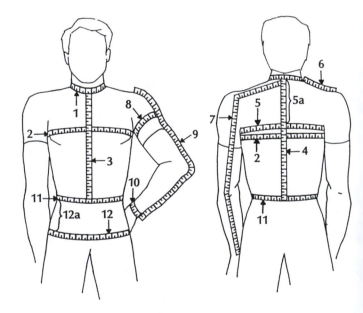

Fig. 3.4 Location for taking upper body measurements for men

TABLE 3.4
Measurement Chart for Men

	(1) Body measure- ment	(2) Ease to be added	(3) Minimum required (1 + 2)	(4) Pattern measure- ment	(5) Alteration (Compare 3 + 4)
Upper Body					
1. Neck*		½″ (1.3 cm)			
2. Chest*		3–5″ (7.5–12.5 cm)			
3. Center front waist length		¼–½″ (6–13 mm)			
4. Center back waist length		¼–½″ (6–13 mm)			
5. Back shoulder width		1–1¼″ (2.5–3.2 cm)			
a. Center back neck to back shoulder width level					
6. Shoulder seam length					
Sleeves					
7. Shirt sleeve length					
8. Upper arm circumference		2–3″ (5–7.5 cm)			
9. Arm length					
10. Wrist circumference		½–1″ (1.3–2.5 cm)			
Lower Body					
11. Waist*		1″ (2.5 cm)			
12. Full hip (seat)*		2–3″ (5–7.5 cm)			
a. Waist to full hips					
13. Upper leg circumference		2″ or more (5 cm or more)			
14. Pants outseam (side seam)					
15. Crotch depth		½–1″ (1.3–2.5 cm)			
16. Crotch length		½–1″ (1.3–2.5 cm)			

*Basic measurements for pattern selection.

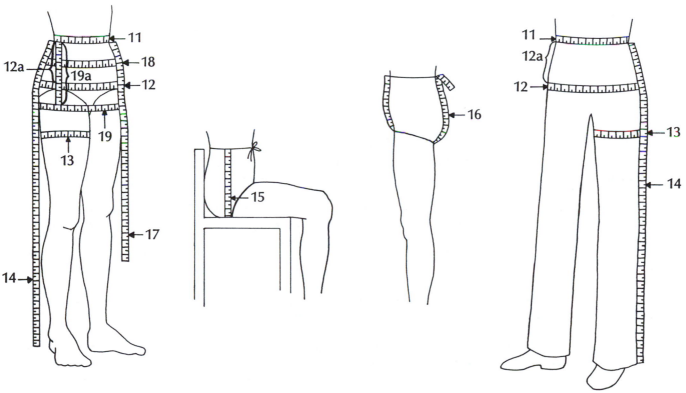

Fig. 3.5   Location for taking lower body
measurements

string or a piece of 1/4 inch (6 mm) elastic around the waist and adjusting it to the appropriate location. This string should be left on the body throughout the measuring process, as several measurements are dependent upon having the waistline defined. Always measure to the *bottom* of the string or elastic when taking body measurements.

2. The base of the neckline can be determined in several ways.

a. A thin chain necklace or string can be placed around the neck and adjusted to be in the appropriate location.

b. The base at the back of the neck corresponds to the top (usually the most prominent) vertebra. This point can be located by bending the head slightly forward, and noting the location of the top vertebra.

c. The base of the neck in the front is across the hollow in the neck and is just above the prominent bones of the shoulder blade.

d. At the shoulder, the base of the neck can be located by shrugging the shoulder and noting where an indentation forms.

3. The shoulder end can be located by raising the arm and marking the indentation. This mark corresponds to the end point of the shoulder.

4. The armscye (or armhole) line corresponds to where a regular set-in sleeve would be joined to the garment. The line should appear to fall straight down from the shoulder end point and should pass through the front arm crease. The arm should hang loosely at the side of the body. A mark should be placed in both the front and back at the arm crease or the point where the arm joins the body. To help define this line, a large rubber band or string can be placed around the armhole and adjusted to be in the appropriate location.

Taking Women's Upper Body Measurements

Note: All vertical measurements should be taken to the bottom of the waistline tape.

1. The *high bust* is measured around the back and chest just above the bust with the tape measure parallel to the floor.

2. The *full bust measurement* is taken over the fullest part of the bust with the tape measure parallel to the floor.

3. The *center front bodice length* is taken from the base of the neck in the front to the waistline.

4. The *center of the shoulder to bust tip* is taken from the center of the shoulder seam to the tip of the bust. A separate measurement may need to be taken on each side, especially if the person's body is asymmetrical.

5. The *center back bodice length* is taken from the base of the neck at center back to the waistline.

6. The *back shoulder width* is taken at the point where the arm joins the body from armhole to armhole, or from arm crease to arm crease, approximately 7 inches (18 cm) below the base of the neck. For this measurement, the arms should hang relaxed to the side and the tape measure should be parallel to the floor.

a. *Center back neck to back shoulder width level* is determined after taking the back shoulder width. It is the distance from center back neck to the point where the back shoulder width measurement is taken.

7. The *shoulder seam length* is measured from the base of the neck at the shoulder to the end of the shoulder or arm socket. To determine the shoulder end raise the arm slightly and feel the indentation where the arm joins the body.

8. The *upper arm circumference* measurement is taken with the arm bent and the fist clinched, and it goes around the fullest part of the upper arm.

9. *Arm length* is taken in two measurements.

a. The *arm length, shoulder to elbow measurement* is taken with the arm bent and extends from the end of the shoulder or arm socket to the point of the elbow.

b. The *arm length, shoulder to wrist measurement* also is taken with the arm bent, and extends from the end of the shoulder or arm socket over the elbow to just below the wrist bone.

10. The *wrist circumference* is taken around the wrist below the wrist bone.

Taking Men's Upper Body Measurements

Note: All vertical measurements should be taken to the bottom of the waistline tape.

1. The *neck measurement* extends around the entire neck. One-half inch (1.3 cm) ease needs to be added to this measurement to compare it to ready-to-wear shirt neck measurements.

2. The *chest measurement* is taken around the fullest part of the chest with the tape measure parallel to the floor.

3. The *center front waist length* is measured from the base of the neck at center front to an established waistline.

4. The *center back waist length* extends from the base of the neck at center back to the waistline.

5. The *back shoulder width* measurement goes across the fullest part of the shoulder blades from one armhole or arm crease to the other. For men, this measurement is taken about 8 inches (20.5 cm) below the base of the neck. The arms should hang comfortably at the side for this measurement.

a. *Center back neck to back shoulder width level* is determined after taking the back shoulder width. It is the distance from center back neck to the point where the back shoulder width measurement is taken.

6. The *shoulder seam length* is measured from the

base of the neck at the shoulder to the end of the shoulder or arm socket. To determine the shoulder end raise the arm slightly and feel the indentation where the arm joins the body.

7. The *shirt sleeve length* is taken with the arm slightly bent and extends from the base of the neck at center back across the shoulder over the elbow to just below the wrist bone.

8. The *upper arm circumference* is measured around the fullest part of the upper arm with the tape measure parallel to the floor.

9. The *arm length* is taken from the end of the shoulder to just below the wrist bone with the arm slightly bent.

10. The *wrist circumference* is measured just below the wrist bone.

Taking Lower Body Measurements

Note: All vertical measurements should begin at the bottom of the waistline tape.

11. The *waist* measurement goes around the natural waistline with the tape measure parallel to the floor. Locate the natural waistline on women by bending from side to side at the waistline.

12. The *full hip* is a measurement that will be taken at a different place on each individual. When taking this measurement the tape measure should be parallel to the floor and located at the fullest part of the hip and seat. Examine the body contour from the side view to determine the level of the fullest part of the seat.

a. The *waist to the fullest part of the hips* is the distance from the waistline along the side seam to the point where the full hip measurement was taken.

13. The *leg circumference* is taken around each leg at the fullest part of the thigh.

14. The *pants outseam or side seam length* extends from the waist to the desired pants length.

15. *Crotch depth* is measured with the person seated erect on a hard, flat surface. The tape measure is placed at the waistline and extends over the curve on the side of the body to the flat surface.

16. *Crotch length* extends from the front waistline between the legs to the back waistline. This measurement gives one amount for the entire crotch length. A separate front and back crotch length can be determined by measuring from the waistline in the front and in the back to the inseam. One way to accomplish this is to attach a weight to a string and to tie the string to a tape measure in such a way that the string can be moved along the tape. The weighted string can be adjusted to swing perpendicular to the floor between the legs; its location provides the dividing point between the front and back crotch length measurements.

17. The *skirt length* is determined by measuring from the waistline to the appropriate skirt length at the side seam or at center front. Skirt lengths vary widely with fashion and with skirt type.

18. The *high hip circumference* is taken 3 inches (7.5 cm) below the waist and goes around the body with the tape measure parallel to the floor. The 3 inch (7.5 cm) measure is located on the side of the body 3 inches (7.5 cm) below the waistline and can be marked with a pin placed in the undergarments.

19. The *thigh circumference measurement* is taken with the legs together and extends around both legs at the fullest part of the thigh. The tape measure remains parallel to the floor. This measurement is needed only when the thigh circumference is larger than the full hip circumference.

a. The *waist to the fullest part of the thighs* is the distance from the waistline along the side seam to the point where the thigh circumference measurement was taken.

Body measurements may be taken from a correctly fitted garment with set-in sleeves or from a pair of pants. These measurements should be recorded in the third column of the Measurement Chart, since the garment will have the desired amount of ease.

4 Selecting Fabric and Notions

Apparel fabrics are made of either natural or man-made fibers and can be either woven or knitted. The behavior of the fabric depends on the fiber content, yarn construction, fabric construction, and the finishes. Each fiber gives a different quality to the fabric; the blending of fibers can give the fabric the advantage of the individual fibers. Knowing the fiber content of a fabric is important; it helps to determine the care of the finished garment as well as the appropriate thread and other notions to use during construction. Other fabric properties that are given on the label (e.g., permanent press, preshrunk, colorfast) also are important and should be noted. Fabric properties such as yarn size, yarn count, and amount of twist in the yarn also influence the choices of construction techniques. A thorough and complete knowledge of the fabric is needed before beginning the assembly process.

The fashion fabric chosen should be appropriate for the garment style. Tailored garments require firm fabrics; designs with soft gathers or draped lines need pliable, lightweight fabrics. Garments with many construction details require fabrics with little, if any, design detail. Garment designs with few seams and details may be made in either solid color or patterned fabrics. The illustrations on the pattern envelope indicate the type or types of fabrics appropriate for the garment. In addition, a list of appropriate fabrics appears on the back of the pattern envelope. Studying ready-to-wear also is helpful in determining fabrics appropriate for various garment designs.

The fabric selected should be becoming to the wearer. To determine how the fabric will look, one can drape at least two yards of the material over the shoulders and look in a full-length mirror. It is important to evaluate the effects of fabric color and texture on skin tones, hair and eye color, and body size. Color can enhance the natural color of the wearer and draw attention to areas of the garment where color contrasts are used. Certain colors may increase the apparent size of the body, whereas other colors may optically decrease body size.

Texture in a fabric includes how a fabric looks as well as how it feels. Smooth, shiny fabrics reflect light and tend to enlarge the figure, whereas dull textures absorb light and are less likely to enlarge body size. Fabrics that stretch or cling to the body will reveal body contours, while crisp fabrics will fall away from the body and be less likely to show figure characteristics. Rough, coarse fabrics, or thick fabrics, such as napped or pile fabrics, will tend to increase body size.

The quality of the fabric should be determined before it is cut from the bolt. The following questions should be considered when evaluating quality.

Construction

—Is the fabric firmly woven or knitted?
—Will the yarns pull away from the seam lines?
—Are there any irregularities or flaws?

—Do fiber balls (pills) form when fabric layers are rubbed together?

—If the fabric stretches, does it return to its original size and shape?

Dyeing or Printing

—Is the dyeing or printing even?
—Is there any discoloration along the fold line?
—Does the color rub or flake off?
—Is there any visible powder when fabric layers are rubbed together?
—Are geometric prints or plaids printed on grain?

Fabric Finishes

—Is the fabric wrinkle resistant?
—Are heat set, or permanent press, fabrics finished on grain?

Fabric Grain

Woven Fabric

Grain refers to the direction of yarns in woven fabric (Fig. 4.1). Fabric is woven with the lengthwise and crosswise yarns at right angles to each other. Lengthwise yarns run parallel to the selvage; crosswise yarns run perpendicular to the selvage. *Selvages* are the firmly woven lengthwise finished edges of woven fabric. The lengthwise yarns (warp) usually are stronger and stretch less than the crosswise yarns (filling). The crosswise

yarns occasionally may be heavier and stronger as in ribbed fabrics, and usually have more stretch than the lengthwise yarns. *True bias* makes a 45 degree angle across the lengthwise and crosswise yarns and is the direction on woven fabric having the greatest stretch. *Bias* (also called *garment bias*) is any direction on a fabric that does not follow exactly a lengthwise or a crosswise yarn. *Garment bias* is any angle between true bias and the lengthwise or crosswise grain.

The grainline marking is indicated on the pattern piece by a straight line with an arrow at each end. Most pattern pieces are placed on the fabric with this grainline marking parallel to the selvage (i.e., on lengthwise grain). Garment pieces sometimes are cut on the crosswise grain to achieve a special effect such as when cutting striped fabric for the shoulder yoke. Garment pieces also are cut on true bias to achieve an effect and to avoid matching of pieces such as cuffs and yokes cut from plaid fabrics.

On-grain fabric has been finished with the crosswise yarns at right angles to the lengthwise yarns. *Off-grain fabric* yarns are not at right angles to each other. Fabric should be straightened, when possible, so that it is *on-grain* before laying out the pattern. If a fabric is not on-grain before cutting, the finished garment may hang unevenly after several launderings.

Knitted Fabrics

Knitted fabrics are made from a series of interlocking loops, which provides greater flexibility or stretch than most woven fabrics. The construction of knitted fabrics varies, as it does with woven fabrics, producing a wide variety of fabrics with different degrees of stretch. The degree of stretch must be considered when selecting patterns and sewing with any knitted fabric.

The *wale* refers to the vertical row of loops in knitted fabric. A *course* is a row of loops in the crosswise direction (Fig. 4.2). When placing pattern pieces on knitted

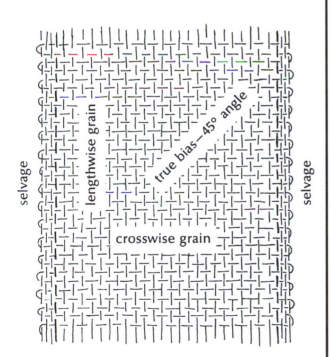

Fig. 4.1 Grain in woven fabric

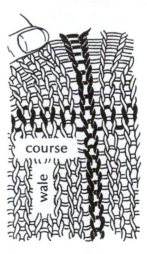

Fig. 4.2 Grain in knitted fabric

fabric, the sewer uses the wale in the same way as the lengthwise grain is used in woven fabric.

Knits are made on either flat or circular machines. Those produced on the flat machines will look similar to woven fabric and will have perforated edges resembling selvages; knits made on circular machines come in tubular form and are usually cut apart along one wale to make a flat piece of fabric before cutting out the pattern. Horizontal stripes made on circular knitting machines will be slightly off grain as the stripe spirals around the fabric. The wider the stripe, the more diagonal the pattern will be.

Fabrics Requiring Special Handling

Some fabrics, because of their construction, require special handling; therefore, they should be selected by a person with some knowledge and skill in apparel assembly techniques. The person who is just learning to sew will want to select a firmly woven fabric and avoid most of the fabrics discussed in this section. A firm double knit also is a good choice for the novice.

Many fabrics treated with resin finishes (e.g., crease resistant or permanent press fabrics) are quite stable and often cannot be straightened if off-grain. They may be stiff and present challenges when trying to ease one seam to another and when trying to sew lengthwise seams without puckering. Simple styles without set-in sleeves are well suited to these fabrics.

Single-knit tricot and jersey fabrics are more difficult to handle than double knits because they tend to stretch or slip and may present challenges when machine stitching. Seam edges in some single knits tend to curl, requiring special handling during cutting and construction.

Loosely woven fabrics lack stability and often ravel freely. Sheer fabrics, often loosely woven, may need special handling to prevent shadowing of seams, darts, and other construction details. A lining or underlining sometimes is used in part or in all of a garment made from a sheer fabric.

Loosely knitted fabrics will snag readily and will tend to stretch out of shape unless handled carefully. These fabrics work well when made into less-fitted styles with simple lines, few seams, and few construction details.

Some fabrics, because of their construction or design, have an "up and down" effect. Napped and pile fabrics (e.g., corduroy, velveteen, flannel), which have yarns extending above the surface of the fabric, have a different appearance when turned in different directions. Some fabrics have printed, woven, or knitted designs that go in the same direction. To avoid a finished garment in which different parts appear to be different colors or in which designs are going in different directions, sufficient yardage must be purchased to cut all pattern pieces in the same direction. Most patterns provide yardage requirements for both "with nap" and "without nap" fabrics.

"With nap" amounts should be purchased for any "up and down" effect fabrics. A "with nap" layout is used when positioning the pattern on the fabrics, which means that all pattern pieces lay in the same direction on the fabric. These fabrics will present challenges to the sewer when cutting.

Napped and pile fabrics also present challenges during construction. These fabrics are usually more bulky; therefore, care must be taken to reduce bulk on garment edges and in areas such as collars, cuffs, pockets, and waistbands. Special pressing techniques must be used to avoid flattening the nap or pile. Pressing on a needle board, a terry cloth towel, or a piece of self fabric will help avoid this problem.

Plaid and striped fabrics require skill in cutting to insure that the designs in the completed garment are both balanced and matched. *Woven* plaids and stripes are easier to cut than *printed* plaids and stripes, which may be printed off-grain. Fabrics with small plaids and stripes that are *even* usually present less of a challenge than do fabrics with larger or *uneven* designs. *Even* plaids and stripes are symmetrical in the arrangement of the pattern and color both lengthwise and crosswise. A "with nap" layout is not required for even plaids or stripes. *Uneven* plaids and stripes do not have a symmetrical arrangement of stripes. The stripes or plaids may differ in the number, size, and/or color of lengthwise or crosswise lines. For pattern layout for uneven plaids and stripes, follow the directions for a "with nap" layout. See Chapter 8 for more information on working with plaids and stripes.

Patterns with many pieces and a great deal of detail should be avoided when working with plaid and striped fabrics. Extra fabric needs to be purchased to allow sufficient yardage for matching the plaid or stripe. The extra amount needed depends on the number of pattern pieces to be cut, the size of the repeat in the plaid or striped fabric, the width of the fabric, and the general shapes of the pattern pieces. The *repeat* is the square or rectangle that contains the complete plaid design. More yardage is required for fabrics with large repeats than ones with smaller repeats. Additional fabric will be required to match pattern pieces that have more difference in widths between the top and bottom of the pattern (as in a flared skirt) than when patterns are more rectangular in shape (as in straight skirts or pants). When working on wider fabrics, pattern pieces for the front and back of the body often are placed side by side on the fabric, automatically matching the horizontal stripes on the plaid. Thus, no extra yardage would be required for matching. (See Chapter 8.)

Selecting Shaping/Support Fabrics

Appearance, serviceability, and stability of garments are enhanced by the use of shaping and support fabrics—interfacings, underlinings, and linings.

An *interfacing* is a layer of fabric cut the same shape as the garment piece to be interfaced and placed between that garment piece and its facing. Interfacings are used to provide body, support, shape retention, firmness, strength, stability, and smoothness to certain parts of the garment. Areas that usually are interfaced include collars, cuffs, lapels, collarless necklines, waistbands, and button/buttonhole openings.

An *underlining* is cut exactly like the garment section and is stitched to the garment piece before construction begins. During construction, the two layers of fabric (the fashion fabric and the underlining) are treated as one. Underlinings are used to

—produce shape;
—prevent stretching;
—prevent shadowing;
—make the garment opaque; and
—provide a foundation for handwork.

An entire garment or selected parts of a garment may be underlined.

A *lining* is an inner garment cut and assembled before being attached to the outer garment. A lining is used to

—produce a more comfortable garment;
—finish the inside of a garment;
—eliminate the wearing of some undergarments, particularly slips;
—serve as a stay for specific design effects; and
—reduce stretching, clinging, and wrinkling of the fashion fabric.

An entire garment or selected parts of a garment may be lined.

Interfacings

No one type of fabric is right for interfacing all fashion fabrics or for all areas needing interfacing. The choice of an interfacing is governed by many factors: (1) the construction and weight of the fashion fabric, (2) the support necessary to create the effect indicated by the design of the garment, (3) the construction and weight of the interfacing, and (4) the color of the fashion fabric and the interfacing.

Interfacing fabrics generally need to be the same or lighter in weight than the fashion fabric. It should complement and reinforce the garment fabric without overpowering it. Although special interfacing fabrics are available, some apparel fabrics, especially lightweight ones, are suitable for use as interfacings. Broadcloth, percale, batiste, and organdy are examples of apparel fabrics that may be appropriate for use as interfacings. Their availability in a wide range of colors and weights makes them especially appealing for use with many fabrics. Using self-fabric as the interfacing is not uncommon with sheer and lightweight fabrics.

Interfacings come in two main types: (1) *sew-in* or *nonfusible* and (2) *fusible*. Most types are available in woven, nonwoven, weft-insertion or knitted varieties

and in several weights. Interfacings can have stretch in one or more directions, or they may be stable in all directions. Some come in both dark and light colors, though white remains the most commonly found interfacing regardless of the type. The amount of interfacing required for the garment generally is listed on the back of the pattern envelope.

Fusible interfacings are adhesive backed and are applied to the fashion fabric by the use of heat, moisture, and pressure. After application, fusible interfacings have a tendency to stiffen the fabric and to produce a rippled effect on some fabrics. They are not recommended for many woven fabrics that are sheer or lightweight because the adhesive may come through and show on the outside of the finished garment. However, they are effective with and are recommended for use on most knitted fabrics, and they can be used successfully on woven fabrics that are not going to be washed frequently.

Sew-in or nonfusible interfacings, as their name implies, are attached to the garment through the process of stitching, either by hand or machine. The effectiveness of the interfacing can be determined by holding the interfacing between two layers of the fashion fabric and shaping it as it will be in the garment. A summary of the advantages and disadvantages of both types of interfacings is presented here.

Sew-in or Nonfusible Interfacing
Advantages:
—Provides softer, more subtle shaping
—Usable on both woven and knitted fabrics
—Does not change the hand or feel of the fabric
—Can determine the effectiveness of the interfacing on the fashion fabric by holding the two layers together
Disadvantages:
—May soften somewhat after washing
—If nonwoven, may buckle in an area where completely enclosed (collar or cuff)
—Requires more steps in applying to fashion fabric

Fusible Interfacing
Advantages:
—Quick to use; no need to baste
—Adds firmness to an area and makes topstitching easier
—May stabilize a loosely woven or lightweight fabric
—Usable on most knits and on selected woven fabrics
Disadvantages:
—Difficult to evaluate the amount of firmness created by fusing
—Becomes firmer after fusing
—May add too much body or stiffness to fashion fabric
—Fusing agent may press through to the right side after repeated pressings
—May not adhere to all fabrics, especially firm fabrics with a hard finish
—Interfacing may separate after many wearings or launderings
—Not suitable for some fabrics such as napped or pile fabrics or fabrics with surface texture

The location and purpose of the interfacing will influence whether a woven, a nonwoven, a knit, or a weft-insertion fabric is appropriate. The woven, nonwoven, and knit interfacings are available as fusible and nonfusible or sew-in types. Weft-insertion interfacings are available only as a fusible interfacing.

Woven interfacings are strong and should be used to reinforce those areas that need to be stabilized, especially cuffs, yokes, and placket bands cut on the bias as well as behind buttonholes. They drape well and are resilient. Some woven interfacings feel stiff when purchased, but will soften after laundering. All woven interfacings should be preshrunk before cutting.

Nonwoven interfacings are fiber webs, much like paper or felt. They may be stable in all directions, stable in the lengthwise direction and stretch in the crosswise direction, or stretch in all directions, in which case they are called all-bias. The amount of stretch in the interfacing needs to be considered when selecting the appropriate type for each area in the garment. The all-bias nonwoven interfacings should not be used in areas needing to be stabilized. Nonwoven sew-in interfacings may buckle in an area that is completely enclosed, such as inside a collar, causing a crease to form in the interfacing after the collar has been turned and pressed. The interfacings that have one-way stretch or are all-bias may be suitable for use on woven and knitted fabrics in areas that do not need to be stabilized.

Knit interfacings are softer and more flexible than wovens and nonwovens. The fusible varieties are stable in the lengthwise direction but stretch in the crosswise direction. When fused to the fashion fabric, the knit interfacing provides body to the fabric but does not overpower it, making it especially suited to all weights of knitted fabrics. They can be used to stabilize garment areas such as buttonholes, if they are cut so that the stable direction of the interfacing runs in the same direction as the buttonhole. Fusible knit interfacings have a tendency to shrink during the fusing process. To avoid shrinkage problems on large garment pieces, the interfacing can be fused to the fashion fabric before cutting out the pattern piece. Stabilized nylon tricot is a nonfusible fabric that is stable in all directions. Because of its flexibility it is a desirable interfacing for medium- to lightweight fabrics.

Weft-insertion interfacings are constructed with yarns laid in the crosswise direction of a warp knit. They maintain the softness of a knitted fabric yet have the stability of a woven fabric. They do not become as stiff as some woven and nonwoven interfacings when fused to fashion fabric. Because of their structure, weft-insertion interfacings are very versatile and can be used on both woven and knitted fashion fabrics.

Before a fusible interfacing is used, it is recommended that a sample be applied to a piece of the fashion fabric to test the compatibility of the two fabrics and the amount of stiffness created by the fusing. Several types and weights may need to be tested before the right one is selected. Since interfacings come in many weights and types, it is desirable to have a variety of fabrics available for use.

Compatibility is the key word when choosing an interfacing. Interfacings need to be selected at the same time as the fashion fabric to insure that the two are compatible. By placing the two together and shaping the fabric in a way similar to the areas of the garment to be interfaced, one can judge if the appropriate amount of body and crispness is present in the interfacing. Fusible interfacings, which add stiffness to the fabric when applied, are less reliable than sew-in interfacings when tested in this way.

Another consideration when selecting an interfacing is the care requirements of the interfacing and fashion fabrics. While the two fabrics may have different fiber contents, each must require the same care. When possible, a dark color interfacing should be used with a dark fabric and a light color interfacing with a light fabric. A garment may require a different interfacing in different areas in order to achieve various design effects.

Also found on the market are shaping and support products for specific areas of the garment. Waistband interfacings come in both fusible and sew-in varieties and provide the nonroll effect desired in this area. They are available in a variety of widths, in both packaged form and by the yard. A preassembled waistband is available to finish the inside of men's pants. Also available are fusible interfacing strips in narrow widths for use in cuffs and bands.

Fusible Webs

Fusible webs have a bonding agent that, when melted between two layers of fabric, joins them together. Fusible webs are not to be confused with fusible interfacings, and should not be used as such. The fusible webs usually are used to hold hems, facings, and appliques to a garment. Since the fabric usually becomes stiffer when a fusible web is used, a small piece should be tested with the fashion fabric to determine if the stiffness created is acceptable.

Linings and Underlinings

In most cases, the same fabric is appropriate to use for either a lining or an underlining, except in coats and jackets where a heavier lining fabric may be desired. Certain fabrics, both woven and knitted, are designed specifically as lining fabrics; however, the sewer is not limited to these selections. Many fashion fabrics also are appropriate to use for these purposes.

Since linings and underlinings provide a good feel to the inside of the garment, they usually are smooth in texture. They may be of a matching or contrasting color. If used with a sheer or lightweight fabric, most often linings and underlinings are of the same color unless the sewer is trying to achieve a particular effect. With opaque fabrics, either a matching or a contrasting color fabric, even a print, can be used. Care of the inner fabric must be compatible with that of the fashion fabric.

As a general rule, knitted fabrics are not lined or underlined, as the inner construction has the tendency to take away the inherent flexibility of the knitted fabric. If a lining or underlining is desired, tricot is a good choice.

Selecting Sewing Accessories

Different patterns require a variety of sewing accessories or notions. In this section, four of these will be discussed: thread, zippers, buttons, and tapes and bindings.

Thread

The most commonly available threads are those made from polyester or a blend of polyester and cotton. These threads are strong, flexible, and available in a wide range of colors. Because of their ability to stretch, they can be used to sew knitted as well as woven fabrics. Long-fiber polyester threads are recommended for use with overlock sewing machines because they have less tendency to produce lint than other threads.

One hundred percent cotton and silk threads are manufactured but may not be widely available to the sewer. Specialty threads, such as those designed specifically for topstitching, come in a limited number of colors. Also on the market in a limited number of colors are lightweight threads that work especially well on lightweight and sheer fabrics.

Thread should either match the garment fabric or be a shade darker, because it tends to look a shade lighter when it is sewn into the garment. Thread used for plaid or printed fabrics should match the most dominant color in the fabric.

Zippers

A zipper is a closure with interlocking synthetic coils or metal teeth, attached to a tape and operated by a slider. There are two types of zippers: (1) conventional and (2) invisible.

Conventional zippers have either metal or synthetic coils, and the tapes can range from lightweight polyester to heavyweight cotton. The purpose for which the zipper will be used determines the type and weight of zipper to purchase. All-purpose zippers, available in a variety of lengths, are used for most garments. Heavy trouser zippers are appropriate for garments requiring the heavier fabric tape and metal teeth that are characteristic of these zippers. Separating zippers, which open at both the top and the bottom, are used primarily for jack-

ets. Decorative zippers, usually exposed in the finished garment, are available in a limited range of colors and designs.

Invisible zippers, when installed in a garment, become hidden in the seam and only the pull tab shows. A special zipper foot is required for inserting this zipper into the garment.

Buttons

Buttons are available in two basic types: (1) sew-through and (2) shank (Fig. 4.3). A sew-through button usually is flat with two or four holes. A shank button has a solid top and a built-in shank on the back. Buttons are sized by diameter, with the pattern generally specifying the size needed for a particular garment. Buttons can match or contrast with the fashion fabric. Weight, style, and care should be compatible with the fashion fabric. Shank buttons are more appropriate than flat buttons for loop style buttonholes; flat buttons are more comfortable than shank buttons down the back of a garment.

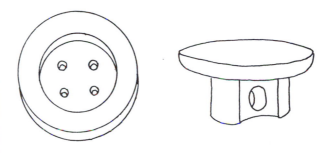

Fig. 4.3   Sew-through and shank buttons

Tapes and Bindings

Bias tapes and seam bindings are used in garments for a variety of purposes. They often are included in seams to stabilize and reinforce the area and to prevent stretching. Bindings are used as a finish for seams and hems as well as for elastic and drawstring casings. Tapes or bindings also may be used to add a decorative touch to the finished garment. They come in a variety of widths, colors, fiber contents, weights, and constructions.

Straight, woven seam bindings are used for stays in straight seams and to finish hem edges. Lace binding gives a decorative finish to a hem and, because it has stretch, can be used with knits.

Bias tape has prefolded edges; double-fold tape is folded in half, slightly off-center, for easy application. Bias tape is used to finish seam edges and for casings.

Other notions that may be needed during the construction process include hooks and eyes, snaps, elastic, and trims. All notions required to complete the garment will be listed on the back of the pattern envelope.

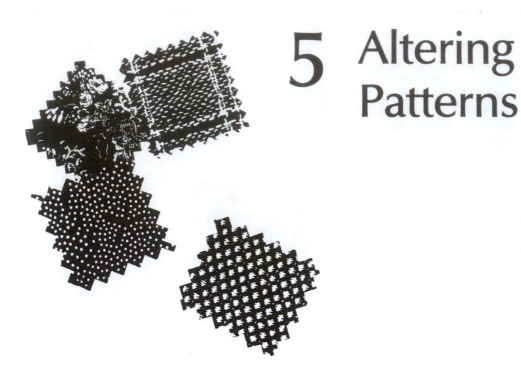

5 Altering Patterns

To be attractive, a garment must not only be well constructed, but it also must fit well. The first step to achieving good fit is to start with a pattern that is the correct figure type and size; then the pattern measurements should be compared to personal body measurements and necessary pattern alterations made. This chapter will describe the steps involved in doing basic pattern alterations before the garment is cut. Fitting the garment during construction is discussed in Chapter 6.

Deciding on Pattern Alterations

Deciding how much to alter any area of the garment can be done by one of three methods: (1) by measuring the pattern and comparing those measurements to the person's measurements plus ease; (2) by pinning the paper pattern together and trying on the pattern; or (3) by comparing the pattern measurements to those on a well-fitting garment of a similar style.

Measuring the Pattern

The measurements in Tables 3.3 and 3.4 will serve as a guide for deciding on needed pattern alterations. Column 3 of these charts contains the minimum length or width required for specific areas of the body and results from adding the actual body measurement to the speci-

fied amount of ease (columns 1 and 2). The figures in column 3 are the ones to be compared with the *actual* pattern measurements, which are determined by *measuring the corresponding areas of the pattern that might require a change.*

Some patterns contain design ease in addition to wearing ease. The design ease is fullness (such as darts, tucks, pleats, gathers, or flare) added to a pattern that makes the pattern larger than one's personal measurements plus ease. The amount of design ease added to a pattern is difficult to determine. By referring to the illustration on the pattern envelope the sewer can see how the designer intended the pattern to fit. The design ease should not be relied upon for fitting ease.

Before measuring the pattern it is necessary to determine the areas on the pattern that need to be measured. A closely fitting garment will require more pattern measurements to be taken than will a very loosely fitting garment. The areas on patterns that contain considerable design ease do not need to be measured, as fit is assured because of the extra ease that has been added to the pattern.

When measuring the pattern, seam allowances and construction details such as darts, pleats, tucks, and gathers should not be included in the measurement. When the garment is stitched, these garment details would not be available in the finished garment for fitting. Some pattern companies are printing on the pattern the total circumference measurements for the bust/chest, waist, and hip areas.

If stitching lines are not printed on the pattern, as is the case on multi-sized patterns, the sewer will need to mark the stitching line in the areas where the measurements are to be taken before actually measuring the pattern. The first step is to decide which pattern size to use. For skirts and pants, measure at the hipline to decide which size fits best. For a garment fitting the upper half of the body, one would usually use the chest or bust circumference measurement. When taking these measurements, measure in ⅝ inch (1.6 cm) to mark the stitching line, and then measure to that mark and not to the cutting line. For example, before measuring the waist circumference, the sewer must measure down from the cutting line ⅝ inch (1.6 cm) to mark the stitching line (a in Fig. 5.1) and ⅝ inch in from the side seam for the pattern side seam stitching line (b in Fig. 5.1). Then measure the waist circumference within these markings.

Certain length measurements must be marked on the pattern *before* taking circumference and width measurements. These length measurements include: center front neck to the location for upper chest width (a to b in Fig. 5.2), center back neck to the location for the back

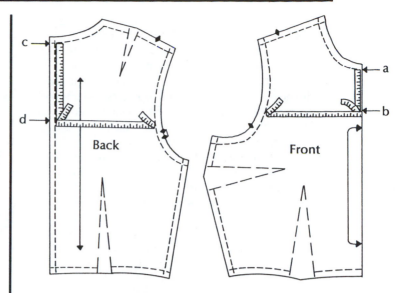

Fig. 5.2   Measuring bodice patterns

shoulder width (c to d in Fig. 5.2), waist to high hip (a to b in Fig. 5.3), and waist to full hip (a to c in Fig. 5.3). After these marks are made on the pattern, the appropriate width and circumference measurements can be taken at the same location on the pattern as they were taken on the body.

Since many pattern pieces represent only half the body, most *circumference measurements* taken from the *pattern* will need to be *doubled* before comparing them to body measurements. An asymmetrical pattern will have separate pieces for both the right and left sides, therefore each piece would need to be measured and the individual measurements added together when comparing the pattern measurements to the body measurements.

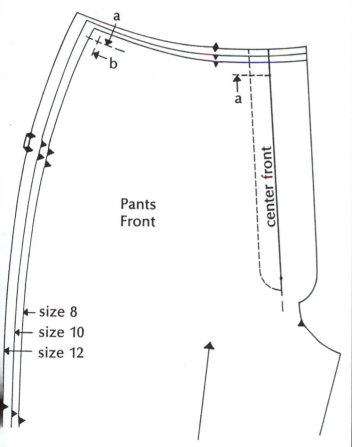

Fig. 5.1   Marking seam lines on multi-sized patterns before taking pattern measurements

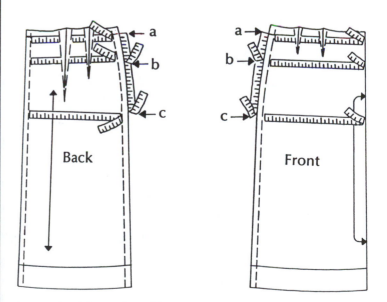

Fig. 5.3   Measuring skirt patterns

The sleeve length measurement on fitted sleeves with elbow shaping is taken in two parts. First, the measurement from the top of the sleeve to a point level with the elbow dart or elbow curve is taken (a to b in Fig. 5.4). If there is a difference between this measurement and the body measurement, the pattern would be lengthened or shortened above the elbow point. Once this alteration is completed the total sleeve length is measured (a to c in Fig. 5.4) and this measurement is compared to the total arm length measurement. If an alteration is indicated the pattern is altered below the elbow point. Sleeve circumference is measured at the widest part of the sleeve (d to e in Fig. 5.4), called the sleeve capline.

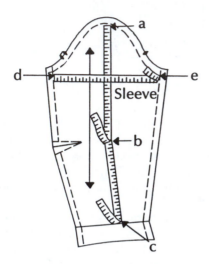

Fig. 5.4   Measuring sleeve pattern

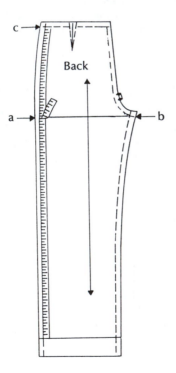

Fig. 5.5   Measuring pants patterns

Before measuring the crotch depth on the pants pattern, the crotch line must be drawn at right angles to the grainline from the side seam to the crotch point on the back pattern piece (a to b in Fig. 5.5). The crotch depth measurement is taken only on the pants back pattern piece from the waist seam line to the crotch line (a to c in Fig. 5.5). The total crotch length measurement is taken on both the front and the back pants patterns, along the center and crotch seams, from the front waistline to the back waistline (a to b in Fig. 5.6). The tape can be placed on its edge when measuring along the curve.

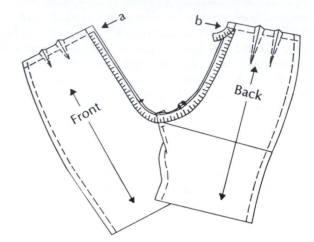

Fig. 5.6   Measuring total crotch length on pants pattern

All pattern pieces that are combined to produce a unit need to be measured to determine the total measurement. For example, if a sleeve has a cuff, both the cuff and the sleeve need to be measured to determine the total length. When measuring the waist circumference on a skirt or pant pattern style with an inset pocket, the pocket yoke should be pinned to the garment front, matching the appropriate pattern markings, before measuring the waist circumference (Fig. 5.7).

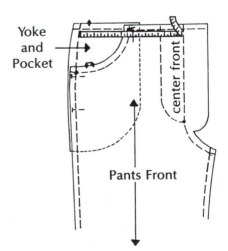

Fig. 5.7   Measuring waist circumference on a pattern style with inset pocket

Pinning the Paper Pattern Together

Another way to determine needed alterations is to pin the pattern pieces together and try the paper pattern on the person. This procedure works especially well when checking length of garment pieces, such as skirt, pants, sleeve, or bodice lengths. Shoulder seam length is also a good measurement to check in this way as well as dart length and position (Fig. 5.8). Because the pattern pieces represent only half of the finished garment, checking circumference by this method may be less accurate. Pinning pattern pieces together and trying them on sometimes is done after alterations have been made to check for their accuracy.

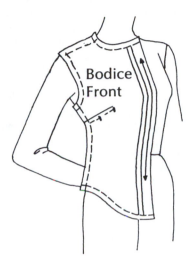

Fig. 5.8 Checking fit of pattern on the body

Measuring a Garment that Fits Well

Measuring a garment of a similar style that fits well is another way to determine needed alterations. The measurements obtained by measuring a garment already contain the necessary amounts of ease and would be compared directly to the corresponding pattern measurements.

When all the pattern measurements have been compared to the minimum required for the individual, the location and amount of the individual alterations can be determined (column 5 on the Measurement Chart). Looking at all needed changes at one time is important because often two or more alterations can be done in the same slash in the pattern piece.

When many adjustments are made to a pattern, it is advisable to make and fit a test garment in muslin or other inexpensive fabric before cutting the fashion fabric. After the test garment has been fitted and altered, the pattern should be readjusted to match the test garment.

Principles of Pattern Alterations

When altering pattern pieces to achieve good fit, certain procedures must be followed to insure accurate results.

1. The basic silhouette of the design should remain the same after alterations have been made.
2. Design ease should be maintained.
3. Seam lines that originally were straight must remain straight after alterations have been made; seams that originally were curved should retain a similar curve after alterations have been made.
4. Alteration slashes must go from one seam line to another so that the pattern will remain flat.
5. Most slash or overlap alteration lines are drawn parallel or perpendicular to the grainline.
6. The original grainline of the pattern should be retained.
7. Corresponding pattern pieces must be altered to insure that adjoining seams will match.
8. Width alterations are seldom made at center front or center back of the garment.
9. Alterations should be placed where they are needed.
10. Alterations to add length to the pattern usually are made between the points of the body joints—shoulder, elbow, wrist, waist, hip, knee—rather than at the lower edges of the patterns. Length alterations on the bodice/shirt usually are made between the bust/chest and waist or lower edge.
11. Alterations to add to the circumference usually are made near the side seams rather than close to center front or center back.
12. The amount added to each pattern piece for a circumference alteration depends on the total number of pattern pieces involved. If adding 2 inches (5 cm) to the waistline of a garment with a front and a back pattern piece, ½ inch (1.3 cm) would need to be added to each pattern piece. Pattern pieces usually represent half the body for most symmetrical styles, so the amount added to each pattern piece is half the total amount needed for that pattern piece. If two pattern pieces are involved (each piece representing ¼ of the body), the amount added to each pattern piece is ¼ of the total amount.
13. Larger contours require larger darts; smaller contours require smaller darts.
14. The original termination points of darts and seams are used when truing/perfecting a seam line or dart after an alteration has been made.
15. When perfecting a seam line with a dart, the dart should be closed before redrawing the seam.
16. When perfecting the pattern, the stitching line should be restored first and then a new cutting line drawn an appropriate distance from it.

General Sequence for Pattern Alterations

Before starting to make the alterations on the pattern, the pattern should be measured in the appropriate locations and a record made of all the needed alterations. Often more than one alteration can be made in the same slash. For example, corrections to the back shoulder width and the waist circumference can be made in the same vertical slash. Also, some alterations will affect the measurement of another area and should be made before the second area is measured and altered. An example of this is when a correction is made to the back shoulder width, because this change affects the total bust circumference. Thus, alterations to the back shoulder width and waist circumference and to the front chest width and waist circumference should be made before measuring and altering for total bust circumference.

Suggested sequence for altering a pattern
that fits the upper half of the body:

1. Back shoulder width and/or waist circumference
2. Front chest width and/or waist circumference
3. Dart size (for bra cup size other than B cup)
4. Remeasure pattern for total chest/bust circumference and alter at the side seam
5. Shoulder length (sometimes combined with numbers 1 and 2 above)
6. Dart position and length
7. Total bodice length at center front, side seam, and/or center back

Suggested sequence for altering a skirt pattern:

1. Waist, high hip, hip, and/or thigh circumference
2. Skirt length

Suggested sequence for altering a pants pattern:

1. Crotch depth
2. Waist, high hip, hip, and/or thigh circumference
3. Leg circumference
4. Total crotch length
5. Pants length

Altering the Pattern Using the Slash Method

The slash method for altering patterns is based on the principle that the alteration is made in the area of the pattern where the adjustment is needed. Alterations usually are made by the "slash and spread" method to increase the pattern and the "slash and lap" or the "folded pleat" method to decrease the pattern. These techniques provide a permanently altered pattern that can be used again and again. The original seam allowances remain intact and seam lengths are not altered unnecessarily.

The following guidelines should be followed when using the slash method to alter patterns.

To slash and spread to increase the pattern:

1. Draw the line across the pattern at the place where it is to be slashed (many patterns have this guideline marked on the pattern).
2. When the entire width or length of the pattern piece is to be increased:
    a. Extend the grainline the full length of the pattern.
    b. Draw two parallel lines on a slightly larger piece of paper, making the space between the lines equal to the amount the pattern is to be increased. Make a third line perpendicular to and through the two parallel lines to be used as a guideline for keeping the pattern grainline straight.
    c. Slash the pattern. Use pins or tape to fasten both sections of the pattern to the added piece of paper along the parallel lines, using the guideline to keep the pattern grainline straight.
3. When the spread extends only partially through the pattern section:
    a. Slash the pattern *to but not through* the opposite seam line (not the cutting line). When possible, slash to a corner where two seam lines meet rather than to the center of a seam line.
    b. To keep the pattern flat, clip from the cutting edge of the pattern seam allowance to the same point on the seam line, creating a pivot point where the slashes meet.
    c. Spread as needed for alteration.
    d. Use pins or tape to fasten the pattern to a piece of paper.
    e. Straighten the grainline marking.

To slash and lap to decrease
a portion of the pattern:

1. When the decrease does not extend across the entire pattern piece, slash the pattern *to but not through* the opposite seam line. When possible, slash to a corner where two seam lines meet rather than to the center of a seam line.
2. A second slash is often made perpendicular to the original slash line *to but not through* the adjacent seam line.
3. To keep the pattern flat, clip from the cutting edge of the pattern seam allowance to the same point on the seam line for each of the slash lines, creating a pivot point where the slashes meet. Lap as needed for the decrease.
4. Secure the lapped area in place with pins or tape.
5. Straighten the grainline marking.

To fold a pleat to decrease the entire width
or length of the pattern piece:

1. Draw two parallel lines across the pattern at the place where it is to be decreased, making the space between these lines equal to the amount the pattern is to be decreased.
2. Fold the pattern on one line and bring it to the second line. *The folded pleat will be one-half the width of the total decrease.*
3. If the pleat crosses a grainline marking, be sure that it remains straight after the fold is made in the pattern.
4. Fasten the folded pleat in place with pins or tape.

Pattern Alterations for Common Fitting Problems

Bodice Alterations

Altering Bodice Back Shoulder Width

The back shoulder width measurement is used to determine necessary alterations across the back shoulder blade area. Sufficient width is needed for comfort and movement. The armscye line for a standard fitted sleeve would extend about ½ inch (1.3 cm) beyond the back arm crease, or the point where the arm joins the body. When arms are straight at the side of the body, a well-fitted garment fits smoothly without noticeable wrinkles or folds. For a rounded back or for protruding shoulder blades, a shoulder dart or tucks from a back yoke are necessary for a smooth fit. When fitting a garment, if there are tight horizontal wrinkles or if the sleeve pulls in toward the body, the back width is too narrow (Fig. 5.9). If there are loose vertical folds of fabric near the armholes of the garment, then the back shoulder width is too wide (Fig. 5.10).

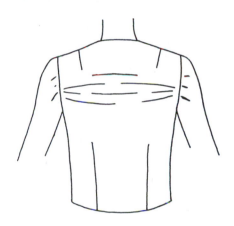

Fig. 5.9   Broad back

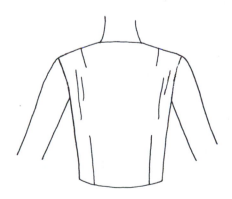

Fig. 5.10   Narrow back

To alter bodice back for broad or narrow back:

1. Mark on center back the distance from center back neck to the point where the back shoulder width measurement was taken (*a* to *b* in Fig. 5.11). At this point draw a line across the back pattern perpendicular to center back (*b* to *c* in Fig. 5.11).

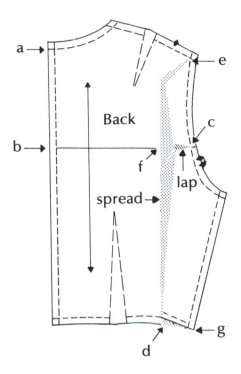

Fig. 5.11   Increasing back shoulder width

2. On a line parallel to center back and about 1½ inches (3.8 cm) from the armhole, slash from the waistline to a point about 2 inches (5 cm) from the shoulder seam. Angle the slash to the end of the shoulder seam (*d* to *e* in Fig. 5.11).

3. Slash horizontally from the vertical slash to the armhole seam on the horizontal line marking the point where the back shoulder width measurement was taken (*f* to *c* in Fig. 5.11).

4. Clip the seam allowances to points *c* and *e* in Figure 5.11 to permit the pattern to lie flat.

5. To increase the back shoulder width, spread the vertical slash one-half the needed amount at the intersection with the horizontal slash (*f* in Fig. 5.11), but do not spread at the waistline. This causes the edges of the horizontal slash to overlap, shortening the outer section of the pattern at the waistline.

6. Correct the waistline seam by redrawing the side section of the waistline (*d* to *g* in Fig. 5.11).

7. To decrease the bodice back shoulder width, lap the vertical slash (Fig. 5.12).

If the shoulder seam length and/or the waist circumference also need to be altered, they can be increased or decreased by spreading or lapping the vertical slash at the appropriate location at the same time as the adjustment is made to the back shoulder width.

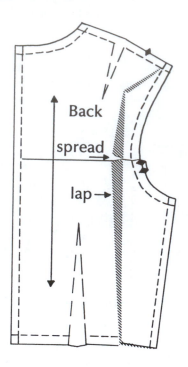

Fig. 5.12   Decreasing back shoulder width

Altering Bodice Front Upper Chest Width

If excess fabric appears above the bust as vertical folds causing the front armscye line to extend beyond the armhole crease, the pattern may need to be altered for a narrow chest (Fig. 5.13). If there are tight horizontal wrinkles pulling the armhole in toward the center of the body, then more width is needed on the front pattern piece (Fig. 5.14). The armscye line for a regular set-in sleeve should fall in a smooth line from the end of the shoulder joint through the point where the arm joins the body, or the front arm crease, and then curve under the arm toward the side seam.

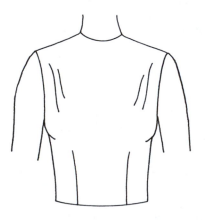

Fig. 5.13   Narrow upper chest

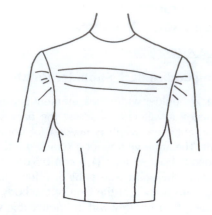

Fig. 5.14   Broad upper chest

To alter bodice front for broad or narrow upper chest:

1. Mark on center front the distance from center front neck to the point where the front chest width measurement was taken (a to b in Fig. 5.15). At this point draw a line across the front pattern perpendicular to center front (b to c in Fig. 5.15).

2. On a line parallel to center front and about 1½ inches (3.8 cm) from the armhole, slash from the waistline to a point about 2 inches (5 cm) from the shoulder seam. Angle the slash to the end of the shoulder seam (d to e in Fig. 5.15).

3. Slash horizontally from the vertical slash to the armhole seam on the horizontal line marking the point where

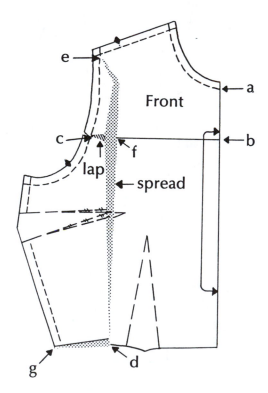

Fig. 5.15   Increasing front chest width

the front chest width measurement was taken (*f* to *c* in Fig. 5.15).

4. Clip the seam allowances to points *c* and *e* in Figure 5.15 to permit the pattern to lie flat.

5. To increase the front chest width, spread the vertical slash one-half the needed amount at the intersection with the horizontal slash (*f* in Fig. 5.15), but do not spread at the waistline. This causes the edges of the horizontal slash to overlap, shortening the outer section of the pattern at the waistline.

6. Correct the waistline seam by redrawing the side section of the waistline (*d* to *g* in Fig. 5.15).

7. To decrease the bodice front chest width, lap the vertical slash (Fig. 5.16).

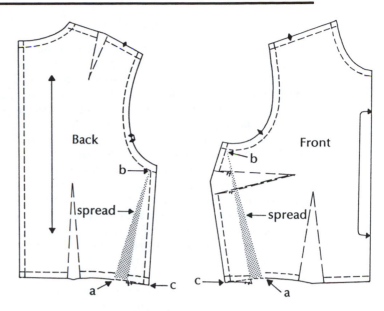

Fig. 5.17   Increasing bodice waist circumference

2. Clip the seam allowance to point *b* in Figure 5.17 to permit the pattern to lie flat.

3. To increase the waist circumference spread (at point *a* in Fig. 5.17) one-fourth the needed amount.

4. Correct the waistline seam by redrawing the seam line of the side section from *a* to *c* in Figure 5.17.

5. If the diagonal slash has cut through the underarm dart, redraw the dart stitching lines.

6. To decrease the waist circumference, lap the waistline one-fourth the needed amount (Fig. 5.18).

7. This alteration would be made to both the bodice front and bodice back pattern pieces.

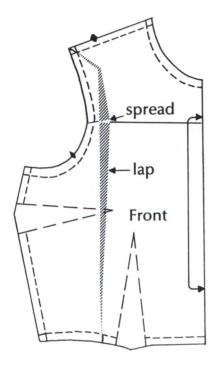

Fig. 5.16   Decreasing front chest width

If the shoulder seam length and/or waist circumference also need to be altered, they can be increased or decreased by spreading or lapping the vertical slash at the appropriate location at the same time as the adjustment is made to the front upper chest width.

Altering Bodice Waist Circumference

As mentioned, if the waist circumference needs to be altered along with the back shoulder width and front chest width, it can be done in the same vertical slash. If only the waist circumference requires an adjustment, this can be made by slashing from the waistline to the intersection of the side seam and armhole seam.

To alter bodice waist circumference:

1. Starting on the waistline at a point 2 inches (5 cm) from the side seam, slash diagonally to the intersection of the armhole seam and the side seam (*a* to *b* in Fig. 5.17).

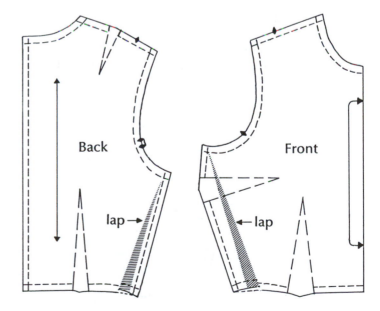

Fig. 5.18   Decreasing bodice waist circumference

Altering Bodice Front Dart Size

Alterations to the size of the bodice front darts is based on body contour; the larger the contour the larger the darts. Bust contour is usually measured in terms of bra cup size. Patterns are generally designed for a size B-cup bra; therefore, they would be altered for persons wearing a different cup size. Some patterns are now providing alternate cutting and stitching lines to provide adequate fitting for the different bra cup sizes. If this option is not available, then an alteration to dart size would be appropriate. To change a pattern from a B-cup to an A-cup, decrease the waist dart size about ½ inch (1.3 cm); to go from a B-cup to a C-cup, increase ½ inch (1.3 cm); to go from B-cup to D-cup, increase ¾ inch (1.9 cm). Increasing the bust size lowers the bust-fitting dart; decreasing the bust size raises the bust-fitting dart. Since posture also affects the shape of body curves and the fit of bodice darts, it is recommended that a test garment from the altered pattern be fitted before cutting the fashion fabric.

A well-fitted bodice front drapes smoothly over the body contours, with no unwanted wrinkles or folds. Diagonal wrinkling pointing to the bust point usually indicates that dart size is too small (Fig. 5.19). If the wrinkling originates from the armhole, then usually only the side bust-fitting dart needs to be increased. If the diagonal wrinkling originates from the side seam to the bust point, then the waist bust-fitting dart needs to be increased.

If there is excess fullness at the point of the darts, then the dart size needs to be decreased (Fig. 5.20). If there are two darts, each dart needs to be evaluated separately to determine whether one or both darts need to be decreased.

To increase bodice front darts for full bust:

1. Locate the bust point (a in Fig. 5.21) by extending the center line of both the underarm and waistline darts to the point of intersection.

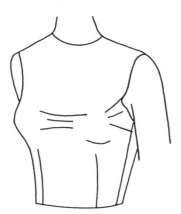

Fig. 5.19   Full Bust—diagonal wrinkles indicate dart size is too small

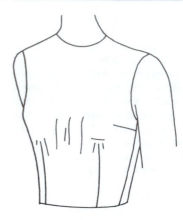

Fig. 5.20   Small bust—fullness at dart points indicates dart size is too large

2. Starting in the center of the waistline dart, slash vertically from the waistline to the bust point (b to a in Fig. 5.21), then diagonally to a point on the armhole seam line near the notch (c in Fig. 5.21).

3. Slash through the center of the side bust-fitting dart from the side seam *to but not through* the bust point (d to a in Fig. 5.21).

4. Clip the armhole seam allowance to point c in Figure 5.21 to permit the pattern to lie flat.

5. Spread at point a in Figure 5.21 the needed amount to increase the bust darts and continue to spread the same amount through the vertical slash (a to b in Fig. 5.21). This will cause the diagonal slash and the side bust-fitting dart to spread.

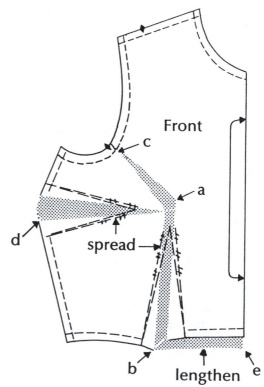

Fig. 5.21   Increasing size of bodice front darts

6. Since the spread through the center of the waistline dart separated the dart at the point, draw a new dart point in the center of the spread. Draw new dart lines connecting this point to the original dart lines at the waistline. The new dart points should end about 1 inch (2.5 cm) from the bust point.

7. Repeat the procedure for the side bust-fitting dart.

8. Perfect the waistline seam line by folding the dart and adding length to the center front section from points *b* to *e* in Figure 5.21. This added bodice length usually is needed for the full bust.

To decrease bodice front darts for small bust:

1. Locate the bust point (*a* in Fig. 5.22) by extending the center line of both the underarm and waistline darts to the point of intersection.

2. Starting in the center of the waistline dart, slash vertically from the waistline to the bust point (*b* to *a* in Fig. 5.22), then diagonally to a point on the armhole seam line near the notch (*c* in Fig. 5.22).

3. Slash through the center of the side bust-fitting dart from the side seam *to but not through* the bust point (*d* to *a* in Fig. 5.22).

4. Clip the armhole seam allowance to point *c* in Figure 5.22 to permit the pattern to lie flat.

5. Lap (at point *a* in Fig. 5.22) the needed amount to decrease the bust darts and continue to lap the same amount through the vertical slash (*a* to *b* in Fig. 5.22). This will cause the diagonal slash and the side bust-fitting dart to lap.

6. Since the lap through the center of the waistline dart caused the dart stitching lines to cross, locate a new dart point in the center of the lapped area. Draw new dart lines connect-

ing this point to the original dart lines at the waistline. The new dart points should end about 1 inch (2.5 cm) from the bust point.

7. Repeat the procedure for the side bust-fitting dart.

8. Perfect the waistline seam line by folding the dart and decreasing the length of the center front section from points *b* to *e* in Figure 5.22. This shorter front length usually is needed for the small bust.

To increase the size of only the side bust-fitting dart or to add a dart when no dart is present:

If the wrinkling in the garment indicated that only the side bust-fitting dart needed to be increased, the alteration procedure is slightly different than when both darts are increased. This procedure could also be used to create a dart on a bodice design where no dart is present.

1. Draw a line through the center of the side bust-fitting dart to the bust point, then to center front, at right angles to the lengthwise grainline (*a* to *b* in Fig. 5.23). If there is no dart in the pattern, hold the pattern up to the individual, lining up the shoulder seam line and center front. Mark the bust point on the pattern. Draw a line from the side seam through the bust point indicating the angle for the new dart. Draw a line from the bust point to the center front as indicated.

2. Slash along this line, separating the pattern into two pieces.

3. Spread the upper and lower bodice sections adding the needed amount to enlarge the dart or create a new dart. Be sure to maintain the proper grainline alignment for both sections of the bodice.

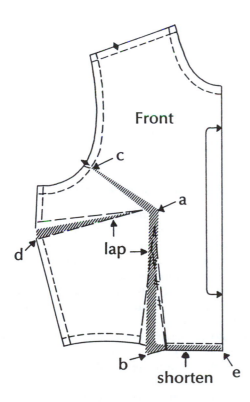

Fig. 5.22 Decreasing size of bodice front darts

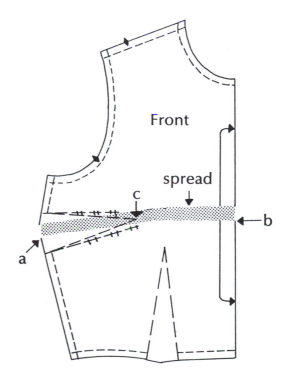

Fig. 5.23 Increasing size of only the side bust-fitting dart

4. Locate the point of the dart in the center of the spread (c in Fig. 5.23), about 1 inch (2.5 cm) from the bust point.

5. Connect this point to the original dart lines at the side seam.

6. Fold the dart and perfect the side seam by connecting the seam line at the waist and underarm point in a straight line.

Altering Total Chest/Bust Circumference

After the back shoulder width, the front upper chest width, the waist circumference, and the size of any front bust darts have been altered, then the total bust/chest circumference on the pattern needs to be remeasured to determine if any further adjustment is needed. If a change is indicated, this alteration is made to the side seams of the bodice/shirt front and back. This alteration is needed to correct the pattern for individuals who have a larger or smaller rib cage than allowed for on the pattern. Any alteration to the bodice/shirt side seam will change the armhole circumference, thus the sleeve or armhole facing would need to be adjusted in the same area for the armhole to fit correctly.

To increase chest/bust circumference
for a large rib cage:

1. Measure out from the seam line at the underarm point on both the garment front and the garment back one-fourth the total amount of increase (a in Fig. 5.24).

2. Connect this point to the seam line at the waistline (a to b in Fig. 5.24). If there is a side bust-fitting dart, fold the dart before drawing the new side seam.

3. Measure out from the new side seam stitching line the desired width for the seam allowance and draw a new cutting line.

4. Add the same amount to underarm seam of the sleeve or armhole facing so that the armhole lengths will match.

To decrease chest/bust circumference
for a small rib cage:

1. Measure in from the seam line at the underarm point on both the garment front and the garment back one-fourth the total amount of decrease (a in Fig. 5.25).

2. Connect this point to the seam line at the waistline (a to b in Fig. 5.25). If there is a side bust-fitting dart, fold the dart before drawing the new side seam.

3. Measure out from the new side seam stitching line the desired width for the seam allowance and draw a new cutting line.

4. Take away the same amount from the underarm seam of the sleeve or armhole facing so that the armhole lengths will match.

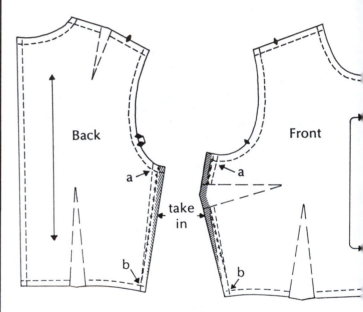

Fig. 5.25   Decreasing chest/bust circumference at side seam

Altering Shoulder Seam Length

The armscye seam line for a regular set-in sleeve should lie across the end of the shoulder joint, which is where the arm joins the body, continue downward through the front arm crease, and then curve toward the underarm seam. To locate the shoulder joint, raise the arm and feel the indentation at the socket. This is one way to determine the location for the armscye seam line for a regular set-in sleeve.

When sleeves have extra fullness at the top in the form of gathers or tucks, the sleeve is placed about ½ inch (1.3 cm) in from the end of the shoulder joint. The armhole seam line on sleeveless designs may vary from the normal placement of the armscye with a set-in sleeve to one that curves inward several inches (centimeters).

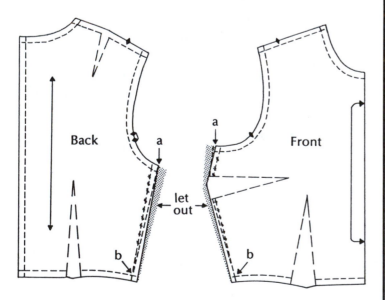

Fig. 5.24   Increasing chest/bust circumference at side seam

The underarm point on a basic sleeveless garment may be higher than one in which sleeves are a part of the design.

Many garments are designed with extended shoulder seams. This additional length will vary depending on the design. Before determining correct shoulder length, one must carefully examine the design on the pattern envelope to determine the intended location for the armscye seam line. If the neckline style varies from "the basic," the length of the shoulder seam will also be affected.

When fitting a garment with a regular set-in sleeve, if horizontal wrinkles pull across the shoulders and the natural shoulder extends beyond the armhole seam line into the sleeve of a regular set-in sleeve, then the shoulder seam usually needs to be lengthened (Fig. 5.26). If the armscye seam line drops off the end of the shoulder joint and the upper part of the sleeve droops and wrinkles, then the shoulder seam length needs to be shortened (Fig. 5.27).

The shoulder-length measurement on the Measurement Chart should indicate any needed alteration to shoulder length for a regular set-in sleeve. Adjustments to this measurement would need to be made for other sleeve variations. Since the shoulder-length measure-

ment is very difficult to take on the body, it is wise to hold the pattern up to the individual after it is altered to recheck the accuracy of the alteration before cutting.

To alter shoulder seam length:

1. Starting about 2 inches (5 cm) from the armhole edge of the shoulder seam, slash both front and back patterns parallel to lengthwise grain, then diagonally to the armhole seam line near the notch (a to b in Fig. 5.28).
2. Clip the armhole seam allowance near the notch to permit the pattern to lie flat.
3. To increase shoulder seam length spread the slash to make shoulder seam the desired length (Fig. 5.28).
4. To decrease shoulder seam length lap the slash to make the shoulder seam the desired length (Fig. 5.29).

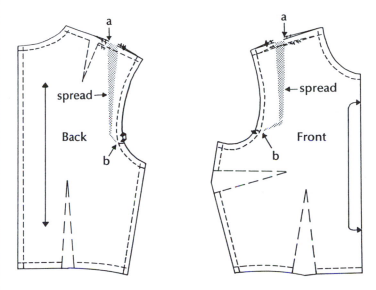

Fig. 5.28   Lengthening shoulder seams

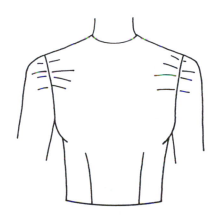

Fig. 5.26   Broad shoulders

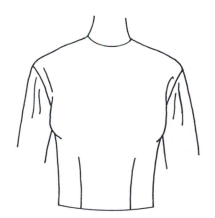

Fig. 5.27   Narrow shoulders

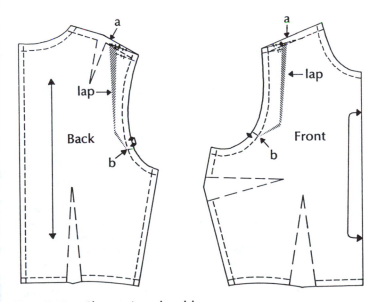

Fig. 5.29   Shortening shoulder seams

5. Perfect the shoulder seam line by drawing a new seam line from the neck to the armhole. If there is a shoulder dart, *fold the dart before redrawing the shoulder seam line.*

6. After drawing a new seam line, measure out the desired amount for the seam allowance and draw a new cutting line.

To alter the shoulder seam length on a pattern containing a yoke, the alteration would be done to the yoke as well as to the front and back bodice or shirt pieces.

To shorten shoulder seam when pattern contains a yoke:

1. On the yoke pattern slash inward along the shoulder line for about 2 inches (5 cm) from the armhole edge (a to b in Fig. 5.30).

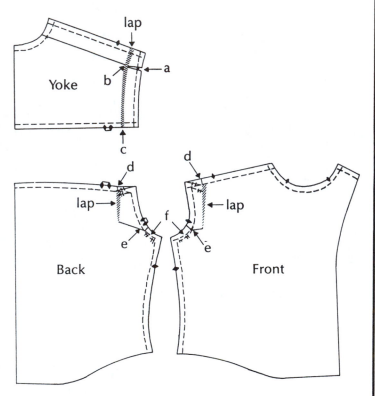

Fig. 5.30   Shortening shoulder seams on yoke pattern

2. Fold on each side of the slash line one-half the amount to be subtracted to correct the shoulder seam length (c in Fig. 5.30). Keep outside edges of yoke even.

3. Redraw yoke armhole seam. Reposition shoulder point marking midway in spread area.

4. Starting about 2 inches (5 cm) from the armhole edge of both garment front and back patterns, draw lines parallel to center front and center back from the yoke seam line, then diagonally to the notched area of the armhole (d to e in Fig. 5.30). Slash the pattern along the drawn line to the armhole seam line.

5. Clip the armhole seam allowance to point e in Figure 5.30 to permit the pattern to lie flat.

6. Lap the slashes the same amount as was shortened on the yoke piece. Perfect the seam line on each piece.

7. Raise both back and front underarm seam lines half the amount of spread in the yoke armhole seam so the armhole remains the original circumference (f in Fig. 5.30).

To lengthen shoulder seam when pattern contains a yoke:

1. Reverse the process outlined for shortening shoulder seam length by slashing so that the yoke pattern spreads the needed amount at the shoulder rather than lapping (a to b in Fig. 5.31).

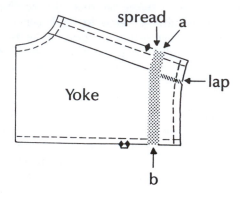

Fig. 5.31   Lengthening shoulder seams on yoke pattern

2. Lower both back and front underarm seam lines half the amount lapped in the yoke armhole.

Altering for Shoulder Slope

Poor fit results when shoulders are more square or have more slope than the pattern. Altering for square or sloping shoulders is difficult to determine by taking body measurements. If this is a problem, the construction of a test garment is recommended to determine the correct shoulder angle. If the shoulder angle is adjusted on one pattern, the same adjustment would usually be made to other patterns. The use of shoulder pads is an alternate procedure for correcting the fit for sloping shoulders.

To alter for sloping shoulders:

If wrinkles form from the tip of the shoulder seam at the neckline diagonally to the armhole and the armhole ripples, the shoulder seam should have a greater slope (Fig. 5.32). Excess fabric is usually noted along the shoulder at the armhole end of the shoulder seam. When making this alteration, it is necessary to adjust the lower armhole area as well as the shoulder to maintain the correct armhole size.

1. Starting 1½–2 inches (3.8–5 cm) from the outer edge of the shoulder seam on both garment front and back, slash parallel to center front and center back to a point just below the armhole seam (a to b in Fig. 5.33).

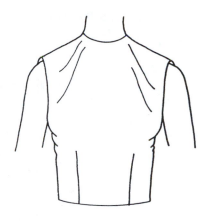

Fig. 5.32   Sloping shoulders

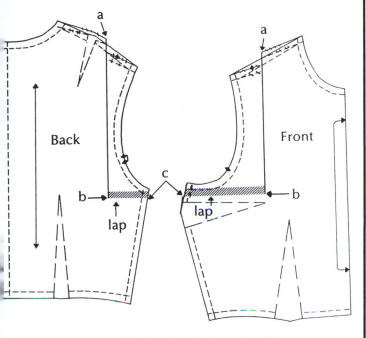

Fig. 5.33   Altering for sloping shoulders

2. Make a second slash perpendicular to the vertical slash through the side seam (*b* to *c* in Fig. 5.33), separating the armhole section.

3. Measure down from the horizontal slash line the amount needed to lower the shoulder seam. Draw a line at this point parallel to the horizontal slash line and lap the armhole section to this line.

4. Perfect the shoulder seam line by drawing a new seam line from the neck to the armhole. If there is a shoulder dart, *fold the dart before redrawing the seam line.*

5. After drawing a new seam line, measure out the desired amount for the seam allowance and draw a new cutting line.

To alter for square shoulders:

If wrinkles point diagonally to the end of the shoulder and excess fabric forms along the shoulder seam near the neck-

line, the garment needs to be altered for square shoulders (Fig. 5.34). The armhole area should be raised in the underarm in addition to raising the shoulder end to maintain the correct armhole size.

1. Starting 1½–2 inches (3.8–5 cm) from the outer edge of the shoulder seam on both garment front and back, slash parallel to center front and center back to point just below the armhole seam (*a* to *b* in Fig. 5.35).

2. Make a second slash perpendicular to the vertical slash through the side seam (*b* to *c* in Fig. 5.35), separating the armhole section.

3. Attach a piece of paper to the horizontal slash, and measure up from the horizontal slash line the amount needed to raise the shoulder seam. Draw a line at this point parallel to the horizontal slash line. Match the armhole section to this line.

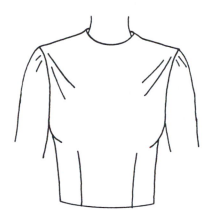

Fig. 5.34   Square shoulders

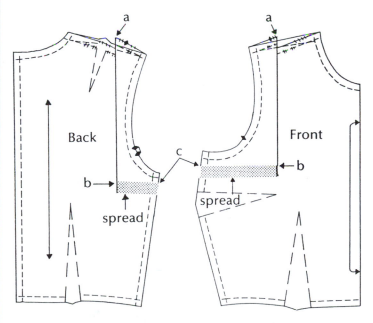

Fig. 5.35   Altering for square shoulders

4. Perfect the shoulder seam line by drawing a new seam line from the neck to the armhole. If there is a shoulder dart, *fold the dart before redrawing the seam line.*

5. After drawing a new seam line, measure out the desired amount for the seam allowance and draw a new cutting line.

Altering for Shoulder Slope on Pattern with a Yoke

Altering the shoulder slope on patterns containing a yoke is somewhat different than on patterns with a shoulder seam.

To alter for sloping shoulders on patterns with a yoke:

1. Slash along the shoulder line from the armhole *to but not through* the neck seam line (a to b in Fig. 5.36).

2. Clip the neck seam allowance to point *b* in Figure 5.36 to permit the pattern to lie flat.

3. Lap the slash lines at the armhole to subtract the needed amount.

4. Perfect the yoke armhole seam. Reposition the shoulder point marking midway in the lapped area.

5. Lower both back and front underarm seam lines one-half the amount lapped in the yoke so that the armhole remains the original size (c in Fig. 5.36).

To alter for square shoulders on patterns with a yoke:

1. Slash along the shoulder line from the armhole *to but not through* the neck seam line (a to b in Fig. 5.37).

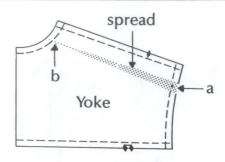

Fig. 5.37 Altering a yoke pattern for square shoulders

2. Clip the neck seam allowance to point *b* in Figure 5.37 to permit the pattern to lie flat.

3. Spread the pattern at the armhole the needed amount.

4. Perfect the yoke armhole seam. Reposition the shoulder point marking midway in the spread area.

5. Raise both back and front underarm seam lines one-half the amount spread in the yoke so that the armhole remains the original size.

Altering Bust Dart Position

Bust darts should point to the fullest part of the bust and terminate about 1 inch (2.5 cm) from the bust point. Use the shoulder to bust-point measurement to determine the correct position of the bust darts. When fitting a garment, darts must be positioned correctly before analyzing the dart size.

To alter bust dart position:

1. Draw horizontal lines on the pattern ½ inch (1.3 cm) above and below the underarm dart, at right angles to lengthwise grain (a to b and c to d in Fig. 5.38). Connect the lines with a vertical line through the dart point (b to d in Fig. 5.38).

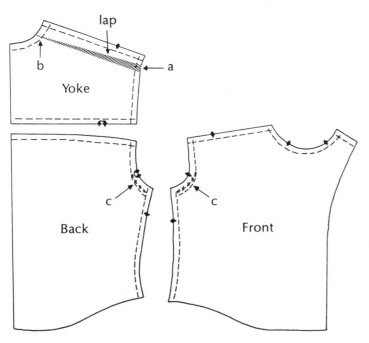

Fig. 5.36 Altering a yoke pattern for sloping shoulders

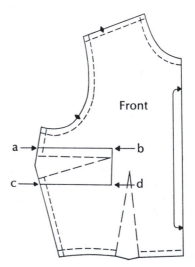

Fig. 5.38 Marking lines for altering side bust-fitting dart position

2. Cut out the dart along the marked lines.

3. To raise the dart (Fig. 5.39), tape paper under the opening, measure up from the lower slash line the necessary amount and draw a new line parallel to the original horizontal line. Position the lower edge of the dart section along the new line.

4. To lower the dart (Fig. 5.40), measure down from the lower slash line the necessary amount and draw a new line parallel to the original horizontal line. Position the lower edge of the dart section along the new line. Place paper under the opening in the pattern.

5. If there is a waist-fitting dart, raise or lower the dart point the necessary amount and connect the new dart point to the original dart lines at the waistline (a in Fig. 5.39 and 5.40).

Altering Bodice Waist Length

The waistline seam of fitted garments should rest at the natural waistline on the body, with an appropriate amount of ease on the bodice. The amount of bodice lengthwise ease will vary with the design of the garment. Center front and center back length measurements plus ease are used to determine the necessary length adjustments. Length alterations may be an even amount across the garment or an uneven amount from center front or center back to the side seam. The alteration procedure is different, depending on the change required.

To lengthen bodice waist an even amount:

1. Slash both front and back bodice patterns on a horizontal line drawn perpendicular to the center line above the waistline (a to b in Fig. 5.41). Commercial patterns usually have alteration lines marked on the pattern for this purpose.

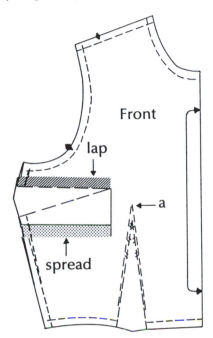

Fig. 5.39 Raising side bust-fitting dart

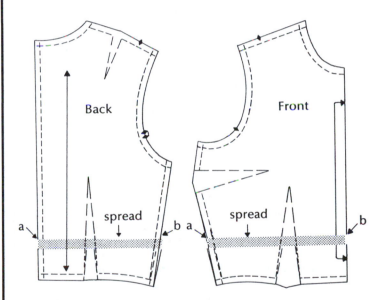

Fig. 5.41 Lengthening bodice an even amount

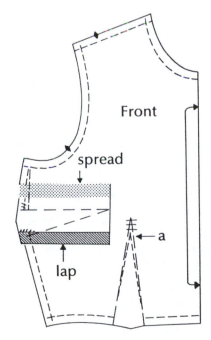

Fig. 5.40 Lowering side bust-fitting dart

2. Spread the pattern the full amount of needed increase in length.

3. Perfect the side seam by drawing a new seam, connecting the seam line at the armhole and waistline in a straight line. If there is a dart in the seam, *fold the dart before drawing the new seam line.*

4. After drawing the new seam line, measure out the desired amount for the seam allowance and draw a new cutting line.

5. Correct the stitching lines of the waist-fitting dart.

To shorten bodice waist an even amount:

1. Draw two parallel lines across both the front and back bodice patterns above the waistline and perpendicular to the lengthwise grainline marking, making the space between the lines equal to the amount the bodice should be shortened (*a* and *b* in Fig. 5.42). Commercial patterns usually have alteration lines marked on the pattern for this purpose.

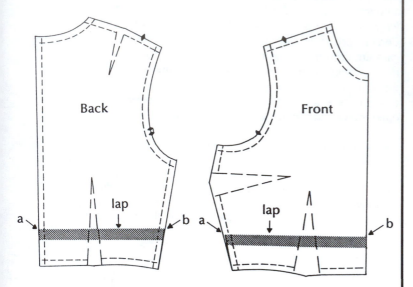

Fig. 5.42   Shortening bodice an even amount

2. Lap the pattern the full amount of needed decrease in length by folding along the bottom line and bringing the fold to the top line. The depth of the fold is equal to one-half the total amount of decrease.

3. Perfect the side seam by drawing a new seam, connecting the seam line at the armhole and waistline in a straight line. If there is a dart in the seam, *fold the dart before drawing the new seam line.*

4. After drawing the new seam line, measure out the desired amount for the seam allowance and draw a new cutting line.

5. Correct the stitching lines of the waist-fitting dart.

To alter bodice length an uneven amount:

1. Slash bodice pattern on a horizontal line drawn perpendicular to the center line above the waistline (*a* to *b* in Figs. 5.43 and 5.44).

2. Draw a line from this horizontal line to the center of the waistline (*c* to *d* in Figs. 5.43 and 5.44). Slash on this line *to but not through* the waistline seam line.

3. Clip the waistline seam allowance to point *d* in Figures 5.43 and 5.44 to permit the pattern to lie flat.

4. To add length to the bodice pattern spread the pattern the full amount of needed increase in length. When the increased length is an uneven amount from the center of the pattern to the side seam, keep the spread even in width from the center line to the center of the pattern (*a* to *c* in Fig. 5.43). Taper the amount of increase from the center of the pattern to the side seam (*c* to *b* in Fig. 5.43).

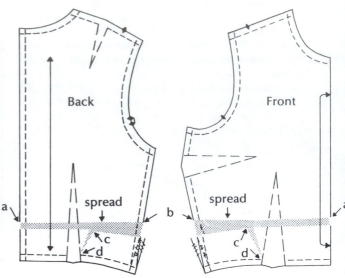

Fig. 5.43   Lengthening bodice an uneven amount

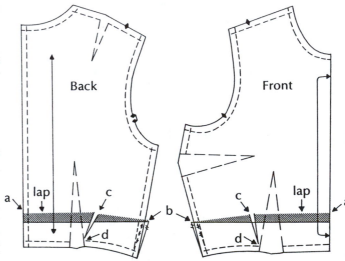

Fig. 5.44   Shortening bodice an uneven amount

5. Perfect the side seam by redrawing a new seam, connecting the seam line at the armhole and at the waistline in a straight line. If there is a dart in the seam, *fold the dart before drawing the new seam line.*

6. After drawing the new seam line, measure out the desired amount for the seam allowance and draw a new cutting line.

7. To shorten bodice length an uneven amount, reverse the process and lap the desired amount at the center line and at the side seam (*a* to *b* in Fig. 5.44), keeping the amount of lap an even amount from the center line to the center of the pattern (*a* to *c* in Fig. 5.44).

Altering for Prominent Shoulder Blades

If diagonal wrinkles point to the shoulder blades on the bodice back or if the back armhole gaps and a fold of fabric radiates to the shoulder blade, the fullness created by the back shoulder dart is not sufficient for the contour of the back shoulder blade (Fig. 5.45). By manipulating the fold of fabric up to the shoulder seam and enlarging the existing shoulder dart, the fit over the back shoulder area is improved. If there is no shoulder dart, a dart can be created along the shoulder seam or the back neckline seam to provide the necessary shaping for the back shoulder area.

To increase size of back shoulder dart:

1. Slash through the center of the dart to the dart point, then diagonally to the armhole near the notch (a to b to c in Fig. 5.46).

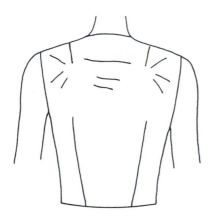

Fig. 5.45 Prominent shoulder blades

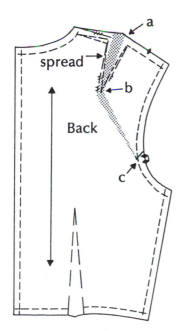

Fig. 5.46 Increasing size of back shoulder dart

2. Clip through the armhole seam allowance to point c in Figure 5.46 to permit the pattern to lie flat.

3. Spread the dart the amount needed to increase dart size (Fig. 5.46).

4. Fold dart and perfect the shoulder seam by drawing a new seam connecting the end points of the seam line.

5. After drawing the new seam line, measure out the desired amount for the seam allowance and draw a new cutting line.

6. A large shoulder dart usually will fit the shoulder area better if the dart lines are stitched in a concave curve, rather than as a straight line dart (Fig. 5.47).

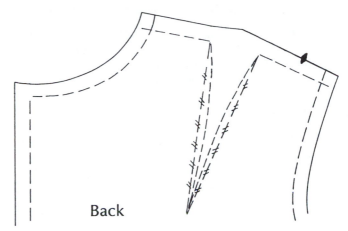

Fig. 5.47 Concave stitching lines for larger shoulder dart

To create a new back shoulder dart:

1. Draw a line down from the back shoulder seam or neckline seam at the location for the new dart (a to b in Fig. 5.48). Continue the line over to the armhole to a point near the notch (b to c in Fig. 5.48).

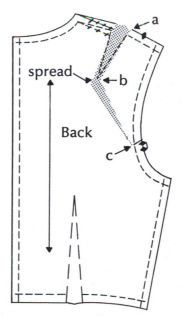

Fig. 5.48 Creating a new shoulder dart

2. Slash along this line *to but not through* the armhole seam line.

3. Clip the armhole seam allowance to point *c* in Figure 5.48 to permit the pattern to lie flat.

4. Spread along the slash line the amount needed to create the new dart (Fig. 5.48).

5. Fold the dart and perfect the shoulder seam by drawing a new seam connecting the end points of the seam line.

6. After drawing the new seam line, measure out the desired amount for the seam allowance and draw a new cutting line.

Altering for Forward Thrust of the Shoulder

On a well-fitting garment the shoulder seam should lie in a straight line on the top of the shoulder, slanting neither to the front nor to the back when viewed from the side. If the shoulder seam slants to the back caused by a forward thrust of the shoulder joint (Fig. 5.49), the shoulder seam needs to be moved forward at the armhole end. This alteration cannot be easily determined by taking body measurements; thus the need for it becomes noticeable only after a garment has been assembled. Once the need has been identified, the alteration usually would be done to other patterns of a similar style.

Fig. 5.49   Forward thrust of the shoulder

To alter a pattern for forward
thrust of the shoulder:

1. Slash the garment front pattern from the armscye to the seam line at the neck-shoulder point (*a* to *b* in Fig. 5.50).

2. Clip through the seam allowance at the neckline to point *b* in Figure 5.50 to permit the pattern to lie flat.

3. Lap the slashed line at the armhole seam line (*a* in Fig. 5.50) the amount needed to bring the shoulder seam forward.

4. Slash the garment back in the same manner and spread along the slash line the same amount (*c* in Fig. 5.50).

5. Perfect the seam lines at the armhole.

6. This alteration changes the total length of the back armhole and the front armhole, therefore the marking at the top of the sleeve where it matches the bodice shoulder seam should be moved forward an amount equal to this change.

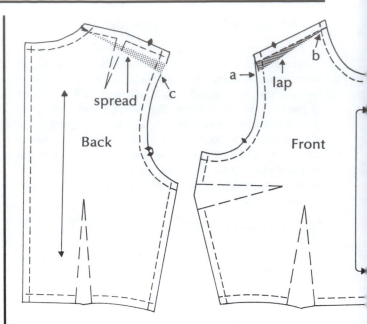

Fig. 5.50   Shifting shoulder seam forward for forward thrust of the shoulder

Altering for Gaping at Center Front

When the garment neckline is gaping at center front (Fig. 5.51), the excess fullness is removed by shifting or sliding the front shoulder seam along the back shoulder seam away from the neckline until the fullness is removed. This correction should be made on both shoulder seams. After shifting the shoulder seam, the neckline seam line and the armhole seam line on the front and back will no longer align and will need to be redrawn.

To alter garment front for gaping at center front:

1. Fold under and pin the shoulder seam allowance of the garment front. Match it to the bodice back shoulder seam allowance, first matching the notches.

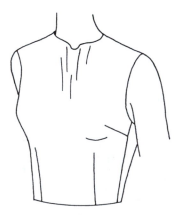

Fig. 5.51   Gaping at center front

2. Slide the front shoulder seam away from the neckline the amount needed to remove the gaping at the center front (Fig. 5.52).

3. Redraw the neckline (a in Fig. 5.52) and the armhole (b in Fig. 5.52) seam lines and cutting lines for the garment front and back.

4. Change the location of the shoulder seam notch on one of the pattern pieces so that the notches match.

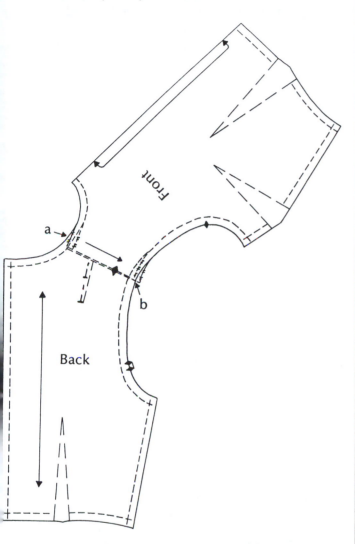

Fig. 5.52   Altering pattern for gaping at center front

Sleeve Alterations

Alterations to sleeve patterns usually involve sleeve length and sleeve circumference. A long fitted sleeve usually extends to just below the wrist bone, with the elbow shaping aligned below the elbow. The sleeve must be wide enough to fit comfortably around the upper arm without strain or wrinkling. The amount of ease varies with the style and the type of fabric being used; knit fabrics require less ease than woven fabrics.

Altering Sleeve Length

If a sleeve is fitted and has elbow shaping, the sleeve length is evaluated in two parts. First, the distance from the top of the sleeve to the middle of the elbow curve or elbow dart is measured and compared to the corresponding body measurement. If an adjustment is needed it is made between the underarm and the elbow. After making that adjustment, the total length is measured and compared to the total arm length measurement. If an additional alteration is necessary it is made between the elbow and the hemline. Alteration lines may be marked on the pattern for these adjustments.

To lengthen sleeve:

1. Draw a line across the pattern where the increase is needed. When this is above the elbow (a to b in Fig. 5.53), the line should be at right angles to the lengthwise grainline marking; when it is below the elbow (c to d in Fig. 5.53), the line is drawn parallel to the slant of the sleeve hem.

2. Slash and spread the needed amount from points a to b in Figure 5.53, and from points c to d.

3. Correct and redraw the sleeve seam lines and cutting lines.

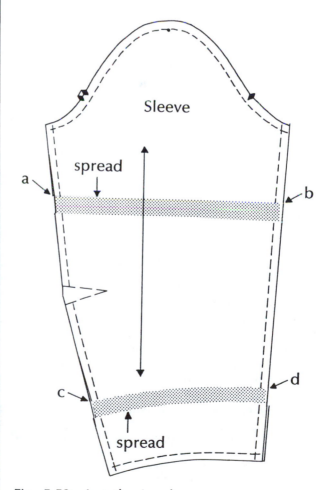

Fig. 5.53   Lengthening sleeve

To shorten sleeve:

1. Draw a set of parallel lines perpendicular to the grainline marking above the elbow (a to b in Fig. 5.54) and a second set below the elbow parallel to the sleeve hem (c to d in Fig. 5.54) to adjust for the desired sleeve measurement. Fold a pleat at each set of lines. Each folded pleat should be exactly one-half the amount of decrease needed in that area.

2. Redraw the sleeve seam lines.

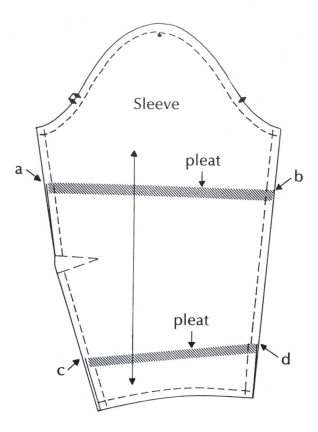

Fig. 5.54   Shortening sleeve

Altering Sleeve Circumference

If the pattern does not provide at least 2 inches (5 cm) of ease in the upper arm circumference, the pattern needs to be altered. Certain styles may contain more than the minimum ease allowance in this area. If there is a significant change made to the sleeve, it is advisable to make and fit the altered sleeve in test fabric before making it in the fashion fabric.

To increase sleeve circumference:

1. On a piece of paper, trace the cutting line of the *sleeve cap*.

2. On the sleeve pattern draw a cutting line parallel to the grainline marking from the top of the sleeve to the sleeve hem (a to b in Fig. 5.55).

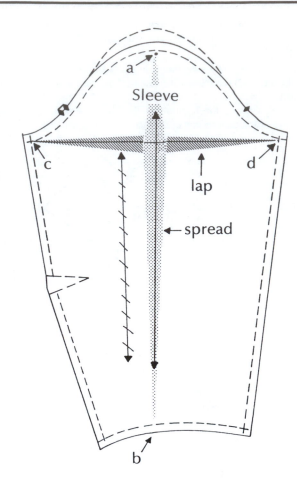

Fig. 5.55   Increasing sleeve circumference in upper sleeve only

3. Draw a line perpendicular to the lengthwise grainline at the widest part of the sleeve, which is the capline (c to d in Fig. 5.55).

4. Slash through the hem on the vertical slash line to the seam line at point a and on the horizontal slash line to the seam line at points c and d in Figure 5.55.

5. Clip the seam allowance at points a, c, and d in Figure 5.55 to the stitching lines to permit the pattern to lie flat.

6. To increase the sleeve only in the upper arm, spread the vertical slash the needed width at the capline, tapering the slash to nothing at the hem. This causes the horizontal slashed edges to overlap.

7. To increase the circumference the entire length of the sleeve, spread the vertical slash the desired amount at both the capline and the hemline (Fig. 5.56).

8. Restore the sleeve cap height by comparing the tracing of the original sleeve cap to the altered sleeve and redrawing the sleeve cap seam line as needed. The amount added to the sleeve cap equals the amount of overlap along the horizontal slash.

9. Draw a new capline connecting the seam line at the widest point of the sleeve (c to d in Figs. 5.55 and 5.56).

10. Draw a new lengthwise grainline perpendicular to the newly drawn capline.

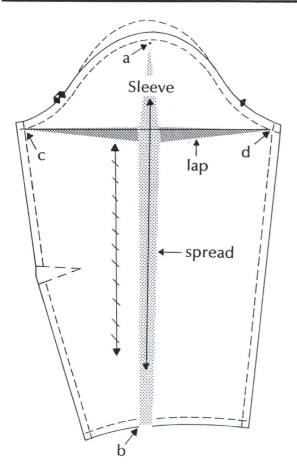

Fig. 5.56   Increasing sleeve circumference the full length of sleeve

Skirt Alterations

Altering Hip Circumference

Fitted skirts should have enough ease through the upper hip and full hip areas to allow the skirt to fall into place without having to pull down on the garment. A closely fitted skirt should fit smoothly, without wrinkles or excess fabric folds. If stress wrinkles form in the skirt (Fig. 5.57), they point to the garment area that is too tight. When the figure is equally proportioned, both the front and back pattern pieces are adjusted one-fourth the total amount needed. If the figure is larger in the back (or front), the back (or front) pattern piece is adjusted one-half the needed amount. If a fold of fabric forms around the skirt near the waist, the high hip is usually too tight (Fig. 5.58). The high hip and full hip can be increased (or decreased) in the same vertical slash line.

To increase high hip, full hip, and/or thigh:

1. On the pattern measure down from the waist the "waist to hip" measurement (a to b in Fig. 5.59) as determined by the location for taking the full hip measurement and mark point b

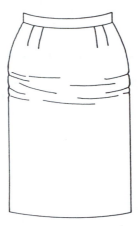

Fig. 5.57   Skirt too tight through the full hip

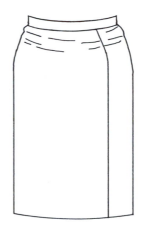

Fig. 5.58   Skirt too tight through the high hip

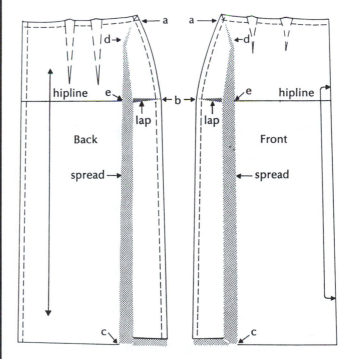

Fig. 5.59   Increasing full hip circumference

in Figure 5.59 on the pattern. Draw a horizontal line from point *b* in Figure 5.59 to the center line, perpendicular to the lengthwise grainline.

2. Draw a vertical line about 2 inches (5 cm) from the side seam and parallel to lengthwise grain, beginning at the bottom of the skirt and extending to a point about 2 inches (5 cm) from the waistline (*c* to *d* in Fig. 5.59). Angle this slash diagonally to the corner where the waistline joins the side seam (*d* to *a* in Fig. 5.59).

3. At the line marking the fullest part of the hips, slash horizontally from the vertical slash to the side seam line (*e* to *b* in Fig. 5.59).

4. If an increase is needed in the high hip, add a horizontal slash from the vertical slash 3 inches (7.5 cm) down from the waist (*f* to *g* in Fig. 5.60).

5. If an increase is needed in the thigh area, add a horizontal slash from the vertical slash at the appropriate thigh level (*h* to *i* in Fig. 5.60).

6. Clip the seam allowances to points *a* and *b* in Figure 5.59 and to points *a*, *b*, and *g*, and/or *i* in Figure 5.60 to permit the pattern to lie flat.

7. Spread the vertical slash the needed amount at the hipline (*e* in Figs. 5.59 and 5.60), high hip (*f* in Fig. 5.60), and thigh (*h* in Fig. 5.60) keeping the spread the same width from the lowest horizontal slash to the hemline to preserve the silhouette of the skirt. This causes the edges of the horizontal slashes to overlap, shortening the side section.

8. Correct the hemline by adding the needed length to the side section to restore the original hemline.

9. If a sharp bulge forms at the high hip or full hip areas of the side seam, round off the seam line.

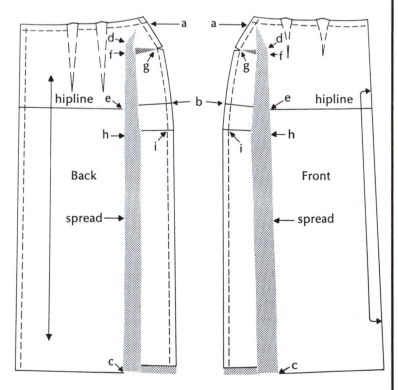

Fig. 5.60   Increasing high hip, full hip, and thigh circumference

To decrease high hip and/or full hip:

1. Measure down from the waist the "waist to hip" measurement (*a* to *b* in Fig. 5.61) as determined by the location for taking the full hip measurement and mark point *b* in Figure 5.61. Draw a horizontal line through point *b* from the side seam to the center line, perpendicular to the lengthwise grainline.

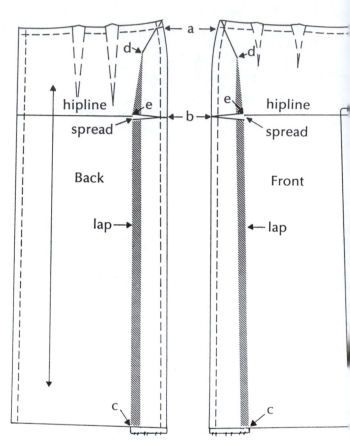

Fig. 5.61   Decreasing full hip circumference

2. Draw a vertical line about 2 inches (5 cm) from the side seam, parallel to lengthwise grain. Slash along this line beginning at the bottom of the skirt and extending to a point about 2 inches (5 cm) from the waistline (*c* to *d* in Fig. 5.61). Angle this slash diagonally to the corner where the waistline joins the side seam (*d* to *a* in Fig. 5.61).

3. At the line marking the fullest part of the hips, slash horizontally from the vertical slash to the side seam line (*e* to *b* in Fig. 5.61).

4. If a decrease is needed in the high hip, add a horizontal slash from the vertical slash 3 inches (7.5 cm) down from the waist (*f* to *g* in Fig. 5.62).

5. Clip the seam allowances to points *a* and *b* in Figure 5.61 and points *a*, *b*, and *g* in Figure 5.62 to permit pattern to lie flat.

6. Lap the vertical slash the needed amount at the hipline (*e* in Figs. 5.61 and 5.62) and high hip (*f* in Fig. 5.62), keeping the amount of lap the same from the hipline to the hemline to

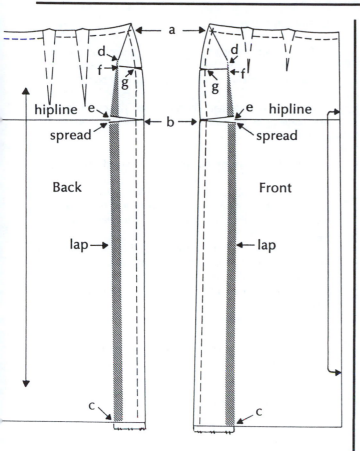

Fig. 5.62 Decreasing full hip and high hip circumference

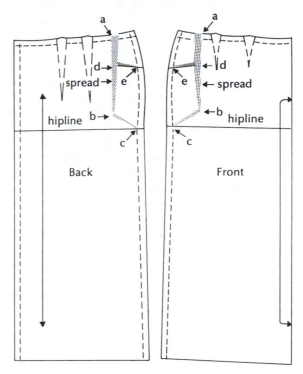

cal slash at the waist (a in Fig. 5.63) and high hip (d) the needed amount.

5. To decrease the waist and/or high hip lap the vertical slash the needed amount (Fig. 5.64).

6. Perfect the waistline seam as a smooth curve.

Fig. 5.63 Increasing skirt waist and/or high hip circumference

preserve the silhouette of the skirt. This causes the edges of the horizontal slashes to spread, lengthening the side section.

7. Correct the hemline by trimming off the excess from the side section to restore the original hemline.

Altering Waist and/or High Hip

If the waist circumference needs to be adjusted in addition to the full hip, the alteration can be completed in the same vertical slash line used to alter the full hip. However, if only the waist or high hip requires an adjustment, it can be made by slashing from the waistline to the side seam at the hipline.

To alter waist and/or high hip circumference:

1. Slash along a vertical line beginning at the waistline and extending to within 2 inches (5 cm) of the hipline (a to b in Fig. 5.63). Angle this slash line to the side seam line (b to c in Fig. 5.63).

2. If an alteration is needed in the high hip, slash from this vertical slash to the side seam line 3 inches (7.5 cm) down from the waist (d to e in Fig. 5.63).

3. Clip the seam allowance to points c and e in Figure 5.63 to permit the pattern to lie flat.

4. To increase the waist and/or high hip spread the verti-

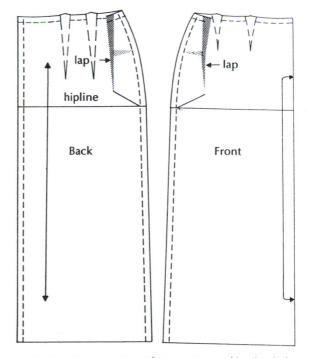

Fig. 5.64 Decreasing skirt waist and/or high hip circumference

Altering Skirt or Pant Dart Length and Dart Size

Dart length is related to the length of the torso. Darts should extend to within ½–1 inch (1.2–2.5 cm) of the fullest part of the body contour. Dart length can be determined by holding the pattern up to the body and noting the fullest part of the front and/or back body contour on the pattern, or while pin fitting the darts in the fashion fabric. Dart length should be corrected before analyzing dart size.

Skirt or pant dart size is related to the size of the body contour. The larger the contour, the larger the dart; the smaller the contour, the smaller the dart. Since it is difficult to determine dart size using body measurements, alterations are determined after making a test garment or by pin fitting darts in the fashion fabric. Once dart size has been determined for individual figure contours, similar alterations to correct dart size would be made on other patterns containing fitting darts.

Correctly fitted darts lie smoothly over the body contour. If there is excess fullness at the point of the dart (Fig. 5.65), the dart is usually too big for the body curve and needs to be made smaller. If there are diagonal wrinkles pointing to a prominent body curve (Fig. 5.66), there needs to be more shaping of the fabric for the size of the curve and the dart size needs to be increased.

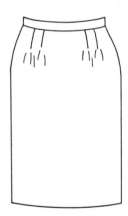

Fig. 5.65   Dart size too big

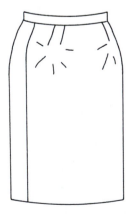

Fig. 5.66   Dart size too small

To alter dart length:

1. After determining the correct dart length on the body, measure down from the waistline seam line on the pattern the appropriate length for the dart and mark a new point (a to b in Fig. 5.67).

2. Draw in new dart stitching lines by connecting this new point (b in Fig. 5.67) to the original dart lines at the waistline.

To alter dart size for garment with single dart:

1. Slash along the side of the dart that is closest to the side seam from the waistline to the dart point (a to b in Figs. 5.68 and 5.69); angle the slash over to the side seam line at the hipline (b to c in Figs. 5.68 and 5.69).

2. Clip the side seam allowance to point c in Figures 5.68 and 5.69 to permit the pattern to lie flat.

3. To increase dart size spread the dart at the waistline the desired amount (Fig. 5.68). Place paper under the spread area.

4. To decrease dart size lap the dart at the waistline the desired amount (Fig. 5.69).

5. Locate the new point of the dart in the middle of the spread or lap.

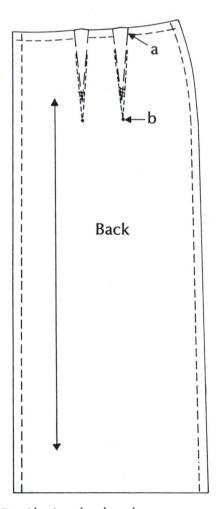

Fig. 5.67   Altering dart length

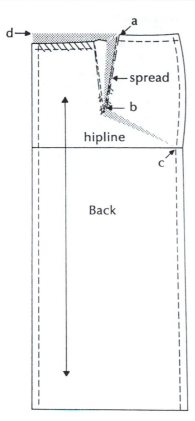

Fig. 5.68 Increasing dart size for a single dart

6. Draw the dart stitching lines by connecting this new point to the original dart lines at the waistline.

7. Perfect the waistline by folding the dart and adding to the waist height from the dart to the center when the dart is increased (a to d in Fig. 5.68), or trimming the excess from the waistline from the dart to the center when the dart is decreased (a to d in Fig. 5.69).

To alter dart size for garment with two darts:

1. Slash along the side of the darts that is closest to the side seam from the waistline to the dart points (a to b in Figs. 5.70 and 5.71); angle the slash lines to a point below the two darts to form a common pivot position (b to c in Figs. 5.70 and 5.71); continue the slash over to the side seam line at the hipline (c to d in Figs. 5.70 and 5.71).

2. Clip the side seam allowance to point d in Figures 5.70 and 5.71 to permit the pattern to lie flat.

3. To increase dart size spread the darts at the waistline the desired amounts (Fig. 5.70). Place paper under the spread areas.

4. To decrease dart size lap the darts at the waistline the desired amount (Fig. 5.71).

5. Locate the new points of the darts in the middle of the spread or lap.

6. Draw the dart stitching lines by connecting the new points to the original dart lines at the waistline.

7. Perfect the waistline by folding the darts and adding to the waist height from the dart to the center when the darts are increased (a to e in Fig. 5.70), or trimming the excess from the waistline from the dart to the center when the darts are decreased (a to e in Fig. 5.71).

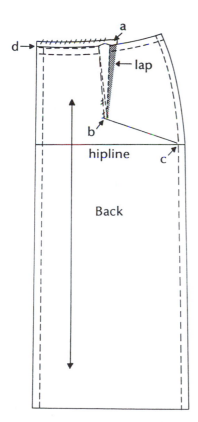

Fig. 5.69 Decreasing dart size for a single dart

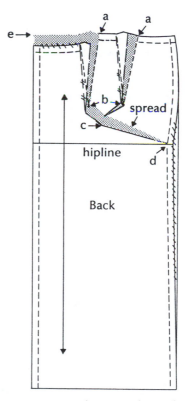

Fig. 5.70 Increasing dart size for a double dart

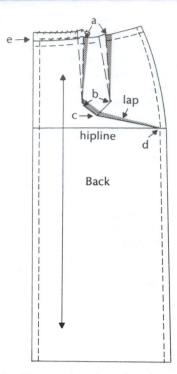

Fig. 5.71   Decreasing dart size for a double dart

Altering Skirt Length

To alter skirt length:

Skirt length can be altered in one of two ways: (1) by changing the length at the bottom edge of the pattern or (2) by slashing and spreading or taking a folded tuck across the pattern between the hipline and the hemline. If the skirt pattern is flared, the skirt circumference will be changed if the alteration is made at the bottom edge of the pattern. This usually poses no problem unless the skirt circumference is made too large to fit on the fashion fabric. In this situation the alteration should be made internally by slashing and spreading the pattern (Fig. 5.72). Perfect the seam lines by drawing a straight line from the hipline to the hemline.

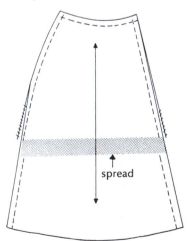

Fig. 5.72   Lengthening a flared skirt by slashing and spreading

Pants Alterations

Well-fitted pants (Fig. 5.73) should hang straight from the hips to the hem without wrinkling or sagging. Both inseams and outseams should hang straight slanting neither to the front nor to the back. Pants patterns need to be carefully measured and altered in the suggested sequence to achieve proper fit. It is helpful in altering pants patterns to mark some additional lines for measurements and alteration purposes (Fig. 5.74).

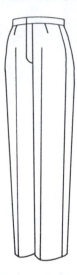

Fig. 5.73   Well-fitting pants

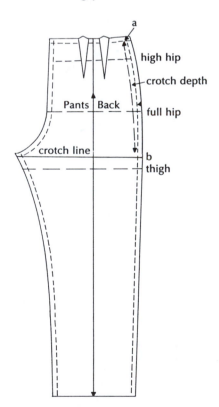

Fig. 5.74   Lines for pants measurements and alterations

Before altering:

1. Extend the lengthwise grainline marking the full length of the pattern.

2. At the widest part of the crotch area on the pants back, draw in the crotch line at right angles to the grainline.

3. Mark the high hip, full hip, and thigh levels at right angles to the grainline.

4. Mark the position for measuring the crotch depth near the side seam from the waist to the crosswise grain at the crotch line.

The pants pattern should be measured and altered in sequence beginning with altering crotch depth. If dart length or size needs to be altered, refer to the section on Skirt Alterations for altering darts. The style of the pattern may allow for more than the minimum amount of ease; this is design ease and should not be removed.

Altering Crotch Depth

The depth of the crotch curve on pants patterns is related to the depth of the lower torso or the distance from the waistline to the lower part of the buttocks. If the crotch depth is too short, the waistline will be too low. If the waistline is pulled up to fit the natural waistline, the pant fabric will pull inward toward the crotch seam (Fig. 5.75). If the crotch depth on the pants is too long, the lower crotch seam will hang below the body level at the inseam.

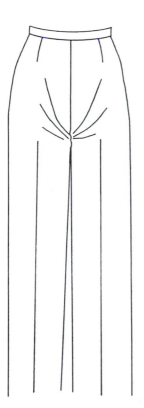

Fig. 5.75   Pants crotch depth too short

To alter crotch depth:

1. Compare the personal crotch depth measurement plus ease to the crotch depth measurement on the *pants back pattern* (a to b in Fig. 5.74).

2. To lengthen the pants crotch depth slash and spread *both front and back patterns* an even amount at the *hip level* (Fig. 5.76).

3. To shorten the pants crotch depth fold horizontally across the pattern on *both front and back patterns* an even amount at the *hip level*.

4. Redraw the crotch and side seam lines to smooth out the curves.

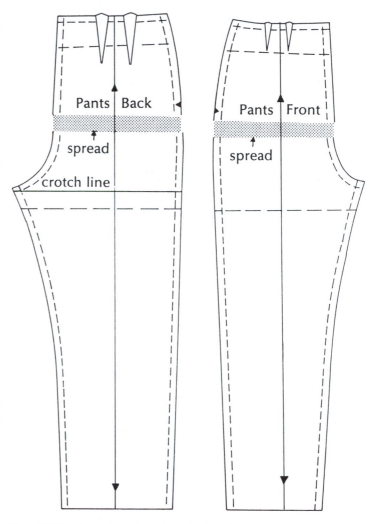

Fig. 5.76   Lengthening crotch depth

Altering Hip Circumference

Pants should fit without any horizontal or diagonal stress wrinkles pointing to the side seam. If wrinkling occurs at any point along the side seam (Fig. 5.77), more ease needs to be added to the pattern at that location. If the garment has excess vertical folds near the side seam (Fig. 5.78), there is too much fullness and some of the

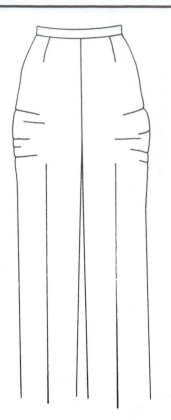

Fig. 5.77   Pants too tight in hip and thigh areas

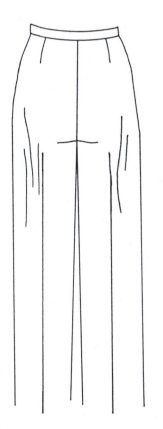

Fig. 5.78   Pants too loose in hip and thigh areas

ease should be removed. If too much ease is removed, however, diagonal wrinkles may form. Before altering the pants pattern, body circumferences should be measured at the waist, high hip, full hip, and leg circumference areas. Appropriate amounts of ease should be added to these measurements before measuring the pattern. The amount of ease added will vary with the style of the garment; more ease is added for pleated styles than for styles with basic fitting darts.

To alter pants circumference at the waist, high hip, full hip, and/or thigh levels:

1. About 2 inches (5 cm) from the side seam draw a vertical slash line parallel to lengthwise grain beginning at the bottom of the pants and extending to a point about 2 inches (5 cm) from the waistline (a to b in Fig. 5.79). Angle this slash line diagonally to the corner where the waistline joins the side seam (b to c in Fig. 5.79). Slash on this line from the waistline *to but not through* the hemline.

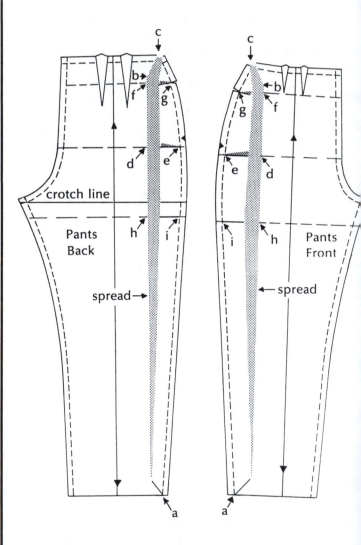

Fig. 5.79   Increasing waist, high hip, full hip, and/or thigh circumference on pants

2. At the line marking the fullest part of the hips, slash horizontally from the vertical slash to the side seam line (*d* to *e* in Fig. 5.79).

3. If an increase is needed in the high hip, add a horizontal slash from the vertical slash 3 inches (7.5 cm) down from the waist (*f* to *g* in Fig. 5.79).

4. If an increase is needed in the thigh area, add a horizontal slash from the vertical slash at the thigh area (*h* to *i* in Fig. 5.79).

5. Clip the seam allowances to points *a*, *e*, *g*, and/or *i* in Figure 5.79 to permit the pattern to lie flat.

6. To increase pants circumference spread along the vertical slash the needed amount at the waist (*c*), high hip (*f*), hipline (*d*), and thigh (*h* in Fig. 5.79) tapering the spread to nothing at the hemline to preserve the original pants circumference at the hemline.

7. To decrease pants circumference lap along the vertical slash the needed amount, tapering the lap to nothing at the hemline to preserve the original pants circumference at the hemline (Fig. 5.80).

Altering Waist and/or High Hip

If the waist circumference needs to be adjusted in addition to the full hip, the alteration can be completed in the same vertical slash line used to alter the full hip. However, if only the waist or high hip require an adjustment (Fig. 5.81), the alteration can be made by slashing from the waistline to the side seam at the hipline.

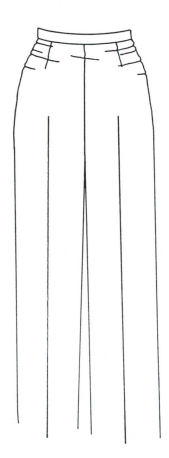

Fig. 5.81   Pants too tight in waist and high hip areas

To alter waist and/or high hip circumference:

1. Slash along a vertical line beginning at the waistline and extending to within 2 inches (5 cm) of the hipline (*a* to *b* in Fig. 5.82). Angle this slash line to the side seam line (*b* to *c* in Fig. 5.82).

2. If an alteration is needed in the high hip, slash from this vertical slash to the side seam line 3 inches (7.5 cm) down from the waist (*d* to *e* in Fig. 5.82).

3. Clip the seam allowance to points ·c and e in Figure 5.82 to permit the pattern to lie flat.

4. To increase the waist and/or high hip spread the vertical slash at the waist (*a*) and high hip (*b*) in Figure 5.82 the needed amount.

5. To decrease the waist and/or high hip lap the vertical slash the needed amount.

6. Perfect the waistline seam as a smooth curve.

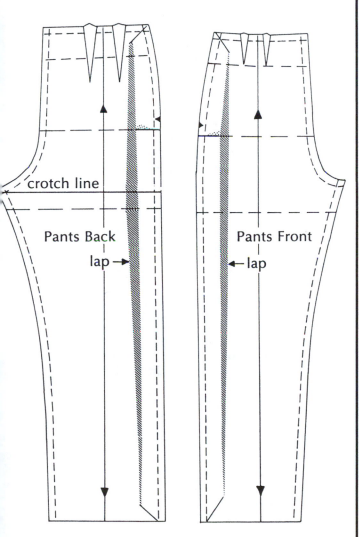

crotch line

Pants Back

lap →

Pants Front

← lap

Fig. 5.80   Decreasing waist, high hip, and/or full hip circumference on pants

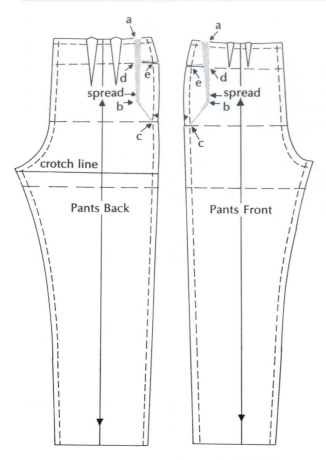

Fig. 5.82   Increasing waist and/or high hip circumference

Altering Upper Leg Circumference

When the body torso is deep from the front to the back, diagonal wrinkling to the crotch area often occurs (Fig. 5.83). This wrinkling, which is usually more apparent in the back than in the front, may cause the pants inseam to pull up uncomfortably while walking or sitting. To provide the necessary depth through the crotch area in the pattern, the crotch point should be extended at the inseam. If the body proportion is larger in the back than in the front, more would be added to the back crotch point than to the front. If the body is proportioned equally from front to back, equal amounts would be added to both inseams. The upper leg circumference measurement plus ease would be used to compare to the pattern measurement to determine the amount of this alteration.

To alter upper leg circumference:

1. To increase the upper leg circumference, extend the crotch point at the inseam and taper to the original seam line at about knee level. Add most of the increase to the back unless wrinkles appear in both front and back; then add equally to the front and back (Fig. 5.84). Two inches (5 cm) is

only the minimum ease recommended for the upper leg circumference. Most pant styles will have more than the minimum amount of ease in this area.

2. To decrease the upper leg circumference take in the inseam of the leg at the crotch point and taper to the original seam line at about knee level. Usually equal amounts are taken off both the front and the back pattern pieces.

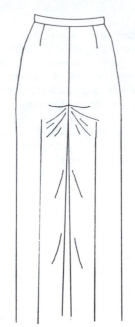

Fig. 5.83   Diagonal wrinkling to the crotch point on pants back created by more body depth from front to back

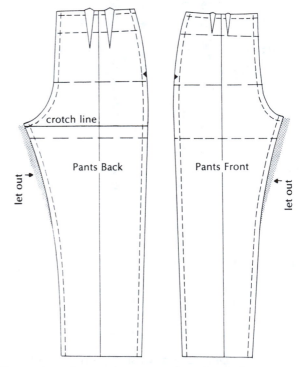

Fig. 5.84   Increasing upper leg circumference

Altering Total Crotch Length

The total crotch length measurement is taken on the body beginning at the front waistline and continuing around the body through the legs to the back waistline. This measurement aids in analyzing body depth and width. To determine the amount of the alteration to the total crotch length on the pattern, add ease to the body crotch length measurement and compare to the pattern crotch length measurement. Alterations for total crotch length can be made on a horizontal slash line at about the hip level and/or at the inseam on either the front or the back; however, most of the alteration usually is done to the pants back pattern. If the figure is full in front, then the alteration would be divided between the front and the back. When the figure is deep from front to back, most of the alteration is made by extending the back crotch point at the inseam.

To alter total crotch length:

1. Slash horizontally from the crotch seam *to but not through* the side seam at about hip level (*a* to *b* in Fig. 5.85).

2. Clip the side seam allowance to point *b* in Figure 5.85 to permit the pattern to lie flat.

3. If the torso is long, add most of the alteration at this level by spreading along the center back seam line (*a* in Fig. 5.85) the necessary amount.

4. If the body shape is deep in proportion from front to back, add all or most of the alteration to the back inseam by extending the crotch point at the inseam seam line, tapering the new seam line to the original seam line at the knee level (*c* to *d* in Fig. 5.85).

5. To decrease crotch length, lap the pattern along the horizontal slash line and/or take in along the inseam (Fig. 5.86).

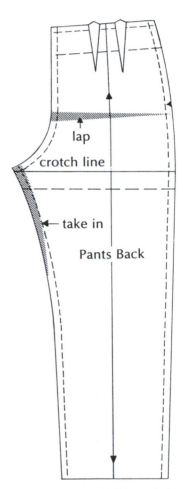

Fig. 5.86   Decreasing total crotch length

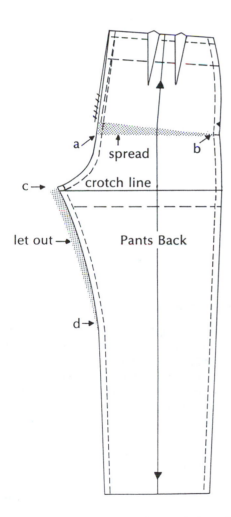

Fig. 5.85   Increasing total crotch length

Altering for a Lowered Buttocks Curve

The contour of the buttocks curve influences the shape of the crotch curve on the pants pattern. Horizontal wrinkling often occurs below the buttocks if the crotch curve on the pattern is too shallow (Fig. 5.87), sometimes causing the waistline and horizontal grainline to drop. It is difficult to anticipate this alteration before cutting out a pants pattern; therefore, correction often occurs after the first fitting. The fitting problem can be corrected in the garment by deepening the stitching line in the area of the crotch curve on the pants back (*a* in Fig. 5.88). The curve should be deepened a small amount at a time until the desired shape is achieved. To avoid a "peak" from forming at the inseam area, the front crotch curve seam line should be made more shallow (*b* in Fig. 5.88). The crotch curve will fit more smoothly if the seam allowance is trimmed to ⅜ inch (1 cm) after the correct fit has been achieved.

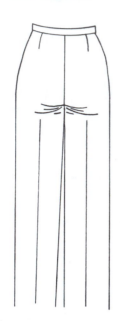

Fig. 5.87   Horizontal wrinkling below a lowered buttocks curve

Fig. 5.88   Deepening the back crotch curve on pants

To alter pants pattern for a lowered buttocks curve:

1. Deepen the crotch curve on the pants back pattern the amount that was deepened on the garment (*a* in Fig. 5.89).
2. Flatten the curve on the front crotch seam line (*b* in Fig. 5.89).

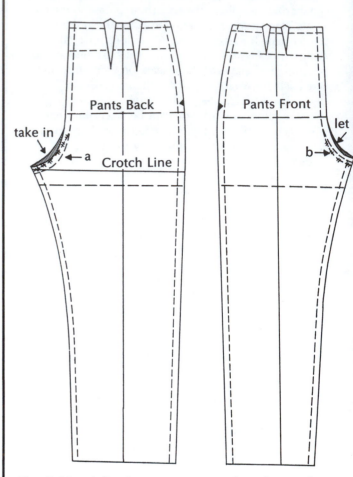

Fig. 5.89   Adjusting pants pattern for a lowered buttocks curve

Altering for Full Inner Leg

This alteration reshapes the inseam to accommodate a leg shape where the thighs and knees are close together (Fig. 5.90). The straightened inseam allows the fabric to relax and to hang free from wrinkles. It is difficult to determine the amount for this alteration without fitting an actual garment; therefore, it is recommended that a test garment be fitted before cutting out the fashion fabric.

To alter for full inner leg:

1. Reduce the slant of the inseam by adding width to the leg along the inseam at the crotch point and knee level (*a* to *b* in Fig. 5.91) on both the pants front and back pattern pieces.

Fig. 5.90   Full inner leg

The amount added to these points depends on the shape of the leg.

2. Continue drawing the inseam to the hemline adding an even amount to the seam from the knee to the hemline (b to c in Fig. 5.91).

3. To adjust the pant leg circumference to match the original pattern, the outseam can be tapered in from the thigh level to the hemline, taking in the side seam the amount that was added to the circumference at the inseam (d to e in Fig. 5.91).

Altering Pants Length

Pants length can be altered in two ways: (1) by changing the length at the bottom edge of the pattern or (2) by slashing and spreading or taking a folded tuck across the pattern between the knee and the hemline. If the pants leg is tapered, the hem circumference will be changed if the alteration is made at the bottom edge of the pattern. For tapered pants styles it is recommended that the alteration be made by slashing and spreading to lengthen or by slashing and lapping to shorten on an alteration line located between the knee level and the hem. Perfect the seam lines by drawing a straight line from the thigh level to the hemline.

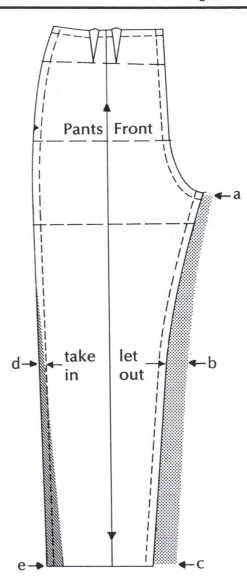

Fig. 5.91   Altering pants pattern for full inner leg

6 Components of Fit

Wearing apparel is created when a two/dimensional fabric is shaped through the use of design features such as darts, pleats, tucks, and seams to fit the three-dimensional body form. What is meant by "fit" and how good fit is achieved in personally sewn garments is the focus of this chapter.

The fit of clothing is important for many reasons. Clothing is an extension of oneself, and the way clothing fits affects personal appearance and the first impression one makes on others. Clothing fit also influences how individuals feel about themselves and how they act. Poorly fitting clothing may make a person self-conscious, whereas clothing that fits well allows one to feel self-confident, comfortable, and poised.

Factors Affecting Fit

Fit varies according to many factors, including the style of the garment, the fabric being used, and the end use of the garment. A tent dress is designed to fit differently than a strapless one; one would not expect the same standards of fit to apply to each. Garments constructed from woven fabrics will fit differently than those made from knitted fabrics where the inherent stretch in the fabric contributes to the overall fit of the garment. Different types of garments with their varying end uses are expected to fit differently. The fit of a warm-up suit will not be the same as that of a leotard.

Fit also varies according to individual preferences. Persons of different ages may want clothes that fit differently. Personal size and mood also may affect the preference for a certain standard of good fit. Fashion dictates what is acceptable as good fit from one period to another. Cultural differences exist, too; some of these may be rooted in the predominant religious beliefs of the culture.

Body contour, posture, body proportion, and symmetry affect the fit of clothing. Patterns are designed for an average symmetrical body shape, with standard posture and body proportion. Very few individuals are the same size and shape as this standard; therefore, pattern alterations need to be made before garment pieces are cut and fitting adjustments are made during the assembly process. Careful, objective analysis of one's body shape will aid in the selection of clothing styles that will enhance one's appearance and in identifying pattern adjustments necessary for good fit.

Body Contour

An individual's body contour usually is somewhat different from the standard figure used for fitting commercial patterns. Individual shapes vary from very shallow curves to full body curves. Darts, tucks, and curved seams are design details used to shape fabric to fit these body contours. The larger the curve, the more shaping required through these design details; the smaller the curve, the less shaping required. One's body shape will change over time as the body matures, as weight is gained or lost, and by the type of foundation garments worn; thus, continual analysis of body contour is necessary to achieve well-fitting garments.

Posture

Commercial patterns are designed for individuals with standard posture (A in Fig. 6.1). When there is a tendency to have slumping posture (B in Fig. 6.1) the back becomes more rounded resulting in larger curves and a lower bustline. On individuals with overly erect posture (C in Fig. 6.1) the back shape becomes straighter, resulting in shallower curves and a higher bustline level. Individuals whose posture varies from the standard may need to alter patterns to correct for individual body variations. Dart size may need to be increased for larger curves or decreased for shallower curves; dart position raised for higher bustline or dropped for a lower bustline. Loosely fitting garment styles, with design details such as gathers, tucks, or flare, may require fewer alterations due to posture variations than more closely fitting garments.

Body Proportion

Body proportion is the vertical space relationship among key body features: shoulders, bust, waist, and hip. Commercial patterns are designed for standard body proportions (Fig. 6.2) that are composed of four basic divisions:

—Half the body is above the fullest part of the hip and half below.
—The waist falls halfway between the underarm and the fullest part of the hip.
—The lower half of the body is divided at the knee.
—Elbows fall at the waist and fingertips at mid-thigh.

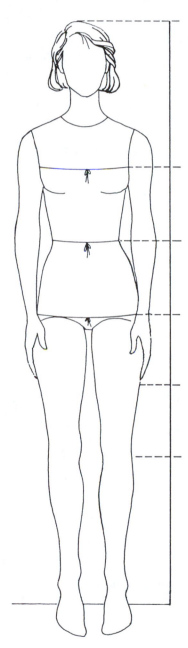

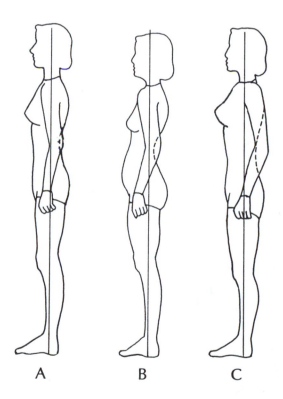

A   B   C

Fig. 6.1   Posture variations: (A) standard posture; (B) slumping posture; (C) overly erect posture

Fig. 6.2   Standard body proportions

Very few individuals conform to these average body proportions; therefore the various female body types available in commercial patterns (misses', miss petite, junior, junior petite, young junior/teen, girls', women's, and half-size) are designed to accommodate differences in body proportion. Body types for the male figure (men's, teen-boys', and boys') are also designed for a body build, not an age. More choices are currently available in the men's and boys' ready-to-wear market than are available in commercial patterns. Since personal body measurements often differ from the pattern measurements, alterations will need to be made for individual variations by adjusting pattern lengths and widths.

Symmetry

Very few people have a symmetrical body. When there is a significant difference on the two sides of the body, a garment may hang unevenly or appear more wrinkled on one side of the body than on the other. Uneven shoulders is one of the most common areas of asymmetry. To correct for uneven shoulders, the angle of the shoulder seam can be adjusted; or shoulder pads of differing thicknesses can be used to give the appearance of balanced shoulders. Other uneven figure features that may require pattern adjustments include: one shoulder blade larger than the other, one hip higher than the other, or one side of the waist curves in more than the other. Selecting garment styles that are more loose fitting helps to camouflage body asymmetry and may reduce the number of needed pattern alterations.

Characteristics of a Well-fitting Garment

As mentioned, good fit depends on many variables, making it difficult to define. Garments will fit differently depending on the style. Close-fitting styles (Fig. 6.3) conform to the body contours more closely than loose-fitting styles (Fig. 6.4). Even on loose-fitting designs, there will be areas of the garment that fit close to the body. There are some general characteristics that can be used to evaluate the fit of garments. More of these characteristics will apply to close-fitting styles than they do to garments that are more loosely fitted.

The following characteristics of a well-fitting garment are listed in the same sequence as one would evaluate the fit of a garment during the fitting process.

1. There should be ample ease for movement. The amount of ease varies with the style of the garment, with fashion, with fabric, and with personal preference. A fitted garment has an appropriate amount of wearing ease without appearing either too tight or too loose. Ease allowances differ in various parts of the body (e.g., more is allowed in the hip area than at the waist). Tables 3.3 and 3.4 provide minimum wearing ease for areas of the body

Fig. 6.3 Close-fitting styles

for a fitted garment of woven fabric. The ease discussed here does not include design ease. Chapter 3 contains an expanded discussion of wearing and design ease.

2. The shoulder area should fit smoothly with no excess fabric around the neck or on top of the shoulder.

3. The shoulder seam should lie in a straight line on the top of the shoulder, slanting neither to the front nor to the back when viewed from the side.

4. The center front and center back lengthwise grainlines should be vertical, at right angles to the floor, and centered on the body. In pants, the front creases, which are on lengthwise grain, hang perpendicular to the floor.

5. For the upper body, the crosswise grainline should be parallel to the floor at upper chest in the front and across the shoulder blades in the back.

6. There should be no excessive vertical folds nor diagonal wrinkles. Any wrinkling that appears is usually an indication of improper fit. Folds in the garment created by design ease or gathers should not be confused with wrinkles that are an indication of poor fit.

7. Darts should be directed to the fullest part of the body contour and terminate about 1 inch (2.5 cm) short of the fullest part of the curve. Bodice styles for females require more darting than shirt styles for males. Bodice front darts will be directed to the bust point; back darts point to the shoulder area. The back waist dart stops

further from the curve than does the shoulder dart to preserve ease across the shoulder blades.

8. The size of the dart is related to the size of the body curve. If there is excess fullness noted at the point of a dart, dart size may be too big. Diagonal folds pointing to a body curve fitted by a dart usually indicate that the dart size is too small.

9. The waistline seam should follow the natural body waistline and fit close to the body.

10. The armscye seam line should lie across the end of the shoulder bone, which is the joint where the arm joins the body, and continue downward in a smooth curve through the front arm crease to the underarm. To locate the shoulder joint, raise the arm and feel the indentation at the socket. The armscye seam line on the back extends slightly beyond the armhole crease, providing ease across the shoulder blade area.

11. Lengthwise grain on a basic high cap sleeve should be straight down the center of the arm from the top of the sleeve to the elbow level. Crosswise grain is parallel to the floor at the upper arm.

12. Elbow darts point to the elbow and the sleeve length should end just below the wrist bone.

13. Pants should hang straight from the hips without sagging, wrinkling, or pulling. Inseams and side seams should hang straight, slanting neither to the front nor to the back.

Fig. 6.4   Loose-fitting styles

Signs of Poor Fit

Grain Placement

Improper grain placement on the body is the first sign of poor fit. Of course the lengthwise and crosswise grain in the fabric must be properly aligned (at right angles to each other) before the garment is cut for the grain in the finished garment to hang correctly. (See Chapter 7, Straightening Fabric Grain.)

Grain is easily observed in fabrics with coarse yarns or those that have woven or knitted stripes or plaids, but it is more difficult to identify in fabrics with fine yarns or printed designs. For easy identification, the grainlines can be marked on the appropriate garment pieces with hand-basting lines before the garment is assembled. Horizontal grainlines should be marked on the fabric at the hip, the front chest, the back shoulder blade, and the sleeve capline (the widest part of a regular set-in sleeve). Lengthwise grainlines should be marked on the fabric at center front, center back, center of the pants leg, and down the center of the sleeve. If a center front or center back seam follows lengthwise grain, the seam line can be used to evaluate correct grain placement.

Structural Seam Line Placement

Structural lines within the garment that do not follow the body contour or divide the body into pleasing proportions are additional signs of poor fit. The placement of the shoulder seam on a bodice or shirt and the waist placement of pants or skirts should be evaluated and corrected first, as the fit in these areas will affect the way the rest of the garment will hang. The proper positioning of other garment seams, darts, pleats, and tucks is then evaluated and corrected, if necessary.

Unwanted Folds and Wrinkles

Extra folds and wrinkles within the garment are other signs of poor fit. The cause of these folds and wrinkles needs to be identified to correct the fit. Folds created by design ease such as gathers should not be confused with diagonal wrinkles and folds that are signs of poor fit.

Horizontal tension wrinkles (Fig. 6.5) indicate that the garment circumference is too small and that the garment needs to be made larger. This is usually accomplished by letting the garment out along the vertical seams or slashing and spreading the pattern near the side seams.

Vertical tension wrinkles (Fig. 6.6) show that the garment is shorter than the body and needs to be lengthened. This can be accomplished by letting the garment out along a horizontal seam or by slashing and spreading the pattern near the seam.

Loose horizontal folds (Fig. 6.7) are a sign that the garment is longer than the body and needs to be shortened. This can be done by taking in the garment along a

Fig. 6.5   Horizontal tension wrinkles caused by garments being too tight

Fig. 6.6   Vertical tension wrinkles caused by a garment section being too short

horizontal seam line or by lapping the pattern along a horizontal fold line.

Loose vertical folds (Fig. 6.8) mean that the garment is too wide. The extra fullness can be removed by taking in the side seams or by lapping the pattern along a vertical slash line.

Diagonal wrinkles (Fig. 6.9) indicate that the garment length is too short and needs to be lengthened or that the fitting dart is too small for the size of the body contour and needs to be enlarged. Diagonal wrinkles usually point to the area of the body causing the problem.

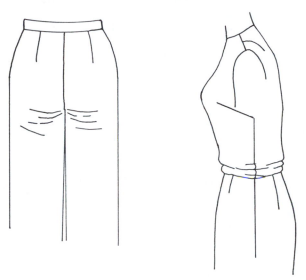

Fig. 6.7 Loose horizontal folds caused by a garment section being too long

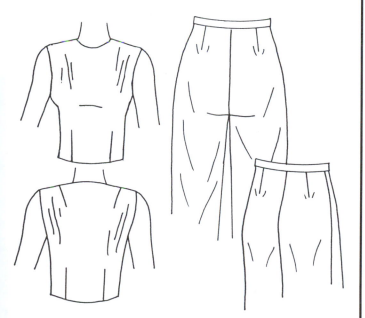

Fig. 6.8 Loose vertical folds caused by garments being too large

Fig. 6.9 Diagonal wrinkles caused by garment being too small for the body contour

Fitting is the process of learning to identify the desired characteristics of good fit and to evaluate the cause of poor fit, to analyze the effect, and to arrive at the solution.

Fitting a Garment During Construction

Even though alterations have been made to the pattern, the garment must be checked for fit during the assembly process to assure that the completed garment will conform to the body of the person who will wear it. The number of fittings required depends on the style of the garment and the number of figure variations of the person who will be wearing it. Loosely fitted garments will require fewer fittings than those that conform closely to the body. A person with many figure variations who is constructing a fitted garment may want to make it first in muslin or another inexpensive fabric to check the alterations that have been made.

Seams and design details that likely would not be changed or refitted can be stitched permanently as garment construction begins. These would include center front and center back seams, tucks, pleats, yoke seams, insets, and other design details. Darts should be pinned since the fit of darts cannot be determined until after the first fitting. Press only those seams and design details that have been permanently stitched. Seams that might require a change, such as shoulder, side, and waistline seams, can be pinned or thread basted either by hand or machine. If machine basting is used, a longer stitch length is recommended so it can be removed easily. When pin basting for fitting purposes, the pins are placed *parallel to and directly on* the seam line. Making changes is easier when the seams are pinned toward the outside of the garment. However, having the seam stick out may produce an illusion of poor fit. When the body is symmetrical, the garment can be fitted either right or wrong side out. When the body is asymmetrical, the garment must be fitted right side out. Pants should be fitted right side out.

The areas of the garment checked during the first fitting are:

—Circumference ease
—Presence of unwanted fabric folds or diagonal wrinkles
—Placement of vertical and horizontal grainlines on the body
—Location and fit of darts, pleats, tucks, and gathers
—Location and direction of lengthwise seams
—Location of the neckline seam, if one is present. If the garment contains a collar, the collar can be pinned to the neckline seam to check for appropriate proportion.
—Location of circumference seams such as bodice waistline. A change in the bodice length affects how an attached skirt or pant will fit; thus, checking bodice length is critical for those garments with a waistline seam.
—Placement lines for pockets
—Location of armhole seam line for placement of the sleeve
—Placement and fit of the crotch seam in pants

Following the first fitting, the darts and the lengthwise seams can be stitched permanently and finished. If the open construction technique is followed, the side seams of a garment would be completed after the neckline has been finished. The neckline (collar and/or facing) can be completed before the second fitting. A zipper, if present, would be installed. Sleeves would be completed and pin basted to the armhole.

The following areas in the garment would be evaluated during the second fitting:

—Review the appearance and check the major fitting areas previously described.
—Check armscye seam line and grain placement of sleeves.
—Mark the position for waistbands on skirts and pants.
—Locate placement for closures and fasteners

A third fitting is usually necessary to mark garment hemlines. Other finishing details can be checked at this time, as well.

A plan such as the one described does not mean that a garment is to be tried on only two or three times during construction. Often, many fittings are required. These three are, however, the minimum number of fittings necessary for checking the success of pattern alterations and making changes in the garment at a point when they can be accomplished without extra work. Waiting until the end of construction to fit a garment can result in the redoing of many seams and darts.

To accomplish these three fittings and to incorporate unit method of clothing construction, the sewer will need to study the guide sheet carefully and devise a plan that incorporates the various methods advocated here.

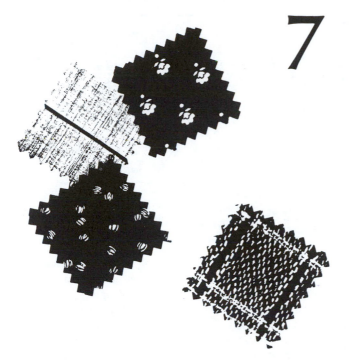

7 Fabric Preparation and Use

For the finished garment to fit and hang correctly, the garment must be cut from a fabric that is on grain. This chapter will describe the processes involved in straightening and preshrinking both woven and knitted fabrics.

Woven Fabrics

Woven fabrics have grain (see Chapter 4). Lengthwise grain runs parallel to the selvages; crosswise grain runs perpendicular to the selvages. When fabrics are woven, the crosswise and lengthwise yarns are perpendicular to each other. However, during the weaving or finishing processes, fabrics sometimes become distorted and this perpendicular relationship no longer exists. Grain perfection in the fabric needs to be restored before the garment is cut. Two steps are involved in this process: *straightening the end of the fabric*, unless the fabric is torn from the bolt when purchased, and *straightening the grain* or realigning crosswise and lengthwise yarns if they are not perpendicular to each other.

Straightening Fabric Ends

If a fabric has been torn from the bolt, the ends of the fabric already will be straight. This can be identified by pulling a crosswise yarn across the entire width of the fabric.

The ends of fabric, if cut rather than torn from the bolt, can be straightened in one of three ways. Firmly woven fabrics can be torn by snipping through one selvage and pulling. The fabric will tear on a crosswise yarn. This technique, however, will not work on all fabrics. In the second method, which works well for fabrics with a woven-in, crosswise design (such as on a woven plaid), the sewer needs only to cut along one of these crosswise design lines in order to have the fabric end follow a crosswise yarn. This technique will not work on fabrics on which the design has been printed instead of woven. The third method involves pulling one crosswise yarn and cutting along the line it makes (Fig. 7.1). To

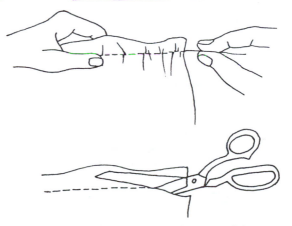

Fig. 7.1   Straightening ends of woven fabric

begin this process, the sewer needs to identify the lowest point along the end being straightened; this is the point where the yarn pulling process begins. As the crosswise yarns may have a tendency to break, one must be gentle when pulling them. If the yarn breaks, cut along the pulled line, then pick up the yarn and continue to pull and cut across the fabric until the process is completed. Regardless of the method used, both ends of the fabric need to be straightened.

Straightening Fabric Grain

Step two in preparing the fabric to be on-grain involves checking the grain alignment. By folding the fabric so that the selvage edges are parallel to each other and the fabric is smooth and flat with no diagonal wrinkles, the sewer can tell if the crosswise yarns are perpendicular to the lengthwise. Figure 7.2 illustrates an on-grain woven fabric; Figure 7.3 is an off-grain woven fabric.

To restore the proper grain alignment (i.e., lengthwise and crosswise yarns perpendicular to each other), the short corners of the fabric need to be pulled in the direction of *true bias* (Fig. 7.4). Recheck the fabric often, as a

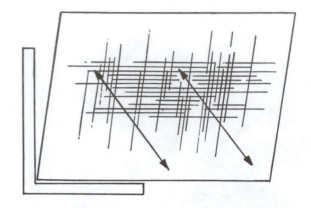

Fig. 7.4 Direction for pulling woven fabric to straighten grain

minimum amount of pulling may be needed for those fabrics that are loosely woven, have little if any finish, or are off-grain by very little. Other fabrics may require several attempts, using firm pulling action. For larger pieces of fabric, two people are needed to complete this process. Sometimes the selvages of fabrics are very tightly woven and may need to be clipped at intervals to allow the fabric to be made grain perfect.

Some fabrics cannot be straightened by this process: (1) fabrics that are very tightly woven, (2) those with certain finishes such as permanent press, (3) fabrics permanently bonded to a backing, or (4) knitted fabrics. If the fabric is so badly off grain that the finished garment will be affected, the fabric should be returned to the store and another selection made. Another alternative is to cut one layer at a time to ensure the same grain on both halves of the garment. With experience, the sewer will learn to recognize off-grain fabric and will avoid purchasing it, thus avoiding this problem.

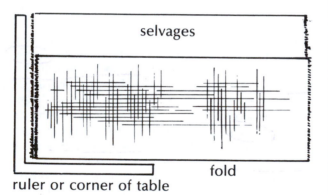

ruler or corner of table

Fig. 7.2 On-grain, woven fabric

Knitted Fabrics

Knitted fabrics have wales in the lengthwise direction and courses in the crosswise direction (see Chapter 4). Since knits have no selvage as do woven fabrics, a lengthwise grainline needs to be established. A line basted down a wale near the center of the fabric piece can be used as the lengthwise grain marking. A magnifying glass may be needed to complete this process on some knitted fabrics.

Knitted fabrics with an obvious crosswise design in the fabric (e.g., stripes) need to be folded so that the crosswise designs are matched. Tubular knits usually are cut apart along a wale to form a flat fabric before cutting.

Knits that are finished off-grain generally cannot be straightened. If the grain distortion will affect the appearance of the finished garment, the fabric should not be purchased or should be returned to the store for another selection.

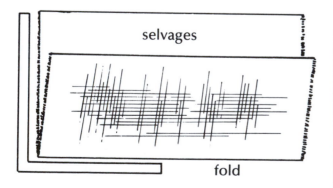

Fig. 7.3 Off-grain, woven fabric

Preshrinking

Preshrinking a fabric involves providing it with the same care procedure before the garment is cut as will be given to the finished garment. Washable fabrics can be either hand or machine laundered and line or machine dried. Washing and drying temperatures are important, because heat and shrinkage are directly related. If much shrinkage occurs during the first treatment, the process may need to be repeated because progressive shrinkage is common in some fabrics. When working with fabrics known to have considerable shrinkage, such as 100 percent cotton knits, it is recommended that additional fabric be purchased. The center fold of some fabrics may need special treatment during preshrinking to remove soil.

Nonwashable fabrics also need to be preshrunk. One method is to send the fabric to a professional dry cleaners for steam pressing; cleaning is not necessary unless the fabric is soiled. Another method involves wrapping the fabric in a damp sheet and leaving it for a period of time. This method is generally recommended for wool and wool-like fabrics.

To shrink nonwashable fabrics:

1. Straighten fabric ends.
2. Fold fabric lengthwise. Baste or pin selvages and ends together with rustproof pins.
3. Dampen a sheet; remove all excess moisture.
4. Open up the sheet and place the fabric on the dampened sheet. The sheet should extend 12–18 inches (30.5–46 cm) beyond the fabric.
5. Lap the end of the sheet over the fabric and continue to fold the sheet and fabric together. Keep the fabric as smooth as possible to avoid wrinkling.
6. Cover with plastic to prevent rapid drying and let stand 6–8 hours.
7. Carefully remove the fabric from the sheet. Smooth the fabric so that the grainline is straight. Allow to dry on a flat surface.
8. Press, if necessary.

Both preshrinking methods for nonwashable fabrics require that the fabric ends have been straightened first. The fabric grain may be easier to straighten after being preshrunk.

Notions such as zippers, tapes, and interfacings also need to be preshrunk. Small items can be placed in a bag before being placed in the washing machine or safety pinned to the firm edge of a garment. Fusible interfacings should not be placed in the washer or dryer. They can be preshrunk by soaking in a bowl of hot water for 15–20 minutes and then drip dried, or rolled gently in a towel and spread out on a flat surface to dry.

Preshrinking serves not only the purpose that its name implies, but it also removes excess resins and sizing that may be present in some fabrics. Thus, the preshrunk fabric may be easier to handle than the one that is not preshrunk. Even fabrics known not to shrink may benefit from this treatment.

8 Special Fabrics

A number of fabrics require special treatment for cutting and sewing. This chapter will discuss these special fabrics: plaids, stripes, silky wovens, and directional fabrics. Sewing with knits is discussed in Chapter 9.

Plaids

This section discusses *woven* plaids. Printed plaids also are available; however, unless printed on-grain (and they often are not), they are not recommended.

Plaid fabrics can have an even or an uneven design. In an *even plaid* (Fig. 8.1), the color bars and spaces are symmetrical around the center of the plaid block or repeat, thus forming a mirror image both right and left as well as up and down. *Uneven plaids* have irregularly placed color bars and spaces and do not form a mirror image around the center of the plaid block (Fig. 8.2*A, B, C*). Plaids can be uneven in the lengthwise direction (Fig. 8.2*A*), the crosswise direction (Fig. 8.2*B*), or both (Fig. 8.2*C*). The more irregular and the larger the plaid design, the more challenging the cutting task will be and the more extra fabric will be needed to complete the task.

Three major considerations need to be given to plaid fabrics when deciding how to cut them.

1. For the finished garment to look balanced, the plaid needs to be centered (Fig. 8.3). This means that the sewer needs to decide which of the vertical lines of the fabric to place in the center front and back and down the center of the sleeve.

2. A second consideration is where to place the dominant crosswise bars on the body. Thought needs to be given to figure features when making this decision, as

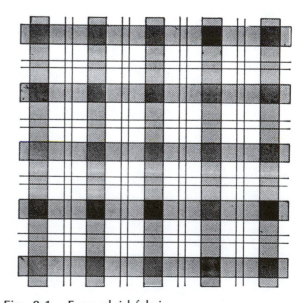

Fig. 8.1   Even plaid fabric

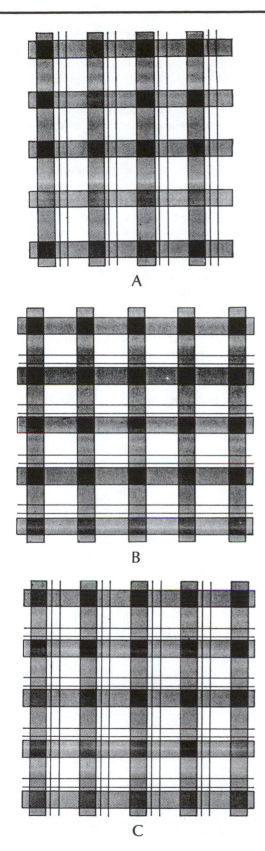

Fig. 8.2 Uneven plaid fabric: *(A)* uneven lengthwise; *(B)* uneven crosswise; *(C)* uneven lengthwise and crosswise

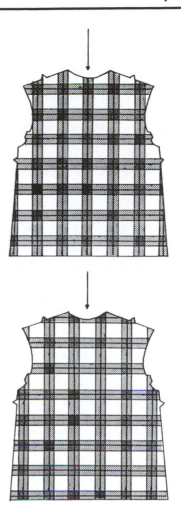

Fig. 8.3 Placement of vertical plaid bars at center front

the dominant line could draw attention to areas needing to be deemphasized. The dominant line also should not be placed at the hemline of a garment with a curved hem, as the hem will tend to look uneven when this bold line does not follow the curve of the hem. Where the edges of garments are straight, however, placing the dominant line at the edge may be a good idea.

3. The crosswise lines of the plaid need to be matched so that the lines of the fabric continue around the body. Since matching all seams may not be possible, the sewer will need to decide those that are most critical to the appearance of the finished garment. Such seams as the side seams, center front, and center back of garments would be matched without exception. However, if the front of the sleeve is matched to the bodice, it may not be possible to also match it in the back. Also, shoulder seams are difficult, if not impossible, to match. To avoid problems with matching garment details such as cuffs, bands, yokes, and patch pockets, sometimes these pieces are cut on a different grain, usually true bias or crosswise grain.

Preparing the Pattern and Fabric for Matching Plaids

Extra lines will need to be placed on the pattern pieces to aid in centering and matching. The center will need to be marked on pieces where the center is not indicated (e.g., the sleeve, front facing, etc.). One or more crosswise lines will need to be drawn perpendicular to the grainline to help in aligning the pattern piece on the fabric. Adding notches at the top and bottom of pattern pieces with long seams will help when matching adjoining pattern pieces. Changing the slant of darts also may be advisable. The stitching line for darts that enter the seam line at a diagonal will not match; changing those darts to be perpendicular to the seam will give a more pleasing effect in the finished garment.

Plaid fabrics must be grain perfect if the finished garment is to be balanced and matched (see Chapter 7). The crosswise bars need to be at a perfect right angle to the lengthwise ones.

If the plaid is uneven in the crosswise direction, a "with nap" layout will need to be chosen. If the fabric is folded for cutting, the two layers will need to be pinned together in a number of locations to insure that a matched pair of garment pieces is being cut. Using a single thickness layout will eliminate this step and may make cutting a matched pair of pieces an easier task than when trying to do it on folded fabric. When cutting pattern pieces singly, care must be taken to reverse the second pattern piece (i.e., turn it upside down) so that pieces for both right and left sides are being cut.

Changing the grain for some pattern pieces may be advisable when working with plaids. Matching such pieces as cuffs, bands, and patch pockets can be a challenge; cutting them on the true bias or the crosswise grain will eliminate the problem. True bias gives an interesting effect to garments constructed from plaid fabrics and is often used for either part or all of the garment. A chevron effect, where bars of the plaid meet on a 45 degree angle at the seams, is possible with even plaids.

The chevron effect can be achieved with uneven plaids only when the fabric has no apparent right or wrong side. The right side of the fabric is used on one of the sides of the front and the wrong side of the fabric for the other side of the front. To continue the chevron effect at the side seam, the skirt front and back pattern pieces must be the same width and have the same slant along the side seam.

Pattern Layouts with Plaids

Before placing the pattern pieces on the fabric, decisions need to be made concerning which lengthwise line is to be placed in the center of the garment, where the dominant crosswise lines will be placed, whether a single or folded layout is to be used, and whether a with nap layout is needed. Chapter 11, which discusses gen-

eral procedures for layout and cutting, should be studied carefully before proceeding.

A trial layout is advised, placing only a minimum number of pins in the grainline of each pattern piece until the final location is determined. When doing a pattern layout with plaid fabrics, pattern pieces are moved often before finally being placed in the appropriate location. The main pieces of the garment, and usually those for the front of the garment, are the first to be placed on the fabric. Each piece needs to be placed so that it is balanced—the center is on the vertical bar chosen for this purpose. When checking the matching of one piece to another, it is the position of the plaid line at the *seam line*, not at the cutting line, that should be aligned. The pattern piece can be moved up and down on this bar of the plaid until the crosswise lines are aligned as needed. To match the designs along the vertical seam lines, the notches and other markings of the adjoining seams need to fall on exactly the same crosswise bars. Again, matching occurs at the *seam line* or *stitching line*, not at the cutting line. Once the first piece is pinned in place, the second piece can be placed on top of it and the strategic matching lines drawn onto it before it is placed in an appropriate place.

Measuring from the grainline to the selvage is not necessary when working with a woven plaid, as each of the bars represents lengthwise grainline. The same is

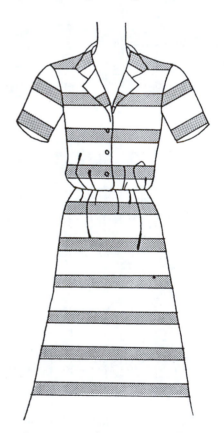

Fig. 8.4   Garment with continuous horizontal bars across the waistline seam

true for crosswise grain. If, after the fabric is placed on lengthwise grain, the crosswise bars do not align with the crosswise markings on the pattern, the fabric is not grain perfect. It will need to be straightened further before proceeding with the layout.

If the garment has horizontal seams, pattern pieces need to be placed so that the horizontal bars are continuous as the eye moves vertically across the seam (Fig. 8.4). Again, it is important to check the placement of the horizontal bar at the stitching line and not the cutting line.

Plaids that are uneven lengthwise present challenges when trying to center or balance the vertical bars. If the fabric has no right and wrong side, the pieces for the right and left sides of the body can be balanced by not reversing the fabric when cutting the second piece on those patterns that have center back and center front seam lines. In this situation, the right side of the fabric will be the outside on one side of the body, and the wrong side of the fabric will be the outside on the other side of the body. Otherwise, the garment needs to be cut so that the bar used in the center gives the most balanced effect possible and the plaid repeat is continuous around the entire body.

Accuracy in cutting plaid fabrics is absolutely crucial to the appearance of the finished garment. Both time and patience, plus enough fabric, are needed to insure success.

Sewing Plaid Fabrics

Once the plaid fabric is cut and marked (see Chapter 11), care must be taken when sewing to have the designs perfectly aligned. Seams will need to be carefully pinned and possibly even basted before machine stitching. When pinning, first place the pins *parallel to and directly on the seam line*, with a pin at each matching point. Open up the seam and check that the plaid is perfectly matched on each side of the seam (Fig. 8.5). Before sewing, place a second set of pins *perpendicular to the seam line* at each of the matching points (Fig. 8.6). Use the parallel pins as a stitching guide and remove the pins as the seam is being stitched. Carefully sew over the pins placed perpendicular to the seam line to insure exact matching during sewing. Remove the pins after the seam has been stitched.

Slip basting the seam before machine stitching is another way to align plaids and stripes. For slip basting, one seam allowance is folded under and placed on top of the other seam allowance, matching stitching lines and plaids or stripes (Fig. 8.7). The seam is pinned and then hand stitched by running the needle through the fold of the upper layer catching only a thread of the bottom layer. The fabric is unfolded and machine stitched.

A double-faced tape, sticky on both sides, can be used to hold the two pieces of plaid fabric together for

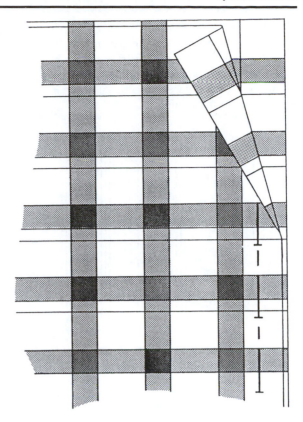

Fig. 8.5 Joining seams in plaids: step 1—pinning parallel to the seam

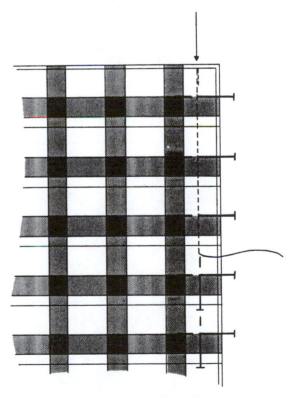

Fig. 8.6 Joining seams in plaids: step 2—pinning perpendicular to the seam

stitching (Fig. 8.8). The tape needs to be placed just to the outside of the stitching line, within the seam allowance, so that it is not caught in the machine stitching. This tape should be tried on a scrap of the fabric before being used on the garment to be sure that it will cause no damage to the fabric.

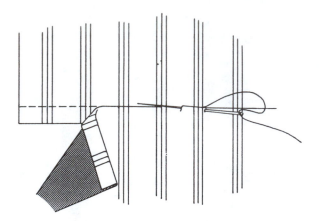

Fig. 8.7   Joining seams in stripes: slip basting

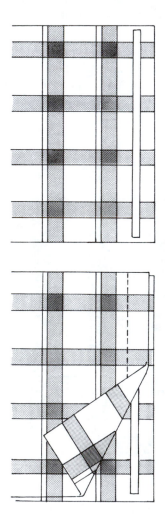

Fig. 8.8   Joining seams in plaids: tape method

Striped Fabrics

Striped fabrics, like plaids, can be either even or uneven; and the stripes can run vertically or horizontally on the fabric. Reading through the directions for working with plaids is recommended before starting on a stripe.

Since stripes are positioned in only one direction, decisions need to be made only about centering or matching. Even, horizontal stripes can be cut using a "without nap" layout, consideration being given to the placement of the dominant stripes on the body. If the pattern includes a horizontal seam, cutting so that the stripe continues in an evenly-spaced manner across the seam is important.

To achieve a particular effect and to avoid matching, parts of the garment can be cut on a different grain. Cuffs, bands, and yokes often are cut with the stripe running in the opposite direction to the rest of the garment. Stripes can be cut to achieve a chevron effect along bias seams.

The matching and centering of stripes follows the same procedures as is used with plaids.

Silky Woven Fabrics

Silky woven fabrics, because they are slippery, need to be handled carefully when cutting and sewing. When cutting, the fabric may need to be anchored to a cutting board or a piece of paper to keep it on grain. If the fabric has a tendency to show puncture marks, all pinning needs to be done within the seam allowance. Lightweight thread, available in a limited number of colors, helps to prevent puckering of seams. French seams are a good choice, where appropriate, as the narrower seams are more attractive if the finished seam can be seen from the outside of the garment. A fine, sharp sewing machine needle should be selected. Using the straight stitch throat plate and presser foot on the machine will help to keep the fabric from being pushed down into the throat plate during sewing. Placing a piece of paper between the fabric and the throat plate of the machine may be necessary to keep the fabric from slipping when sewing. Changing the pressure on the presser foot will help to keep the two layers of fabric together as they go through the sewing machine. An even-feed foot is available for some machines and may be helpful on fabrics where slippage is a serious problem. Overlock machines provide a smooth seam for many silky woven fabrics.

Nonfusible interfacings are preferred to fusibles for silky woven fabrics, because fusibles tend to make the fabric stiff. Often, too, the fusible interfacing will leave a crinkled rather than a smooth appearance on the fabric. In addition, it has a tendency to come loose during laundering, often leaving a "bubbled" effect in the interfaced area.

Directional Fabrics

Many fabrics, including uneven stripes and plaids, are directional; they have an "up" and "down" effect. Other directional fabrics include napped fabrics such as velvets and corduroys and many prints. The latter are directional if all of the designs in the print are turned in the same direction. Animal prints, for example, often have all of the animals standing the same way. Shiny fabrics such as satins are directional if the fabric takes on a different appearance in the light depending on the direction in which it is viewed. Knits are considered directional fabrics because the looped construction is wide on one end of the loop and narrow on the other. Knits may reflect light differently if some sections of the garment are cut in the opposite direction.

All fabrics need to be examined to see if they are directional. If they are, a "with nap" layout will need to be selected. The important point is to lay and cut all of the pattern pieces in the same direction on the fabric. The direction to use depends on the fabric and the effect desired. Fabrics with a short nap (corduroy, velvet, velour) will have a richer color if cut with the nap running up, the fabric will feel smooth when brushed from the bottom to the top of the garment. The color will appear lighter if the nap runs down. The direction of the nap can be determined by running the hand over the fabric; the nap feels smooth in the downward direction, rough in the upward direction.

9 Working with Knitted Fabrics

Knitted fabrics, because of their construction, require different handling during cutting and sewing of garments. This chapter will discuss those aspects that deviate the most when working with knitted rather than woven fabrics. Discussion on selection of knitted fabrics is found in Chapter 4 and on fabric preparation in Chapter 7. Almost every chapter has some discussion of techniques to use with knitted fabrics.

Knitted fabrics differ widely in fiber content and construction; sewing techniques vary according to these differences. As with any fabric, experimentation is necessary to determine the best techniques to use. No one seam or interfacing or hem is recommended for all knits.

Layout, Cutting, and Marking Knits

Prior to layout and cutting, the knitted fabric must be preshrunk (see Chapter 7) and the grainline identified. To locate lengthwise grain on knitted fabric a row of basting can be placed along one wale near the fold line (Fig. 9.1). This basting will be followed when folding the fabric and when aligning pattern pieces on the fabric.

Tubular knits with horizontal stripes need to be cut so that the stripes match as they go around the body. This may mean that the garment will not be perfectly aligned on lengthwise grain; however, having the stripes match generally is considered more important than cutting the garment on lengthwise grain.

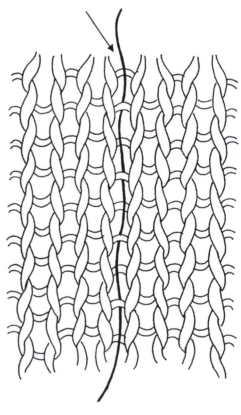

Fig. 9.1   Basted line to identify wale in knitted fabric

74

Careful attention needs to be given to the fold in knitted fabric, because sometimes the crease is impossible to remove with washing or pressing. In this case, cutting to avoid the fold is advised.

Most garments made from knitted fabrics are cut with the greatest amount of stretch going around the body. Exceptions to this rule include those garments, such as one-piece bathing suits and leotards, where lengthwise stretch is critical to the fit and function of the garment.

Because knits tend to reflect light differently up and down, a "with nap" layout should be chosen (Fig. 9.2). The fabric needs to be kept on the table during layout and cutting, as distortion can occur easily if the knit is allowed to hang over the edge.

Knits that have a tendency to curl may need to be pinned together or to paper before the pattern is placed on the fabric. Thick or bulky knits may need to be pinned with long pins or pinned and cut one layer at a time. Ballpoint pins are available for use with knitted fabrics.

Knits, such as interlocks, that have a tendency to run usually are cut so the direction of the run would be from the bottom of the garment to the top. As the lower edges of garment pieces are hemmed and generally receive less strain during construction, excessive running may be avoided. A seam sealant can be placed on the edges that may run to reduce the chances of problems during construction. Fusible interfacing can be used in areas of strain on the garment to help prevent runs from occurring.

Pattern pieces that would be cut on the bias in woven fabric will be cut in the direction of the greatest stretch in knits. Usually this will be on the crosswise grain. Pieces used for bindings are a good example of this.

Any of the marking methods discussed in Chapter 11 are appropriate for knitted fabrics with the exception of the tracing wheel, which has the tendency to damage some knitted fabrics. Using the smooth rather than the serrated wheel may eliminate this problem. Otherwise, another marking technique should be chosen.

Seams

Several characteristics of knits influence the type of seam chosen: (1) their tendency to be bulky, (2) their tendency not to ravel, (3) and their ability to stretch. Knits that curl or run have additional characteristics that need to be considered when deciding the best seam to use.

In most garments made from stretchy knit fabrics, some seams need to retain the stretch or give; others need to be stabilized so that they will not stretch. To stabilize a seam, a piece of seam binding or twill tape (Fig. 9.3) is stitched into the seam. Areas to be reinforced include the shoulder seams and seams where a gathered edge is stitched to an ungathered edge. An exception to this guideline would be an armhole seam if a gathered sleeve is a part of the design. The armhole seam would not be reinforced with tape as the seam needs to retain its flexibility.

Seams also can be stabilized by using fusible interfacing that has been cut so that it is stable in the direction of the seam. An example of this would be a yoke seam where the interfacing is cut so that it is stable in the crosswise direction. The addition of piping to a seam not only adds a decorative feature to the garment, but it also stabilizes the seam.

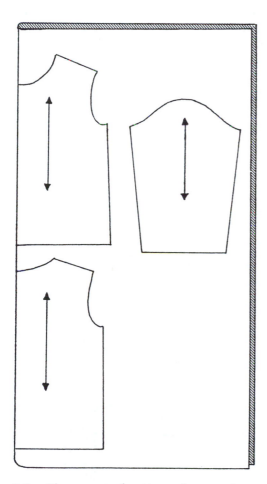

Fig. 9.2 Placement of pattern pieces using "with nap" layout for cutting knitted fabric

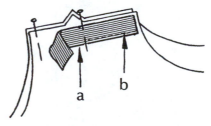

Fig. 9.3 Use of stay to reinforce seam in knitted fabric

Multipurpose and ballpoint needles are recommended for sewing knitted fabrics; a test seam needs to be made to determine which is the best for the fabric. More than one seam type may be required on a garment—for example, a regular straight stitched plain seam might be used in one area and a narrow zigzag stitch used in another.

Skipped stitches often are a major problem when sewing knitted fabrics. A discussion of solutions to this problem is presented at the end of this chapter.

Machine tension may need to be adjusted when sewing knitted fabrics. A *loosely balanced tension*, where both upper and lower tensions are loosened, may provide additional give to a seam and is recommended especially when a straight stitched seam is used.

Those seams that need to have a lot of stretch can be stitched in one of several ways. The type of seam chosen will depend on the amount of stretch in the fabric, the weight of the fabric, the amount of curling that occurs on the seam edge, and the type of machine available.

Regular Straight Stitch

A regular straight stitch will produce the flattest seam and can be used on many knitted fabrics. By using thread with some give (e.g., polyester or cotton wrapped polyester), a loosely balanced tension, and, if necessary, stretching the fabric slightly as it is guided under the presser foot, the seam may have sufficient give. If, however, the stitching line breaks when tension is applied to

it, adjustments may be required in the machine tension, stitch length, and pressure, or another seam choice may need to be made.

The regular straight stitch would be used where a plain seam that is to be pressed open is desired. The seam edges usually require no edge finish since knit fabrics do not ravel. The plain seam can be used, too, when the seam is pressed in one direction. However, neither of these will work well with knitted fabrics that have a tendency to curl. If the seam is to be pressed to one side, a second row of stitching, either straight or zigzag (Fig. 9.4), can be added to only the seam allowance, making this appropriate for the fabric that curls as well as the one that does not. The second row of stitching is placed into the seam allowance approximately ¼ inch (6 mm) from the first, and the seam allowance is trimmed close to this stitching.

Zigzag Stitch

If more stretch is desired, one row of narrow zigzagging, or two rows of zigzagging placed close together, can be used (Fig. 9.5). Usually, this type of seam is trimmed close to the stitching, leaving a narrow finished seam. The zigzagged seam is not the best choice for the seam that needs to be pressed open, as the thread would show along the seam line.

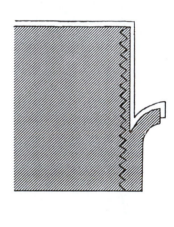

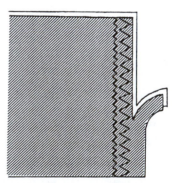

Fig. 9.5   Zigzag seam in knitted fabric

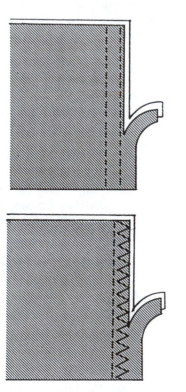

Fig. 9.4   Double-stitched seams

Special Stretch Stitches

Some sewing machines have special stretch stitches. Since stretch stitches often are difficult to remove, *always* test them in both directions on a sample piece of fabric before using them in the garment. Stretch stitches usually combine forward and backward feed action on the machine and can be used as a functional seam or as a decorative stitch (Fig. 9.6). As with the zigzagged seam and double-stitched seam, this seam is trimmed close to the stitching. A second stretch stitch found on many machines is the straight stretch stitch, produced when the machine takes two stitches forward and one stitch back (Fig. 9.7). This very durable seam works well in areas that receive a great deal of strain, such as the crotch seam on a swimsuit. The stitches are almost impossible to remove, so this seam should be used with care.

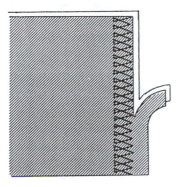

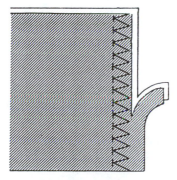

Fig. 9.6 Stretch stitch for knitted fabric

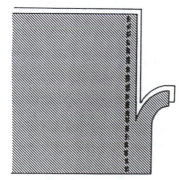

Fig. 9.7 Straight stretch stitch

Overlock Seam

The overlock machine produces a seam that works well for most knitted fabrics. The built-in stitch found in the three-thread and four-thread overlock seams (Fig. 9.8) provides the give needed for seams in many knits. Because the overlock machine cuts away the excess fabric as it sews, no additional trimming of the seams is necessary.

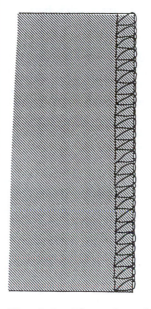 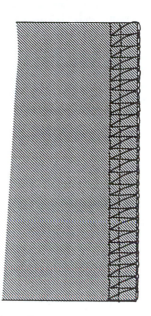

Fig. 9.8 Three-thread and four-thread overlock seam

Interfacing

Fusible interfacings are recommended for most knitted fabrics (see Chapter 4). These need to be applied according to the directions received when the fusible interfacing is purchased. Test a small piece of interfacing on a scrap of the fashion fabric, as it may add undesirable stiffness. It may be advisable to launder the sample piece to check the appearance and permanency of the bond. If directions for applying the fusible interfacings are not available, follow these suggestions:

1. Set the iron temperature on steam or wool setting.
2. Trim ¼–½ inch (6–13 mm) from the seam allowance of the interfacing to reduce bulk.
3. Position the interfacing on the wrong side of the fashion fabric and fuse-baste the interfacing to the fashion fabric by lightly pressing with the iron for about 2 seconds, beginning in the center and working to the outside.
4. Cover the interfacing with a damp press cloth and apply pressure with the iron, for 10 seconds, to all areas of the fabric being interfaced. Dampen the press cloth as

necessary so that it is always wet in the areas being pressed. *Do not slide the iron.*

5. Remove the press cloth and press over the fused areas to smooth out the press marks.

6. Allow fabric to cool before handling.

7. Check the permanency of the bonding in one corner of the garment piece. Repeat the process, if necessary.

The fusible interfacings with a knitted construction work well on knitted fabrics. However, in areas needing to be stabilized, such as under buttons and buttonholes, interfacing needs to be applied so that stretch will not occur in the direction of the buttonhole. This can be done by using a different interfacing in that area, one with no stretch in the direction of the buttonhole; by putting a second layer of interfacing (one with no give in the direction of the buttonhole) just in the area of the buttonhole; or by applying the knit, fusible interfacing so that there is no give in the direction of the buttonhole.

Closures

In most cases, machine-worked buttonholes are preferable to bound buttonholes in knitted fabrics. If a bound buttonhole is desired (and one may be appropriate in more tailored garments), the method chosen will need to be one that causes the least distortion as the welts of the buttonholes are being formed. Buttonholes made in the lengthwise direction may be more attractive than those in the crosswise direction, since the latter have a tendency to appear stretched unless carefully stabilized.

Exposed zippers and invisible zippers often are used in garmets of knitted fabrics (see Chapter 17). The choice of zipper is important, especially for lightweight fabrics, which need as light a weight zipper as possible.

Finishing Garment Openings

Facings, self-fabric bindings, self-fabric bands, ribbings, and turned and stitched edges are ways that are used to finish hems and garment openings such as necklines, armholes, and the bottom of sleeves and pullovers. Many of these techniques are described in other chapters in this book. References to these chapters will be made when appropriate.

Facings

Facings are discussed in Chapter 15. To stabilize the facing and to prevent the edges from curling, fusible interfacing can be applied to the entire facing piece, extending the interfacing to the edge of the facing. If the knit fabric tends to shift in front of the presser foot, stitch

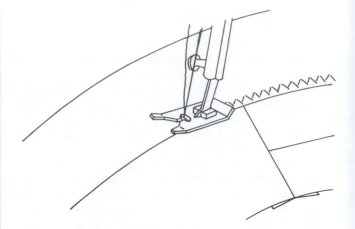

Fig. 9.9   Zigzag understitching

the facing to the garment with the facing side up. If the facing seam is bulky, zigzag understitching (Fig. 9.9) can be used to help flatten the seam and to keep the facing rolled to the inside of the garment.

Self-fabric Bindings

Read Chapter 16 for directions on cutting and applying self-fabric bindings. Bindings cut from knit fabric are cut in the direction of greatest stretch, usually the crosswise direction. When applying binding to a curved edge, it is necessary to stretch the binding so that it will lie flat when completed. The stitch-in-the-ditch technique can be used to secure the back side of the binding. There is no need to turn under the raw edge as knit fabrics do not ravel. Remove the excess bulk by trimming close to the machine stitching (Fig. 9.10).

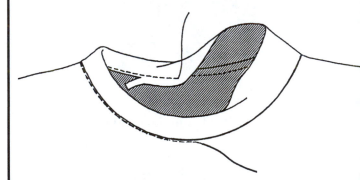

Fig. 9.10   Trimming edge of knit binding to reduce bulk

Ribbing

Ribbing is a stretchy knit fabric, sold by the inch (centimeter) or as precut strips and used to finish garment edges. The most satisfactory ribbings are those that have the ability to recover or return to their original shape after having been stretched.

Ribbings often are used as finishes for the neckline, the lower edge of sleeves, or the lower edge of shirts or pants constructed from knitted and woven fabrics. Ribbings can be cut from self-fabric, if it has appropriate stretch and recovery, or they can be purchased ready to apply.

The length of the band is determined by the stretch and recovery characteristics of the knit fabric and the measurements of the part of the body it must pass over to be put on and then to fit snugly (i.e., it must be able to be pulled over the head but then fit closely to the neck). Since knitted fabrics have varying amounts of stretch, each ribbing piece must be fitted to determine the desired circumference. After cutting the ribbing, pin the ribbing piece to the area of the body where it will be worn and pin the two edges together. Slip the ribbing off. These pins will mark the seam lines for stitching the ends of the ribbing.

To apply a ribbing with an exposed seam:

1. Cut the ribbing the desired width and length. If the ribbing is to be folded, cut it twice the finished width plus two seam allowances.

2. Stitch the seams in the garment and in the ribbing using an appropriate seam for the fabric (see Chapter 9). Press the seams. If the ribbing is to be folded in half, the seam inside the ribbing is usually pressed open and the seams layered/graded (Fig. 9.11).

Fig. 9.11   Stitching and layering/grading seam inside folded ribbing

3. If the ribbing is to be a double thickness, fold in half along the fold line.

4. Divide the ribbing into four equal parts and mark each point with a pin (Fig. 9.12). Divide the garment edge into four equal parts, marking each point with a pin (Fig. 9.13). The garment opening needs to be handled carefully so that it does not become stretched during this process; it should *not* be staystitched.

Fig. 9.12   Folded ribbing divided into four equal parts

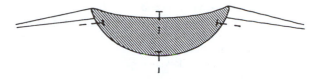

Fig. 9.13   Dividing garment opening into four equal parts

5. Place the ribbing on the inside of the garment with right sides together. Join the ribbing to the garment, matching the pin markings (Fig. 9.14). The seam in the ribbing is usually aligned with a seam in the garment or positioned at center back (a in Fig. 9.14).

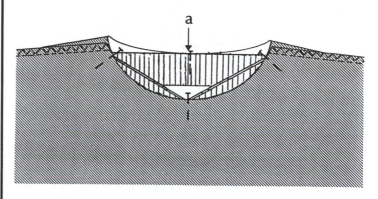

Fig. 9.14   Matching pin markings on ribbing and garment

6. Stitch the ribbing to the garment, stretching the ribbing to match the circumference of the garment. Position the garment under the presser foot with the ribbing on top (Fig. 9.15). The type of seam needs to be one with flexibility (see Chapter 10). It may be a straight machine stitch with loosely balanced tension, a narrow zigzag stitch, a stretch stitch, or an overlock stitch.

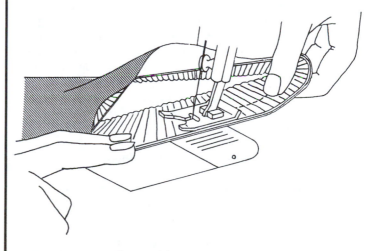

Fig. 9.15   Stitching ribbing to garment

7. Stitch the seam a second time, ⅛–¼ inch (3–6 mm) away from the first line of stitching. A wide zigzag stitch or a straight machine stitch may be used. This step is not necessary if an overlock machine is used.

8. Trim the seam allowance close to the second row of stitching.

9. Press the ribbing with the iron held above the fabric using the steam to help restore the ribbing to its original shape (Fig. 9.16). Press or turn the seam allowance toward the garment.

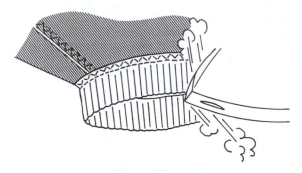

Fig. 9.16   Completing garment ribbing

When applying a ribbing to an area with a small circumference, such as on the wrist of a child's garment, it may be necessary to apply the ribbing *before* sewing the vertical seams in the garment and ribbing. After the ribbing is applied, the vertical seam would be sewn as one continuous seam through the garment and ribbing.

Since fabrics used for ribbings vary in the amount of stretch, there may be locations on a garment where a ribbing may not have sufficient stretch to accommodate the fullness in the garment opening. The size of the garment opening may be reduced by taking a larger seam allowance in the garment, thus matching the circumference of the stretched ribbing, or the garment edge may be partially gathered to match the length of the ribbing as it is being stretched.

Turned and Stitched Edges

Turned and stitched edges are an appropriate finish for necklines, armholes, and lower edges of knit garments. The folded edge does not need an edge finish since knits do not ravel. If the knit fabric has good recovery, which means that it will return to its original shape after being stretched, the garment edge may not require stabilizing. If stabilizing is required, a narrow strip of fusible interfacing or a length of bias seam tape may be applied to the edge.

To make a turned and stitched edge:

1. Fold under the ⅝ inch (1.3 cm) seam allowance (or more if specified) and press, being careful *not* to stretch the edge.

2. Topstitch ¼ inch (6 mm) from the folded edge; place a second row of topstitching close to the folded edge (Fig. 9.17); or use a double needle to stitch two parallel rows of

stitching an appropriate distance from the folded edge (Fig. 9.18). Be sure to use a *loosely balanced machine tension* so the garment opening has sufficient stretch to get the garment on and off without breaking the stitching.

3. Trim the raw edge close to the stitching (Fig. 9.17).

4. Use the iron to steam the edge back into shape if it was stretched during stitching.

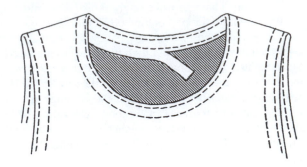

Fig. 9.17   Two rows of topstitching as an edge finish

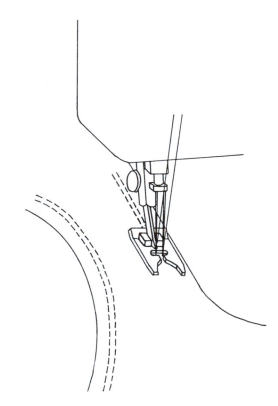

Fig. 9.18   Double-needle topstitching as an edge finish

Hems

Before a hem is marked in a garment made from a knitted fabric, the garment needs to hang overnight or longer. The hemming stitch chosen needs to be one that has the desired amount of stretch for the garment. The machine blind-stitched hem as well as machine topstitching are appropriate choices for many knits. The double needle often is used for the machine topstitched hem. For a hand-stitched hem the lock stitch works especially well as flexibility can be built into the stitching. The fused hem is a good choice for hems on softer knit fabrics where a machine-stitched hem is not appropriate and the stitches from a hand-stitched hem would show on the outside of the garment. It works particularly well on hems of flared skirts. See Chapter 22 for directions for putting in hems.

Since most knitted fabrics do not ravel, the use of a hem finish usually is not required. However, knits that have a tendency to curl or to run will require some finish if other than a narrow topstitched hem is to be used. A machine-stitched edge finish appropriate for the fabric may be helpful, or a narrow strip of fusible interfacing can be placed along the edge of the hem to prevent both curling and running. Then, the garment can be hemmed in any method appropriate for the fabric.

Hems in knits tend to show when stitches are pulled too tight or when an inappropriate edge finish is applied. Instead of a hem, the edges of many knitted garments may be finished with a binding or a casing (see Chapter 16).

Problems with Sewing on Knits

Following is a summary of some problems experienced when sewing on knitted fabrics. Characteristics or causes of the problem are listed as well as procedures to be used for sewing.

Stretching

Characteristics:
- —Inherent in the knit fabric
- —Usually beneficial if properly handled
- —Greatest along crosswise grain or curves or a bias cut piece

Procedures for sewing:
- —Stabilize seam with tape or with a small strip of fusible or lightweight interfacing.
- —Decrease pressure on the presser foot.
- —Stop and lift presser foot periodically to release pressure on the fabric.
- —Avoid stitching close to the cut edge; it is better to allow extra seam allowance and trim to desired width after stitching.

Skipping Stitches

Cause:
- —Upper thread does not catch the lower thread soon enough to form a stitch.

Procedures for sewing:

- —Use a ballpoint needle, multipurpose needle, or smaller size needle.
- —Use a straight stitch presser foot and throat plate.
- —Increase pressure on the presser foot.
- —Sew through tissue paper or wax paper.
- —Prewash fabric to remove any residue or sizing.
- —Try a different type of interfacing.

Curling

Cause:
- —Inherent characteristic of jersey knits

Procedures for sewing:
- —Use a straight or zigzag stitch to make a second row of stitching close to the original seam and trim close to the second row of stitching; press seam to one side.
- —Use an overlock machine.
- —Fuse lightweight interfacing along the edge that curls.
- —Avoid stretching fabric during sewing.
- —Extend fusible interfacing to the edge of the garment pieces such as facings.

Runs

Cause:
- —Interconnecting loop structure of some type of knits (jersey, interlock, and ribs)
- —Fine filament yarns run much easier than bulkier, staple yarns.

Procedures for sewing:
- —Fix snag or hole immediately with a small piece of fusible interfacing or stitch by hand.
- —Test fabric before cutting to determine the direction runs are apt to form; cut pattern with the lower edge of the pattern along the edge of the fabric most likely to run.
- —Avoid stretching until securely sewn.
- —Edge stitch or fuse interfacing along the cut edge likely to run.
- —Use small pieces of fusible interfacing in areas of strain where runs are apt to form.
- —Do not force pins into knit fabric.
- —Check needle for possible rough areas.
- —Use a ballpoint needle, multipurpose needle, or smaller size needle.

Off Grain Fabric

Cause:
- —Inherent in the structure of circular knit fabrics

Procedures for sewing:
- —Knits cannot be straightened.
- —Do not buy a knit fabric that has obvious vertical and horizontal lines that do not meet at right angles.

—Match horizontal lines of the fabric instead of keeping the vertical grain straight (garment may not hang perfectly straight).

Poor Recovery of Fabric

Cause:
  —Incorrect finishing of the fabric
  —Characteristic of a particular fabric
Procedures for sewing:
  —Test fabric before you buy (stretch in the center of the fabric and release).
  —Select pattern styles that are not tight fitting.

Poor Recovery of Seams

Cause:
  —The stitch concentration is too heavy to allow proper recovery (seams appear wavy).
  —Excessive stretching of fabric during stitching
  —Pressure on presser foot is too heavy.
Procedures for sewing:
  —Use a longer stitch length.
  —Stretch only *one* layer of fabric, not both.

—Generally avoid staystitching of knit fabric.
—Release pressure on presser foot.

Excessive Bulk

Cause:
  —Coarse, bulky yarns
  —Structure of knit fabric
Procedures for sewing:
  —If possible, use a plain seam pressed open.
  —If seam allowances will not stay pressed open, zigzag seam allowances together *close* to first row of stitching and trim as needed; a ¼ inch (6 mm) seam allowance is adequate unless seam is pressed open.
  —Many seams do not need to be enclosed (e.g., waistbands, cuffs, neckbands, ribbings).
  —Use the cut edge as the finish on the inside lower edge of cuffs, collars, and waistbands since knits do not ravel, thus exposed raw edges do not need to be folded under.
  —Use zigzag understitching instead of straight stitch understitching.

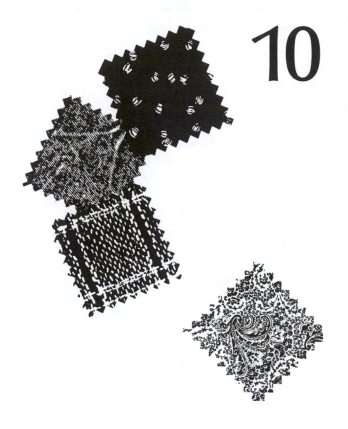

10 Using the Sewing Machine and Serger

Most sewing machines used for custom-sewn garments are either conventional machines or overlock (serger) machines. Most conventional machines have both straight and zigzag stitches; many also are equipped with a variety of special functions that do tasks such as decorative stitches, buttonholes, and monograms. Some conventional machines are computerized and can be programmed to do repeated operations such as buttonholes. Sergers sew an overlock stitch and trim away the excess seam allowance similar to the seams found in ready-to-wear.

Specifics on operating any sewing machine will be found in the owner's manual. To receive the maximum benefit from a machine, the sewer must be well versed in its operation and care. That means a thorough study of the sewing machine manual as well as experimentation with its many operations.

Conventional Sewing Machine

Parts and Functions of the Sewing Machine

Knowing the parts and functions of the sewing machine is important in both its use and maintenance. This section contains general information on the major parts of most conventional machines; the owner's manual will provide detailed descriptions for a particular type and brand of machine.

Bobbin

The bobbin is the metal or plastic device that holds the thread used for the lower part of the stitch. Thread is placed on it, and the bobbin is placed in the bobbin case during the threading operation. Bobbins are made specifically for different brands and types of machines and are not readily interchangeable from one brand of machine to another.

Bobbin Winding Device

The bobbin winding device is used to place thread on the bobbin. Its operation varies from machine to machine; the instruction booklet will contain specific information on winding a bobbin. The thread needs to be wound smoothly onto the bobbin to prevent tangling during construction.

Bobbin Case

The bobbin case holds the bobbin. Some machines have a removable bobbin case; others are a drop-in variety. The bobbin needs to be placed in the bobbin case so that the thread comes off the bobbin in the appropriate direction. Thread must be placed correctly through the slit in the bobbin case to have the proper tension on the bobbin thread. The instruction book will provide this information.

Feed Dog

The feed dog is located in the throat plate and under the presser foot. It moves the fabric under the presser foot the amount needed for the stitch length setting. Its cycle is controlled by the stitch length regulator.

Hand or Balance Wheel

Located on the right-hand side of the sewing machine, the hand or balance wheel controls the movement of the take-up lever and the needle. For most machines, the wheel turns counterclockwise or toward the sewer. It is used to bring the needle into the proper position to begin sewing, to raise the take-up lever to its highest point before starting a new sewing operation, and to manipulate the needle without the use of electric power when sewing areas that require careful handling.

Machine Needles

Sewing machine needles need to match the fabric in density (i.e., coarser fabrics need larger needles). (See Chapter 4.) Double needles can be used to sew two parallel rows, a technique often used for topstitching. Using the double needle means having that number of spools of thread available for the top threading. Some adjustment in the top tension may be needed to accommodate these multiple threads.

Machine needles consist of two parts: (1) the shank or upper part and (2) the shaft or lower part. The shank has a flat side and a rounded side. When placing the needle in the machine, the flat side is placed so that it is facing *away* from the last thread guide.

Needle Position Regulator

On some machines the needle can be moved to the right or the left of the usual center position. Changing the position often is necessary when making buttonholes. The needle position regulator allows for changing the needle position on those machines where this is possible.

Pattern Selection Dial

This mechanism provides the sewer with the various pattern options available on the machine. The sewer makes changes in this device to select the appropriate pattern. The stitch width regulator should be on "0" setting when the pattern selection dial is adjusted.

Presser Foot Lever

The presser foot lever allows the sewer to raise and lower the presser foot at the beginning and end of the sewing operation.

Pressure Regulator

Some machines have a pressure regulator that can be used to change the force the presser foot exerts on the fabric during sewing.

Reverse Mechanism

Most machines will sew in both the forward and the reverse direction. A mechanism found on the machine (see owner's manual) allows the machine to change from forward to reverse stitching. The stitch length remains the same regardless of the direction of stitching.

Spool Pins

The spool pins hold the thread during sewing. Most machines have at least two spool pins. The spool of thread should be placed on the spool pin so that the thread will not catch on the nick in the spool as the thread comes off the spool.

Stitch Length Regulator

This mechanism provides the opportunity for the sewer to change the length of stitch. Discussion of appropriate stitch lengths is found later in this chapter.

Stitch Width Regulator

This mechanism allows the sewer to change the width of the stitch and is of importance when using the zigzag or other stitching patterns available on many machines.

Take-up Lever

The take-up lever regulates the flow of the thread from the spool through the needle. To prevent the needle from coming unthreaded, the take-up lever must be at its *highest* point when beginning an operation. By always returning the take-up lever to its highest point at the end of an operation, it will be in the correct position to begin the next sewing operation. The position of the take-up lever is changed by turning the hand wheel. Computerized sewing machines automatically return the take-up lever to the correct position, thus, relieving the sewer of this task.

Tension Discs

Tension discs regulate the tightness or looseness of the upper thread. The thread must be engaged through the tension discs properly for the tension to be regulated. Tension is *increased* as the tension dial is turned to a *higher number*. Most machines have tension regulators for the bobbin as well as the top thread. The owner's manual will provide information on the regulation of both the top and bobbin tensions.

Thread Guides

Thread guides are strategically located to help direct the thread through the various points on the machine head. The number of thread guides varies with the type of machine. The last thread guide is used to determine the direction for inserting the thread through the needle. The flat side of the shank of the needle usually is positioned away from and the long groove of the needle is facing toward the last thread guide.

Throat Plates and Presser Feet

Machines that do both straight and zigzag stitching usually have a different throat plate and presser foot for these two types of stitches. As expected, the throat plate and presser foot used for zigzag stitching have wide openings; while the ones used for straight stitching have small openings (Figs. 10.1 and 10.2). Leaving the zigzag throat plate (also called the general purpose throat plate) and presser foot on the machine allows for freedom to move from straight to zigzag stitching without making a change. However, the small-hole throat plate and presser foot are recommended when sewing fabrics such as silky wovens, which have a tendency to be pulled down into the bobbin case during the stitching operation.

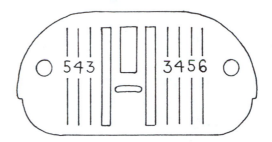

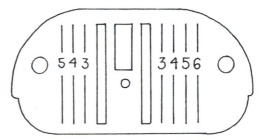

Fig. 10.2   Zigzag and straight stitch throat plates

Many throat plates have lines designating widths of seams (Fig. 10.3). By having the cut edge of the seam follow along a particular line on the throat plate, one is assured of sewing a seam of that width. An adjustable seam guide is available for machines that have no throat plate guidelines or for people who prefer this type of sewing accessory (Fig. 10.4). For sewing curved seams, the seam guide can be tilted for increased accuracy (Fig. 10.5). In the absence of guide lines on the throat plate or a seam guide, pieces of tape can be placed at appropriate locations on the machine.

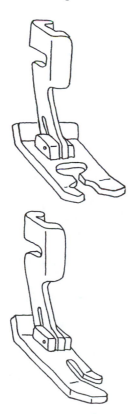

Fig. 10.1   Zigzag and straight stitch presser feet

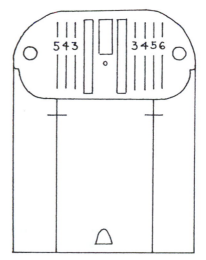

Fig. 10.3   Throat plate with seam widths marked

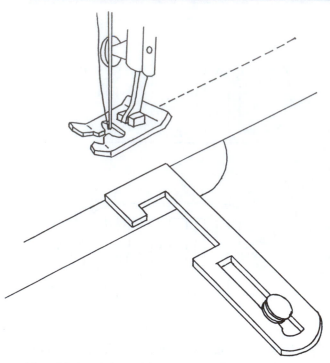

Fig. 10.4 Adjustable seam guide

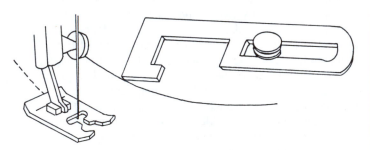

Fig. 10.5 Seam guide position for sewing curved edges

Fig. 10.6 Roller presser foot

Special presser feet are available for doing specific tasks such as installing conventional and invisible zippers (see Chapter 17). A roller presser foot (Fig. 10.6) may be useful when sewing fabrics that are difficult to feed under the presser foot, such as suedes, leathers, and

some knits. A top feed attachment allows both layers of fabric to pass under the needle at the same rate. It works especially well for fabrics such as silky wovens, knits, suedes, plaids, and stripes.

Threading the Machine

The conventional sewing machine has both a top and a bobbin thread, each of which is threaded separately. As a general rule, the top threading proceeds from the spool pin to the tension discs to the take-up level and finally to the needle. In between are found thread guides to keep the thread following the appropriate path.

The bobbin is inserted in the bobbin case with the thread passing through the appropriate tension device. Before starting to sew, the bobbin thread needs to be brought to the top of the throat plate. This is accomplished by turning the hand wheel one revolution while holding on to the top thread. A gentle tug on the top thread will reveal the loop of the bobbin thread which then can be pulled to the top (Fig. 10.7). Before beginning to sew, both the bobbin thread and the spool thread should be placed under the presser foot and pulled to the back or side of the machine (Fig. 10.8).

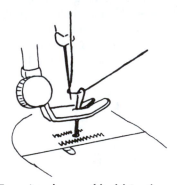

Fig. 10.7 Forming loop of bobbin thread

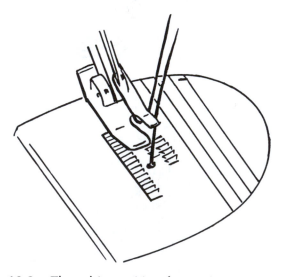

Fig. 10.8 Thread in position for sewing

Seam Appearance

The appearance of the seam is controlled by three things: (1) the thread tension, (2) the stitch length, (3) and the amount of pressure placed on the presser foot. All must be set carefully to insure a balanced stitch.

Thread Tension

All machines have a top thread tension dial that can be regulated to insure correct tension; most also have a bobbin tension that can be adjusted as needed. Tension needs vary from one fabric to another so they must be checked each time a different fabric is used.

A perfect stitch is formed when the needle and bobbin threads lock between two layers of fabric. The stitch is the same on the top as on the underside (Fig. 10.9). A *double* thickness of the fashion fabric should be used for testing the stitch.

Fig. 10.9   Appearance of balanced machine tension

If an imperfect stitch is formed, the threading of the head and the bobbin case should be checked. If the threading is correct, the difficulty may be improper balance of the tensions on the upper and lower threads. If the thread lies straight on the underside of the fabric, the upper tension is too loose or the lower tension is too tight (A in Fig. 10.10). If the thread lies straight on the upper side of the fabric, the upper tension is too tight or the lower tension is too loose (B in Fig. 10.10). Adjustments are made in the upper tension, if possible. Refer to the machine instruction book for directions for adjusting the machine tension.

A

B

Fig. 10.10   Unbalanced machine tension: *(A)* upper tension too loose or lower tension too tight; *(B)* upper tension too tight or lower tension too loose

Machine tension can also be checked by stitching a seam through *double* thickness of fabric in the direction of greatest stretch (true bias in woven fabric and usually in the crosswise direction of knits), backstitching at the beginning and end of the seam. If the tension is balanced, the stitched line will "give" with the stretch in the fabric, or if the fabric is very stretchy, both the top and the bobbin threads may break when the fabric is pulled (Fig. 10.11). The tension needs to be adjusted when *one* thread breaks. If the top thread breaks and the bobbin thread does not, generally the top tension is too tight and needs to be loosened, or turned to a lower number. If the bobbin thread breaks but the top does not, generally the bobbin tension is too tight and needs to be loosened. Sometimes if puckering occurs and the tension is balanced, *both* the top and the bobbin tensions may need to be adjusted to a looser setting. This is true especially when sewing fabrics such as silky wovens. A looser, but balanced, tension may be desirable when using the zigzag stitch as an edge finish to avoid curling the edge or when sewing a straight stitch on knit fabrics to provide more "stretch" or "give" to the seam.

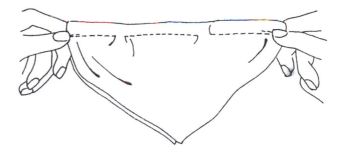

Fig. 10.11   Checking for balanced machine stitch

Stitch Length

The stitch length regulator, found on the front of the machine, may be expressed in either metric or English. For English measure, stitch length is expressed as stitches per inch; the higher the number the shorter the stitch. The numbers on the dial generally range from 6 to 18. For metric, the number on the dial refers to the actual length of the stitch in millimeters; the higher the number the longer the stitch. The numbers generally range from 0 to 4, with 4 representing approximately 2.5 stitches per centimeter, 2 representing approximately 5 stitches per centimeter, and l.5 representing 7 stitches per centimeter.

The stitch length used when sewing depends on the weight of the fabric, the intended use of the line of stitching, the end use of the garment, and the location of the row of stitching. The regular stitch length of 10–14 stitches per inch (4–5.5 stitches per centimeter or a setting of 2–2.5) is used for much of the general sewing that is done on garments—staystitching, seams, darts, and other construction details. A longer stitch would have fewer stitches per inch or centimeter and would be used for decorative topstitching and machine basting. On the English setting, this would be 6–8, on metric 3–4. A shorter stitch would have more stitches per inch or centimeter and would be used for reinforcement stitching. On the English setting, this would be 16–18, on metric 1–1.5.

The length of an ease or gathering stitch varies with the weight of the fabric. The most attractive gathers occur when the *shortest* possible stitch that works for pulling gathers is used, a technique that deviates from most pattern guide sheets that recommend using the longest possible stitch (see Chapter 14). Table 10.1 provides a summary of the recommended stitch lengths for various machine functions.

TABLE 10.1
Recommended Stitch Lengths for Various Machine Functions

Machine functions	Stitches per inch	Metric machine setting
Regular stitching	10–14	2–2.5
Staystitching	10–14	2–2.5
Decorative topstitching	6–8	3–4
Reinforcement stitching	16–18	1–1.5
Multiple zigzag stitching	16–18	1–1.5
Gathering or easing	8–10	2.5–3
Machine basting	6–8	3–4

Presser Foot Pressure

Pressure refers to the force on the fabric as it moves under the presser foot. Pressure is closely associated with the feed dog, the device that moves the fabric under the presser foot. The primary function of pressure is to hold the layers of fabric such that they move evenly with one another under the presser foot. If, for example, the top layer of fabric is being pushed along ahead of the lower layer (Fig. 10.12), an adjustment in pressure is

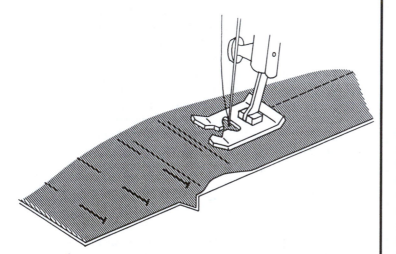

Fig. 10.12 Blister in front of presser foot

needed. As a general rule, lighter weight fabrics need lighter pressure, heavier fabrics need heavier pressure. Pressure cannot be adjusted on all machines; the owner's manual will provide needed information.

Zigzag Stitching

Both stitch length and width are important when using the zigzag stitch. Stitch length is regulated by the same dial that sets the stitch length for straight stitching; width changes are made by a special dial on the machine for this purpose. Width regulates how far the needle moves from side to side; length regulates how close the stitches are together. Figure 10.13 illustrates straight stitching at various length settings and corresponding zigzag stitching using the same length settings with several different width settings.

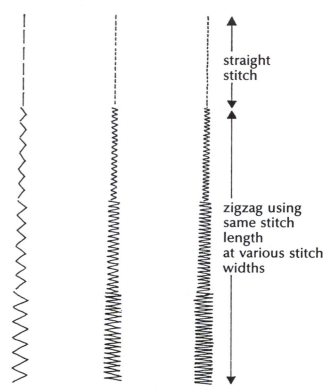

straight stitch

zigzag using same stitch length at various stitch widths

Fig. 10.13   Varied stitch lengths and widths in straight and zigzag stitching

Zigzag stitches are used for a number of purposes including finishing the edges of woven fabrics, sewing seams in some knitted fabrics, and adding a decorative touch to the garment. Experimentation will be needed to determine the appropriate width and length to use, each depending on the fabric and the purpose for which the zigzag stitch is intended. Some machines also provide choice in types of zigzag stitches, usually regular and multiple zigzag or serpentine stitch. The owner's manual will provide information on available stitches and recommended uses.

Basic Sewing Procedures

Before stitching by machine, the fabric layers usually are joined by pins, basting, tape, or glue stick. Pins need to be removed as sewing proceeds; sewing over pins can be a safety hazard and can damage the sewing machine needle.

To begin sewing, both the top and the bobbin thread need to be pulled back under the presser foot (see Fig. 10.8). The area to be stitched is placed under the presser foot and the needle placed in the fabric about ¼ inch (6 mm) in from the end of the seam. The bulk of the fabric is to the *left* of the needle. After the needle is in the appropriate spot in the fabric to begin sewing, the presser foot is lowered. The reverse stitch is used to backstitch ¼ inch (6 mm) at the beginning and end of each seam (Fig. 10.14). Holding the two threads taut as sewing begins will help to keep the threads from tangling at the beginning of the seam.

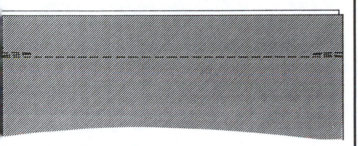

Fig. 10.14   Stitched seam with backstitching at beginning and end

The appropriate machine speed to use depends on the skill of the sewer and the shape of the seam. Greater machine speed usually can be used when sewing straight seams than when working with curved ones. In especially difficult spots, turning the wheel by hand may be easier than trying to use electric power. Some machines have a regulator for the speed of the machine; using the slower speed is recommended for inexperienced sewers and for sewing areas of the garment requiring special care.

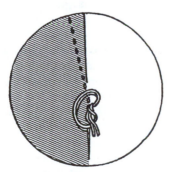

Fig. 10.15   Tailor's knot

Keeping the seam smooth and even in width takes careful manipulation. The guidelines on the throat plate or an adjustable seam guide are helpful in this operation.

At the end of the seam, the reverse stitch can be used again to reinforce the area and eliminate the need to tie the threads. Backstitching should *not* be used on the *outside* of the garment such as when topstitching, since the stitching is not especially attractive. Backstitching also is not used on the pointed end of the dart. In those cases, a tailor's knot is used (Fig. 10.15).

Chapter 12 contains additional discussion on sewing seams.

Continuous Stitching

Much time, motion, and some thread can be saved by sewing a series of seams, especially short ones, in one continuous operation (Fig. 10.16). When nearing the end of one seam, the sewer places a second seam under the presser foot and continues to sew. The beginning and end of each seam can be backstitched to prevent their coming apart when the pieces are separated. This same technique can be used when extensive staystitching is required on a garment.

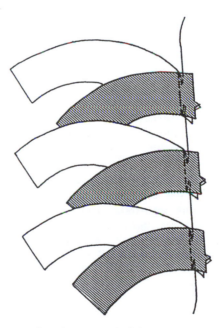

Fig. 10.16   Continuous stitching

Machine Problems and Possible Solutions

Failure to obtain a smooth line of stitching usually is caused by one or a combination of the following: incorrect machine threading, unbalanced tension, a blunt or bent needle, incorrect needle placement, incorrect needle size, or the wrong amount of pressure from the presser foot.

If the *fabric snags at right angles to the stitching line,* the needle may be too large or the wrong type, or the point of the needle may be damaged. To correct the problem, replace the needle.

If the *spool thread breaks,* the machine may not be threaded correctly; the needle may be the wrong size or inserted incorrectly; or the upper tension may be too tight. The threading of the machine head, the position of the needle, the upper tension, and the placement of the spool of thread on the spool pin all need to be checked. Sometimes the thread catches on the nick in the spool causing it to break. This is remedied by turning the spool over.

If the *needle breaks,* the needle may be the wrong style for the machine; the needle may be bent or not inserted all the way up into the clamp; or the needle may be too fine for the weight of the fabric, the thread, or the stitching procedure.

If the *stitch length is uneven,* the presser foot pressure may be set too light; the throat plate may be set in the "darn" position; the presser foot may be loose; or there may be a buildup of lint in the feed dog area.

If the *bobbin thread breaks,* the bobbin may be wound incorrectly or may be too full; the bobbin tension may be too tight; or the bobbin case may be threaded incorrectly.

If the *thread forms large loops along the seam line* on the top or the bottom of the fabric, most likely the machine is threaded incorrectly. The thread may not be through the tension discs on the top tension, or the bobbin may be inserted incorrectly in the bobbin case. Also, the bobbin thread may not be caught around the tension slot on the bobbin case. Another cause of this problem is lint or thread buildup in the bobbin case area or the need for the machine to be oiled.

If the *fabric puckers along the stitching line,* the tension or the stitch length may not be adjusted correctly for the fabric, or the sewer may be using the wrong thread. A loosely balanced tension often is desired for knit fabrics, silky wovens, and other lightweight fabrics. This is achieved by loosening both the top and bobbin tensions while also keeping them balanced. Fabric pucker may also be caused by a blunt needle or too much pressure on the presser foot.

If the *machine skips stitches,* the needle may not be the appropriate size or style for the fabric or thread, or the needle may be inserted incorrectly. Skipped stitches may be corrected by reinserting the needle correctly, using a smaller needle or one designed especially for the fabric, using the small hole throat plate and narrow presser foot for straight stitching, or by sewing over tissue or waxed paper.

If the *fabric is pulled down into the bobbin area* when stitching, the wrong throat plate may be in place. This problem occurs often on silky woven fabrics; a solution is to use the straight-stitch throat plate, which has a smaller hole than the zigzag or all-purpose plate, and the narrow presser foot.

If a *fold of fabric forms in front of the presser foot,* the two layers of fabric are not moving over the feed dog at the same rate. The pressure on the presser foot needs to be adjusted to eliminate the problem. Pinning the fabric layers at closer intervals may help, or using the top feed attachment or the roller presser foot may eliminate this problem.

If the *fabric is not moving between the presser foot and the feed dog,* the feed dog may not be in the proper position, or the pressure on the presser foot may be too light. Another cause of the problem is the stitch length regulator being set at "0." Some fabrics such as vinyl may need to be guided under the presser foot by holding the fabric both in front and behind the presser foot and guiding the fabric through the machine.

If the *thread snarls at the beginning of a seam,* the machine may be threaded incorrectly or the bobbin thread may not be pulled up to the top. Both the top and the bobbin thread need to be on the top of the machine throat plate and pulled back under the presser foot at the beginning of the seam. Holding the threads taut may be necessary for fabrics on which snarling at the beginning of the seam is a problem.

If the *needle comes unthreaded at the beginning of the sewing operation,* the take-up lever was not at its highest point.

If the *zigzag edge finish tends to curl the edge of the fabric* and forms a corded edge, the stitch length or stitch width may be set incorrectly. The spool or bobbin tensions may be too tight or the fabric may be too lightweight for this method of edge finish. The multiple zigzag stitch may be used as an edge finish on fabrics where this continues to be a problem.

Overlock or Serger Sewing Machine

The overlock or serger sewing machine differs from the conventional sewing machine in several ways. Basically, the overlock sews a seam, cuts off the excess fabric, and overcasts the raw edges in one operation. The overlock machine has no bobbin; rather it has two to five top threads. The number used depends on the number available on the machine and on the sewing operation being done. For seam construction, generally the three-thread is used for knits, the four-thread for wovens. The five-thread overlock machine usually has the combination of a three-thread overlock stitch and a two-thread safety stitch. On most models the two seam types can be used alone. Some machines can also convert to a four-thread. The two-thread is used for the over-edge stitch (an edge finish) and for flatlock seaming. With some tension adjustments the three-thread can also sew the flatlock seam.

The most commonly used overlock machines have one or two needle threads and one or more loopers referred to as the upper looper and lower looper (Fig.

10.17). The stitch is formed over a prong or stitch finger. There may be a single or double prong. The width of the prong along with the thread tension will determine the width or bight of the stitch. A traditional lockstitch seam cannot be sewn on an overlock machine.

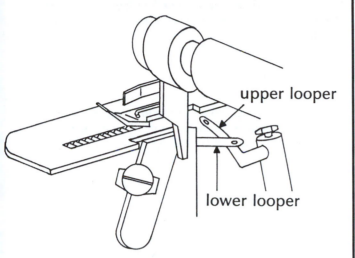

Fig. 10.17   Upper looper and lower looper on an overlock machine

Because three operations are combined into one on the overlock machine, certain sewing operations can be done more quickly. The overlock machines sew up to 1500 stitches per minute whereas the conventional machine averages 700–1100 stitches per minute.

The overlock machine is a supplement to the conventional machine and was not designed to replace it. Operations such as topstitching, installing a zipper, and making buttonholes cannot be accomplished on the overlock machine. In addition, those seams that need a full seam allowance or need to be pressed open are not appropriate for stitching on an overlock machine. The overlock machine does provide an excellent edge finish for plain seams sewn on the conventional machine. It can also perform unique operations, such as making a narrow rolled hem, or form decorative stitches, such as the flatlock stitch.

Types of Overlock Machines

Overlock machines are classified according to the number of threads used to make the stitch. The most common are three-thread and four-thread machines, but two-thread and five-thread machines are available.

Two-thread

Two-thread machines are limited in use to finishing seam edges and flatlock seaming. The stitch is formed with one needle thread and one looper thread that goes over the top of the fabric leaving a loop that is caught by the needle thread. The looper then goes under the fabric, catches the needle thread, and pulls it to the fabric edge (Fig. 10.18). The two-thread stitch is not designed to sew a regular seam. It will sew a decorative flatlock stitch (Fig. 10.19) that can be used to join seams in the body of a garment. See page 102–3 for further description of the flatlock seam.

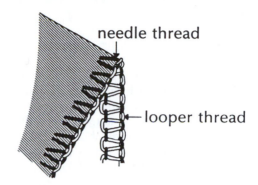

Fig. 10.18   Two-thread overedge stitch

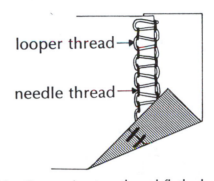

Fig. 10.19   Decorative two-thread flatlock seam

Three-thread

The three-thread overlock stitch can be used both as a seam and as an edge finish. The two looper threads interlock at the edge with the needle thread forming a stitch that looks the same on both the right and wrong sides of the fabric (Fig. 10.20). The seam has a great deal

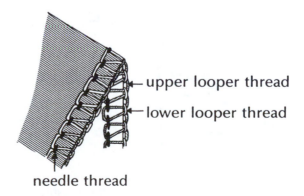

Fig. 10.20   Three-thread overlock stitch

of give, making it suitable for knit fabrics. It can also be used on woven fabrics, but it should be reinforced with a conventional lockstitch seam in areas of stress. This is the stitch most often used with specialty threads, such as pearl cotton, to provide a decorative finish to garment edges. With some tension adjustments the three-thread can be used for flatlock seaming and narrow rolled hemming. Some three-thread machines can convert to two-threads.

Four-thread

There are two kinds of four-thread overlock stitches: (1) the four-thread overlock and (2) the four-thread safety stitch. The four-thread overlock is similar to the three-thread, but it has an additional row of straight stitching down the middle for added durability (Fig. 10.21). This seam is excellent for woven fabrics and has almost as much stretch as a three-thread, so it is suitable for use on knit fabrics as well. Some machines can convert from a four-thread to a three-thread and/or two-thread. By removing one needle and adjusting the tension, the machine can make a flatlock seam and narrow rolled hem.

The four-thread safety stitch machine sews a two-thread chainstitch and a separate two-thread overlock

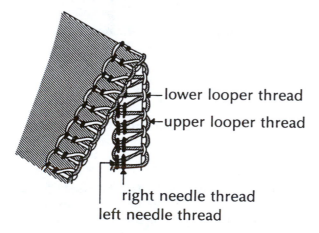

lower looper thread
upper looper thread

right needle thread
left needle thread

Fig. 10.21   Four-thread overlock stitch

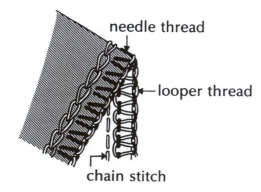

needle thread

looper thread

chain stitch

Fig. 10.22   Two-thread chain and two-thread overlock stitch

stitch (Fig. 10.22). The seam is strong and durable and especially suited for easily raveling, loosely woven fabrics. The seam width is wider than the four-thread overlock stitch described earlier. It has less stretch than a three-thread or the other four-thread machine, so it may not give with the stretch of some knit fabrics. The two-thread chain stitch can be used alone as can the two-thread overlock stitch.

Five-thread

There are many combinations of five-thread overlock machines. Some will do all of the functions mentioned above, while some offer the two-thread safety stitch and three-thread overlock stitch. Each seam type can be used alone.

Parts and Accessories

Loopers

Instead of bobbins, the overlock machines have one or two loopers (Fig. 10.17). The lower looper carries the thread that forms on the lower side of the fabric while the upper looper carries the thread that forms on the upper side of the fabric. The two looper threads lock around each other and are linked with the needle thread(s) to form the stitch. There are tension dials to control the tension for both of the looper threads.

Thread Stand

The thread stand holds the spools or cones of thread for both the needles and the loopers. If spools of thread are used the spool should be placed on the stand with the notch on the spool down. The spools are usually covered with spool caps to insure that the thread will come off the spool more smoothly. Adapters or cone holders are placed on the thread stand when cones of thread are used.

Thread Guides

The overlock machine has a different set of thread guides, which are usually color coded for each spool or cone, to aid in the correct threading of the machine. Machines must be threaded in the sequence suggested in the manual for proper stitch formation. The thread guide pole should be pulled all the way up when sewing. The thread eyelets in the top of the guide pole must be directly above the respective spool pins for proper feeding of the thread.

Needle

The overlock machine may use a needle specially designed for the machine, or it may use a conventional sewing machine needle. As with the conventional machine, needles must be the correct size for the type of thread being used. When inserting the needle, the long groove must be in the front and the scarf, or indentation along the side of the needle, must be in the back (Fig. 10.23). The use of tweezers that come with the machine is helpful when changing needles.

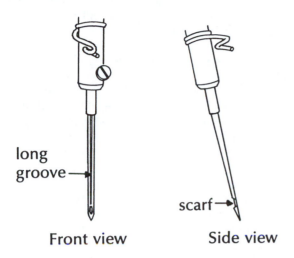

long
groove→

scarf→

Front view   Side view

Fig. 10.23   Needles for an overlock machine

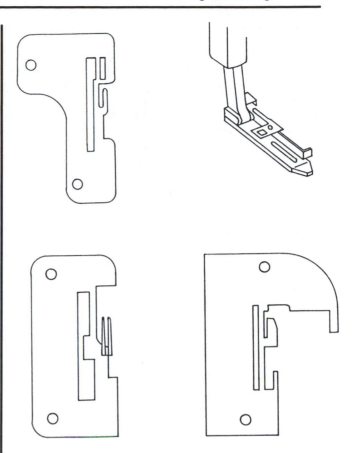

Fig. 10.24   Stitch former or stitch finger

Tension Regulators

Tension dials should be either number or color coded for easy reference when adjusting. Some tension dials rotate around only once, while others go around many times to loosen or tighten. The dials are turned to the right or to a higher number to tighten and to the left or a smaller number to loosen. It is necessary to experiment with the tension adjustments when making different stitches, such as the flatlock or rolled hemming stitch.

Stitch Former or Stitch Finger

The metal prong that helps to form the stitch is located on the throat plate or on the presser foot (Fig. 10.24). The width of this prong or stitch finger determines the width of the stitch. For this reason a different throat plate may be necessary when making the narrow rolled hemming stitch.

Knives

There are two knives used to cut the fabric (Fig. 10.25); one is made of hard carbide steel and the other of a softer metal. The lower blade is stationary, but the upper one can usually be disengaged or rotated out of the way for threading and for certain stitching procedures, such as when sewing pin tucks. If the knives no longer trim the seam smoothly while sewing, the softer

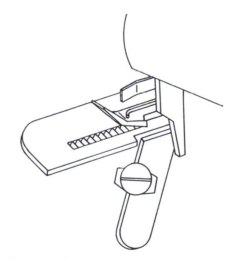

Fig. 10.25   Machine knives on an overlock machine

knife blade may need to be changed. It is important never to leave pins in the fabric during sewing as sewing over the pins will damage the knives. Be sure to remove the pins before the fabric approaches the knives.

Presser Foot

The presser foot on an overlock machine is longer than on a conventional machine (Fig. 10.26) and usually does not need to be lifted at the beginning or at the end of a seam. There is a presser foot lifter that can be used to raise the presser foot, when necessary. There may be a thread cutter on the back of the presser foot that can be used to cut the thread chain (a in Fig. 10.26). Some machines allow the sewer to adjust the pressure on the presser foot by turning the adjusting bolt. Usually less pressure is needed for thinner, more delicate fabrics.

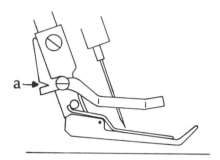

Fig. 10.26   Presser foot for overlock machine

Hand Wheel

Most hand wheels on overlock machines turn in a clockwise direction or away from the sewer, which is opposite the direction for turning hand wheels on most conventional machines. The direction the wheel rotates should be marked on the hand wheel for easy reference.

Machine Lighting

Not all overlock machines will have built-in lighting. Depending on the light source, it may be desirable to have auxiliary lighting.

Special Attachments

Special attachments that may come with the machine or that may be purchased separately include the rolled edge attachment used for making a narrow rolled hem, the blind hemming foot that facilitates blind hemming, an elastic applicator foot that automatically stretches elastic as it is being sewn to the garment, and tweezers that aid in threading the machine. Many machines have built-in storage for the tweezers and screwdrivers.

Waste Receptacle

A small container that fits just below the knives is ideal for catching fabric scraps accumulated while sewing. If one is not provided with the machine, a paper bag can be taped in front of the sewing table for this purpose.

General Sewing Information

Thread

The quality of the sewing thread used on an overlock machine is important because of the higher speed of the machine. For the most consistent stitch quality, long-staple polyester thread is recommended, because it is strong and has good abrasion resistance. High-quality cotton-covered polyester has good sewability in addition to the strength and abrasion resistance of the polyester. For special effects cotton, silk, nylon, rayon, or metallic thread can be used. Woolly nylon thread is a texturized thread that creates a soft, stretchy seam, and is often used on lingerie or stretch garments. Pearl cotton is a heavier thread that is soft and not highly twisted. It is often used to give a decorative finish to garment edges. These special threads are often used only in the loopers, and regular thread is used in the needles. When combining thread types, it is usually necessary to adjust the tension to obtain a balanced stitch.

For most general serging, a lighter weight serger thread is recommended. A special finish is applied to the serger thread to make it more suited to the high-speed sewing. The finer thread can be used with smaller needles; it creates less bulk along the seam line than do the heavier threads. Finer thread is more suitable for sewing on lighter weight fabrics. Regular sewing thread will work on medium- to heavyweight fabrics. Its use may require some adjustments to the thread tension.

Thread for the overlock machine is available in cones or tubes. Cone adapters are placed on the thread stand when cones are used to keep the cone secure, but they are removed when using tubes or regular spools of thread. Spool caps should be used when sewing with the regular spools of thread to insure that the thread will come off the spool freely (Fig. 10.27).

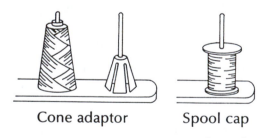

Cone adaptor   Spool cap

Fig. 10.27   Cone adaptor and spool cap for overlock machine

Thread is usually purchased to match the color of the garment. For some projects, the looper threads may be of a neutral color that blends with the color of the garment, but the needle thread should be of a matching color. Since the loopers use much more thread than do the needles, the cones or spools of thread can be switched between the needles and the loopers for more uniform usage of the thread.

Threading

All machines come with threading diagrams that are usually color coded to aid in the threading of the machine. Machines should be threaded in the proper sequence for correct stitch formation and to avoid thread breakage. Most overlock machines are threaded from left to right. Threading may be done more easily using the tweezers and/or the needle threader. Before sewing, pull all threads to the rear and place them under the presser foot.

The easiest way to change thread is to tie the new thread to the old thread and pull the new thread through the machine. This is done by first clipping the old thread just above the cones or spools and then tieing the new thread onto the old thread (Fig. 10.28). The thread ends should be trimmed before pulling the thread through the tension discs. It may be easier to pull the thread by first loosening the tension knobs. The knots will usually go through the looper eyes easily, but the knots will have to be cut in order to thread the needles.

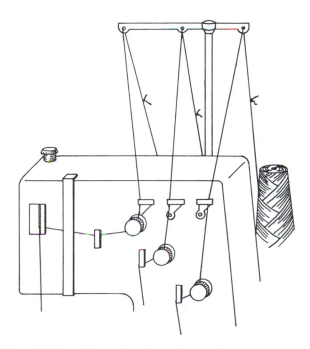

Fig. 10.28 Changing thread by tieing on new thread to old thread

When first learning to use the overlock machine, try using a different colored thread in each of the loopers and needles. With this technique, the function and tension of each of the threads is easier to identify.

Tension Adjustments

When the tension is balanced, the stitches will be even and flat on both the top and bottom of the fabric, with no puckering or loose loops along the seam line.

When the seam is pulled apart from the right side, there should be no thread showing along the seam line. Thread tension is adjusted by turning the tension discs to the right to tighten and to the left to loosen. On some overlock machines, the tension dials may need to be rotated around several times in order to make much change in the thread tension and to obtain a balanced stitch (Fig. 10.29). Figures 10.30 to 10.35 illustrate tension problems on a three-thread overlock stitch. The same principles apply to a two-thread or to a four-thread stitch.

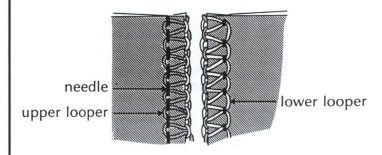

Fig. 10.29 Balanced overlock stitch

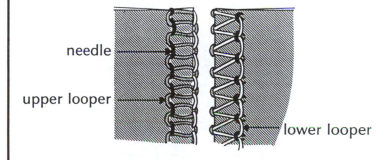

Fig. 10.30 Needle thread too loose

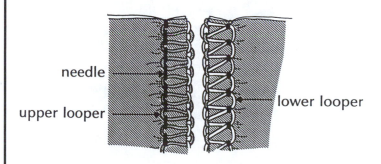

Fig. 10.31 Needle thread too tight

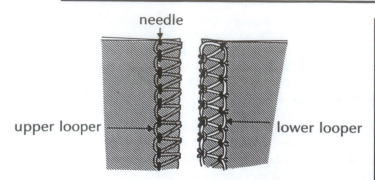

Fig. 10.32   Both loopers too tight

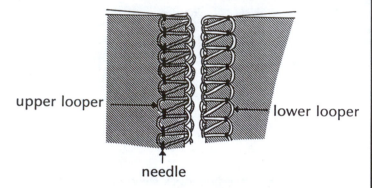

Fig. 10.33   Both loopers too loose

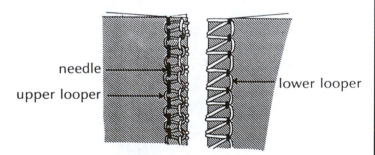

Fig. 10.34   Lower looper too loose or upper looper too tight

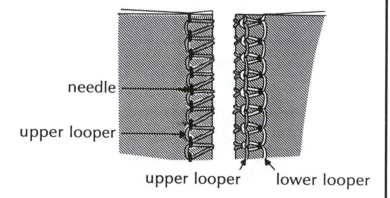

Fig. 10.35   Lower looper too tight or upper looper too loose

Stitch Length and Width

Stitch length is usually adjusted by turning a dial on the front of the machine or loosening a screw and moving a lever. The numbers on most stitch length dials or levers are in metric. The lower the number, the shorter the stitch; the larger the number, the longer the stitch. A 3 mm stitch length on an overlock machine is equivalent to approximately 9 stitches per inch; a setting of 2 mm is the equivalent to 12 stitches per inch. The shorter stitch length setting of 1 mm is usually used to create the narrow rolled hem or satin-type stitch.

The weight of the fabric will determine the appropriate stitch length to use. The longer the stitch length, the more likely a seam will pull apart and thread will be visible along the seam line. The longer stitch length uses less thread and may be appropriate when using the overlock machine to finish garment edges. For most general sewing the normal stitch length of 2.5–3 mm is recommended; however, a sample seam should be made when using a new fabric to determine the best stitch length, tension, and stitch width.

Stitch width can be adjusted in several ways: (1) by moving the lower knife and sometimes the stitch finger by turning a dial or by loosening a screw, (2) by changing the throat plate to one with a narrower or wider stitch finger, or (3) by changing the needle position if more than one needle can be used on the machine. A general recommendation is to use a wider stitch width on heavier fabrics and a narrower stitch width on lighter weight fabrics. The wider stitch width is generally going to be a more durable stitch for woven fabrics.

Clearing the Stitch Former or Stitch Finger

The terms *stitch former* or *stitch finger* are used interchangeably to describe the prong located on the throat plate or presser foot that aids in the formation of the overlock stitch (Fig. 10.24). Stitches always remain on the stitch former unless the fabric is maneuvered in such a way to remove these stitches. To perform certain stitching techniques, such as turning square corners, it is necessary to clear the stitches from the stitch former.

To clear the stitch former:

1. Raise the presser foot and needle.
2. Create some slack in the needle thread by gently pulling on the needle thread just above the thread guide above the needle (Fig. 10.36).
3. Pull the garment or thread chain back under the presser foot just enough to remove the stitches from the stitch former.

Stitching a Seam

Before sewing a seam on the overlock machine it is important to plan the construction and fitting sequence. If seams are being sewn on the overlock machine, the

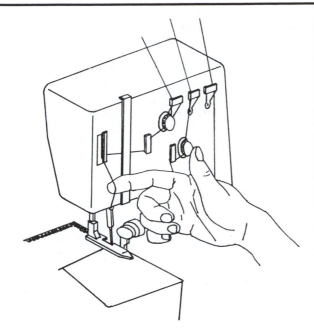

Fig. 10.36   Creating slack in needle thread
before clearing stitch former

fitting must take place before stitching since the excess seam allowance is trimmed while the seam is being sewn. If the overlock stitch is to be used as an edge finish for a plain seam sewn on the conventional machine, the finish can be applied either before or after the plain seam is stitched.

Overlock seams are recommended for the following situations:

1. For garments made of medium- to lightweight fabrics where narrow seam allowances with the seam edges finished together would be appropriate

2. On silk or silklike fabrics to prevent puckering of seams and to prevent raveling

3. For loose-fitting garments where it is not important for the seam allowances to be pressed open

4. For medium- to lightweight knits, especially those knits where seams allowances will not stay pressed open

Using the overlock seam as an edge finish is appropriate:

1. Whenever an overcast edge finish is needed for finishing garment edges

2. On medium- to heavyweight fabrics

3. On closely fitted garments where flat seams, which are pressed open, are desired

4. Where there are pockets or a zipper in a seam

5. Where a wider seam allowance is needed for fitting purposes

Usually a combination of plain seams and overlock seams are used in assembling a garment, so careful plan-

ning must occur before construction begins. The construction sequence may be different from the one presented in a pattern guide sheet. Many patterns include instructions for garment construction using the overlock machine, or they include overlock sewing hints along with the instructions for sewing on the conventional machine. Following is an example of the construction sequence for assembling a rugby shirt (Fig. 10.37) using both conventional and overlock machines.

Fig. 10.37   Rugby shirt

1. Make front placket—conventional machine.
2. Stitch shoulder seams—overlock machine.
3. Stitch purchased collar to neckline—overlock machine.
4. Apply ribbing to the bottom of the sleeves—overlock machine.
5. Attach sleeves to body (open construction)—overlock machine.
6. Stitch sleeve seam and side seam (one continuous seam)—overlock machine.
7. Finish hem edge, if necessary—overlock machine.
8. Complete hem—conventional machine or by hand.
9. Make buttonholes—conventional machine.
10. Attach buttons—by hand.

Since most overlock machines do not have the seam allowance guides marked on the regular throat plates as do conventional machines, the sewer must find a groove or mark on the machine that can be used as a guide for stitching a ⅝ inch (1.9 cm) seam. It must be remembered that the seam line is where the needle enters the fabric, not where the knife cuts off the excess fabric. If pins are used to hold the seam layers together, they should be placed parallel to the stitching line so there will be no danger of sewing over them. Remove the pins before they reach the location of the knives. Seam allowances could also be held together with hand basting or with a glue stick. It is not necessary to raise the presser foot when sewing most fabrics. The longer feed dogs will grab the fabric and feed it under the presser foot.

After a seam has been sewn the threads are not pulled through the machine as is the procedure for sewing on a conventional machine. At the end of a seam the sewer must continue stitching or "chaining off" until the thread chain is long enough to cut. Threads in the overlock machine will not jam when sewing with no fabric under the presser foot. The thread chain can be cut with regular shears, by using the thread cutter on the back of the presser foot, or by bringing the chain around to the front of the machine and running it under the presser foot, cutting it with the machine knives.

Securing a Seam

Since it is not possible to backstitch on an overlock machine, it is necessary to use other methods for securing the stitching at the end of a seam. If the seam or stitching will be crossed by another seam, it may not be necessary to secure the threads at the end of a seam, except at points on a garment where there will be stress placed on the seam. There are several methods that can be used to secure the overlock seam.

Tieing a Knot. The threads in the chain can be separated and a regular square knot or tailor's knot can be tied (Fig. 10.38).

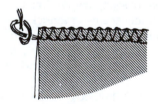

Fig. 10.38   Tieing a tailor's knot at end of overlock seam

Using Seam Sealant. A drop of liquid seam sealant can be applied to the threads at the end of a seam. Apply only a small amount to the thread ends (Fig. 10.39). The seam sealant should be allowed to dry before handling the garment.

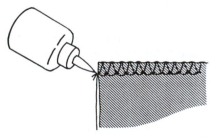

Fig. 10.39   Using seam sealant at end of overlock seam

Burying the Chain. After stitching the chain at the end of a seam, the chain can be threaded through the stitches along the seam line.

To bury the chain:

1. Pull the threads at the end of a seam to smooth out the chain.
2. Thread the chain into the eye of a tapestry needle and slip the needle back through the seam for about ½ inch (1.3 cm) (Fig. 10.40).

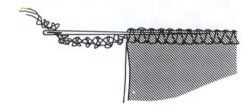

Fig. 10.40   Burying the thread chain

Securing with Machine Stitching. This technique resembles backstitching on a conventional machine.

To secure the thread chain at the beginning of a seam:

1. Sew one or two stitches into the fabric.
2. Bring the thread chain around to the front and under the presser foot (Fig. 10.41).
3. Sew over the chain for about ½ inch (1.3 cm).
4. Move the chain to the right and cut off the excess while sewing the rest of the seam (Fig. 10.42).

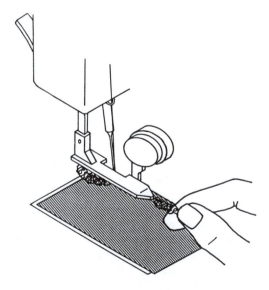

Fig. 10.41   Bringing thread chain under the presser foot

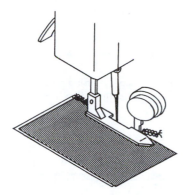

Fig. 10.42   Stitching over thread chain at beginning of a seam

To secure threads at the end of a seam:

1. Stop the sewing after taking about one stitch off the end of the fabric (Fig. 10.43).
2. Raise the presser foot and clear the stitch former.
3. Flip the fabric over and bring in front of the machine.
4. Lower the presser foot and stitch over the last few stitches along the edge of the seam.
5. Chain off to the edge of the seam and trim the threads (Fig 10.44).

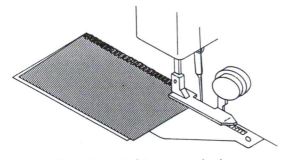

Fig. 10.43   Securing stitching at end of seam: stopping stitching with one stitch off the fabric

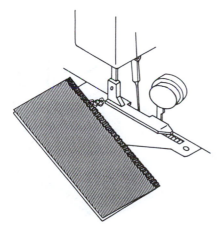

Fig. 10.44   Securing stitching at end of seam: stitching over previous stitching

Removing Stitches

Several methods can be used to remove the stitches from an overlock seam. One method is to slide the end of a seam ripper under the loops on one side of the seam cutting the threads along the edge (Fig. 10.45). The needle thread(s) will pull out easily. The loose looper threads will have to be removed. A second method involves pulling the needle thread(s) from the seam line (Fig. 10.46). The needle thread(s) can be clipped every 4–6 inches (10–15 cm) to make it easier to pull the thread(s) (a in Fig. 10.46). After removing the needle thread(s) the looper threads will come out easily.

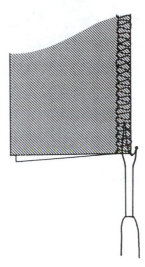

Fig. 10.45   Cutting overlock stitches with a seam ripper

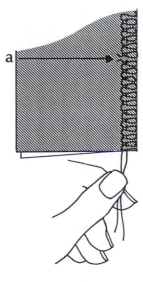

Fig. 10.46   Removing stitches by pulling the needle thread

Overlocking Techniques

Stabilizing Overlock Seams

Certain areas on a garment may need to be stabilized to prevent stretching and to provide extra strength. This may be necessary for shoulder seams or waistline seams, especially in garments made from knitted or loosely woven fabrics. Several methods can be used to stabilize overlock seams:

1. Include a strip of seam tape or twill tape when overlocking the seam (Fig. 10.47).

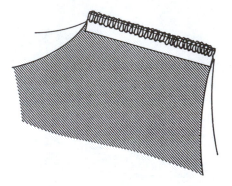

Fig. 10.47   Overlocking tape to stabilize a seam

2. Overlock over a length of pearl cotton, yarn, or buttonhole twist. Allow several inches (centimeters) of thread to extend beyond the seam at the ends so it can be caught when stitching across the seam (Fig. 10.48).

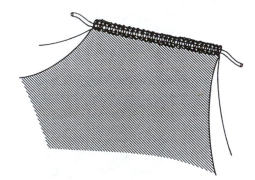

Fig. 10.48   Overlocking over a length of heavy thread to stabilize a seam

Overlocking Outside Corners

There are two methods of stitching around outside corners on items such as scarves and placemats. The first technique leaves a thread chain at each of the corners that must be secured after the stitching. Continuous stitching around an outside corner is difficult to do, but with practice it can be quicker and it provides a finished look on both sides of the fabric.

To finish a square corner by stitching off the edge:

1. Stitch along one side of the fabric and chain off the edge.
2. Stitch the next side, crossing over the chain of the first side, securing the end of that seam. Chain off the edge (Fig. 10.49).

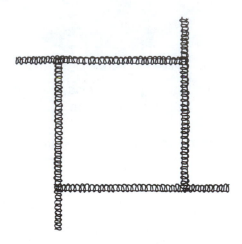

Fig. 10.49   Finishing a square corner by chaining off the edge

3. Continue in the same manner around all sides.
4. Secure the thread ends in one of the following ways:
    a. Cut off excess thread and seal the thread ends with seam sealant.
    b. Insert thread ends into a needle and hide the threads under the overlock seam.

To finish a square corner with continuous stitching:

1. Stitch along one side of the fabric, not trimming off any seam allowance. At the end continue *one* stitch off the end of the fabric.

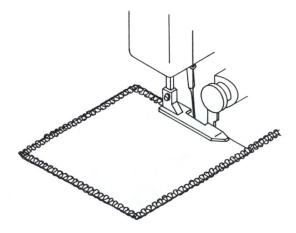

Fig. 10.50   Continuous stitching around an outside corner

2. Raise the needle and the presser foot.

3. Clear the stitch former.

4. Turn the fabric and position the corner of the fabric right under the needle.

5. Lower the presser foot and stitch the remaining sides in the same manner (Fig. 10.50), leaving a 3 inch (7.5 cm) thread chain at the end of the last side.

6. Secure the thread ends by one of the methods previously described.

Overlocking Inside Corners

Inside corners may be easier to overlock if the upper knife is disengaged. The edge to be finished should be trimmed to the desired width so no fabric is cut off while stitching.

To overlock an inside corner:

1. Disengage the upper knife.

2. Trim the edge of the fabric to the desired shape.

3. Overlock along the edge, stopping the stitching when the inside corner is located directly below the needle (Fig. 10.51).

3. Pull the fabric down in front of the machine, forming a straight edge (Fig. 10.52).

4. Continue stitching along the edge.

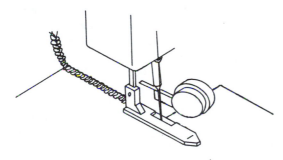

Fig. 10.51   Overlocking an inside corner: stopping stitching at the corner

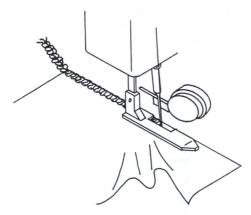

Fig. 10.52   Overlocking an inside corner: pulling fabric down to form a straight edge

Stitching Around Inside and Outside Curves

When stitching around curved edges it is important to stitch slowly and to watch where the knife is cutting rather than watching the needle. When the seams are quite curved, it may be necessary to lift the presser foot every few inches (centimeters) and readjust the fabric under the foot. On outside curves push the fabric toward the presser foot and the knife. When sewing inside curves, gently pull the fabric, almost forming a straight line while stitching, being careful not to pull or stretch the fabric out of shape.

Stitching a Circle

When the overlock stitch is used as an edge finish, it is often necessary to sew an enclosed circle, such as a hem edge or finishing the outside edge of a placemat. Two methods are presented for stitching in a circle.

To sew in a circle on a turned up hem:

1. Overlock the edge of the hem, trimming very little off the edge.

2. After stitching the entire circle, stitch over the beginning stitches for about 1 inch (2.5 cm) (a in Fig. 10.53).

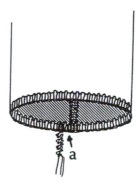

Fig. 10.53   Overlocking in a circle on a turned hem

3. Chain diagonally off the edge.

4. Thread ends can be cut close to the edge, tied in a knot, or sealed with seam sealant.

To sew in a circle on an exposed edge:

1. Trim the edge of the fabric to the desired shape and width.

2. Overlock around the edge, trimming very little off the edge. Stop a few stitches before the point where the stitching began.

3. Disengage the upper knife and overlock until the stitching just meets the original stitching.

4. Overlock diagonally off the edge making a 3 inch (7.5 cm) chain.

5. Unravel the threads in the chain (Fig. 10.54). Secure the thread ends by one of the following methods:

a. Tie knots in each tail. Cut off excess thread and seal the knots with seam sealant.

b. Insert thread ends into a needle and hide the threads under the overlock seam.

Fig. 10.54   Overlocking in a circle on an exposed edge

Gathering or Easing

Gathering may be done on the overlock machine by stitching along the edge with either the three-thread or four-thread stitch. On some materials it may be easier to pull the thread if the stitch length is lengthened. If using a three-thread machine, pull on the needle thread; if using a four-thread machine, pull *both* needle threads to gather the edge the desired amount (Fig. 10.55). When stitching the gathered edge to the ungathered edge, stitch very close to the lowest row of stitching used to make the gathers. Since the overlock stitch finishes the edge while putting in the gathering threads, the edge will not ravel while pulling on the gathering threads. One disadvantage of using this method is that the seam width is very narrow, making it more difficult to manipulate the fabric while gathering and when joining the gathered edge to the ungathered edge.

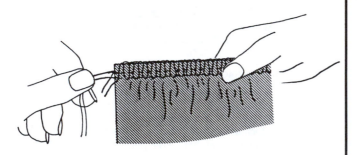

Fig. 10.55   Pulling the needle threads on a four-thread overlock stitch to gather an edge

This technique can also be used to ease a hem on a flared or circular skirt. Instead of easing the entire hem edge by pulling on one thread, draw up the extra fullness by pulling on the *needle thread* at regular intervals along the edge (Fig. 10.56).

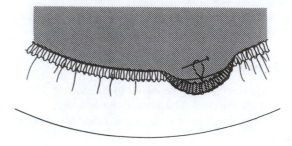

Fig. 10.56   Shaping a curved hem using an overlock stitch

Flatlock Stitching

The flatlock seam is a decorative seam with stitching showing on the right side of the garment. It is the only seam made on an overlock machine that can be located on the garment at a place other than on a garment edge. Flatlock stitching is often used to join two garment sections along a seam line, and it is most commonly seen on sportswear made of knit fabrics, such as sweatshirts and jogging outfits. It can be done on a two-thread and on most three-thread machines. Flatlock topstitching is done much the same way, except that it does not have to be located along a seam line. Striking effects can be made using different colors or types of thread. When experimenting with the flatlock stitch, it is a good idea to use different colors of thread in the needle and loopers until the tension and stitch length settings are correctly set.

To sew a two-thread flatlock seam:

1. *Loosen* the needle and looper tensions.
2. To have the loops showing on the right side of the garment sew the two layers of fabric with wrong sides together (*A* in Fig. 10.57). To have the ladder on the outside, sew with right sides together.
3. Pull the two layers apart until the seam is flat (*B* in Fig. 10.57).

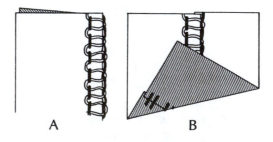

Fig. 10.57   Two-thread flatlock stitch

To sew a three-thread flatlock seam:

1. *Loosen* the needle tension almost all the way. The needle thread will form the ladder on the under side of the stitch (a in Fig. 10.58). *Tighten* the lower looper tension until the loops totally disappear. The lower looper thread will lie along the edge of the seam (b in Fig. 10.58). The upper looper usually needs no adjustment. This thread forms the loops on the top side of the seam (c in Fig. 10.58).

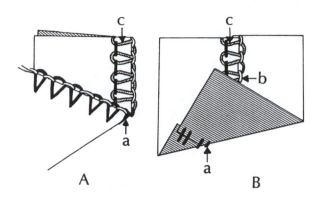

Fig. 10.58   Three-thread flatlock stitch

2. Sew two layers of fabric together as described for making a two-thread flatlock seam (A in Fig. 10.58).
3. Pull the two layers apart until the seam is flat (B in Fig. 10.58).

To make flatlock topstitching:

1. Mark the placement for the flatlock topstitching on the fabric.
2. Fold the fabric wrong sides together on the placement line.
3. Disengage the top knife on the machine.
4. Place the fabric under the presser foot so that the fold is moved in away from the edge of the throat plate, reducing the width of the stitch along the fold.
5. Stitch along the fold (Fig. 10.59). About half of the stitch will be off the edge of the fabric.

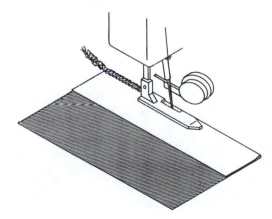

Fig. 10.59   Flatlock topstitching along a folded edge

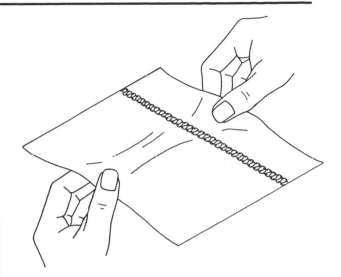

Fig. 10.60   Pulling fabric taut for flatlock topstitching

6. Unfold the fabric. Pull taut to flatten the stitches (Fig. 10.60). Several parallel rows of stitching may be made, if desired.

Narrow Rolled Hemming

The narrow rolled hemming stitch is often used to finish the edges of ruffles, scarves, napkins, and tablecloths. Since the edge usually rolls under, a beadlike effect is created along the edge. The rolled hem is usually done using three threads, but can be done on some two-thread machines. On most machines, a special throat plate and/or presser foot are required to make the stitch. The tensions must be adjusted to make the edge roll under. On a three-thread machine, the lower looper tension is tightened (a in Fig. 10.61) and the upper looper thread is loosened so that the upper looper thread is pulled over the edge (b in Fig. 10.61) causing the edge to curl under. The needle thread (c in Fig. 10.61) usually

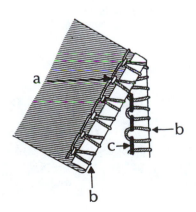

Fig. 10.61   Narrow rolled hem on a three-thread machine

requires no adjustment. The stitch length is usually shortened to 1/16–1/8 inch (1–2 mm) to create the satin edge. Special effects can be created by using decorative thread. It is important to always make a sample on the fabric to be used. Corners can be finished by the methods described earlier in this chapter.

A "lettuce leaf" hem (Fig. 10.62) can be created by using the narrow rolled hem in the crosswise direction on soft knits and stretching the fabric as the stitch is being made. Increasing the pressure will increase the amount of stretch creating a "leafier" edge.

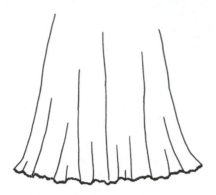

Fig. 10.62   "Lettuce leaf" edging

Unique Assembly Procedures Recommended for Overlock Sewing

Overlocked Sleeve Placket

This type of placket is quick to make and creates very little bulk in the placket area of the sleeve. The technique can be used on both woven and knitted fabrics.

To make an overlocked sleeve placket:

1. Slash the sleeve for the placket opening (Fig. 10.63).
2. Disengage the knife and overlock the slashed edge, trimming nothing from the edge while stitching. Stitch to the point of the slash.
3. Pull the remaining part of the slash down forming a straight line. Overlock the edge (Fig. 10.64).

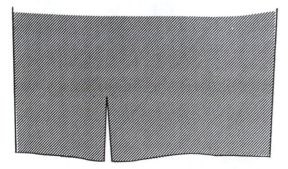

Fig. 10.63   Slashing placket opening in the sleeve

4. Fold sleeve placket area with right sides together. Stitch a 2 inch (5 cm) dart at the top end of the placket (Fig. 10.65).
5. Press each edge of the placket to the wrong side (Fig. 10.66). Press the dart flat.
6. Secure the edges of the placket in one of the following ways:

   a. Hand stitch along the edges using a blind or slip stitch.

   b. Topstitch the placket edges stitching close to the folded edge.

   c. Place a narrow strip of fusible web under the placket edges and press.

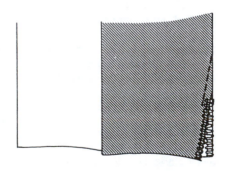

Fig. 10.64   Overlocking slashed edge of sleeve placket

Fig. 10.65   Stitching dart at top of placket

Fig. 10.66   Pressing placket edges

Applying a Cuff

Cuffs can be applied to a sleeve in one sewing step. The cuff will be attached to the sleeve with an exposed seam, a technique often used in ready-to-wear. This technique could be adapted to attaching a collar to a shirt or a waistline casing on skirts and pants.

To attach a cuff with an exposed seam:

1. Complete the sleeve placket as previously described but do not secure the edges of the placket until after the cuff is attached. This technique for attaching a cuff also works well when the sleeve placket opening is located in the sleeve seam (Fig. 10.67).
2. Make the cuff.
3. Match the cuff to the sleeve with right sides together. Fold the edges of the placket over the ends of the cuff.
4. Overlock the seam through all thicknesses (Fig. 10.68).
5. Open out the cuff, turning the seam toward the sleeve.
6. Secure the edges of the placket in place.

Fig. 10.67   Sleeve placket located in sleeve seam

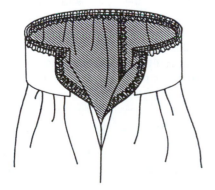

Fig. 10.68   Overlocking cuff seam

Machine Problems and Solutions

Problems with *skipped stitches* may be caused by the needle size being incorrect for the thread or the fabric, by the needle being inserted incorrectly, by using a damaged needle, or by the machine being incorrectly threaded.

If the *needle breaks,* the needle may not have been inserted correctly; it may not have been the right size for the thread or the fabric; the presser foot or throat plate may not be positioned properly; or there may have been excessive pulling on the fabric while stitching.

Thread breakage may be caused by improper threading; the thread eyelets in the pole guide may not be positioned directly over the cones or spools of thread; the thread tension may be tight; thread may be caught in the spool notch; or the needle may be inserted incorrectly.

If the *fabric puckers while sewing,* the thread tensions may be too tight; the presser foot pressure may be too heavy; the stitch length may be too long; or the thread may be too heavy for the weight of the fabric.

If the *fabric stretches while sewing,* the pressure may be too heavy; the stitch length may be too short; the edge may need to be stabilized with tape or interfacing; or the fabric may have been stretched while sewing.

If the *fabric does not feed under the presser foot,* the stitch length may be too short or the presser foot pressure may be incorrectly set for the fabric.

If the *edges of the overlock seam are ragged after stitching,* the knife blades may not be positioned properly or they may be damaged or dull and need to be replaced.

11 Pattern Layout, Cutting, and Marking

Accuracy in cutting and marking is necessary to construct a garment that duplicates the design and size of the pattern. This chapter discusses procedures used for cutting out the pattern and for transferring pattern markings.

Preparation for Pattern Layout

Before beginning a construction project, it is important to prepare the fabric, study the pattern guide sheet, and identify the pattern pieces to be used. Several basic procedures need to be followed before laying out the pattern.

1. Straighten and preshrink the fabric (see Chapter 7).
2. Make all necessary pattern alterations (see Chapter 5).
3. Assemble the pattern pieces necessary for the view being made and return other pieces to the pattern envelope. Small pattern pieces that may be printed together on one sheet can be cut apart; excess paper around the pattern pieces need not be removed.
4. If pattern pieces are extremely wrinkled, press with a *warm, dry* iron. Smooth remaining pattern pieces by hand.
5. Identify and circle the appropriate pattern layout on the pattern guide sheet. The layout is determined by the *view of the pattern*, the *width of the fabric*, the *size*

of the pattern, and *fabric type* (with or without nap).

6. Study the layout and the individual pattern pieces being used. While most pieces are placed on lengthwise grain (i.e., the grainline arrow on the pattern is parallel to the selvage), the sewer may want to change this placement to achieve a different effect.

7. Pattern pieces are made for the right half of the body, and most are cut one time from folded fabric. Check each pattern piece to determine any that may deviate from this procedure. For example, cuffs often need to be cut twice in order to produce four fabric pieces. Asymmetrical designs will have a different pattern piece for the right and left sides, and each of these is cut only one time.

8. Patterns typically have ⅝-inch (1.6 cm) seam allowances. Increase the seam allowance from ⅝ inch (1.6 cm) to 1 inch (2.5 cm) for seams that have a lapped zipper and for those that might need minor adjustment during construction (garment side seams). These new cutting lines can be drawn around the pattern before or after the pattern is placed on the fabric.

Pattern Layout

Different layouts require different folds; some will require more than one type of fold. If a partial or double lengthwise fold (Figs. 11.1 and 11.2) is required, the sewer must be careful that each fold is on grain. That

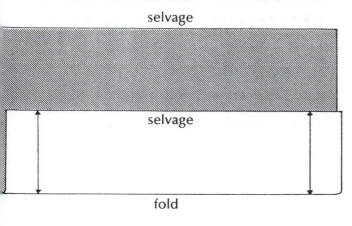

selvage

selvage

fold

Fig. 11.1   Partial lengthwise fold — the selvage is measured an even distance between the arrows

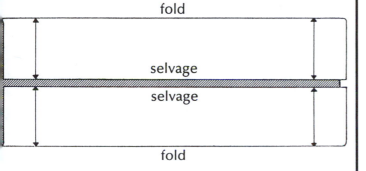

fold

selvage

selvage

fold

Fig. 11.2   Double lengthwise fold — the selvages are measured an even distance between the arrows

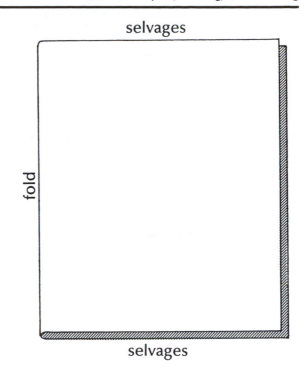

selvages

fold

selvages

Fig. 11.3   Crosswise fold

means measuring the width of the folded layer in several places to insure that it is an equal distance from the selvage edge. Some garments require a crosswise fold (Fig. 11.3) for some or all of the pattern pieces. If the fabric being folded has an "up and down" design or texture, the fabric will need to be cut and refolded so that the design or nap is going in the same direction on each piece. As a general rule, if the pattern layout calls for more than one fold, the sewer starts with the fold that contains the most pattern pieces. Before cutting, the remaining fabric should be measured to be sure that sufficient fabric remains for the rest of the pattern pieces.

The fabric can be folded with the right sides to the inside or the outside for cutting. Having the right sides to the inside will reduce soiling of the fabric; however, some of the marking techniques are easier to accomplish if the fabric is folded with right sides to the outside. Having the right sides of the fabric to the outside is recommended when one needs to be able to see the designs in order to match or place them accurately. After the fabric has been folded in the appropriate way, all the pattern pieces should be placed on the fabric for a trial layout. No pins are used at this stage. The pinning process can begin when the sewer has determined that sufficient fabric is available for all of the pattern pieces to be placed.

The first pins are placed on the grainline (either on the grainline arrow or the fold line); a good procedure is to attach all pattern pieces to the fabric with just these two or three pins until all the pattern pieces are in place. That way, if a pattern piece needs to be moved, only a minimum number of pins will need to be removed and replaced. Once all pattern pieces are in the proper location and on grain, the rest of the pins can be placed perpendicular to and just inside the seam line. Pins are usually placed about every 4–5 inches (10–12.5 cm) around the entire pattern piece. Pattern pieces should be placed as close together as possible to economize on fabric.

Having each pattern piece cut on grain is extremely important if the finished garment is to fit and hang properly. Pattern pieces that go on the fold need to be placed with the "place on the fold" line exactly on the fold of the fabric. Those pieces with grainline arrows need to be placed so that the arrow is exactly parallel to the grain. This is done by anchoring one end of the grainline marking to the fabric with a pin and then measuring from there to the selvage (Fig. 11.4). The other end needs to be pinned to the fabric at exactly the same distance from the selvage. For especially long pattern pieces, the sewer may want to measure in the middle of the pattern pieces too.

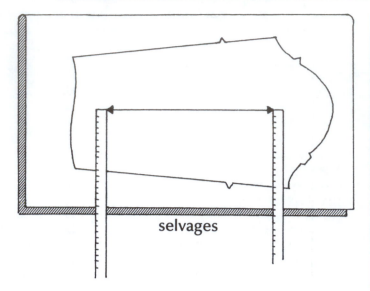

Fig. 11.4   Aligning pattern piece on straight grain of fabric

The number of pins needed varies with the type of fabric. The sewer should use only as many pins as are absolutely necessary for holding the pattern to the fabric. Smooth, slippery fabrics usually require more pins than firmer fabrics. If a fabric tends to show pin marks, all pins should be placed within the seam allowance, or weights could be used in place of pins.

The fabric needs to be kept on a flat surface during the layout and cutting procedure. Allowing it to hang off the end of a table may cause the fabric to be pulled off grain.

Some layouts require cutting one piece at a time on an open, single layer of fabric. When following this procedure, the sewer must be extremely careful to reverse the pattern piece (turn it upside down) when cutting the duplicate piece so that a right and a left side are being cut. Making a second pattern piece and placing both on the pattern at the same time (being sure that the two form a mirror image) would eliminate this problem. If only one piece is to be cut (e.g., an asymmetrical design with a different right and left side), both the pattern and the fabric must be either "face up" or "face down" to insure that the appropriate side is being cut.

Some fabrics require special layout techniques. Those are discussed in Chapters 8 and 9.

Cutting

The sewer needs to check the layout carefully before doing any cutting, because a mistake at this stage is a costly one. The novice may want to have another person check the pinning before starting to cut.

The pattern is cut along the indicated cutting line, a bold line printed on the pattern. If the seam allowance was increased to 1 inch (2.5 cm) for a lapped zipper or for fitting purposes, the newly marked line should be used for cutting. Included on the cutting line are notches, triangular shaped symbols that aid in assembling the garment. Patterns contain single, double, and triple notches; each set is usually numbered. Their counterparts can be found on the adjoining seam.

The most accurate cutting occurs when the fabric is kept as flat on the table as possible; bent-handle shears make this possible. Notches are cut *out* away from the seam allowance, with double or triple notches cut as a single unit (a in Fig. 11.5). The garment should be cut *with the grain*, which as a general rule means cutting from the highest point of the pattern downward and the widest point of the pattern inward (Fig. 11.6). Cutting with the grain reduces stretching and raveling. Many patterns indicate the direction in which to cut the seam by placing an arrow on the cutting line or printing a pair of shears turned in the appropriate direction.

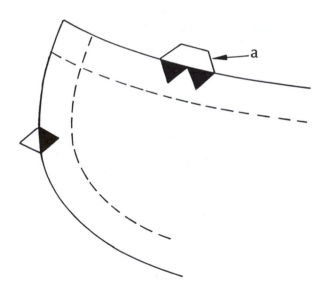

Fig. 11.5   Cutting notches

Lining, underlining, and interfacing fabrics should be cut at the same time but separate from the fashion fabric. Sometimes a lining is cut and stitched prior to the fashion fabric to check for fit.

Very bulky fabrics may need to be pinned and cut one layer at a time. Silky woven fabrics and some single knits may need to be pinned to a cutting board or to sheets of paper before the pattern pieces are pinned to the fabric. This will stabilize the fabric and keep it on grain, lessening distortion in the finished garment.

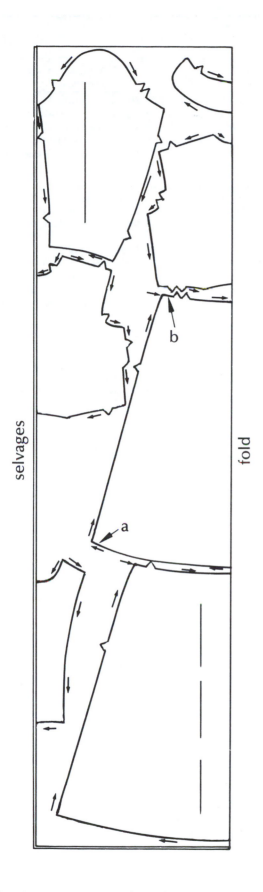

selvages

fold

b

a

Fig. 11.6   Directions for cutting

Marking

To assemble a garment, the sewer needs to know the location of key construction details—darts, tucks, pleats, buttonholes, pockets. *Marking,* defined as the transfer of significant pattern symbols to the fabric, is done after cutting and before the pattern is removed from the fabric. Several marking options are available to the sewer: dressmaker's carbon paper and tracing wheel, tailor's tacks, pins, chalk, and washable marking pens. The method used is determined by the characteristics of the fabric, the type of mark being transferred, and whether the mark is to be viewed on the right side or wrong side of the fabric. The different methods with their advantages and uses are listed in Table 11.1.

Dressmaker's Carbon Paper and Tracing Wheel

Dressmaker's carbon paper is a specially prepared waxed paper that is available in several colors. The waxy side of the paper goes against the *wrong* side of the fabric (Fig. 11.7). The paper can be folded so that both layers of fabric are marked at the same time. Carbon paper is used only on the inside of the garment, with the *lightest* possible color being chosen for the fabric. As few pins as possible should be removed when putting the carbon paper in place. When using a tracing wheel, the sewer should protect the table with a piece of cardboard, a magazine, or a tracing board.

The serrated tracing wheel can damage certain fabrics and should be avoided where such a tendency exists. A smooth tracing wheel or the edge of a table knife could be used so that holes are not made in the fabric. Dressmaker's carbon paper also should be avoided on any fabric where the marking might show through to the right side of the fabric. Holding the fabric up to the light as well as examining it on the table is recommended to

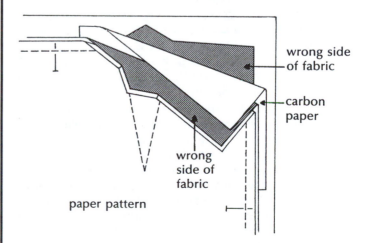

wrong side of fabric

carbon paper

wrong side of fabric

paper pattern

Fig. 11.7   Placement of tracing paper

TABLE 11.1
Methods for Marking Construction Details

Method of marking	Suitable fabrics	Advantages	Disadvantages and precautions in use
Dressmaker's carbon paper and tracing wheel	Any firm fabric unless too thick to show marks, or a lightweight fabric on which marks do not show on right side of fabric.	Quick, easy, and accurate. Entire stitch line of detail transferred to fabric. Identical marks on both layers of fabric.	May show on right side of fabric. May be difficult to remove. Some fabrics permanently punctured by tracing wheel. Markings may be distorted on stretchy fabrics. Wheel can rip tissue pattern.
Tailor's tacks	All fabrics except those that retain puncture marks. Most suitable for sheer or delicate fabrics, spongy, or knit fabrics.	Easily removed. Visible on both sides of each layer of fabric.	Must be marked along the exact stitching or detail line. Must take small stitches for accurate markings. Time consuming. Threads must be removed after machine stitching. Danger of snipping fabric when cutting threads between layers of fabric.
Pins	All fabrics except those that retain puncture marks.	Quick and easy.	If pins slip out, location of detail is lost.
White chalk or chalk pencil	All fabrics except white.	Easy to remove white chalk marks.	Difficult to achieve accuracy. Necessary to sharpen edge of chalk often to make fine lines.
Wax chalk	Medium and heavy wool and wool blends only.	Not easily rubbed off.	May leave grease marks on fabrics other than wool. Necessary to sharpen edge of chalk often to make fine lines.
Washable marking pen	Most washable fabrics.	Quick and easy. Markings disappear in a few days or with water.	Difficult to achieve accuracy if pens are not sharp. Removing markings before pressing is necessary.

insure that none of the marking will be visible in the finished garment. When using carbon paper on heavier fabric, each layer may need to be marked separately for the markings to show and to avoid excessive damage to the pattern. As with other forms of marking, it is important to test the procedure on a scrap of fabric before using it on the garment piece.

To insure accuracy in tracing, a ruler should be used to mark straight seams and darts (Fig. 11.8). The end of a dart can be marked with a line that intersects the stitching lines for the sides of the dart, to clearly indicate where the end is located (Fig. 11.9). Dots and other such symbols on the pattern can be marked with an "X".

The solid and dotted lines on patterns used for such details as pleats can be marked with two different colors of tracing paper to distinguish between the two. Since carbon paper is *never* used on the outside of the garment, the sewer will have to use thread basting along the traced line for such details as center front or back, pleats, tucks, fold lines, and pocket lines, all of which need to be seen on the right side of the garment (Fig. 11.10). Use the tracing wheel and carbon paper to transfer the appropriate symbol to the wrong side, then baste along this line.

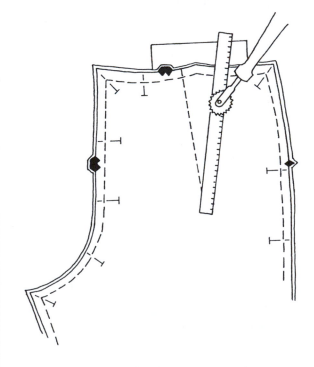

Fig. 11.8   Using ruler for accuracy when tracing

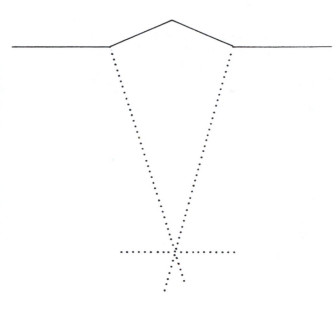

Fig. 11.9   Marking end of dart

Tailor's Tacks

Tailor's tacks, which use thread for marking, are safe for most fabrics, with the exception of those susceptible to puncture marks. Sometimes, too, dark threads will leave marks if used for making tailor's tacks on light-colored fabrics. Otherwise, tailor's tacks are one of the safest of all markings. They are durable during construction, yet they usually are removed easily. Care needs to be taken not to get tailor's tacks caught in buttonhole stitching, as removing those markings can be a real challenge. Removable basting thread may be an appropriate choice for making tailor's tacks, since it will disappear with moisture.

A double thread with no knot is used when making tailor's tacks. Running the thread through beeswax before starting this procedure will keep the thread from tangling. A *very short stitch* is taken through the pattern and the layers of fabric at the point where the tailor's tack is desired. A tail of thread 1½ inches (3.8 cm) long should be left (a in Fig. 11.11). A second stitch is taken in the same location, leaving a 1-inch (2.5 cm) loop (b in Fig. 11.11). When the tailor's tack is cut, a tail similar to the first one needs to be left (a in Fig. 11.12). The two layers of fabric are separated and the thread is cut between the two layers, leaving a tailor's tack in both layers of fabric (b in Fig. 11.12).

If several tailor's tacks are needed in a row, a series can be made and cut apart when all are completed. A simplified version of the tailor's tack is a row of uneven basting, which works well for defining lines, such as for pleats. If marking two layers of fabric in this manner,

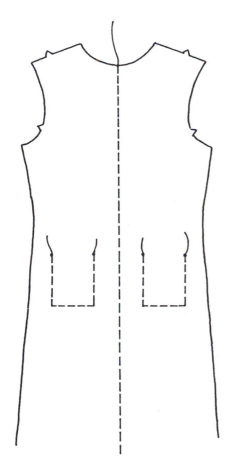

Fig. 11.10   Thread tracing

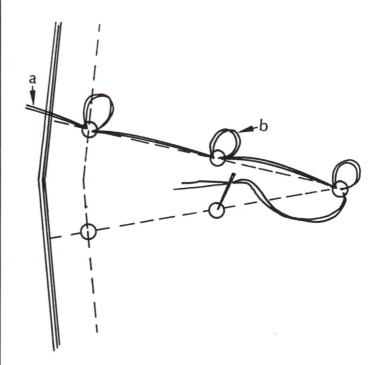

Fig. 11.11   Making tailor's tacks

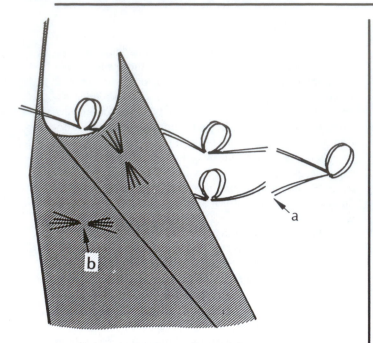

Fig. 11.12 Cutting tailor's tacks

longer thread tails need to be left to insure adequate thread for markings on both layers when the two are separated to cut the thread (Fig. 11.13).

The sewer may want to use different colors of thread to distinguish among various markings. Tailor's tacks work well regardless of whether the garment was cut with the right side of the fabric toward the inside or toward the outside.

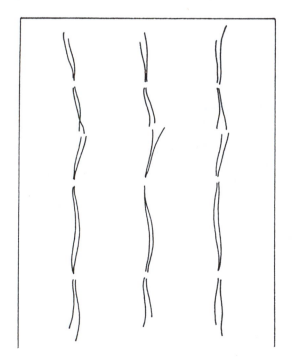

Fig. 11.13 Using uneven basting for a modified tailor's tack

Pins

Pins provide a quick method for making *temporary* markings on fabrics that do not show puncture holes. They do not work well for fabrics, however, that do not hold pins well, such as loosely woven or slippery fabrics.

For pin marking, the pins are placed into the fabric at the appropriate places; a second pin is inserted into the same point from the opposite side of the fabric to provide a marking on both layers (a in Fig. 11.14). When the sides are separated, a pin remains in both layers of the fabric (b in Fig. 11.14). This separating must be done gently, as the pins have a tendency to fall out. After separating the fabric layers, "small stitches" are taken in the fabric at the location of each pin to identify the pattern marking.

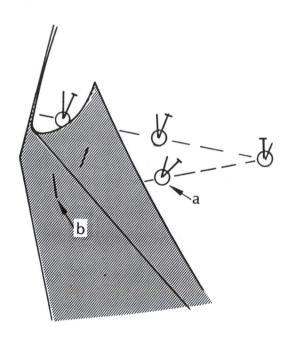

Fig. 11.14 Pin marking

Tailor's Chalk

Pin markings combined with tailor's chalk provide another type of marking. After the pins have been placed in the fabric as previously described, the chalk can be used to mark a line joining the pin markings. To be effective and accurate, the chalk must be sharp. As with the tracing wheel, a ruler is helpful when marking with chalk (Fig. 11.15). Chalk tends to rub off easily, so it should not be used for markings that need to be seen for a long time. Waxy chalk should be used only on wool or wool blends; the chalky type can be used for other fabrics.

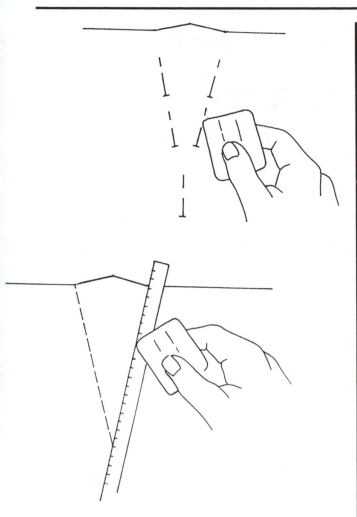

Fig. 11.15   Chalk marking

Marking Pens

Washable marking pens *(never lead pencils, felt tip pens, or ballpoint pens)* make a dot that, on lighter weight fabrics, will go through both layers at one time. The marking pen most often is used with pin markings much as is tailor's chalk; however, with some fabrics a mark can be made directly through the pattern onto the fabric. Marking pens need to be tested to insure that the mark will not remain after the area has been dampened with a cloth. All markings made with washable marking pens should be removed before pressing over the markings.

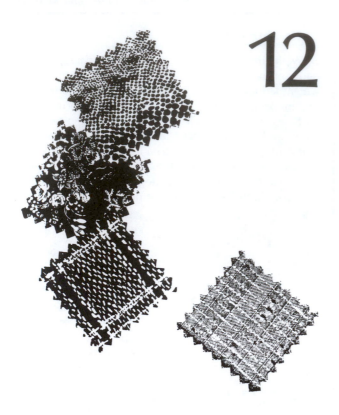

12 Exposed Seams and Edge Finishes

Exposed seams are visible on the inside of the finished garment and include all of the structural seams of the garment. *Enclosed seams* (discussed in other chapters of this book, including Chapters 15, 16, 20, and 21) are those inside a part of the garment (e.g., the collar, cuff, waistband) and are not seen on the inside of the finished garment. This chapter will concentrate on how exposed seams are stitched and finished.

Directional Stitching

To prevent distortion of the fabric edges during stitching, seams need to sewn and finished *with the grain.* This directional stitching (with the grain) is especially important on curved areas or garment bias seams. Straight, on-grain seams and true bias seams can be stitched in either direction. Many pattern companies include an arrow on the cutting and stitching lines to indicate how to handle these areas. (See discussion on directional cutting in Chapter 11.)

One way to identify grain direction is to run a finger along the cut edge of the fabric and observe the separation of the yarns (Fig. 12.1). "With the grain" is the direction in which the yarns lie smoothly along a cut edge; "against the grain" is the direction in which the yarns tend to spread apart. The direction of the arrow in Figure 12.1 is going "against the grain." Another method to de-

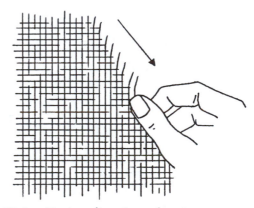

Fig. 12.1 Testing direction of grain on a cut edge

termine the grain direction for cutting and sewing is to work from the "high point to the low point" or "from the widest point to the narrowest point" on a garment piece.

Staystitching

Staystitching is a row of directional stitching placed a scant ⅛ inch (3 mm) from the seam line and within the seam allowance for the purpose of preventing stretching. It generally is done on a single layer of fabric and is completed *after* marking and *before* stitching of seams, darts, and other construction details. When attaching interfacing or underlining to an area, staystitching can be done through both layers of fabric.

Staystitching is used primarily on garment bias seams that have the greatest tendency to stretch while fitting, such as the neckline and waistline seams (Fig. 12.2). Seams cut on straight grain or in areas of the garment that are sewn or basted together before fitting need not be staystitched. As a general rule, armhole seams are not staystitched because the extra stitching may inhibit the flexibility needed in this seam.

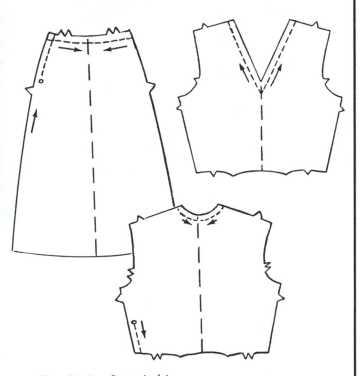

Fig. 12.2   Staystitching

Each seam is staystitched separately. Continuous stitching (see Chapter 10) may be an efficient approach when a great deal of staystitching is required. Backstitching is not used when staystitching. A regular stitch length is used unless the staystitching also serves as reinforcement stitching when a shorter than average stitch length is used.

Seams and Seam Allowances

A *seam* is a row of machine stitching that holds together two or more layers of fabric. The *seam allowance* is the fabric between the seam line or stitching line and the cut edge. On most conventional patterns, the seam allowance is ⅝ inch (16 mm or 1.6 cm); for some "knits only" patterns and patterns "designed for use with the overlock machine," the seam allowance may be less.

Before any seams are sewn in the actual garment, a

sample seam should be stitched and pressed to determine the appropriate machine tension, pressure, and stitch length as well as the appropriate pressing techniques to use on the fabric (see Chapters 10 and 13). Any needed staystitching or reinforcement stitching would be completed before the seams are sewn.

Seam Types

Plain Seams

The plain seam can be used on both straight and curved seams and is usually pressed open after construction.

To construct a plain seam:

1. Place right sides together of the sections to be joined, matching the seam ends, notches, dots, and other pattern markings (*a* in Fig. 12.3). For some seams, the ends of the garment pieces will match at the stitching line and not at the cut edges (*b* in Fig. 12.3).

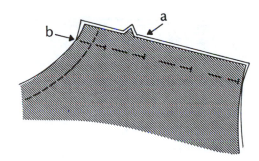

Fig. 12.3   Pinning a seam

2. To mark the seam line, place pins directly on and parallel to the *stitching line* (Fig. 12.3) and remove them before the machine passes over them. For accuracy in pinning and stitching, take small bites of fabric when pinning. Seams also can be held in place for sewing with hand basting or with a double-faced sticky tape placed just inside the seam line and into the seam allowance (see Fig. 8.7). The sticky tape should not be caught in the stitching.

3. Backstitch the ends of the seam (*a* in Fig. 12.4) or tie the threads.

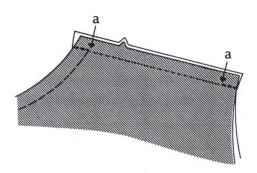

Fig. 12.4   Backstitching ends of seam

4. The plain seam has two raw edges that will require a finish unless the fabric does not ravel. If the seam is pressed open, each edge is finished separately; if the seam is pressed in one direction, the two seam edges can be finished as one. If bulk is a problem, the seam can be layered and the edges finished separately. *Seams should be finished before crossing with another seam.*

5. Plain seams can be pressed open or in one direction (see Chapter 13 for pressing techniques). Press each seam *before* it is crossed with another seam or construction detail.

Because of their construction, some plain seams require special handling. These include: intersecting seams, unlike curved seams, inset corners, and crotch seams.

Intersecting Seams

When plain seams intersect, care must be taken when pinning and stitching to insure that the two seams match (Fig. 12.5). To reduce bulk in the area, the seam allowance ends need to be cut (Fig. 12.6). When the intersect-

ing seams are pressed in one direction, considerable bulk is possible. To reduce that bulk, the seams can be pressed open for about 1 inch (2.5 cm) and then clipped and pressed in the appropriate direction (Fig. 12.7). The open seam would be trimmed as shown in Figure 12.6 to minimize the bulk in the area. An alternative method would be to press the seam to opposite sides in the two garment sections (Fig. 12.8).

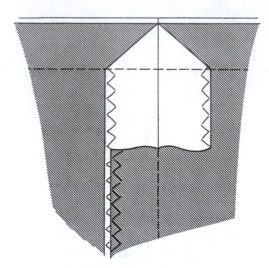

Fig. 12.7 Intersecting seams pressed in one direction

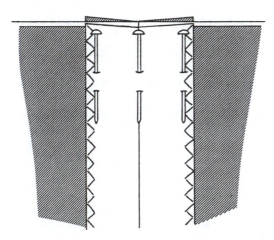

Fig. 12.5 Pinning intersecting seams to stitch

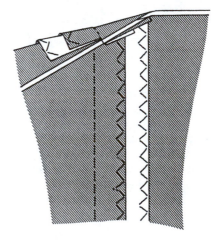

Fig. 12.8 Intersecting seams pressed in opposite direction on the two garment layers

Unlike Curved Seams

Unlike curved seams, such as those found on princess seams and curved yoke seams, require special handling because the two edges being joined have different types of curves. On a princess seam the concave curve or inside curve is found on the center section; the convex or outside curve occurs on the side panel.

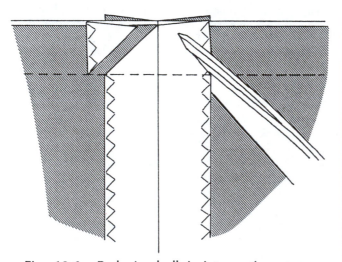

Fig. 12.6 Reducing bulk in intersecting seams

To join unlike curves:

1. Staystitch the inside or concave curve and clip the seam allowance in the curved area to the staystitching (Fig. 12.9). *Clipping* is done with the points of the shears and extends from the cut edge *to but not through* the stitching line.

2. Pin and stitch the two edges together with the clipped concave curve on top (Fig. 12.10). Care must be taken to match the garment edges and the ends at the *seam line*.

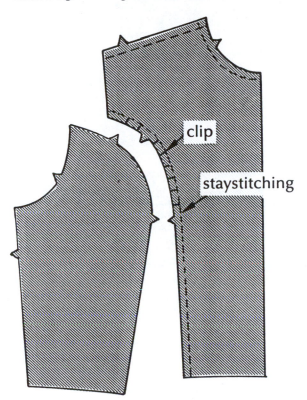

Fig. 12.9   Staystitching and clipping inside curve

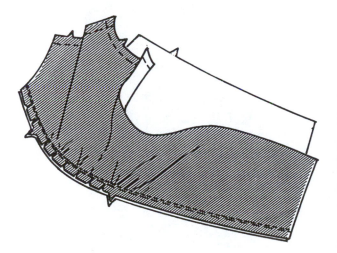

Fig. 12.10   Stitching unlike curve seam

3. Finish the seam edges in an appropriate manner.

4. Press the curved seam using a pressing cushion (see Chapter 13) to preserve the shape of the seam. The seam can be pressed open or in one direction.

a. If the seam is pressed open, the convex curve or outside curve will need to be notched in the curved area (Fig. 12.11). *Notching* involves removing small wedges of fabric from the seam to allow the curve to be smooth while also removing bulk from the seam allowance. Notching is done with the points of the shears and extends *to but not through* the stitching line. Several small notches are preferred to a few larger ones; the objective is to have the cut edges of the notches meet, not gap or overlap.

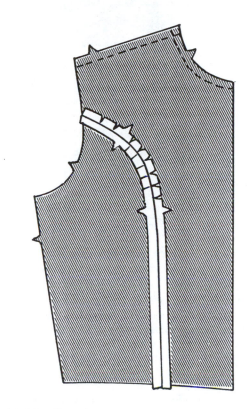

Fig. 12.11   Pressing open a curve seam

b. If the curved seam is pressed in one direction, generally it is pressed toward the center of the garment. Notching of the convex curve is not necessary when the seam is pressed in this manner. Pressing the seam open over the pressing cushion is advised before the seam is pressed toward the center. To reduce bulk, the seam can be layered/graded, with the seam edge toward the inside being cut shorter than the seam edge toward the garment. Layering/grading is not recommended if the seam is to be topstitched.

Inset Corners

Inset corners may have different shapes; however, the procedures for joining them are the same. The inset corner is created when an "inside" corner is joined to an "outside" corner, such as in a "V" yoke.

To make an inset corner:

1. Carefully mark the stitching lines for the corner on both garment sections to make joining easier and more accurate.

2. Reinforce the section with the inside corner with a row of stitching placed close to or directly on the seam line, using a shortened stitch length for about 1 inch (2.5 cm) on either side of the corner (*a* in Fig. 12.12).

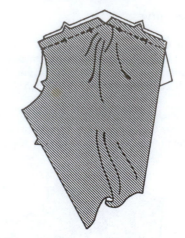

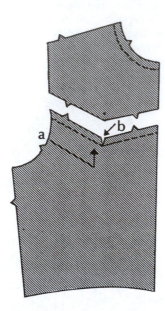

Fig. 12.12   Marking and reinforcing an inset corner

Fig. 12.13   Pinning an inset corner

3. If the fabric is an open weave or is one that tends to ravel easily, additional reinforcement may be needed. A small circle of fusible interfacing can be fused to the wrong side of the fabric over the inside corner before it is reinforced.

4. Clip the inside corner all the way to the reinforcement stitching (*b* in Fig. 12.12). If the fabric ravels excessively, seam sealant can be applied to the clipped area.

5. With right sides together and the reinforced inside corner on top, pin the two sections together, *starting at the corner* and pinning in both directions to each end. Accurately match the markings for the corner on the two garment sections. Care must be taken to match the garment ends at the *seam line;* the cutting lines may not match at the end of seams when pinning a seam with an inset corner. Place pins parallel to and directly on the seam line (Fig. 12.13). From the right side check the smoothness of the fabric along the seam line before stitching.

6. Stitch the seam with the reinforced corner on top (Fig. 12.14). Stop the machine at the corner with the needle in the fabric. Pivot the fabric under the needle and adjust as needed to continue stitching the other side. The stitching must stop exactly at the point, and pivoting must be done carefully to avoid stitching an unwanted pleat in the corner.

7. The inset corner seam generally is pressed in one direction, usually toward the yoke (Fig. 12.15). Layering/grading the seam will help to reduce bulk, but is not recommended if top stitching is to be used. Finish the seam edges and trim excess fabric from the point.

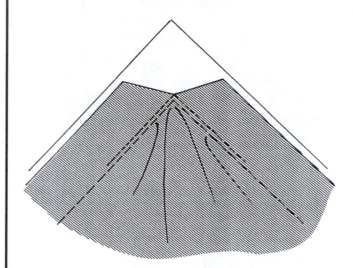

Fig. 12.14   Stitching inset corner

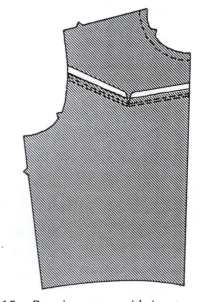

Fig. 12.15   Pressing seam with inset corner

Crotch Seam

The crotch seam in pants, culottes, or shorts usually is a plain seam, and is a variation of an intersecting seam. Many methods can be used for sewing it, two of which are discussed here. In both of these methods, the crotch seam is stitched as one continuous seam.

Open Construction

In this method, the crotch seam is stitched before the side seams. The main advantage to the open construction technique is ease in fitting the side seams of the pants.

1. Stitch pants back to pants front at the inseams with right sides together (Fig. 12.16). Finish the seam edges and press the seam open.

2. Pin the crotch seam matching inseams, notches, and other pattern markings. If a zipper is to be inserted, pin the seam to the bottom of the placket opening (a in Fig. 12.17).

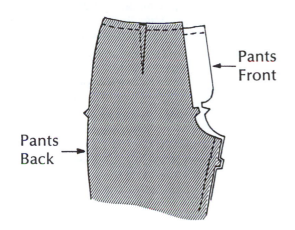

Fig. 12.16 Stitching leg inseam

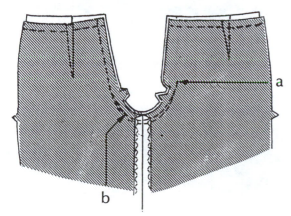

Fig. 12.17 Stitching and reinforcing crotch seam: open construction

3. Stitch the crotch seam, reinforcing the lower curve with a second row of machine stitching (b in Fig. 12.17). If a zigzag stitch is used for the reinforcement stitching, it can serve as an edge finish as well. The reinforcement stitching should be placed about ⅜ inch (1 cm) from the seam line.

4. Trim the lower curve to ⅜ inch (1 cm); *this curve should not be clipped*. Press open the seam above the lower curve and finish the seam edges. A small clip may be needed at the points where the reinforcement stitching ends in the front and the back in order for the seam above it to be pressed open and flat. Since clipping can weaken the seam, it should be avoided if possible.

5. To pin the side seams, refold the garment so that right sides are together and right front is against right back and left front is against left back. Place pins parallel to and directly on the seam line so that the garment can be fitted before sewing. Stitch, press, and finish the seams.

Closed Construction

In this method, the crotch seam is stitched after sewing the inseams and side seams. It is recommended for garments that have a zipper in the side seam since the zipper can be installed in the flat piece. This technique works best for pants that require little fitting during construction (i.e., pants patterns that are known to fit well or ones with sufficient design ease to minimize the need for fitting).

1. Stitch the inseams and side seams of each pants leg. Finish the edges and press seams open.

2. Turn one leg section right side out and slide this section inside the other leg section, right sides together. Match notches and inseams.

3. Stitch the crotch seam (Fig. 12.18).

Fig. 12.18 Stitching crotch seam: closed construction

4. Reinforce the lower curve and finish as described in the open construction method.

A third method for stitching the crotch seam is described in Chapter 17. In that one, the zipper is installed in the crotch seam before any of the other seams (inseams, side seams) are stitched. This method works especially well for fly front zippers.

Finishes for Plain Seams

Plain seams have raw edges that usually need to be finished to prevent raveling and to provide a pleasing appearance to the inside of the garment, which is important in garments such as unlined jackets where the seam edges may be seen when the garment is worn. The discussion in this section centers on finishing edges in woven fabrics; knitted fabrics that have little, if any, tendency to ravel generally require no edge finish.

The type of edge finish used depends on (1) the degree to which the fabric ravels, (2) the weight of the fabric, (3) how sheer or opaque the fabric is, (4) the end use of the garment, and (5) the resources (especially time and money) to be invested in the garment.

Garments have many edges that require finishing in addition to seams. Hem and facing edges are two that are present in many garments. The same edge finish may be appropriate for each area, or a different one may need to be selected. Seams that are pressed open may require a different edge finish from those that are pressed in one direction.

Garment edges may be finished before any construction begins, or seams may be finished after they are stitched and pressed. The tendency of some edge finishes to leave press marks is minimized if the finishing is done after pressing. However, seams such as the unlike curve seam described previously would be finished before pressing, clipping, and notching.

For fabrics that ravel easily, the sewer may want to finish all the seam edges before beginning garment assembly. The hem edge and others that would be trimmed would not be included in this process. Care must be taken not to remove the notches when finishing the seams before assembly, or the notches need to be marked with a washable marking pencil.

Machine Zigzag

Many conventional sewing machines are equipped with regular and multiple zigzag stitches and other functional or decorative stitch options that can be used to provide an edge finish. Each can be an effective and relatively quick method for finishing the edges in a garment. To be most effective, the machine zigzag stitch should be placed along the *very edge* of the seam if the full seam allowance is being left in the garment (Fig. 12.19). For a neater appearance loose yarns can be

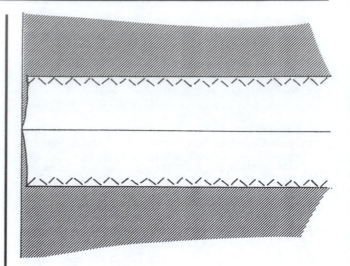

Fig. 12.19 Zigzag edge finish

trimmed close to the machine zigzag stitching. Machine zigzagging is not recommended on sheer fabrics as it will show through from the outside of the garment. It generally does not work well on lightweight or slippery fabrics, as these fabrics tend to curl or fold under the stitching, producing a corded effect. A loosely balanced tension may reduce this problem. Experimentation with the appropriate stitch type, width, length, and machine tension will be necessary before deciding which edge finish to use on a particular fabric. The zigzag edge finish may be used on medium- to heavyweight fabrics. If the edge tends to curl while zigzagging, a looser, balanced machine tension may be needed. Using the multiple zigzag or serpentine stitch may eliminate this problem (Fig. 12.20). The wider stitch width usually will provide the most effective edge finish.

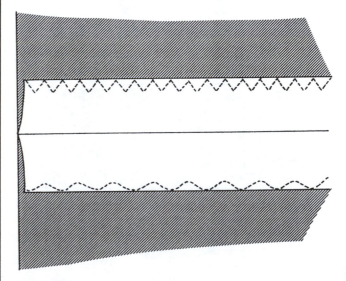

Fig. 12.20 Multiple zigzag or serpentine stitch edge finish

The overedge stitch on the overlock machine also works well for edge finishing. If this is done before the garment is assembled and if the knife blade is in the cutting position, the notches will need to be marked in an appropriate way as they will be cut off during stitching.

Bound Edge

Several products can be used to bind an edge in a garment, such as commercial bias tape, bias cut strips of fabric, or a narrow strip of sheer knit tricot packaged as a sheer seam finish. A bound edge finish strengthens seams, provides a neat appearance, and prevents shedding in corduroy and quilted fabrics. It is appropriate for medium- to heavyweight fabrics and is especially good to use on garments such as unlined jackets. Two methods for making the bound edge finish are described.

Bias Tape. Double-fold bias tape is folded such that one edge is slightly wider than the other. After the notches have been trimmed away from the seam, the bias tape is placed over the edge, with the wider edge on the underside (Fig. 12.21). The tape is then stitched in place from the right side. A lightweight, sheer knit tricot seam binding also is available to use as a binding for seams. It comes flat and will curl over the edge of the fabric if slight tension is placed on the binding as it is being stitched in place. Care must be taken not to stretch the tape too much as it may distort the shape of the seam edge.

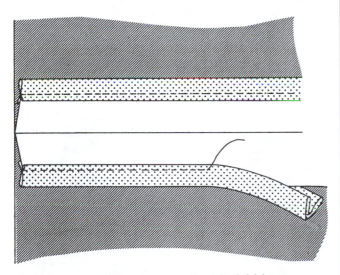

Fig. 12.21 Bound seam: double-fold bias binding

Hong Kong Finish. The Hong Kong finish makes use of bias strips about 1½ inches (3.8 cm) wide, cut from lining-weight fabric. Double-fold bias tape can also be used if one of the folds nearest the edge is pressed out flat before stitching the tape to the garment.

To make the Hong Kong finish:

1. With right sides together, stitch the bias strip to the edge (Fig. 12.22), stitching ⅛ inch (3 mm) from the edge.
2. Fold the bias strip over the edge and press.
3. From the right side, stitch in the crevice of the first stitching (stitch-in-the-ditch), going through all layers and holding the lower side of the bias strip in place (Fig. 12.23). Trim the excess fabric from the back side as needed.

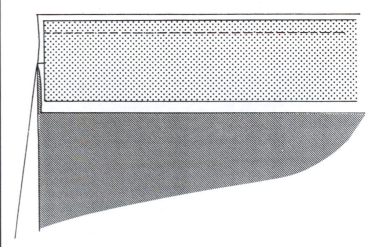

Fig. 12.22 Hong Kong finish: first stitching

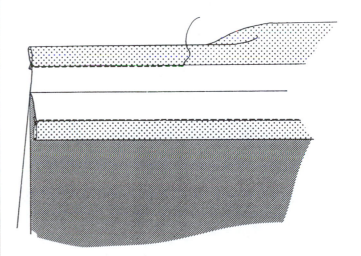

Fig. 12.23 Hong Kong finish: second stitching

Hand Overcast

When a machine stitch is not feasible, hand overcasting can be used (Fig. 12.24). It would be appropriate on very lightweight fabrics that would curl or become too stiff if finished by machine. The hand stitches are about ⅛ inch (3 mm) deep and about ¼ inch (6 mm) apart. A single thread is used, and the stitches should be left relatively loose. The hand overcast edge can be used along with a row of straight machine stitching placed ⅛ inch (3 mm) from the edge for additional security.

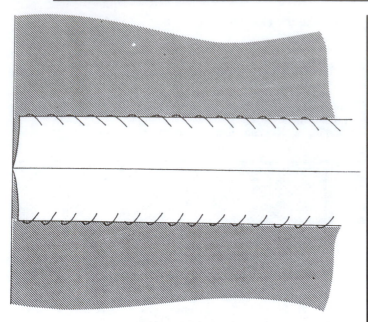

Fig. 12.24   Hand overcast edge finish

Pinked or Pinked-and-Stitched Edge

For fabrics with little tendency to ravel, such as wool, the pinked or pinked-and-stitched edge finish (Fig. 12.25) may be an appropriate choice. The addition of the row of stitching with the pinked edge makes this edge finish more durable than when no stitching is present.

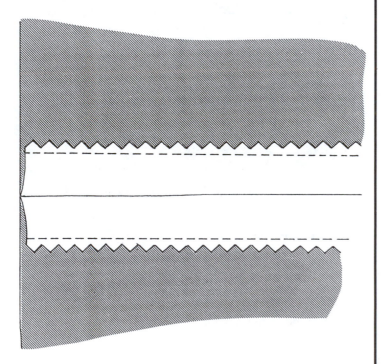

Fig. 12.25   Pinked-and-stitched edge finish

Turned-and-Stitched Edge

The turned-and-stitched edge finish (also called clean finishing) is used on lightweight, opaque fabrics. It is not recommended for use if the finished seam will produce a ridge on the right side after the seam is pressed open.

To turn and edge stitch:

1. Turn under ⅛–¼ inch (3–6 mm) along the edge of the seam and stitch close to the folded edge (Fig. 12.26).
2. Sewing the turned-and-stitched finish on a curved edge will be more accurate and easier if a row of machine stitching is placed about ⅛ inch (3 mm) from the edge before the edge is turned (Fig. 12.27). The edge can be turned on this line and pressed before being stitched, though pressing is not necessary in most cases.

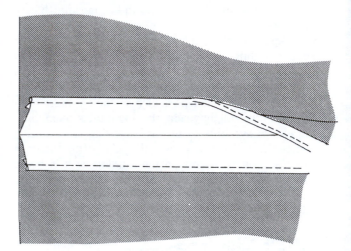

Fig. 12.26   Turned-and-stitched edge finish: straight seam edge

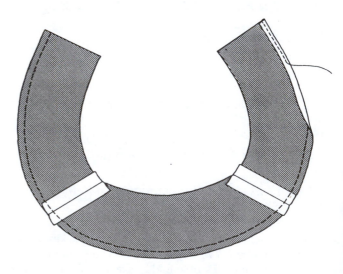

Fig. 12.27   Turned-and-stitched edge finish: curved edge

French Seam

The French seam is a narrow seam with all raw edges enclosed within the finished seam. It is sometimes called a "seam within a seam." The French seam is appropriate for use on lightweight fabrics and on straight or only slightly curved seams. It is not recommended for areas such as the armscye, crotch, or unlike curved seams. Directions for making the French seam need to be followed closely to be sure that the full ⅝-inch (1.6 cm) seam is used during construction.

To make a French seam:

1. Place *wrong sides of fabric together* and pin along the seam line.
2. Stitch ¼ inch (6 mm) from the seam line; for a ⅝-inch (1.6 cm) seam this would be ⅜ inch (1 cm) from the raw edge.
3. Press the seam open; then press the seam to one side.
4. Trim the seam to within ⅛ inch (3 mm) of the stitching line (Fig. 12.28).
5. Turn the garment so that right sides are together. Press or crease the first row of stitching so that it is directly on the edge. Pin carefully to prevent slipping.
6. Stitch along the original ⅝-inch (1.6 cm) seam line, ¼ inch (6 mm) from the first seam. The finished seam should be no wider than ¼ inch (6 mm) (Fig. 12.29).
7. Press the seam flat, then press to one side.

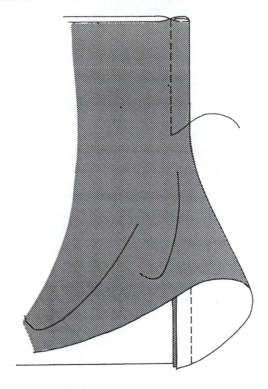

Fig. 12.29 French seam: second row of stitching

In areas where the French seam cannot be used, a mock French seam can be substituted.

To make a mock French seam:

1. Stitch a plain seam on the seam line.
2. Trim the edges to about ½ inch (12 mm).
3. Fold each edge toward the other and press so the finished width is about ¼ inch (6 mm).
4. Stitch along the folded edges by hand or by machine (Fig. 12.30). This stitching is in the seam allowance only and does not go through to the outside of the garment.

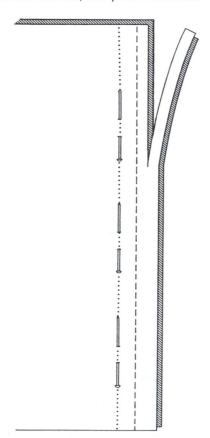

Fig. 12.28 French seam: first row of stitching

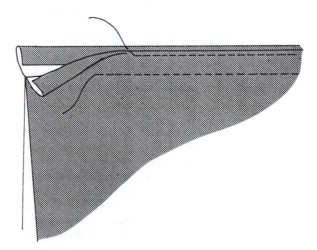

Fig. 12.30 Mock French seam

Flat-felled Seam

The flat-felled seam appears finished on both the outside and the inside of the garment, so it may be appropriate for garments such as wrap-around skirts and unlined jackets in which the seam may be seen when the garment is worn. It also is a durable seam so it is used for sports clothes and other items requiring seams with strength. The true flat-felled seam works best on straight or nearly straight seams. As there is outside stitching on the flat-felled seam, contrasting thread and a longer stitch length can be used for a decorative effect. The outside of the garment will have a double row of topstitching at each seam and the inside a single row. In some situations this effect can be reversed for a different look to the seam.

To make a flat-felled seam:

1. With *wrong sides* of the fabric together, sew a plain seam directly on the seam line. The seam should be stitched in the appropriate direction so that the side of the seam that will be on the outside of the finished garment is on top. That way both rows of stitching will be done with the top thread on the outside, thus insuring two rows of identical stitching.

2. Press the seam open, then press both edges in the same direction (Fig. 12.31). Flat-felled seams can be turned in either

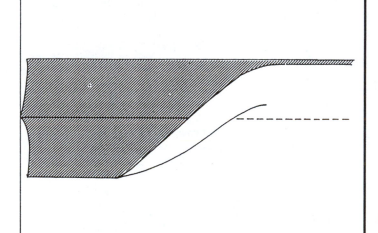

Fig. 12.31 Flat-felled seam: first row of stitching

direction in the garment, toward the back or toward the front as well as up or down. Throughout the garment, however, they should be turned consistently the same way. It is important to plan ahead to achieve the results described in step 1.

3. Trim the under seam allowance to ⅛ inch (3 mm) (*a* in Fig. 12.32) and the top seam allowance to ½ inch (12 mm).

4. Turn under the top seam allowance half its width (*b* in Fig. 12.32) for a finished width of approximately ¼ inch (6 mm).

5. Topstitch close to the folded edge (Fig. 12.33).

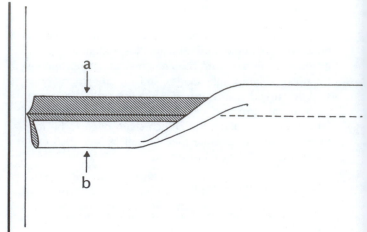

Fig. 12.32 Flat-felled seam: preparing for second row of stitching

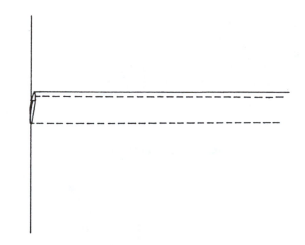

Fig. 12.33 Flat-felled seam: second row of stitching

Welt Seam

The flat-felled seam may be too bulky for some fabrics, so the welt seam can be substituted.

To make a welt seam:

1. Stitch a plain seam with *right sides* of the fabric together.

2. Press the seam open and then to one side. Trim the under seam allowance to ¼ inch (6 mm) (Fig. 12.34). Finish the upper or wider seam allowance in a manner appropriate for the fabric.

3. From the outside, topstitch the seam, enclosing the narrower seam allowance in the wider one (Fig. 12.35). This row of stitching is approximately ¼ inch (6 mm) from the edge. A second row of stitching can be placed near the original stitching line to give the appearance of a flat-felled seam. The latter often is called a double welt seam.

1. Machine baste the covered cording to the *right* side of one seam allowance, matching the stitching line of the cording with the seam line of the garment piece (Fig. 12.36). Use the cording or zipper foot that comes with most sewing machines to stitch close to the cord.

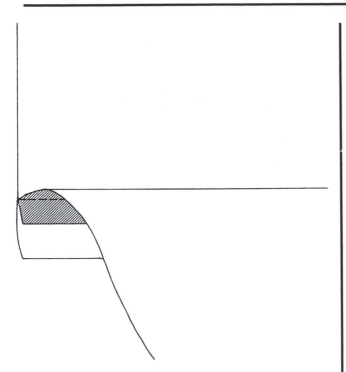

Fig. 12.34   Welt seam: first stitching

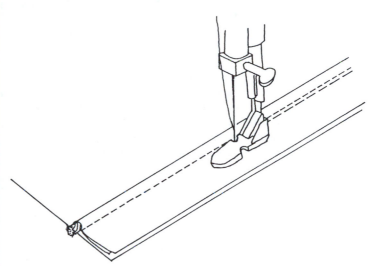

Fig. 12.36   Placement of covered cording in preparation for stitching seam

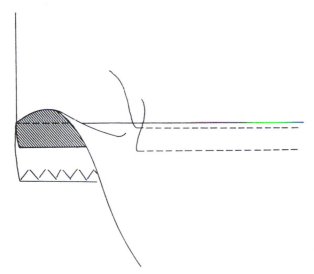

Fig. 12.35   Welt seam with two rows of topstitching

2. With right sides together, match the seam allowances of the two fabric pieces with the cording *between* the two layers.

3. Stitch the seam, with the corded layer on top, using the cording foot so that the second row of stitching is just beside the cording (Fig. 12.37). The last row of stitching should be the closest to the cording, so that none of the previous stitching shows on the outside of the finished garment.

4. Press the seam; layer/grade as needed; and finish if appropriate.

Corded Seams

Corded seams sometimes are used to add a decorative touch or to give a unique appearance to a seam. Covered cording can be purchased in most fabric stores, or it can be made with bias strips stitched over cording (see Chapter 16).

To make a corded seam:

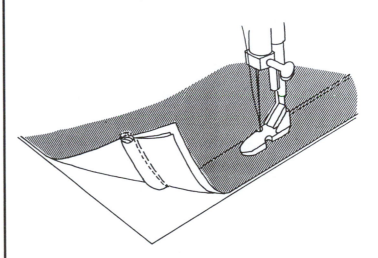

Fig. 12.37   Sewing seam with covered cording

Topstitched Seams

Topstitching is a row of machine or sometimes hand stitching done from the right side of the garment to add interest, emphasize a seam, or help hold a seam or outer edge flat. Topstitching can be done with matching or contrasting thread; a topstitching thread, which is heavier than regular sewing thread, also can be used. If the topstitching thread is not available in the appropriate color and a heavier thread is desired, two threads can be threaded through the needle. With both the topstitching thread and the double thread, a larger needle is recommended and some adjustment in the machine tension may be required.

Topstitching often is done with a longer-than-normal machine stitch length. The same stitch length should be used for all topstitching done on a garment. Backstitching should not be used to secure thread ends for topstitching where it would be visible on the outside of the garment; thread ends should be pulled to the wrong side and tied.

To keep topstitching straight, the edge of the presser foot can serve as a stitching guide. If a wider topstitching is desired, a strip of tape can be placed along the seam edge and used as a stitching guide. Tape should be used only on fabrics that are not damaged as the tape is removed. The quilting foot, which comes with the sewing machine (Fig. 12.38), also can be used to aid when top-

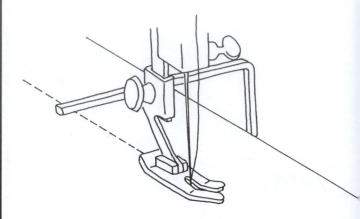

Fig. 12.38   Quilting foot for topstitching

stitching in an area where the seam guides on the throat plate cannot be seen.

The straight stitch as well as decorative stitches can be used for topstitching. It can be done on both sides or only one side of a seam. The double or triple needle can be used to sew parallel lines at the same time. Flat-felled and welt seams are additional examples of topstitched seams.

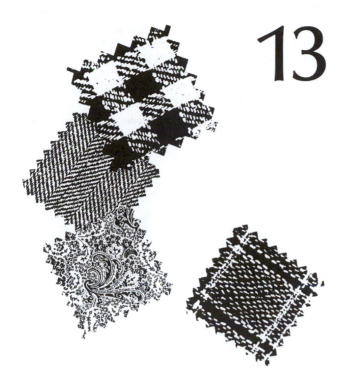

13 Pressing Techniques and Equipment

Good pressing is as essential to the appearance of the finished garment as is good construction. Pressing equipment, used correctly, aids in achieving flat seams, smooth edges, and sharp creases. This chapter describes basic pieces of pressing equipment and their uses.

Pressing Defined

Pressing is a process by which the iron is raised and lowered on the fabric in a series of up-and-down motions (Fig. 13.1). *Ironing* is a sliding motion of the iron on the fabric. Both are done as much as possible in the direction of the fabric grain (Fig. 13.2).

Pressing Equipment

Knowing and using the appropriate pressing equipment is essential to success in completing the task.

Iron

A steam iron or a steam-and-spray iron, both of which may be used with or without water, is convenient for pressing many fabrics. Cordless irons and irons with automatic shut-off features are also available. The instruction booklet that accompanies the iron will give

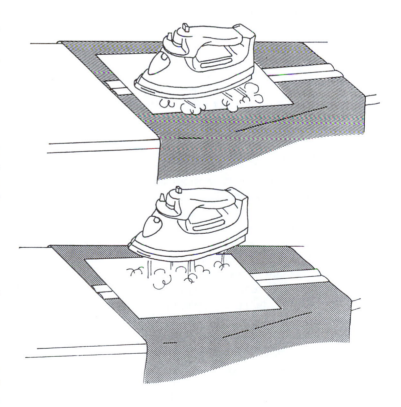

Fig. 13.1   Pressing techniques

127

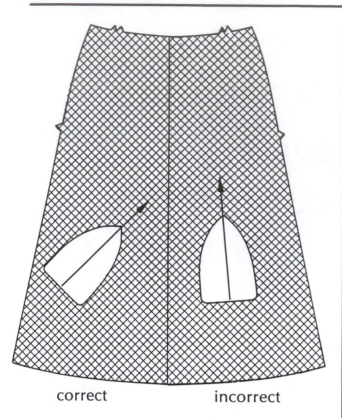

correct   incorrect

Fig. 13.2   Ironing in direction of fabric grain

specific directions for its operation and maintenance.

The iron will last longer and will give better service if only distilled water is used and if the iron is emptied completely before storing. The steam iron should be stored in an upright position to prevent corrosion that could occur from moisture that collects when it is stored flat. The sole plate of the iron should be kept smooth and clean.

Press Cloths

The choice of press cloth depends on the kind of fabric being pressed. Fabrics used for press cloths should be white or colorfast and washed free of sizing and lint. Specially treated press cloths that vary in weight and sheerness are available commercially. A large piece of firmly woven cotton fabric that has been laundered also makes a satisfactory press cloth, especially when a damp cloth is required. A piece of wool fabric, in addition to the damp cotton press cloth, may be used to press wool garments. The wool press cloth should not be darker in color than the fabric being pressed.

Ironing Board

An ironing board should be smooth, well padded, and stand firmly at an appropriate height for efficient work. An adjustable board, which can be raised or low-ered to a comfortable working height, allows for flexibility in the use of the board. The covering for the ironing board should be free of lint and sizing.

Sleeve Board

A sleeve board (Fig. 13.3) is a small ironing board that is shaped and padded like the larger one. Its primary purpose is to press the underarm seam of sleeves without pressing in unwanted creases. It also is used when pressing other narrow garment sections and for small garments such as those for young children.

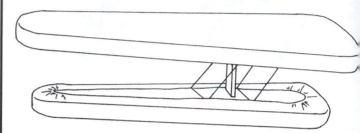

Fig. 13.3   Sleeve board

Point Presser

The point presser is a narrow wooden board that tapers to a point at one end (Fig. 13.4). It is used for pressing open seam allowances in points and corners, such as those found in collars and cuffs. Often the point presser is constructed so that the base can be used for a pounding block.

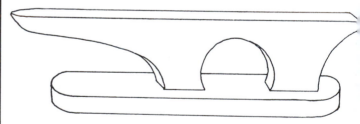

Fig. 13.4   Point presser

Pounding Block

The pounding block (Fig. 13.5), also called a beater or clapper, is a flat block with rounded edges used to produce flat seams and sharp creases in garments from wool or wool-blend fabrics. The pounding block is used by firmly pressing on garment edges, seams, or hems while the fabric is still moist and pliable. The fabric does not become shiny when the pounding block is used to force out the steam.

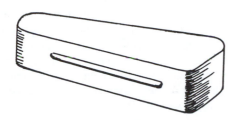

Fig. 13.5   Pounding block

Needle Board

The needle board (Fig. 13.6), constructed of fine steel wires set vertically into a fabric base to simulate a napped fabric, is used to prevent crushing napped and pile fabrics during construction. When the fabric is placed face down on the needle board, it will not become matted during pressing. If a needle board is not available, a piece of self-fabric or a plush towel can be substituted.

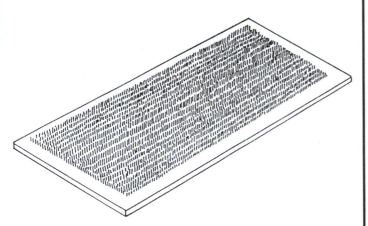

Fig. 13.6   Needle board

Seam Roll

The seam roll (Fig. 13.7) is a firmly packed cylindrical cushion used to press just the seam line; thus, it prevents the seam edges from pressing through to the right side of the garment. It also works well when pressing seams in narrow areas such as in sleeves.

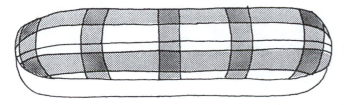

Fig. 13.7   Seam roll

The seam roll can be made by covering one or two tightly rolled magazines or a length of hardwood bannister rail with a piece of firmly woven fabric. To construct, a rectangle of fabric is cut to fit the roll and stitched to form a tube (a in Fig. 13.8). After the seam has been pressed open and the tube turned to the right side, the rolled magazine is slipped inside the tube and the ends closed by turning the edges of the fabric in and stitching securely. The finished seam roll should be sufficiently hard that it will not give under the weight of the iron.

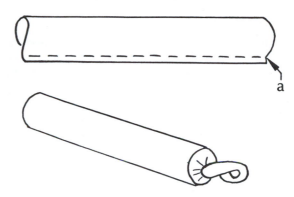

Seam or sleeve roll

Fig. 13.8   Making a seam roll

Pressing Cushion

Pressing cushions, available in various shapes, are used when pressing darts and curved seams (Fig. 13.9). The tailor's ham is about 7 inches (18 cm) wide and 12 inches (30.5 cm) long and often is covered with wool on one side and cotton on the other. The pressing mitt usually is about 6 inches (15 cm) square, but it may come in other shapes and sizes.

To make a pressing cushion, two pieces of cotton drill or ticking are cut the appropriate size (plus seam allowances) and stitched together, leaving an opening for turning to the right side and filling. A second layer of wool fabric is added to one side, if desired, before stitching.

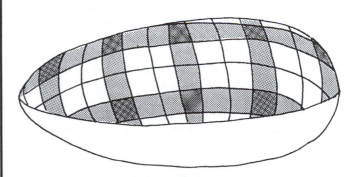

Fig. 13.9   Pressing cushions

Clean, dry sawdust mixed with a small amount of clean white sand provides a firm filling for the pressing cushion. The finished cushion should be solid enough so that it will not dent when the fingers are pressed against it.

Clothes Brush

A clothes brush is used to restore napped or pile fabrics that may have been crushed slightly during pressing.

Paper Strips

Fabrics that tend to show press marks may need additional protection to prevent seam edges and dart lines from pressing through to the outside. Heavy paper strips, placed between the seam or dart and the outside layer of the fabric, will provide this protection. The heavier the paper the less likely it will curl during use and the more protection it will provide. Paper grocery bags or large white envelopes are good sources for the strips.

General Pressing Procedures

Several basic procedures need to be followed when pressing a garment both during construction and after it is completed. First, what is the fiber content? Knowing the fiber content is absolutely crucial; pressing a silk fabric is much different than pressing a polyester fabric. Can steam be used? What heat setting is most appropriate? Does the fabric have a tendency to show press marks and, therefore, require protection during pressing? Is a press cloth needed? Does the press cloth need to be damp or dry? Is additional protection such as paper strips required?

Many of these questions can be answered by sewing a sample seam and a sample dart in the fabric and pressing each in a variety of ways to determine the most appropriate methods required. Since pressing procedures change with each fabric, this testing should occur at the beginning of each construction project.

The fiber content of the fabric determines the temperature to use when pressing, as well as whether moisture is an appropriate choice. Many fabrics are a combination or blend of two or more fibers, in which case, the choices are based on the most sensitive of the fibers. Most man-made fibers have a lower melting point than do the natural fibers; therefore, the heat setting for a fabric such as a cotton-polyester blend would be determined by the polyester fiber.

Some fabrics will water spot (e.g., silk), so a dry iron and a dry press cloth are required. Other fabrics tend to hold the moisture from the steam iron (e.g., wool) and should be allowed to dry after pressing before handling.

Most pressing is done from the wrong side of the garment. Pressing is done in the order of construction;

seams, darts, and other construction details are pressed before being crossed by other seams or construction details. Several units can be pressed at one time as long as each is pressed before being joined to another unit.

Pressing over pins can leave press marks that often are impossible to remove; therefore, *pressing over pins is not recommended.* A light touch needs to be used when pressing over basting, as those marks tend to show as well. After the initial pressing of a basted edge, the bastings can be removed and the edge repressed with more pressure on the iron.

During construction, units should be folded carefully or placed on a hanger to avoid unnecessary wrinkling that would create the need for additional pressing.

Evidence of Good Pressing

—The original texture of the fabric is maintained.
—No shine or press marks show on a dull-textured fabric.
—No wrinkles or crinkled areas appear on a smooth-surfaced fabric.
—Seams and darts are pressed smoothly on the stitching line.
—Fabric does not fold over the stitching line or look bubbled.
—Edges of seam allowances and the folded edges of darts do not form ridges on the right side of the garment.
—No water-spot marks are visible.

Pressing Seams

Plain seams and straight seams generally are pressed open. The seam is pressed flat (Fig. 13.10) to set the stitches before being pressed open. A seam roll is recommended to prevent the seam edges from leaving a mark on the outside of the finished garment (Fig. 13.11). If a seam roll is used, the entire base of the iron can be used, because the curve of the roll prevents the seam edges

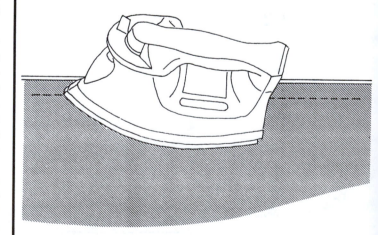

Fig. 13.10   Pressing seam flat to set stitches

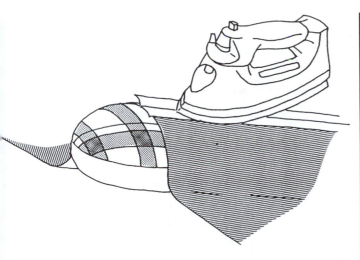

Fig. 13.11 Pressing seam open over a seam roll

from marking the outside. If a seam roll is not available, strips of paper can be placed under both sides of the seam allowance before pressing to provide protection (Fig. 13.12).

Seams that are pressed in one direction (e.g., collars, yokes, cuffs) should be pressed open before being pressed in one direction. Curved seams are pressed over a pressing cushion. Seams with points or corners are pressed open using the point presser.

French seams or narrow double-stitched plain seams

are pressed in one direction, generally toward the back of the garment. If two French seams or narrow double-stitched seams intersect, one can be pressed in one direction and the other in the opposite direction to reduce bulk at the point of joining. French seams and narrow double-stitched seams need to be pressed in the same direction for the entire length of the seam.

Pressing Darts

Darts are pressed flat to set the stitches (Fig. 13.13) before they are pressed either open or in one direction (Fig. 13.14). If pressed in one direction, *vertical darts are pressed toward the center front or center back; horizontal and diagonal darts are pressed down.* The pressing cushion is used when pressing darts to preserve the contour created by the dart. Appropriate protection in the form of a press cloth or paper strips should be used as determined by pressing a trial dart.

Darts in bulky or heavy fabrics sometimes are slashed and pressed open (Fig. 13.15). Slashing the dart produces two raw edges which will require an edge finish. Darts in linings often are pressed in the opposite direction to those in the fashion fabric to reduce bulk.

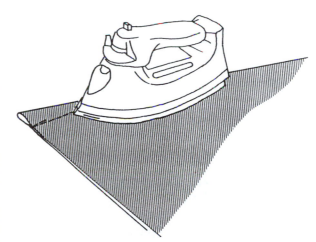

Fig. 13.13 Pressing dart flat to set stitches

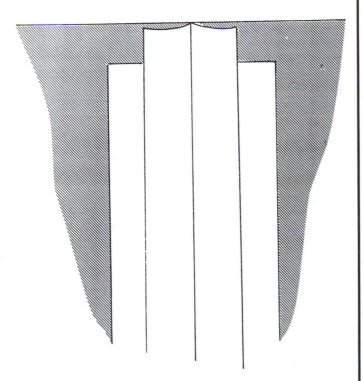

Fig. 13.12 Protecting seam edges with strips of paper

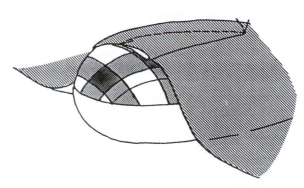

Fig. 13.14 Pressing dart over pressing cushion

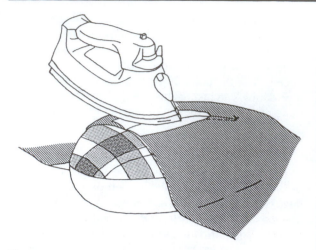

Fig. 13.15   Pressing slashed dart

Pressing Corners and Points

Enclosed seams of collars, cuffs, lapels, and waistbands are easier to crease if pressed open *before* turning. To press the corner or point, the seam is placed over the point presser (Fig. 13.16) and pressed with the tip of the iron.

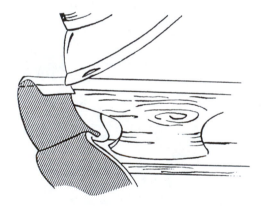

Fig. 13.16   Using point presser to press corners or points

Pressing Pant Creases

Creases are set in pants after lengthwise seams are stitched. The creases are formed down the center of each front and back section, the front crease stopping 5–6 inches (12.5–15 cm) below the waistline and the back crease stopping even with the crotch point on the pants. In styles with trouser pleats the crease may be continued up into the edge of a pleat.

To press pant creases:

1. Fold pants right side out so that the side seams and inseams match (a in Fig. 13.17).

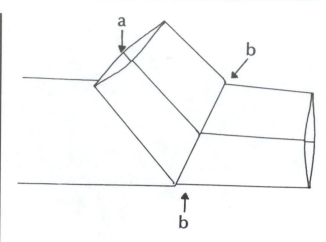

Fig. 13.17   Pressing pant creases

2. Press firmly on the area to be creased with steam and a damp press cloth (b in Fig. 13.17).

3. Press the edge with a pounding block, if appropriate for the fabric.

Special Pressing Procedures

Many fabrics require special treatment during pressing. Good pressing methods help to preserve the original texture of the fabric whether it is a smooth shiny surface such as a glazed chintz or a deep pile fabric such as a plush velour. Some fabrics such as vinyl, suede, and leather cannot be pressed. Instead, seams and edges are topstitched or glued in place.

Fabrics with Surface Interest

Shiny Surfaces

Glazed chintz and most other shiny fabrics may be pressed on the right side, thus preserving the luster of the fabric. Satin-weave fabrics are an exception because the shine on the surface is due to fabric construction and fiber content. The right side of the fabric could be distorted by the iron, so these fabrics should be pressed from the wrong side.

Smooth Nonshiny Surfaces

Nonshiny surface fabrics should be pressed from the wrong side. These fabrics may require extra protection to prevent seam edges from marking on the right side. Some thermoplastic fibers such as acetate are extremely sensitive to heat and can be softened by an iron temperature that is too high. The resulting shine on the fabric would be permanent; therefore, extreme care must be taken when pressing these fabrics.

Raised-surface Designs

Raised-surface fabrics should be pressed on the wrong side and against a soft surface, such as a terry towel. When the raised design is pressed into the soft surface, the design sinks into it and is not flattened.

Napped Surfaces

Napped surfaces of velvet, velveteen, and corduroy are pressed over a needle board if one is available, or over self-fabric or a plush towel if one is not (see discussion under Needle Board). When using self-fabric, the nap is maintained better if the direction of the nap on the fabric is opposite to that on the press cloth. Another alternative is to press the fabric upright in such a way that the iron does not touch the fabric (Fig. 13.18). The iron is standing upright, and a damp press cloth is placed against the wrong side of the fabric. Because the fabric will be moist after pressing, it must be handled carefully and allowed to dry before additional work is done on it.

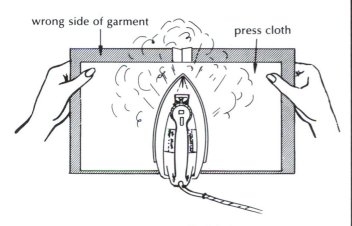

wrong side of garment

press cloth

Fig. 13.18 Pressing a pile fabric

Other Fabrics Requiring Special Pressing

Knitted and Stretch Fabrics

Stretch and knitted fabrics need to be pressed carefully to avoid distorting the fabric. Knits made from man-made fibers may require a damp press cloth in order to flatten the seams. Darts in bulky knits may need to be slashed and pressed open to achieve a flattened appear-

ance. Most pressing is done in the direction of the lengthwise grain (or wale) of the knitted fabric.

Leathers and Suedes

Leathers and suedes, both the real and the synthetic ones, often are glued and pounded rather than being pressed with an iron. Experimentation with the fabric is necessary to determine the most appropriate methods.

Silk

Silk fabrics have a tendency to water spot, so they may need to be pressed with a dry iron or protected with a press cloth.

Wool

Wool is not pressed dry as are other fabrics; therefore, it needs to be placed on a flat surface and allowed to dry before being handled. A damp press cloth and steam are used on most wool fabrics, the press cloth being lifted periodically to allow some of the steam to escape. The fabric should retain a suggestion of moistness after pressing and be allowed to dry completely. To press wool from the right side a piece of self-fabric should be placed over the fabric. A steam iron or damp press cloth is used to steam the fabric. The pounding block can be used to flatten seams and edges. The fabric can be brushed lightly to restore the texture.

Man-made Fibers

As a general rule, man-made fibers require a lower iron setting than the one used for natural fibers. While many man-made fibers melt at a low temperature, not all melt at the same temperature. Pressing out creases, once they are in the fabric, may be difficult; so seams and darts should not be pressed until after the garment has been fitted.

Permanent-Press Fabrics

Permanent-press fabrics have a finish that keeps the fabric from wrinkling during wearing, but it also makes it difficult to press seams flat or to crease during assembly. To achieve flat seams and darts and sharp creases, it may be necessary to use a damp press cloth and firm pressure on the iron while pressing.

14 Creating Shape and Controlling Fullness

Shape in a garment can be created by one of two means: (1) through design details such as darts, pleats, tucks, and gathers; and (2) through the addition of shaping/supporting fabrics such as interfacings, linings, and underlinings. This chapter will discuss these two shaping strategies, which are found in many garments. Seams that also provide shaping in a garment are discussed in Chapter 12.

Darts

Darts are wedge-shaped tucks that shape a flat piece of fabric to fit over body contours. Most darts are purely functional and are found on the inside of the garment; some darts, however, may serve a decorative purpose and be sewn to the outside of the finished garment. Darts can have one point or two; be vertical, horizontal, or diagonal; be large and provide much contour or small and provide very little shape; be pressed open or to one side; or be straight or curved.

Sewing Darts

Accuracy is critical when stitching darts to insure that the darts represent the intended size, shape, and fit of the pattern. To check the fit of darts, they should be pin basted and fitted on the body before the final stitching.

To sew a dart:

1. Mark the dart accurately, with a crossmark at the point to show exactly where the dart is to end (see Chapter 11).

2. Fold the dart on the center line and pin following the outer lines. Pins should be placed directly on and parallel to the seam line making sure that the pins follow exactly the dart markings on both the top and bottom layers of fabric. Check dart size and length by fitting the garment.

3. Stitch the dart exactly on the marked line, usually beginning at the wide end (a in Fig. 14.1). A strip of transparent

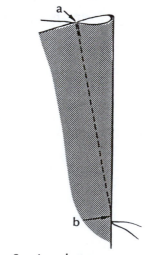

Fig. 14.1 Sewing darts

134

tape can be placed along the dart markings to aid in sewing an absolutely straight dart. The stitching line for the dart should taper gradually to a point with the last two or three stitches falling *exactly* on the fold of the fabric (*b* in Fig. 14.1).

4. Secure the wide end of the dart by backstitching (*a* in Fig. 14.2). Avoid extra bulk at the point by knotting threads using a tailor's knot instead of backstitching by machine. To control the location of the knot, a pin can be placed in the point of the dart (Fig. 14.2). The knot will slide down the pin and tighten at the point.

5. Press darts over the pressing cushion (see Chapter 13). Press vertical darts toward center front or center back; press horizontal and diagonal darts down.

6. To reduce bulk where a dart enters a seam, trim the wide end of the dart diagonally (Fig. 14.3).

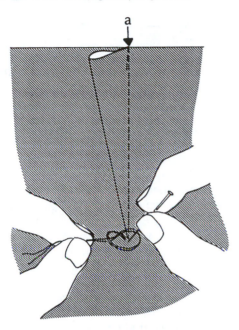

Fig. 14.2   Tieing tailor's knot at pointed end of dart

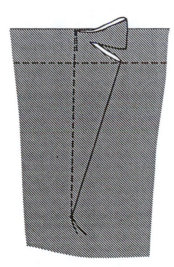

Fig. 14.3   Reducing bulk where dart enters seam

Darts Requiring Special Handling

Some darts because of their size or the type of fabric on which they are used require special handling.

Darts in Bulky Fabrics

Darts made in bulky fabric can be slashed and pressed open to reduce bulk (Fig. 14.4). Before any darts are slashed, they should be checked for fit. Care must be taken not to slash too close to the point on darts made from loosely woven fabric. The slashed edges of the dart made in woven fabric may require an edge finish.

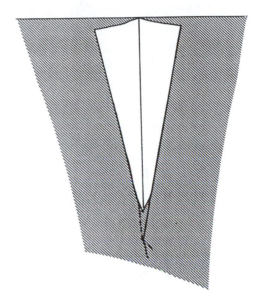

Fig. 14.4   Dart slashed open

Darts in Sheer Fabrics

Darts in sheer fabrics can be unattractive if seen from the outside of the finished garment. Two techniques provide a solution to this problem. A second row of stitching can be placed ⅛–¼ inch (3–6 mm) from the original stitching and the fabric trimmed to this point (Fig. 14.5). This stitching could be a zigzag stitch and used to finish the raw edge if the fabric ravels, unless such stitching would be unattractive if seen from the outside of the garment. Hand overcasting also could be used to finish the edges of this dart.

A second technique is to stitch the dart using "bobbin stitching" or the "continuous thread dart" technique.

To sew a "continuous thread dart":

1. Thread the machine in the appropriate manner for regular stitching.
2. Draw up a length of bobbin thread sufficient to sew the dart, through the hole in the throat plate.

Fig. 14.5   Darts in sheer fabric

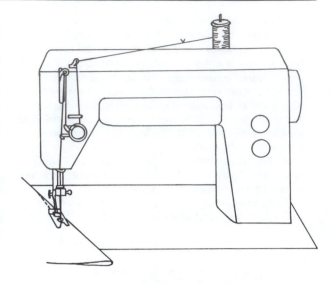

Fig. 14.7   Knotting upper and bobbin threads for sewing continuous thread dart

Tucks

Dart Tucks

The dart tuck is used in place of traditional darting to provide relaxed but defined shaping in parts of the garment (Fig. 14.8). These can be stitched on either the inside or the outside of the garment. When sewn to the outside, contrasting thread could be used to give special emphasis to this design feature. Before stitching, the dart tuck needs to be marked carefully; stitching will follow the instructions found with the pattern. The types and styles of dart tucks vary widely with fashion. If a dart tuck is stitched to the outside, the threads at the exposed end will need to be pulled to the inside and tied.

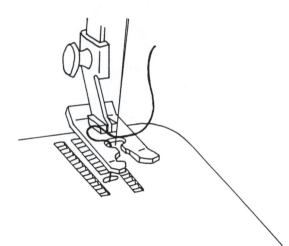

Fig. 14.6   Preparing machine for sewing continuous thread dart

3. Remove the upper thread from the needle, and insert the bobbin thread into the needle in the direction opposite to the top thread (Fig. 14.6).

4. Knot the bobbin thread and the top thread; pull the bobbin thread up through the threading points; and wind the bobbin thread onto the spool (Fig. 14.7). The bobbin thread now is continuous from spool to bobbin.

5. Stitch the dart, starting at the *point*. Place the needle at the dart point, and adjust the thread as needed to insure that it is lying smoothly over the fold of fabric. Lower the presser foot and stitch the dart.

6. Repeat this process for each dart. The technique also works well when doing outside stitching where knotting and backstitching are impractical or unattractive.

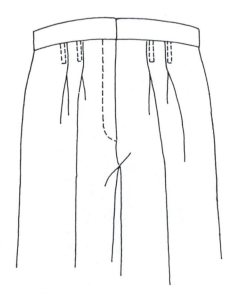

Fig. 14.8   Dart tucks

Decorative Tucks

Generally, decorative tucks are stitched on the outside as a focal point of the design of the garment (Fig. 14.9). Because of the emphasis placed on them, they must be stitched carefully and accurately.

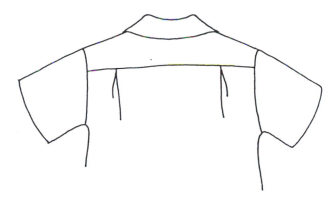

Fig. 14.9   Decorative tucks

To make decorative tucks:

1. Transfer the markings for the decorative tucks so that the markings are visible on the outside of the garment. The modified tailor's tack, discussed in Chapter 11, is especially effective for marking decorative tucks; carbon paper and other techniques that could leave a permanent mark on the outside of the finished garment are not appropriate.

2. Knowing the location of the fold line as well as the stitching lines of the tuck is critical to the success of the finished product. If a fold line is not provided on the pattern, one can be drawn between the two stitching lines. Transfer all of the markings to the right side of the fabric.

3. Stitch and press each tuck one at a time, checking for the accuracy of each before proceeding to the next. Generally, the first tuck stitched is the one closest to the center front or center back.

4. Use the edge of the presser foot, a piece of tape, or a cardboard gauge cut the width of the tuck as aids when sewing the tuck. Hand basting and pressing the tuck before stitching also may be helpful. Backstitch the ends of a tuck seam if it eventually will be crossed by seams or other construction details. Tucks that begin or end in the middle of the garment piece are not backstitched. Pull the threads at the exposed end to the inside and tie.

Pin Tucks

Pin tucks (Fig. 14.10) are very narrow folds of fabric stitched close to the fold on the outside of the garment. They may be decorative, functional, or both. Pressing the tucks before stitching and basting to hold them in place may be helpful to insure that the stitching stays exactly on the fold. Usually one tuck is pressed and stitched before proceeding to the next tuck. This type tuck is not appropriate for thick or spongy fabrics.

Fig. 14.10   Pin tucks

Pleats

Pleats are folds of fabric of varying widths that provide controlled fullness in a garment. Pleats may be pressed or unpressed. They may hang free from a seam, or they may be stitched for a predetermined distance. Different kinds of pleats result from folding the fabric in different ways; knife, inverted, and box pleats are three examples (Fig. 14.11).

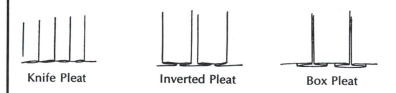

Knife Pleat   Inverted Pleat   Box Pleat

Fig. 14.11   Different kinds of pleats

Unstitched Pleats

Unstitched pleats hang from a seam line, such as the yoke or waistline; they may be pressed or unpressed.

To make unstitched pleats:

1. Transfer the fold lines for the pleats to the right side of the fabric. Using a different color marking to distinguish pleat lines is helpful. Patterns are usually marked with arrows to indicate the direction to fold pleats (a in Fig. 14.12).

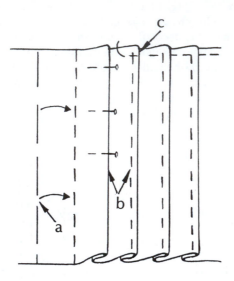

Fig. 14.12   Making unstitched pleats

2. To form the pleats on the right side of the garment, bring one folded line to the other in the direction indicated on the pattern (b in Fig. 14.12).

3. Pin and hand baste the pleats along the fold line. The pleats will remain basted until the garment has been checked for fit. Leaving the pleats basted until the garment is ready to be hemmed, especially for pressed pleats, will help to hold pleat lines accurately in place.

4. Machine baste across the pleat folds along the edge to be joined to other garment pieces (c in Fig. 14.12) to hold them in place until permanently stitched. This basting should be close to the stitching line and within the seam allowance.

5. If pleats are to be pressed, they should be pressed lightly over the basting. Additional pressing will be required when the basting is removed.

Stitched Pleats

Stitched pleats are sewn for a specified distance as designated on the pattern. Stitching may be done on the inside, the outside, or both.

To make stitched pleats:

1. Transfer the pattern markings for the pleats to the fabric. If the pattern does not include a fold line, one can be drawn and marked on the fabric along with the stitching lines. A dot

or some other pattern marking will be used to indicate where the stitching will stop (a in Fig. 14.13); this needs to be marked carefully and accurately on the fabric.

2. Form the pleats on the wrong side by folding on the fold line as indicated on the pattern and pin on the stitching line. Place the pins parallel to and directly on the stitching line and check the placement of the pins on both sides of the pleat.

3. Permanently stitch (b in Fig. 14.13) the pleats the distance indicated on the pattern and either hand or machine baste the remaining amount (c in Fig. 14.13).

4. Lightly press the pleats in the direction indicated on the pattern. Pleats may be topstitched from the right side of the garment, if desired (a in Figure 14.14). Secure threads on the back side by tying; backstitching is not appropriate.

5. Basting should remain in the pleats until the garment has been fitted; leaving the basting in the fabric until ready to hem the garment will help retain the pleat lines.

6. Additional pressing may be required when the basting is removed.

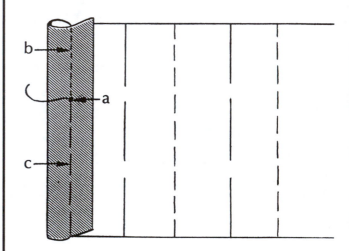

Fig. 14.13   Making stitched pleats

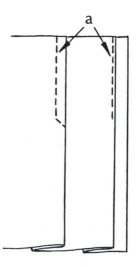

Fig. 14.14   Methods for topstitching pleats

Pleats can be edge stitched for a sharper crease (Fig. 14.15). Edge stitching is done after the hem has been completed but before the piece is joined to other pieces. For example, a pleated skirt would be edge stitched before the waistband is attached. A discussion of hemming techniques appropriate for pleats is found in Chapter 22.

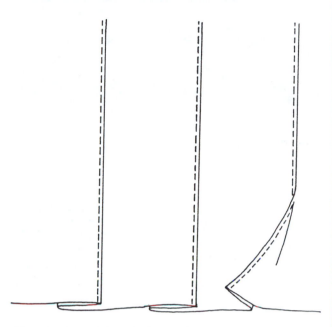

Fig. 14.15   Edgestitching pleats

Gathers

Gathers supply soft fullness in a garment and are formed when fabric is drawn up along a line of stitching. Usually, a longer garment edge is gathered to fit a shorter garment edge. Occasionally, two garment edges of either the same or varying lengths are gathered simultaneously. This often occurs on dresses with a waistline seam where both the bodice and the skirt contain gathers.

Attractive gathers occur when the *shortest* possible machine stitch length, that still gathers, is used for the gathering thread. Experimentation with different stitch lengths will be necessary to determine the appropriate one to use for a particular fabric. Usually, the sewer can start with the regular stitch length and work toward longer stitches. Before starting to put in long rows of gathering threads, the sewer needs to check the bobbin for sufficient thread to complete the task.

To make gathers:

1. Use three rows of gathering stitches, placing them between the marked gathering placement lines as indicated on the pattern. The first row of stitching is placed on the seam line; the second and third rows are placed ⅛–¼ inch (3–6 mm) on either side of it (Fig. 14.16). The row of stitching that is on the garment side of the stitching line would be omitted

for fabrics that have a tendency to show needle punctures. If the area to be gathered is long, it can be divided into lengths of 24–36 inches (61–91.5 cm), with rows of gathering for this distance being used in place of the one continuous length. The gathering threads should be stitched so that the *bobbin thread is on the wrong side* of the piece.

Fig. 14.16   Placement of rows of gathering stitches

2. Leave about 3 inches (7.5 cm) of thread at each end of the rows of gathering stitches to use when pulling up the gathers.

3. When sewing the rows of gathering stitches, place the needle in the fabric before the presser foot is lowered for sewing. In addition, hold the threads behind the needle at the beginning of the stitching. Both of these strategies will help eliminate tangling of the thread at the beginning of the row of stitching.

4. From the wrong side, draw up *all three gathering threads at one time* using the bobbin thread.

To join gathered edge to a straight edge:

1. A layer of interfacing or a strip of stay tape may be applied to the ungathered edge to stabilize the seam (see Fig. 14.19). This may be necessary when working with knits or when sewing gathers to a bias edge.

2. With right sides together, match and pin the gathered edge to the ungathered edge, matching notches and other pattern symbols. Additional markings can be added to help in distributing fullness. For example, the center front and center back of a waistband and skirt or pants can be marked and then matched. Having half-way and quarter-way markings for each of the two pieces helps to insure that the gathers are evenly distributed.

3. Using the bobbin threads, pull the fabric up until the gathered edge is the same size as the ungathered edge and the gathers are evenly distributed. Generally, the threads are pulled from each end toward the middle. Equal tension needs to be applied to all threads during the gathering process, with a gentle force being used to avoid breaking the gathering threads.

4. Wrap the gathering threads around the pin at each end of the gathered area (a in Fig. 14.17) to hold the gathers in place for sewing. Distribute the gathers evenly between the end points indicating the placement for the gathers.

5. With *gathered layer on top*, stitch the two layers together along the seam line. This stitching needs to be checked on the ungathered side to be sure it is straight or a smooth curve. If any puckers appear on the ungathered side, the gathered side was pulled too much and needs to be adjusted.

6. Stitch a second row of stitching ¼ inch (6 mm) into the

seam allowance from the seam line. For a fabric that ravels easily, use a zigzag stitch.

7. Remove the gathering threads that show from the outside of the garment, taking care not to damage the fabric. All gathering threads may be removed, if desired.

8. To reduce bulk, trim the seam allowance of *only the gathered edge* close to the second row of stitching (Fig. 14.18).

9. Press the seam away from the gathers, being careful not to press the gathered area. Placing the seam on a seam roll or close to the edge of the ironing board helps in pressing the seam up to the gathered layer.

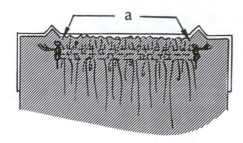

Fig. 14.17   Gathering fullness to a straight edge

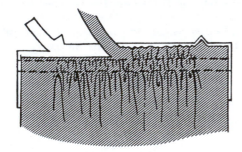

Fig. 14.18   Stitching and layering gathered seam

Joining One Gathered Edge to Another

Sometimes a gathered edge is joined to another gathered edge, a process that requires a somewhat different procedure.

To join two gathered edges:

1. Cut a piece of stay tape the length of the finished seam; gather one of the garment layers to fit the stay (Fig. 14.19). Place the tape on the wrong side of the piece being gathered so that about ⅛ inch (3 mm) extends beyond the stitching line into the garment, with most of the tape resting within the seam allowance. Hand or machine baste the two layers together.

2. Pin the second layer to be gathered with right sides together to the edge with the tape; gather to fit (Fig. 14.20).

3. Stitch the seam through all layers, including the tape in the machine stitching (Fig. 14.21). To prevent the tape from rolling and to flatten the bulk, stitch a second time ¼ inch (6

mm) into the seam allowance from the seam line. Layer/grade the seam allowances.

4. Remove the gathering threads. Turn the seam so that the stay will be next to the body when the garment is worn.

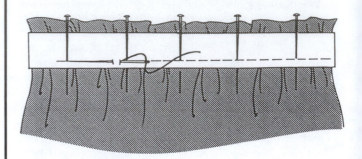

Fig. 14.19   Joining one gathered edge to another: Step 1

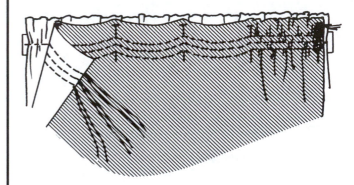

Fig. 14.20   Joining one gathered edge to another: Step 2

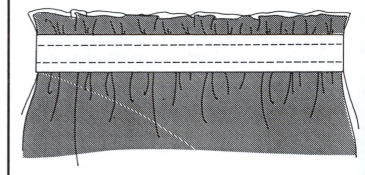

Fig. 14.21   Joining one gathered edge to another: Step 3

Easing

Easing occurs when one fabric edge is slightly longer than the edge to which it is joined. Easing provides subtle shaping and should not be apparent in the finished garment. Sometimes the back shoulder seam is eased to the front, and traditional set-in sleeves are eased into armholes.

To ease a seam:

1. Place a row of ease stitching on the seam line (Fig. 14.22). A slightly longer stitch than the one being used for the garment is recommended. Leave about 3 inches (7.5 cm) of thread at each end of the row of ease stitching. If very little ease is present, the ease thread can be eliminated and the ease controlled through the pinning process.

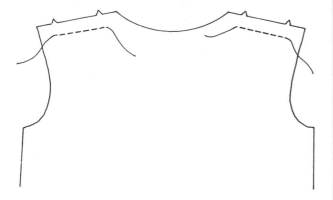

Fig. 14.22   Placement of ease stitching

2. Pin the seam *with the eased side on top.* Place a pin at each end of the area to be eased.
3. Draw up the ease thread from each end until the two edges match (Fig. 14.23). Distribute the ease so that no tucks are present in the pinned seam.
4. Stitch the seam with the eased side on top.
5. Press the seam flat (see Chapter 13) and then in the direction appropriate for the fabric and location (the seam can be pressed open or to one side).

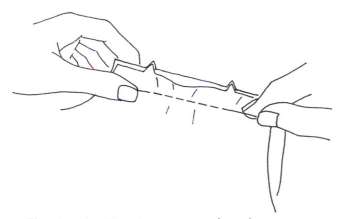

Fig. 14.23   Drawing up ease thread

Interfacings, Linings, and Underlinings

Interfacings

Interfacings are available in both sew-in and fusible varieties. They provide shaping and support to areas such as collars, cuffs, pocket flaps, collarless necklines, and under buttons and buttonholes.

Applying Interfacings

If a pattern piece is not provided for the interfacing, the interfacing should be cut from the same pattern and usually on the same grain as the area it is to interface. An exception would be when the garment fabric piece is cut on the bias; the interfacing is then cut on straight grain if the purpose of the interfacing is to stabilize the area being interfaced.

Interfacings are usually applied to the upper section of the garment detail being interfaced. When applied to the upper section, as in a collar, cuff, or waistband, the interfacing helps to hide seam edges. However, neckband collars may need the interfacing on both sides of the neckband to give appropriate support to the neckband.

Front or back button openings in which a fabric or bound buttonhole is being used need to have the interfacing applied to the underside of the outer fabric. For machine worked buttonholes, the interfacing can be on either the outer fabric or the facing.

Fusible interfacings, when applied to a fabric, have a tendency to leave a ridge along the outer edge; therefore, fusible interfacings usually are placed on the facing rather than on the garment. This is true especially where only a part of the garment is being interfaced, such as a collarless neckline with a facing. In areas of the garment where the interfacing is applied to the entire piece, such as in a collar or a cuff, interfacing is usually applied to the upper section.

Both sew-in and fusible interfacings need to be preshrunk before use. Usually, rinsing each in warm water is sufficient. Sew-in interfacings should be put in the dryer; fusibles cannot. Fusible interfacings need to be tested on a scrap of fabric to determine the effect they produce when joined to the fashion fabric. The instructions that come with the fusible interfacing should be followed exactly; different manufacturers of fusible interfacings have different procedures for applying their interfacings.

Sew-in interfacings need to be applied carefully to insure that they are held in place and serve their purpose in the finished garment, yet do not create unneeded bulk.

Applying Sew-in Interfacings

Reducing Bulk in Sew-in Interfacings. Before the interfacing is applied to a garment piece with corners, the corners of the interfacing can be trimmed diagonally so that no interfacing is caught in the stitching line at the corner or point (Fig. 14.24). This procedure is not recommended for sheer and lightweight fabrics where the absence of interfacing in the corner could be noticeable in the finished garment.

In a garment with a front or back neckline zipper but no collar, the interfacing is trimmed so that no interfacing is caught into the seam where the zipper is to be installed (Fig. 14.25).

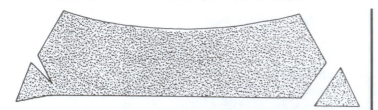

Fig. 14.24   Trimming corners in interfacing

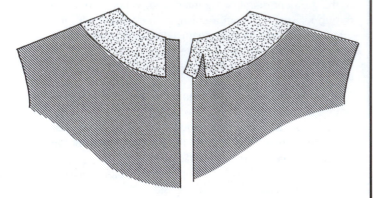

Fig. 14.25   Eliminating interfacing in seam with zipper

If sewing the interfacing into the seams would create bulk, the interfacing and garment seams can be stitched separately and then joined. Interfacing seams are joined by overlapping them and either stitching them with two rows of straight stitching or a single row of zigzag stitching (Fig. 14.26). The fabric is trimmed to the stitching leaving a seam of ¼ inch (6 mm).

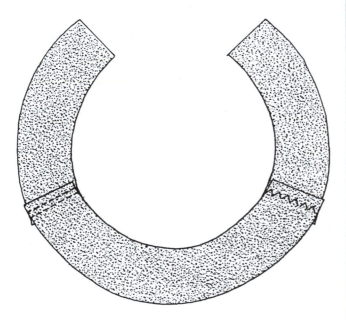

Fig. 14.26   Lapping seams in interfacing

While many instructions suggest trimming the sew-in interfacing to within ⅛ inch (3 mm) of the stitching line, the sewer may prefer to wait and layer/grade the interfacing along with the other enclosed seam allowances (see Chapter 15). Since the interfacing usually is the outermost layer, it would be the one left the longest, not the shortest as would happen if it were trimmed at the time it was being attached to the garment section.

Interfacing at a Fold Line. Often an interfacing stops at a fold line, such as in many collars, cuffs, and front or back button openings. To keep the interfacing in place along the fold line, it needs to be attached loosely by hand using a catch stitch (Fig. 14.27). The catch stitch (Fig. 14.28) is formed by working from left to right (for the right-handed sewer), using a single strand of thread.

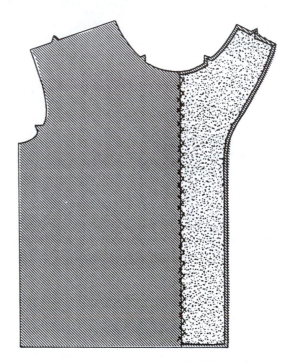

Fig. 14.27   Catch stitching to hold interfacing to fold line

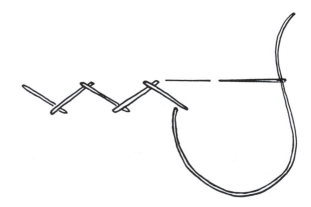

Fig. 14.28   Making the catch stitch

Securing Interfacing to the Facing

Two methods are used to attach the interfacing to the facing, whether it is an extended facing or a separate facing. The first method is often used when there is no back neck facing, since this technique finishes the shoulder seams as well as the outer edge of the facing. The second method can be used when there is a back neck facing, as the same edge finish used on the front facing can also be used on the back neck facing.

Method I – To interface when there is no back neck facing:

This method serves not only to attach the interfacing to the garment but to finish the edge of the facing as well. It works well for most fabrics except ones where the seam might create unnecessary bulk. It is especially effective for sheer and light-weight fabrics where manipulating the facing edge when edge finishing often is a challenge.

1. Pin the interfacing to the *right side* of the facing, placing the edge of the interfacing along the facing fold line (*a* in Fig. 14.29).
2. Machine stitch ¼ inch (6 mm) along the outer edge and continue along the shoulder seam (*b* in Fig. 14.29). Check the pattern for the width of the seam allowance allowed at the shoulder seam of the facing.
3. Trim diagonally at the outer corner of the facing (*c* in Fig. 14.29).
4. Understitch along the seam that joins interfacing to the facing to aid in turning; place the understitching on the interfacing side of the seam (*a* in Fig. 14.30). Turn the interfacing to the wrong side.

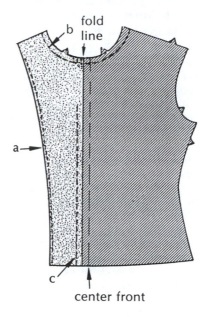

Fig. 14.30 Securing interfacing by stitching to facing near fold line

5. Press, rolling the seam slightly to the interfacing side.
6. Staystitch the neck edge of the facing and interfacing together (*b* in Fig. 14.30).
7. Machine stitch (*c* in Fig. 14.30) or catch stitch (*b* in Fig. 14.31) the loose edge of the interfacing to the facing fold line. When machine stitching, begin stitching at the location for the top buttonhole and ⅛ inch (3 mm) from the fold line so that no stitching shows on the right side when the garment is worn. (Omit this step when the facing has been cut separately from the garment since the interfacing is caught into the seam when joining the facing and interfacing to the garment.)

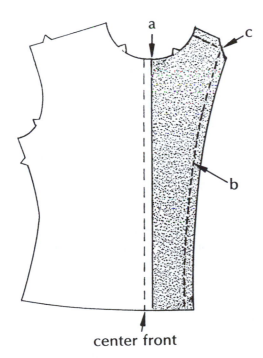

Fig. 14.29 Attaching interfacing to right side of facing

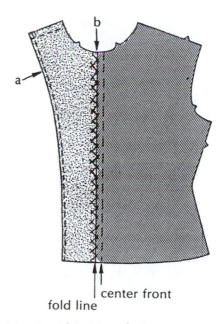

Fig. 14.31 Attaching interfacing to wrong side of facing

Method II—To interface when a back neck facing is used:

In this method the interfacing is attached to the fold line with a hand or machine stitching and then machine stitched to the outer edge. It works well when there is a back neck facing because the same edge finish can be used to finish the facing and the back neck facing. This method for applying an interfacing is preferred for heavier fabrics as the edge can be finished without turning.

1. Pin the interfacing to the *wrong side* of the facing, placing the edge of the interfacing along the facing fold line.

2. Machine stitch the interfacing and facing together ¼ inch (6 mm) from the outer edge and ½ inch (1.3 cm) at the shoulder seam line (a in Fig. 14.31).

3. Machine stitch (c in Fig. 14.30) or catch stitch (b in Fig. 14.31) the loose edge of the interfacing to the facing fold line (see step 7 of Method I).

4. Attach the back neck facing. Press shoulder seams open. Trim facing shoulder seams to ¼ inch (6 mm) (a in Fig. 14.32).

5. Finish the outer edge of the front facing and back neck facing in a method appropriate for the fabric. A zigzag or serged finish is appropriate for heavier fabrics, with both the interfacing and facing layers being finished together. A turned-and-stitched finish is appropriate for lightweight fabrics. To reduce bulk, trim the interfacing close to the first row of stitching before turning and edge stitching (b in Fig. 14.32). Turn

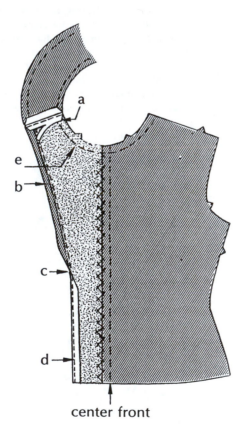

center front

Fig. 14.32 Turning and stitching facing edge over interfacing

facing edge over the interfacing (c in Fig. 14.32) and stitch close to the folded edge (d in Fig. 14.32).

6. Staystitch the neck edge of the facing and interfacing together (e in Fig. 14.32).

Fusible Interfacing

Fusible interfacings contain an adhesive backing that combined with heat, moisture, and pressure joins the interfacing to the fabric.

To apply fusible interfacing:

1. Trim the corners of fusible interfacings diagonally as previously described (see Fig. 14.24). This procedure is not recommended for lightweight and sheer fabrics where the corners might appear unattractive without the interfacing.

2. Trim about ⅜–½ inch (1–1.3 cm) from all seam allowances before attaching the fusible interfacing to the fabric, leaving about ⅛–¼ inch (3–6 mm) to be caught in with the seam. In some cases, the sewer may wish to omit this trimming, especially when working with some knitted fabrics that curl or with some sheer, open-weave fabrics.

3. Position the interfacing over the fabric with the adhesive side toward the fabric. "Fuse-baste" the interfacing to the fabric by lightly touching the iron to the wrong side of the interfacing at several places to hold it in place for the fusing process.

4. Follow the directions supplied with the interfacing to insure good adhesion of the interfacing to the fabric. Special consideration needs to be given to iron temperature, type of press cloth to use (damp versus dry), steam or dry iron, length of time to apply heat, and amount of pressure to use.

5. If no directions are available, follow these guidelines:

a. Place a damp press cloth over the interfacing.

b. Place the iron on the damp press cloth for 10 seconds on every spot being fused. A normal weight iron and some hand or body pressure insures a more permanent bond.

c. Remove the press cloth and press with the iron to remove press marks and smooth out the fabric.

d. Allow fabric to cool before handling.

e. Test one corner for permanency of the bond; repeat the process, if necessary.

If the interfacing is not aligned correctly, it can be removed after pressing for a short time over the fused area and immediately pulling the interfacing away from the fashion fabric. A new piece of interfacing may need to be cut rather than trying to fuse the original piece a second time. Fusible interfacings used with a facing may reduce the curling of some knitted fabrics and may eliminate the need to finish the edge of some woven fabrics.

Linings

A lining is used to provide a finished look to the inside of a garment and also to help maintain its shape. On jackets and coats, a lining aids in putting the garment on and off more easily. The lining is cut and sewn separately from the fashion fabric; generally it is also the same shape and on the same grain. Occasionally, a skirt with much fullness or with pleats will have a lining that is less full or contains no pleats.

Where the lining is attached depends on the style and type of garment. For example, the wrong side of skirt and pants linings usually are attached to the wrong side of the garment at the waistline before the waistband is applied. Linings in dresses usually are sewn in at the waistline seam, if one is present, and at the neckline before the neck edge and armholes are finished.

The lining and the fashion fabric usually are hemmed separately. Occasionally the lining is put inside the hem of the fashion fabric on garments where hems have a tendency to show. In this situation the garment is hemmed only to the lining fabric.

When constructing a lining for a garment with a side zipper opening, the zipper opening in the lining will be located on the opposite side of its location in the finished garment, as the lining is turned inside out and placed wrong sides together when joining the two sections. The zipper opening in the lining is left about 1 inch (2.5 cm) longer than the zipper opening in the garment. After the zipper has been attached in the garment the lining is attached by hand to the zipper tape (a in Fig. 14.33).

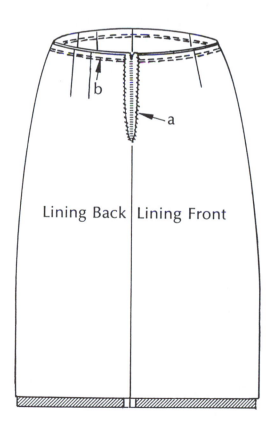

Fig. 14.33 Securing lining to skirt at placket and waistline

To line a garment:

1. Construct the garment to the point where the lining is to be attached.

2. Construct the lining to be the same size and shape as the garment. Seams in the lining generally do not need to be finished because they are inside and not exposed to wear. Most seams will be pressed open. Often darts in the lining are pressed in the opposite direction to those in the fashion fabric to reduce bulk.

3. Attach the lining to the garment by placing it *wrong* sides together and basting it along the seam where it is to be joined (b in Fig. 14.33). From this point, the two fabrics are handled as one.

4. It may be desirable to hand tack the seams in the lining to the seams in the garment, or a French tack can be used to hold the lining in place near the hemline.

5. Complete the garment construction.

6. Hem the lining by turning the hem allowance toward the fashion fabric to give a more finished look to the inside of the garment. Linings are hemmed about 1 inch (2.5 cm) shorter than the garment so that they will not show when the garment is worn. However, the hem of the lining should not be shorter than the width of the hem of the garment so that a gap does not occur between the two. Read Chapter 22 for more information on Hems and Hemming Stitches.

Underlining

An underlining is used mainly to provide support and reinforcement to the garment. The underlining is attached to the wrong side of the fashion fabric before seams are sewn, which helps to keep the inner construction details from showing to the outside on sheer or light colored fabrics.

An underlining is cut the same size and shape as the fashion fabric. Most all markings are placed on the underlining; only those which must be visible on the outside (buttonholes, pocket placement) are placed on the fashion fabric. The underlining is attached to the fashion fabric pieces before the seams are sewn, and the two are treated as one during garment assembly.

To underline a garment:

1. For bulky fabrics, stitch the darts separately in the fashion fabric and the underlining before the two layers are joined. The darts can be pressed in the opposite direction to each other to reduce bulk. More commonly, the underlining fabric is joined to the fashion fabric before the darts are stitched.

2. Place the underlining fabric on the fashion fabric, *wrong* sides together, matching darts, notches, and seam lines. Pin all edges together.

3. Machine or hand stitch the underlining and garment sections together (a in Fig. 14.34). It may be desirable to tailor baste the two layers together (b in Fig. 14.34), or the two layers may be basted together around the outside edges near the seam line. A thread used for the basting should be one which will not leave marks on the finished garment. For example, dark threads are not recommended for use on light

colored fabrics. Fabrics with a tendency to show puncture marks should not be tailor basted. A glue stick can be used to attach the two layers if this product will not leave permanent marks on the fabric. After tailor basting, the two layers are treated as one. The tailor basting should be left in the fabric layers until the garment is completed.

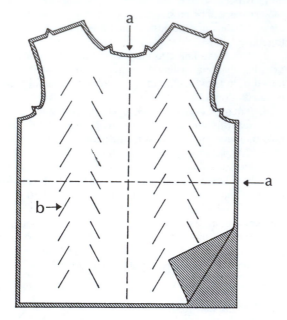

Fig. 14.34 Attaching underlining to fashion fabric

4. Before stitching darts or pleats, machine baste through both layers along the fold line to hold the fabric layers together for more accurate stitching (Fig. 14.35). The two layers are then treated as one when completing darts, pleats, or other design details. Remove this basting after completing the final stitching. Darts are often slashed and pressed open to reduce bulk.

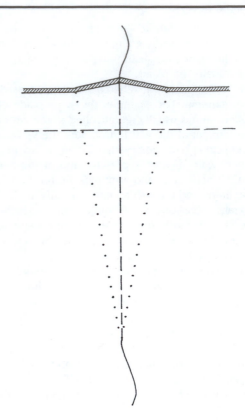

Fig. 14.35 Basting center of dart in fashion fabric and lining before sewing

5. Finish garment edges. Both layers can be finished together, being careful to keep the layers from sliding while edge finishing.

6. Continue garment construction as directed in the pattern instruction sheet, treating garment and underlining as one.

7. Complete garment hem, attaching the fashion fabric only to the underlining fabric (see Chapter 22).

15 Collars and Facings

Collars and facings contain enclosed seams, which in the finished garment are encased within a garment piece. Cuffs, waistbands, and other construction details also contain enclosed seams; these are discussed in other chapters of this book. The principles for doing all enclosed seams are the same and are followed regardless of the location of the enclosed seam.

Enclosed Seams

Treatment of enclosed seams, after they have been stitched, involves three steps: (1) layering/grading, (2) clipping or notching (if curved), (3) and understitching.

To finish enclosed seams:

1. Enclosed seams, because of their location, have a tendency to be bulky. To reduce bulk, layer or grade the seam allowances. This involves cutting each layer of the enclosed seam to a different width, the *widest edge being the one closest to the outside of the finished garment* (Fig. 15.1). The wider edge hides the narrower edges, which lie toward the inside of the garment. The finished widths of enclosed seams depend on the weave of the fabric and the size of the yarns. A tightly woven fabric with small yarns can be layered/graded narrower than a loosely woven fabric with larger yarns. All of the layers of an enclosed seam are layered/graded to a different width.

2. Enclosed seams often are curved. The *inside or con-*

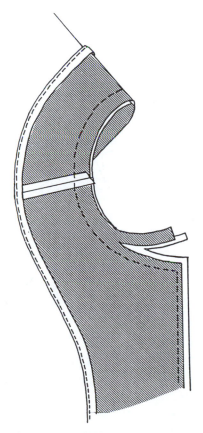

Fig. 15.1 Layering/grading seam

147

cave curve (Fig. 15.2) must be *clipped* to allow the cut edge, which is shorter than the stitching line, to spread open when turned inward. The *outside or convex curve* (Fig. 15.3) is *notched* so that the cut edge, which is longer than the stitching line, can fit inside without the notched edges overlapping or gaping. The clips and notches need to extend *to but not through* the stitching line; both the clips and the notches need to be small and placed close together for the smoothest curve.

The points of a sharp pair of shears are used for the clipping and notching. Sometimes with bulky fabrics, *alternate clipping* of the seam allowances is recommended where clips are placed at different locations on each layer (Fig. 15.4).

3. *Understitching* (Fig. 15.5) is a row of machine stitching done from the right side of a facing (or undercollar or undercuff) that holds the seam allowance to the facing, keeps the facing seam from showing on the outside of the finished garment, flattens the edge of the seam, and aids in pressing. Understitching is done from the right side of the facing, stitching close to the original seam line, with care being taken to keep all the seam allowances turned toward the facing during the stitching. While a straight machine stitch is used most often, sometimes zigzag stitching or even hand stitching may be an appropriate choice. Understitching is not done when it would show from the outside of the finished garment. Pressing along the edge of the seam is done from the wrong side of the garment after understitching has been completed.

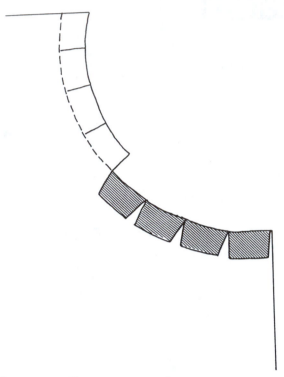

Fig. 15.2 Clipping an inside or concave curve

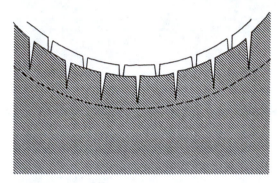

Fig. 15.4 Alternate clipping a concave curve

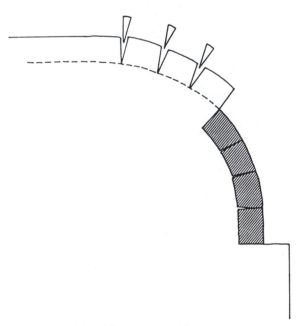

Fig. 15.3 Notching an outside or convex curve

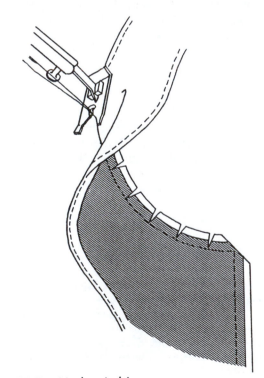

Fig. 15.5 Understitching

The order of finishing the enclosed seam is important. For a smooth appearance, the seam must be layered/graded first, then clipped or notched (if needed), and finally understitched. The seam is pressed after understitching. Layering/grading the seam is easier to do before the clips and notches have created many little areas of fabric, which would take longer to layer or grade; however, reversing those steps will have little influence on the appearance of the finished curve. To clip/notch the seam *before* understitching is critical to the smooth appearance of the curve, and those two steps cannot be reversed. After layering/grading and clipping or notching, the seam is understitched and then pressed. The understitching aids in pressing by bringing the seam to the garment edge and rolling the seam toward the underside while pressing.

Facings

Facings are pieces of fabric used to finish edges of garments such as necklines and sleeveless armholes. They may be cut the same shape and on the same grain as the area that they face (Fig. 15.6); they can be cut as a folded extension of the area to be faced (Fig. 15.7); or they may be bias strips (Fig. 15.8). Bias strips are discussed in Chapter 16.

Facings are used primarily to finish garment edges, such as on a collarless neckline, and are turned to the inside where they are invisible from the outside of the finished garment. However, they can be decorative and appear on the outside of the garment, even being cut

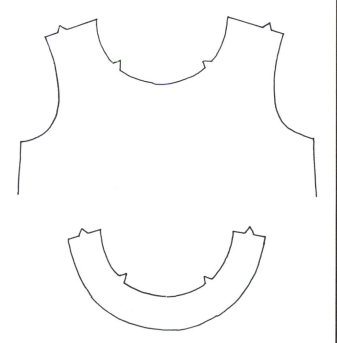

Fig. 15.6   Fitted facing

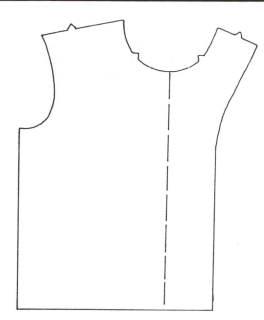

Fig. 15.7   Extended facing

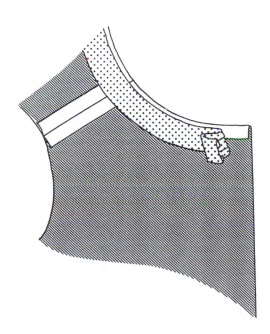

Fig. 15.8   Bias binding

from a contrasting color fabric or topstitched for special emphasis.

When using open construction techniques, the facing would be applied to a neckline before the garment side seams are stitched. Until the side seams are stitched, the garment is flat, making the neckline area more accessible for applying the facing than it would be if the side seams had been stitched.

To apply a shaped facing:

1. Before the facing is attached to the garment, stitch and trim to ⅜ inch (1 cm) any seams that are a part of the facing (Fig. 15.9). The interfacing can be applied to the facing or the garment (see Chapter 14).

2. Finish the outer edge of the facing after trimming the seams and before attaching the facing to the garment. See Chapter 12 for a discussion of appropriate edge finishes.

3. Place the facing over the area to be faced, right sides together, matching pattern markings, notches, and seams. Stitch the seam using a ⅝ inch (1.6 cm) seam (Fig. 15.10).

4. Layer/grade the enclosed seam, clip or notch, understitch, and press, in that order.

5. Tack the facing to the seam using a hand stitch (Fig. 15.11) or "stitch-in-the-ditch" (Fig. 15.12). Stitch-in-the-ditch is a technique in which a row of machine stitching is placed in the groove of a seam to hold that section of the garment to the one underneath it. When done carefully and with matching thread, the stitching usually is not visible on the outside of the finished garment. When using stitch-in-the-ditch for attaching a facing, the stitching is done from the outside; threads should be tied, not backstitched. A small patch of fusible web also can be used to hold the facing to the garment.

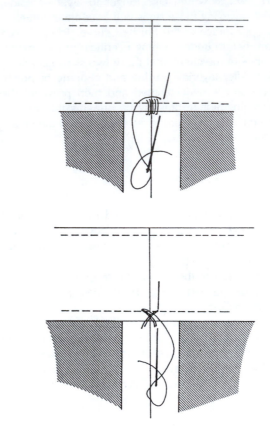

Fig. 15.11   Facing tacked to seam

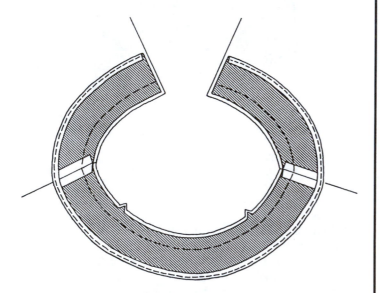

Fig. 15.9   Stitching and trimming facing seams

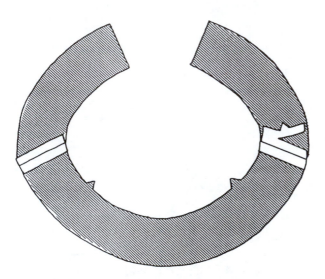

Fig. 15.10   Attaching facing to garment

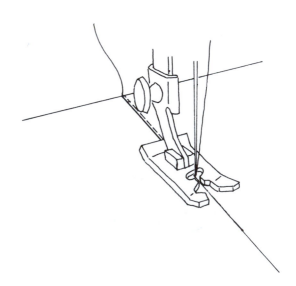

Fig. 15.12   Stitching-in-the-ditch

Special Facing Applications

Some facings because of their location require special procedures when applying them to a garment.

Square Corners

When a facing involves a square corner as in a square neckline (Fig. 15.13), the corner needs to be reinforced with shorter stitches for about 1 inch (2.5 cm) on either side of the corner before the seam is clipped. For open weave fabrics or those that ravel easily, a piece of fusible interfacing can be applied to the corner before stitching for additional reinforcement.

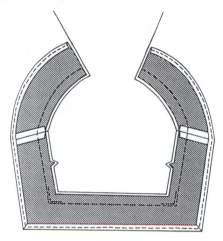

Fig. 15.13   Facing a square corner

Facings with Slashed Openings

Some facings will be slashed after the facing has been stitched to the garment (Fig. 15.14). The point of such a slashed area needs to be reinforced with a row of shorter machine stitches, a patch of fusible interfacing, or a drop of seam sealant before the slashing occurs.

Fig. 15.14   Facing with slashed opening

Facing Applied to Neckline with a Zipper

The facing can be applied before or after the zipper has been installed. Excess bulk at the center back can be a problem when attaching a facing after applying a lapped zipper; therefore, it is recommended to first attach the facing, then insert the lapped zipper using the open seam method. This technique gives a smooth finish where the zipper seam and neckline meet (Fig. 15.15). It is appropriate for use only when an open seam method is being used for installing the zipper.

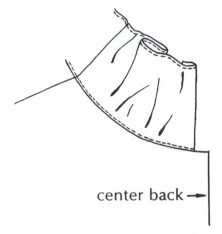

center back ➝

Fig. 15.15   Finished appearance of left side of faced garment

To apply a facing before installing a lapped zipper:

1. Pin the facing to the neck edge, right sides together, matching seams and notches (Fig. 15.16).
2. For a lapped zipper, fold center back seam allowances as follows (see Fig. 15.17):

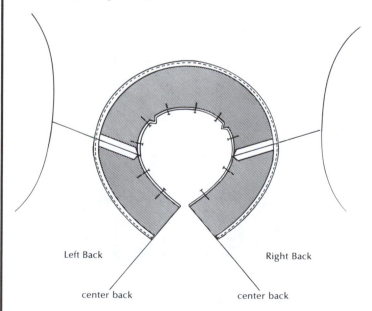

Left Back   Right Back

center back   center back

Fig. 15.16   Attaching neck facing to garment

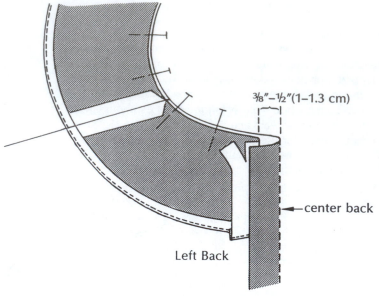

Fig. 15.17   Folding center back seam allowances of left back facing and garment

    a. **Left back facing.** Fold the seam allowance to the outside so the folded edge is ⅜–½ inch (1–1.3 cm) away from center back stitching line. Pin. Trim excess allowance from back edge of facing.

    b. **Left back garment.** Fold the seam allowance to the outside, right sides together, exactly on the center back stitching line. Pin.

    c. **Right back.** Pin the facing flat against the garment without folding.

    3. Stitch the facing seam, layer/grade, clip, understitch, and press.

    4. Apply the zipper following instructions for the Open Seam Method found in Chapter 17, taking care not to catch any of the facing as the zipper is being stitched in place. If the zipper tape extends above the neckline of the garment, the top of the tape can be curved away so that the end of the zipper tape will be covered by the facing when it is folded down over the completed zipper (Fig. 15.18).

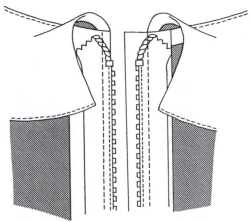

Fig. 15.18   Curving upper edge of zipper tape before stitching

    5. Fold the facing down over the zipper tape and slip stitch in place (Fig. 15.19).

To apply a facing after installing the zipper:

    1. Insert the zipper using a centered or lapped application (see Chapter 17).

    2. Attach the interfacing to the facing or the neckline edge. Stitch the seams in the facing and trim to ¼ inch (6 mm). Finish the outer edge in an appropriate way.

    3. Pin the facing to the neckline, matching seams and notches.

    4. For a lapped zipper, turn back the facing 1 inch (2.5 cm) on the overlap side and ⅝ inch (1.6 cm) on the underlap side (Fig. 15.20). Both seams are trimmed to ½ inch (1.3 cm). For a centered zipper, turn under both facing seam allowances ⅝ inch (1.6 cm) and trim to ½ inch (1.3 cm) (Fig 15.21).

    5. Stitch the facing neckline seam, making sure that the stitching lines are an equal distance above the zipper on both sides of the neckline.

    6. Layer/grade and clip the seam allowance except for the unfaced seam allowance on the overlap side of the zipper (Fig. 15.22). Understitch the neckline seam.

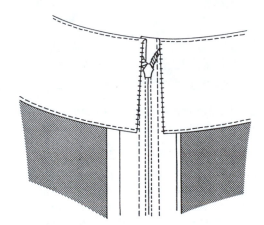

Fig. 15.19   Completed faced opening using lapped zipper

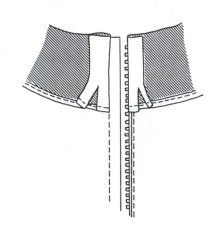

Fig. 15.20   Folding of facing for lapped zipper

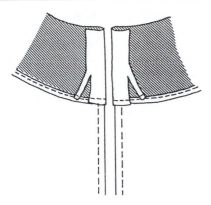

Fig. 15.21 Folding of facing for a centered zipper

7. Turn the facing to the inside and press. For the lapped zipper, the unfaced neckline seam allowance is turned under ⅛ inch (3 mm) to finish the edge (Fig. 15.23). If this produces bulk, the edge can be left flat and hand overcast. The edges of the facing are slip stitched to the zipper tape. The seam allowances for the centered zipper are turned to the inside and slip stitched to the zipper tape.

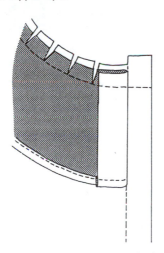

Fig. 15.22 Layering/grading and clipping seam

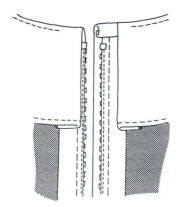

Fig. 15.23 Finishing unfaced seam allowance on lapped zipper

Extended Facings

Extended facings are cut as one with the area to be faced and are possible only where the fold line of the facing follows a straight line. Extended facings often are found in the center front or center back button openings on garments. One piece cuffs and collars are other examples of extended facings.

If a pattern piece has a separate facing that is joined along a straight line, an extended facing can be made by overlapping the two pieces along the seam lines where the two would be joined (Fig. 15.24). The extended facing would be less bulky, but the pattern piece might be more difficult to place on the fabric since it now is wider than when the two pieces are cut separately. In reverse, an extended facing can be changed into two pieces by cutting along the fold line and adding seam allowances to each piece.

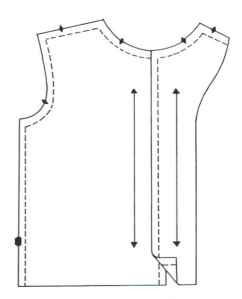

Fig. 15.24 Making an extended facing

When transferring pattern markings for a garment with an extended facing, the fold line and the center front or center back line need to be marked so that they are visible from the outside. A row of basting often is used for this purpose. These lines can also be marked by connecting dots or clips made at each end with a line marked with chalk or washable fabric marking pen.

When attaching a sew-in interfacing to the extended facing, the interfacing needs to be stitched by hand to the fold line to hold it in place (see Chapter 14). Fusible interfacings would need to be placed on the facing side of the piece; if placed on the garment side, they could produce a ridge along the edge of the interfacing. Sew-in interfacings could be placed on either the facing or the garment side. When the interfacing is placed on the facing side, the outside edges of the two layers can be edge finished together.

Combined Neck and Armhole Facings

Many sleeveless garments provide a facing that combines a finish for both the armhole and the neckline edge. Several methods for applying this facing are appropriate, two of which are discussed here. Interfacing should be applied to either the facing or to the garment if needed for body or for stability. Fusible interfacings would be placed on the facing piece. Sew-in interfacings could be placed on either the facing or the garment side. When interfacing is placed on the garment side, the interfacing acts as a buffer between the seam allowance and the outer layer resulting in a smoother finish to the garment edges.

These procedures could also be used when fully lining a sleeveless, collarless garment such as a vest. The facing pieces would be replaced by lining pieces cut the same size and shape as the garment section to be lined.

Method I—To apply a combined facing
with a center neck opening:

1. Stitch the shoulder seams of the garment and press seams open; side seams are left unstitched.
2. Stitch the shoulder seams of the fitted facing, trim to ¼ inch (6 mm), and press open; finish the outer edges of the facing in an appropriate manner.
3. Pin the facing to the garment at the neck edge and the armholes, right sides together (Fig. 15.25). Extend the facing ⅛ inch (3 mm) beyond the garment armhole edge between the notches along the upper part of the armhole seam. This makes the facing slightly smaller than the garment section and prevents the facing from showing along the edges of the finished garment. If the shoulder area is very narrow, the facing may need to be extended ⅛ inch (3 mm) beyond the garment edges between notches on the neckline seam line as well (Fig. 15.25). If a lapped zipper is to be used, refer to the section on Facing Applied to Neckline with a Zipper in this chapter.

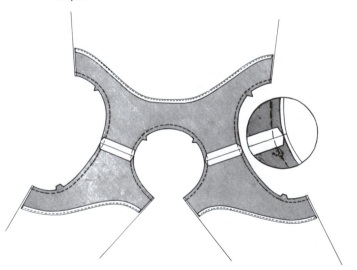

Fig. 15.25 Attaching combined neck and
armhole facing—Method I

4. Stitch the neckline and armhole seams, layer/grade, clip, and understitch where possible.
5. Turn the facing right side out by pulling the two free sections through the shoulder area. Press, rolling the seam slightly toward the facing.
6. Open up the facing and stitch the side seams of the garment and the underarm seam of the facing as one continuous seam (Fig. 15.26). Trim the facing seams to reduce bulk. Press seam open.
7. Fold the facing down over the garment and secure to the garment seam allowance.

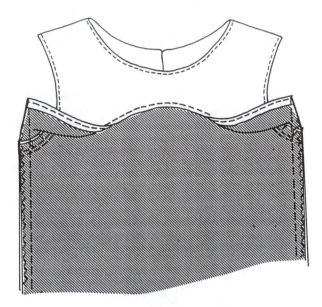

Fig. 15.26 Stitching underarm and side seam
for combined facing—Method I

Method II—To apply a combined facing with
no center neck opening:

1. Stitch the side seams of the garment, finish seam edges, and press. Leave the shoulder seams open.
2. Stitch the underarm seams of the facing and trim; press seams open; finish the outer edge of the facing in an appropriate manner. Leave the shoulder seams open.
3. With right sides together, pin the facing to the garment at the neckline and the armhole. Extend the facing ⅛ inch (3 mm) beyond the garment armhole edge above the notches along the upper part of the armhole. This makes the facing slightly smaller than the garment section and prevents the facing from showing along the edges of the finished garment. If the shoulder area is very narrow, the facing may need to be extended ⅛ inch (3 mm) beyond the garment edges above the notches on the neckline seam line as well.
4. Stitch the front neckline, the back neckline, and the armhole seams, stopping all stitching lines 1⅝ inch (4.1 cm) from the shoulder edge (Fig. 15.27).
5. Compare the front and back shoulder areas to be sure that the two that will join each other are exactly the same width between the rows of stitching. If not, make the necessary corrections in the stitching of the armhole or neck seams.

6. Layer/grade and clip the neckline and armhole seams, stopping at the point where the stitching ends (Fig. 15.28).

7. Turn the *front* shoulder area *right side out;* leave the *back* shoulder *area wrong* side out (a in Fig. 15.29).

8. Place the front shoulder area inside the back shoulder area, with right sides of front and back garment sections together and right sides of facings together (b in Fig. 15.29).

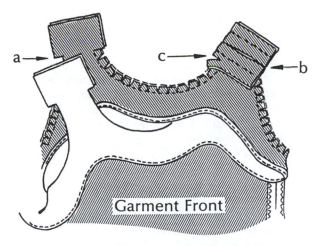

Fig. 15.29   Turning and stitching shoulder seam — Method II

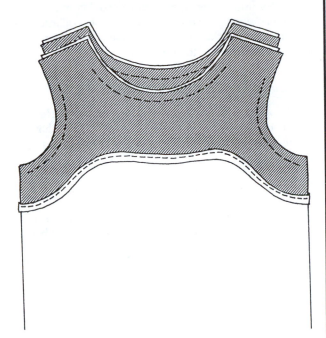

Fig. 15.27   Stitching neck and armhole edges — Method I

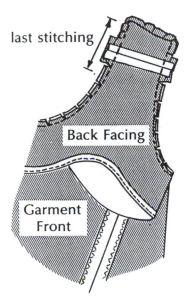

Fig. 15.30   Finishing stitching armhole and neckline seams — Method II

9. Pin and stitch the garment front and back shoulder seams; pin and stitch the facing front and back shoulder seams. Press the seams open and trim the facing seams to ¼ inch (6 mm) (c in Fig. 15.29).

10. Work the shoulder strap area out about 2 inches (5 cm) until the unstitched area of the armhole and neckline seams can be stitched by machine. Pin the seam so that the facing extends ⅛ inch (3 mm) beyond the garment edges to make the facing slightly smaller than the outer area. Stitch the seams, layer/grade, and clip seam allowances (Fig. 15.30).

11. Pull the shoulder seams and the facings back to lie in their finished position. Understitch neck and armhole seams where possible.

12. Press, rolling seams slightly to the facing side. Fold the facing down over the garment and secure the facing to the garment seam allowance.

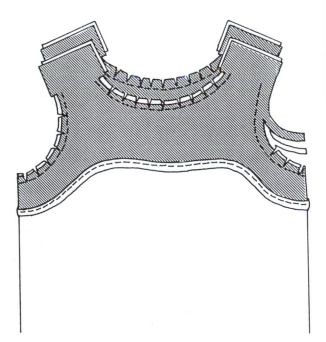

Fig. 15.28   Layering/grading and clipping armhole and neckline seams — Method II

Collars

Collars differ in the amount of roll they have and in the shape along the outer edge. The roll is determined by the shape of the collar neckline. The more nearly the curve of the neckline of the collar matches the curve of the neckline of the garment, the flatter the collar will lie. This collar is called a flat collar (Fig. 15.31). The straighter the neckline of the collar in relation to the shape of the neckline of the garment, the higher the roll of the collar will be. A collar with a slightly concave curved neck edge is called a partial roll collar (Fig. 15.32), whereas a collar that has a straight or slightly convex neck edge is called a full roll collar (Fig. 15.33). A full roll collar may be worn closed at the neck edge or open as a convertible full roll collar.

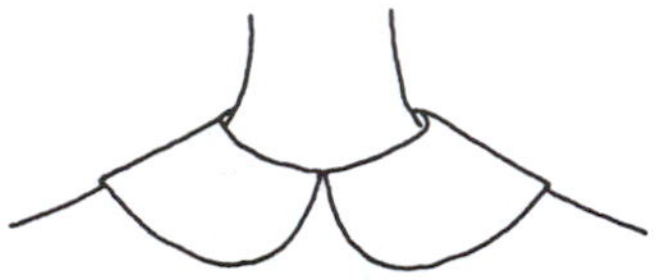

Fig. 15.31   Flat collar

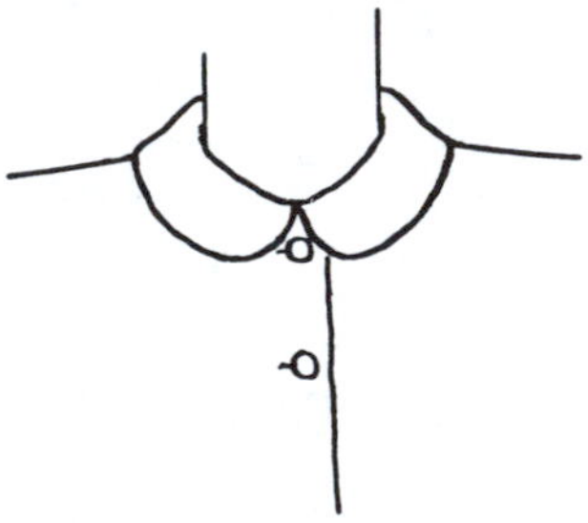

Fig. 15.32   Partial roll collar

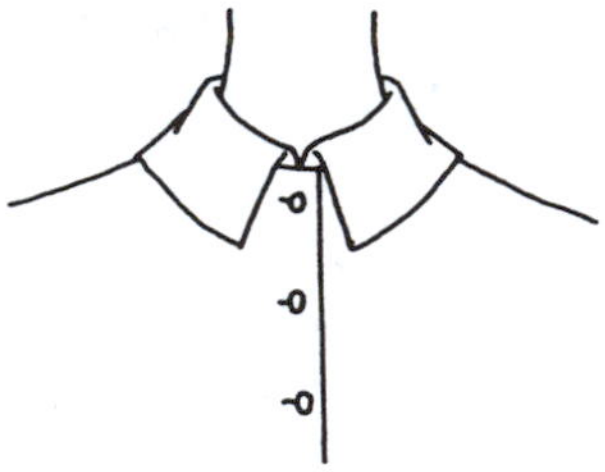

Fig. 15.33   Full roll collar

Partial roll collars (those with a concave neckline curve somewhere between the flat and the full roll) and flat collars can be much wider in design than the full roll collar. Flat collars usually have a facing to cover the neckline seam allowances as those seam allowances are turned toward the garment; full roll collars usually use the neckline edge of the collar to cover the neckline

seam allowances as those seam allowances are turned toward the collar. A combination of the two methods may also be used.

Collars are constructed according to the shape of the front outer edge. The outer edge of a collar is usually round or pointed and this shape determines which method of construction is used.

Collars usually are interfaced to provide more body. The interfacing is placed against the upper collar to conceal the seam allowances and to give a smoother finish to the outer edges of the collar.

Round Collar

The round collar is cut with two separate pieces, the upper collar and the under collar. Collars that are divided at both center back and center front consists of four pieces.

To make a round collar:

1. Transfer the seam line markings for the collar to the interfacing using a tracing wheel and dressmaker's carbon paper (a in Fig. 15.34). Mark the center back of the collar with the tracing wheel or with a small clip into the seam allowance.

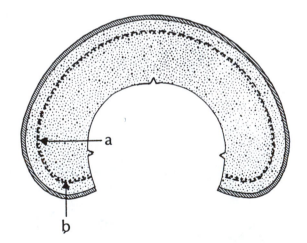

Fig. 15.34   Attaching interfacing to a round collar

2. Stitch the interfacing to the upper collar around the outside edges only ½ inch (1.3 cm) from the outer edges, (b in Fig. 15.34) *leaving the neck edge unstitched. The seam allowance for the interfacing should not* be trimmed although it may be specified in the pattern. It can be layered/graded along with the other seam edges *after* the collar seam has been stitched; and since it is the outermost layer, it will be left the longest and will help to conceal the remaining collar layers.

3. The upper collar needs to be larger than the under collar in order for the collar to roll properly and for none of the under collar to show on the outside of the finished collar.

For the flat collar, this is done by extending the *under collar* (the single layer) approximately ⅛ inch (3 mm) as the upper and under collars are being pinned together in preparation for stitching (a in Fig. 15.35). The amount of difference in the upper and the under collar is determined by the thickness of the fabric, more being required for thicker fabrics and less for thinner ones. Start pinning the two collar layers together at the center of the collar and work toward each end. Ease the upper collar to the under collar around the front curves. If a garment pattern provides a separate under collar pattern piece, this difference may already be accounted for.

4. Stitch the collar seam following the marked stitching line on the interfacing (Fig. 15.35). Fold and check the two sides of the collar to be sure that the two sides are identical before proceeding to finish the collar.

5. Layer/grade the seam so that the longest edge is toward the upper collar. Notch the convex curve as needed (Fig. 15.36).

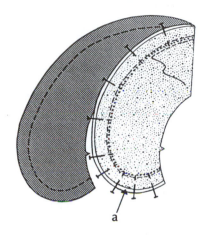

Fig. 15.35   Pinning round collar with under collar extended

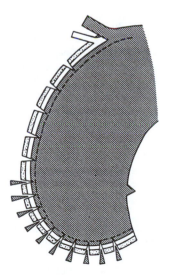

Fig. 15.36   Layering/grading and notching a round collar

6. Understitch the seam allowances to the under collar in two stages by starting at center back and stitching toward the front edges.

7. Turn the collar right side out. Press, rolling the seam slightly to the under side.

8. Topstitch the collar, if desired, before attaching to the garment.

Pointed Collar

A pointed collar may consist of two sections, an upper collar and an under collar, or it may be cut all in one piece with the outer edge of the finished collar being a fold. There are three ways for constructing a pointed collar. Method I can be used on a two-piece collar constructed of medium- to lightweight fabric. With this method the outer seam is understitched before sewing the end seams. Method II is recommended for heavier fabrics. Method III is used when the collar is cut as one piece. For collar stays see pages 165–66.

Method I–To make a two-piece pointed collar for medium to lightweight fabrics:

With this technique the two collar layers are first stitched, and then understitched along the back or outer seam before the ends are stitched. This helps the outer seam to roll toward the under collar, and the understitching aids in the final pressing.

1. Transfer the seam line markings on the collar to the interfacing using a tracing wheel and dressmaker's carbon paper.

2. Stitch the interfacing to the *upper* collar by machine, stitching along the outer three sides ⅛ inch (3 mm) into the seam allowance from the seam line. *Do not* stitch the neck edge.

3. Join the upper collar and under collar, right sides together, along the long outer edge of the collar (Fig. 15.37). The collar ends are not stitched at this time.

4. Layer/grade the seam allowance, clip or notch (if needed), and understitch (Fig. 15.37).

5. Pin the ends of the collar *folding the outer seam of the collar toward the under collar* (a in Fig. 15.38). *Extend the under collar ⅛ inch (3 mm) beyond the upper collar along this seam in order to make the upper collar bigger than the under collar. Taper this extension as needed at the point.*

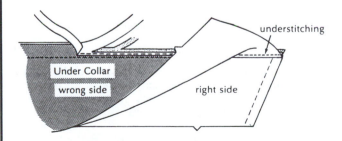

Fig. 15.37   Method I–pointed collar: stitching outer seam

Fig. 15.38 Method I—pointed collar: stitching end seams

6. Stitch the end seams, following the marked stitching lines on the interfacing. Layer/grade the seams and trim the points diagonally, cutting close to the seam line to reduce bulk (*b* in Fig. 15.38).

7. Press the seam open using the point presser.

8. Turn the collar right side out, and work the points out carefully by taking a small hand stitch in the point and gently pulling both ends of the thread (Fig. 15.39), or by pushing out the corner using a large blunt needle or point turner. Care must be taken not to pry the corner out using a pin or needle, as it is possible to pull threads out causing the corner to fray.

9. Press the collar, rolling the seam slightly to the underside.

10. Topstitch the collar, if desired, before attaching it to the garment.

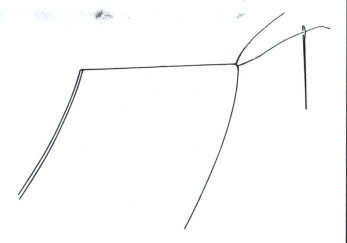

Fig. 15.39 Pulling out corner point with needle and thread

Method II—To make a two-piece pointed collar for heavier fabrics:

With this technique, the collar is stitched around the outer three sides all at one time. The upper collar is bubbled slightly when joining the collar layers to make it larger than the under collar so that the seam around the outer edges will not show on the right side of the finished collar.

1. Transfer the seam line marking of the collar to the interfacing using a tracing wheel and dressmaker's carbon paper. Mark the center back of the collar with the tracing wheel or with a small clip into the seam allowance.

2. Attach the interfacing to the upper collar by machine stitching the outer three sides ⅛ inch (3 mm) into the seam allowance from the seam line. *Do not* stitch the neck edge.

3. Pin the upper collar to the under collar starting at the center of the collar and working toward each end. To make the upper collar slightly larger than the under collar, *extend the under collar* ⅛ inch (3 mm) beyond the upper collar on the outer three sides as the collar layers are pinned together (*a* in Fig. 15.40). The neck edges of the collars should be even (*b* in Fig. 15.40).

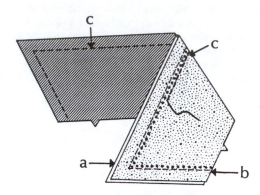

Fig. 15.40 Method II—pointed collar: attaching upper and under collar layers

4. Stitch the collar seam following the marked stitching line on the interfacing (*c* in Fig. 15.40). Fold and check the two sides of the collar to be sure that each side is identical before proceeding to finish the collar.

5. Layer/grade the seam so that the longest edge is toward the upper collar. Trim the points diagonally, close to the seam line, to reduce bulk.

6. Understitch as much of the long outer seam as possible.

7. Press the remaining seams open using the point presser.

8. Turn the collar right side out and work the points out carefully by taking a small hand stitch in the point and gently pulling both ends of the thread (see Fig. 15.39), or by pushing out the corner using a large blunt needle or point turner.

9. Press the collar, rolling the seams slightly to the underside so they do not show from the right side of the collar.

10. Topstitch the collar, if desired, before attaching it to the garment.

Method III—To make a one-piece pointed collar:

The one-piece pointed collar is cut with the upper and under collar in one piece, the outer edge of the finished collar being a fold line.

1. Transfer the seam line markings of the collar to the interfacing using a tracing wheel and dressmaker's carbon paper.

2. Stitch the interfacing to the upper collar along the fold line with a catch stitch and along the ends by machine stitching ⅛ inch (3 mm) into the seam allowance from the seam line (Fig. 15.41). (See Fig. 14.28 for making the catch stitch.)

3. Fold the collar on the fold line, right sides together, to stitch the ends. To make the upper collar slightly larger than the under collar, *extend the under collar* ⅛ inch (3 mm) beyond the upper collar along the end seams (*a* in Fig. 15.42). Taper this extension as needed at the point.

4. Layer/grade the seams and trim the points diagonally, close to the seam line, to reduce bulk (Fig. 15.43).

5. Press the seams open using the point presser. Turn the collar right side out. Work out the points by taking a small hand stitch in the point and gently pulling both ends of the thread (see Fig. 15.39) or by pushing out the corner using a large blunt needle or point turner.

6. Press the collar carefully, rolling seams slightly to the underside so that they do not show from the right side of the collar.

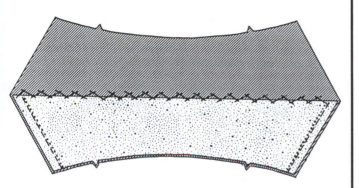

Fig. 15.41   Method III—pointed collar: attaching interfacing

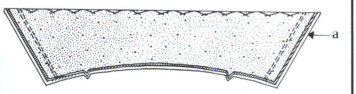

Fig. 15.42   Method III—pointed collar: sewing end seams

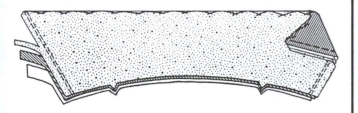

Fig. 15.43   Method III—pointed collar: finishing end seams

Neckband Collars

Neckband collars may be cut as one piece with the neckband a part of the upper and under collars or in two pieces, with the neckband cut separate from the upper and under collars. Directions for constructing both types of collars are given here.

One-piece Neckband Collar

One-piece neckband collars may be constructed according to the directions for a round or pointed collar, depending on the shape of the outer edge, with the following additional procedures.

To make a one-piece neckband collar:

1. When pinning the collar ends, do not extend the under collar. The seam along the front edge of the band should be right along the edge on the completed collar.

2. Using a shortened stitch length, double stitch the corner where the collar and the band meet, positioning the second stitching exactly on top of the first (*a* in Fig. 15.44).

3. Press open the seam along the front edge of the collar and band using the point presser.

4. Layer/grade the seam allowances. Clip to the corner where the collar and the band meet (*a* in Fig. 15.44).

5. Notch the curved area on the neckband (*b* in Fig. 15.44).

6. Turn the collar, carefully pushing out the points or curves. Press, rolling the collar seam slightly toward the under collar along the long outer edge. The seams on the front ends of the collar and band should be on the edge.

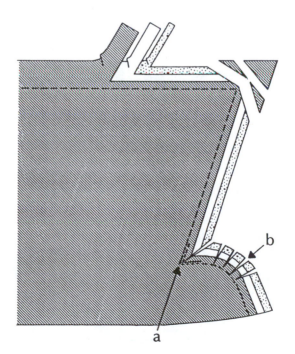

Fig. 15.44   One-piece neckband collar: finishing end seams

Two-piece Neckband Collar

The collar section of a two-piece neckband collar is constructed according to the directions for a round or pointed collar. If topstitching is desired, it should be completed before joining the collar to the neckband.

To make a two-piece neckband collar:

1. Transfer the seam line markings for the neckband to the interfacing using a tracing wheel and dressmaker's carbon paper. Also transfer the center back and the center front markings to the interfacing on the upper and lower edges of the neckband.

2. Attach the interfacing to the wrong side of the neckband by machine stitching along the outer three sides ⅛ inch (3 mm) into the seam allowance from the seam line. *Do not* stitch the neck edge. If a firmer neckband is desired, both neckband and band facing may be interfaced.

3. Join the collar to the neckband by pinning the *right side* of the *undercollar* to the *right side* of the *neckband*, matching center back, notches, and center front markings (Fig. 15.45). Generally, the ends of the collar match the center front markings on the neckband. Pin the *right side* of the *band facing* to the *right side* of the *upper collar*, matching notches and other pattern markings, placing pins parallel to and directly on the seamline. Open out the collar and fold in half, matching the two sides to check that they are identical. Adjust, if necessary.

4. Stitch the seam, following the traced marking on the neckband interfacing and stitching through all layers of the collar and neckband (Fig. 15.46).

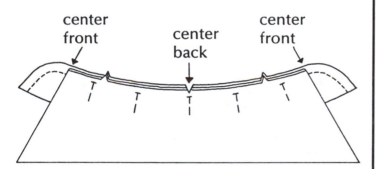

Fig. 15.45   Two-piece neckband collar: joining collar to neckband

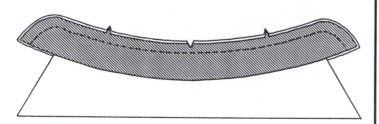

Fig. 15.46   Two-piece neckband collar: stitching band seam

5. Before finishing the seam, turn the band right side out and compare to see if they are identical. Special attention needs to be given to the length of the collar ends on each side and the shape of the curves on the neckband. The two must be the same.

6. Layer/grade the seam and notch the curved area on the neckband (Fig. 15.47).

7. Press open the seam in the curved area of the band using the point presser. Turn the band right side out.

8. Press the band away from the collar. The seam along the front of the band should be on the edge.

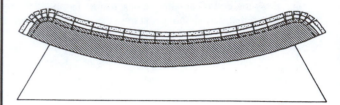

Fig. 15.47   Two-piece neckband collar: layering/ grading and notching band seam

Attaching the Collar

Flat or Partial Roll Collars

The neckline seam of flat and partial roll collars usually is finished with a fitted or a bias facing. The neckline seam allowance is turned toward the garment and is covered by the facing.

To attach a flat or partial roll collar with a fitted neck facing and center front opening:

1. Interface the front facing of the garment as described in Chapter 14. Staystitch the neckline seam on both the garment and the facing.

2. Join the shoulder seams of the front and back neck facings. Trim shoulder seam allowances to ¼ inch (6 mm) and press open. Finish the outer edge in a manner appropriate for the fabric (see Chapter 12).

3. Prepare the collar as previously described in this chapter. Topstitch the collar, if desired, before applying it to the garment.

4. Before attaching the collar, mark the center back on the garment, facing, and collar with a pin or small clip into the seam allowance.

5. Pin the *right side* of the *under collar* to the *right side* of the *garment* neckline, matching center back, notches and other pattern symbols. Clip the garment neckline as necessary so that the two layers are smooth and even. Generally, the collar ends are placed at the center front marking (a in Fig. 15.48). To hold the collar securely at the center front marking, it can be hand tacked in place using small overcast stitches (a in Fig. 15.48).

6. Machine baste the collar to the garment. Check to be sure both sides of the collar and the garment front are identical.

7. Fold the facing on the marked fold line and place over

the collar, right sides together, with center back, seam lines, and other pattern symbols matched. Pin all layers together (Fig. 15.49).

8. Stitch the neckline seam beginning at one front fold line and stitching to the other, stitching a little deeper into the seam allowance than the basting.

9. Check the collar to be sure that the two sides are even. Layer/grade, clip, and understitch the seam. Trim the corners of the seam allowance diagonally, and remove wedges from the shoulder seams to reduce bulk.

10. Turn the facing to the inside of the garment and press. Attach the facing to the shoulder seams using a hand stitch, a piece of fusible web, or by stitching-in-the-ditch.

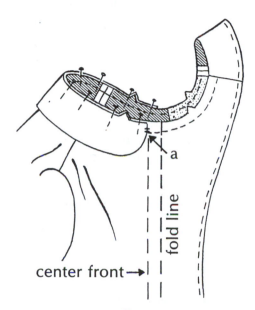

Fig. 15.48 Pinning collar to neckline and attaching at center front

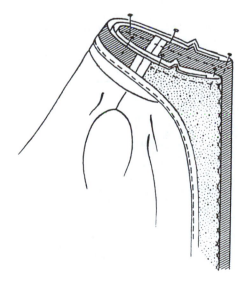

Fig. 15.49 Pinning facing over collar

Full Roll Collars

Full roll collars are ones which have a straight or nearly straight neck edge (A in Fig. 15.50). A convertible collar is one type of full roll collar that can be worn open or closed. The neckline on a convertible collar curves upward from the shoulder seam toward center front (B in Fig. 15.50), forming a slight convex curve (as compared to a concave curve of the flat or partial roll collars). The neck edge (C in Fig. 15.50) of the mandarin collar (Fig. 15.51) is similar to that of the convertible collar. Because these collars are straight along the back neck edge, they usually are not attached with a back neck facing. Instead, the upper collar forms its own finish at the neckline edge. The neckline seam allowance of the collar and garment back are turned into the collar and are covered by either the upper or under collar seam allowance. The neckline seam allowance of the front collar and the garment front are turned toward the garment and are covered by the front facing. The directions given here are for a full roll collar attached to a garment with an extended front facing. The back neckline seams are covered by the upper collar. The same procedures can be used when attaching the convertible and mandarin collars. Mandarin collars could also be attached using the procedures for attaching a band collar (see Neckband Collars).

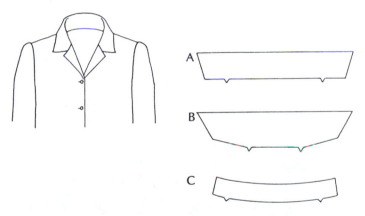

Fig. 15.50 Collar shapes: (A) full roll; (B) convertible full roll; and (C) mandarin

Fig. 15.51 Standing or mandarin collar

To attach a full roll collar:

1. Construct the collar following the directions for a round or pointed collar given previously in this chapter.

2. Interface the extended facing as described in Chapter 14. Staystitch the neckline seam on both the garment and the facing. Mark the center back on both the garment and the collar with a small clip into the seam allowance.

3. Fold the collar along its roll line and pin or hand baste all layers together near the fold line (Fig. 15.52). (Omit this step when attaching a mandarin collar.) *These pins remain in the collar until construction is completed.* Trim the neckline edge of the collar until all edges match that of the upper collar, taking care to retain the notches and the center back marking.

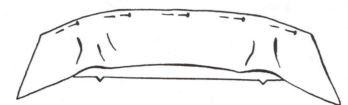

Fig. 15.52 Pinning roll line of full roll collar to shoulder

4. Clip the neckline seam of the garment and facing at regular intervals to the staystitching to make it easier to join the curved neckline seam of the garment to the straight neckline seam of the collar.

5. Pin the *under collar* and the *interfacing* layers to the garment across the back neckline from *shoulder seam to shoulder seam* with right sides of the under collar and garment together (Fig. 15.53).

Fig. 15.53 Pinning collar to neckline seam across back between shoulder seams

6. Stitch the collar to the garment from shoulder seam to shoulder seam.

7. Pin *all layers* of the collar to the garment from *shoulder seam to center front.* Hand tack the end of the collar to center front or other appropriate marking on each side. Machine baste along this seam.

8. Fold the facing on the marked fold line and place over the collar, right sides together (Fig. 15.54). Pin in place, positioning pins parallel to and directly on the seamline. Check to be sure that both ends of the collar and garment front are identical in shape.

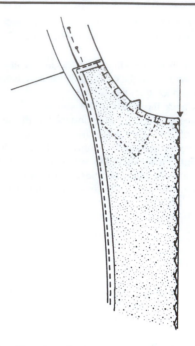

Fig. 15.54 Turning facing over outside of garment and collar

9. Stitch the neckline seam from the front fold line to the shoulder seam on both sides. This row of stitching must match exactly at the shoulder seam with the stitching that extends from shoulder seam to shoulder seam across the back neckline.

10. Layer/grade the neckline seam allowance and clip the curve through *all* layers all the way to the seam line. The garment and facing seams were clipped earlier, but not the collar seam. Trim the excess fabric from the front corners and the shoulder seam allowances.

11. *Clip all seam allowance layers* at the shoulder seam junction, and turn the front facing right side out. Push out the front corners of the facing and carefully press the seam from the front edge to the shoulder seam.

12. Press the seam allowance along the back neck edge toward the collar (Fig. 15.55).

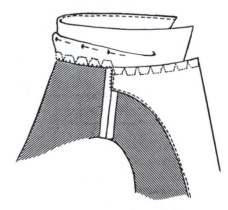

Fig. 15.55 Finishing back neckline and shoulder seams

13. Turn under the seam allowance of the upper collar across the back neckline so the folded edge is positioned just above the neckline stitching line. Pin in place.

14. Slip stitch in place. An alternate method is to machine stitch along the back neck edge stitching close to the folded edge of the collar. Hand stitch the shoulder edge of the front facing to the shoulder seam of the garment (Fig. 15.55). None of the hand stitching should show on the outside of the finished garment.

15. Remove the pins or hand basting along the roll line when the collar is completely finished.

Neckband Collars

A collar with a neckband (Fig. 15.56), whether the band is a part of the collar or a separate piece, is attached using the same principles.

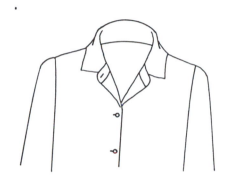

Fig. 15.56   Neckband collar

To attach a neckband collar:

1. Prepare the collar as described previously in this chapter. Complete the front opening of the garment as specified by the pattern.

2. If the collar has no separate band, fold the collar along the roll line and pin close to the fold line, as done in the full roll collar. (See Fig. 15.54).

3. Staystitch and clip the neckline seam of the garment (Fig. 15.57).

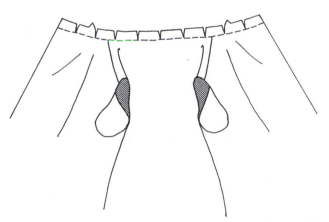

Fig. 15.57   Staystitching and clipping neckline

4. With right sides together, pin the *outer band and interfacing* to the garment, matching center back, pattern markings, and notches. Care must be taken so that the *stitching line* along the front edge of the collar band is exactly in line with the garment front edge (a in Fig. 15.58).

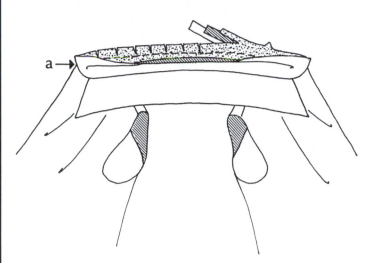

Fig. 15.58   Stitching and layering neckline

5. Stitch the seam. Layer/grade and clip or notch, where necessary (Fig. 15.58). Trim excess seam allowance from collar and band at the front edges.

6. Press the seam toward the collar.

7. Turn under the neckline seam allowance on the band facing the amount necessary to produce a smooth band. The lower edge of the band facing should cover the neckline stitching line in the area of the front band or front facing, but it should be positioned above the stitching line around the remainder of the neckline seam line.

8. *Slip stitch* the band facing to the garment along the neckline seam (Fig. 15.59). These stitches must not show on the outside of the finished garment.

9. Topstitch the band, if desired.

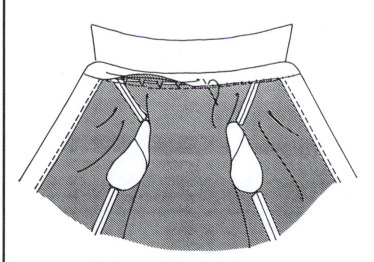

Fig. 15.59   Slip stitching band facing

Shawl Collars

The shawl collar (Fig. 15.60) differs from attached collars because it is an extension of the garment front and not a separate collar. The garment fronts extend around the back of the neckline and become the underside of the finished collar. The facings become the upper side of the collar. Two units are involved in the shawl collar: the garment/under collar section and the upper collar/front facing section. Interfacing usually is attached to the upper collar/front facing section, but it may be attached to the garment section on some fabrics.

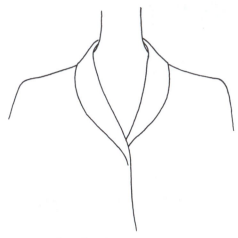

Fig. 15.60   Shawl collar

**To prepare the garment section
for the shawl collar:**

1. Carefully mark the angle on the garment/under collar where the collar and shoulder seams meet. Reinforce the corners by machine stitching for 1 inch (2.5 cm) on either side of the corner, using a shortened stitch length (a in Fig. 15.61).

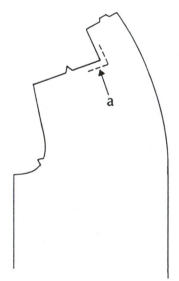

Fig. 15.61   Reinforcing shoulder angle

2. Staystitch the garment back neckline edge and clip the curve to facilitate joining it to the under collar.

3. Join the garment front and back at the shoulder seams (a in Fig. 15.62), stopping the stitching exactly at the point of the reinforced corner.

4. Clip the garment seam allowance diagonally to the reinforced corner. Finish the shoulder seams in an appropriate manner and press open.

5. Stitch the center back seam of the under collar (b in Fig. 15.62). Trim the seam to ¼ inch (6 mm) and press open.

6. With right sides together, stitch the neckline edge of the under collar to the bodice back neckline edge, starting and ending exactly at the reinforced corner (c in Fig. 15.62).

To prepare the upper collar/front facing:

1. Stitch the center back seam of the upper collar/front facing. Trim the seam allowance to ⅜ inch (1 cm) and press open.

2. Lap interfacing at center back of upper collar and zigzag the two layers together (a in Fig. 15.63). Attach interfacing to the wrong side of the upper collar/facing by stitching the two layers together ½ inch (1.3 cm) from the front edge (b in Fig. 15.63).

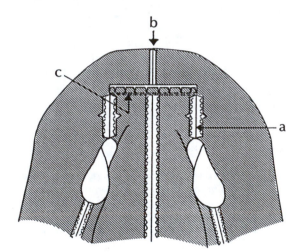

Fig. 15.62   Stitching shoulder seams, center back collar, and collar neck edge on garment/under collar

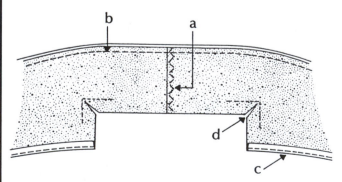

Fig. 15.63   Attaching interfacing to upper collar/ facing and reinforcing corner

3. Finish the outer edge of the facing to the shoulder seam with a method appropriate for the fabric (c in Fig. 15.63).

4. Carefully mark the angle on the upper collar/front facing where the collar and the shoulder seams meet. Reinforce the corner by machine stitching for 1 inch (2.5 cm) on either side of the corner, using a shortened stitch length (d in Fig. 15.63). Clip the seam allowance to the reinforced corner.

To complete the shawl collar:

1. With right sides together, join the upper collar/front facing to the garment/under collar, matching center back, notches, and other pattern markings. Stitch the seam from the lower edge on one side of the garment to the lower edge on the other side of the garment (Fig. 15.64).

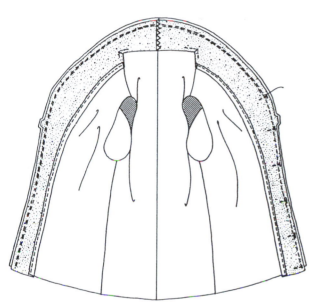

Fig. 15.64   Attaching upper collar/facing to garment/under collar

2. Layer/grade and notch the seam allowance, where necessary.

3. Understitch the outer edge of the under collar across the back (a in Fig. 15.65). Understitch the front facing to seam allowances (b in Fig. 15.65), starting slightly below the roll line for the collar (c in Fig. 15.65).

4. Turn the facing to the wrong side of the garment. Press, rolling the seam slightly to the underside. At the point where the facing becomes the upper collar, the seam should be on the edge. Above this point, the seam will roll toward the under collar.

5. Try on the garment. Pin the collar layers together along the roll line.

6. From the inside of the garment turn under the seam allowance along the shoulder seam and neck edge of the upper collar/facing the amount necessary to produce the amount of roll required. Slip stitch to the garment. These stitches must not show on the outside of the finished garment (Fig. 15.66). The neck edge of the upper collar front facing may also be finished with a fitted facing across the back neck edge.

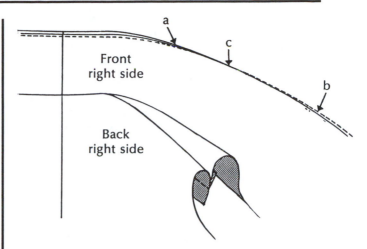

Fig. 15.65   Understitching outer edge of under collar and front facing

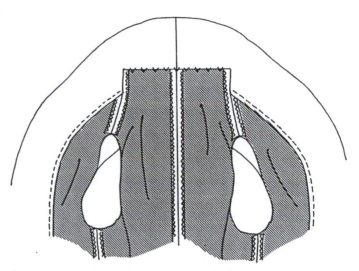

Fig. 15.66   Finishing shawl collar

Shirt Collar Stays

Collar stays are plastic strips with one pointed end and one straight end that are used in the front of collars to keep the points flat against the garment. They are an optional detail on shirts; however, the decision to use a stay must be made before any construction on the collar is done. The stay, which usually can be bought in the notions section of many fabric stores, needs to be long enough to go from the roll of the collar to the point of the finished collar. If the collar is topstitched, the point of the stay would extend to the topstitching line.

To prepare a collar for stays:

1. Place the under collar right side up, and position the stay on top of it with the point stopping ⅝ inch (1.6 cm) from the corner for a collar with no topstitching and an additional ⅜ inch (1 cm) from the corner for a collar with topstitching.

2. Using a washable marking pencil, mark lightly the sides and end of the stay on the right side of the under collar (Fig. 15.67). Remark these lines using a ruler before stitching the lines. The squared off end of the stay is the marking for the buttonhole.

Fig. 15.67   Marking placement for collar stay

3. Baste or fuse a small piece of interfacing to the wrong side over the end of the marking for the buttonhole (Fig. 15.68) to reinforce the area for a small buttonhole. Place a buttonhole a little wider than the stay on the cross marking for the end of the stay. Cut open the buttonhole (Fig. 15.68).

Fig. 15.68   Reinforcing buttonhole placement

4. Stitch in an appropriate sew-in type of interfacing to the edges of the under collar (fusible interfacing is not appropriate for this procedure). To form the pocket for the collar stay, stitch through the interfacing and the fashion fabric along the marked placement lines (Fig. 15.69).

5. Complete the collar construction and insert the stay.

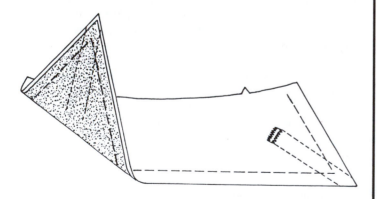

Fig. 15.69   Making pocket for shirt collar stay

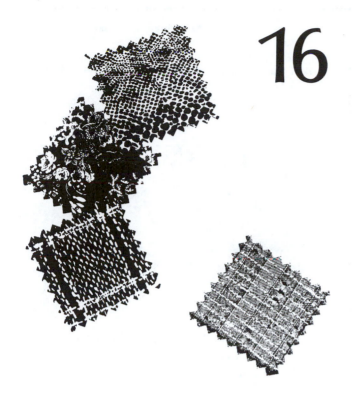

16 Bands, Plackets, Casings, and Yokes

Many garments contain bands, plackets, casings, and yokes. This chapter will discuss each of these and the preparation of bias which often is used for these design details.

Bias Strips

True bias is the direction on woven fabric having the greatest amount of stretch (see Chapter 4). Because of this characteristic, true bias strips are used in many parts of the garment for such design features as bands, casings, and bindings. They are used to cover cording, which can add a decorative touch to seams and other areas of the garment; they serve as an edge finish in bound seams; they are used as tubing for such items as belts; and they finish garment edges such as necklines and hemlines. Bias strips can be made from fashion fabric or bias binding can be purchased in a variety of colors and widths.

To prepare bias strips:

1. Locate true bias by folding one end of the fabric so that the lengthwise yarns are parallel to the crosswise yarns; the diagonal that results is true bias (a in Fig. 16.1). Mark this line with pins, chalk, or a washable marking pen.

2. Draw lines parallel to the bias marking the desired width of the bias strips (Fig. 16.2).

3. Cut the bias strips with each end following straight grain.

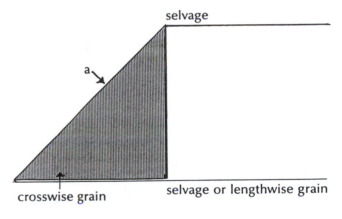

Fig. 16.1   Folding fabric for cutting true bias

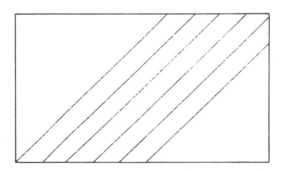

Fig. 16.2   Drawing parallel lines for bias strips

4. Join the bias strips to make a continuous strip. With right sides together, place the bias strips as shown in Figure 16.3. The two strips are at right angles to each other and are joined so that the edges match at the location of the stitching line, ¼ inch (6 mm) from the edge (a in Fig. 16.3). The points of each strip will extend beyond the strip and will be trimmed away after the seam has been stitched.

5. Stitch along the seam, backstitching at each end.

6. Press seams open.

7. Trim protruding seam points even with the edges of the bias strip (Fig. 16.4).

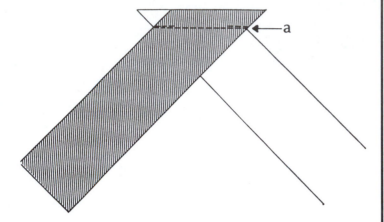

Fig. 16.3   Joining bias strips

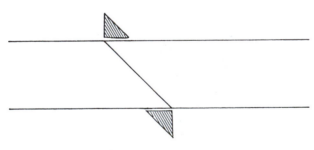

Fig. 16.4   Pressing seam open and trimming the points

When long strips of bias are required, the cutting and joining of individual pieces can be time consuming. By creating and cutting a continuous bias piece, longer strips of bias can be produced in much less time.

To make a continuous bias piece:

1. Mark the bias strips on the fabric (a in Fig. 16.5), and trim excess fabric from the piece (b in Fig. 16.5).

2. Stitch the ends of the fabric that follow lengthwise grain right sides together with one bias strip width extending beyond the edge on each side (Fig. 16.6). Backstitch at each of the marked lines to prevent the seam from coming open

when the strip is cut apart. Stitch the seam with a ¼-inch (6 mm) seam allowance and press open.

3. Cut the strip, beginning at one end and following the marked bias line until one continuous bias strip is formed (Fig. 16.7).

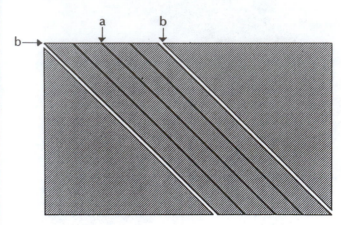

Fig. 16.5   Marking bias strips and trimming excess fabric for a continuous bias strip

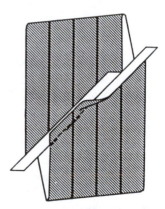

Fig. 16.6   Joining bias piece to form a continuous bias strip

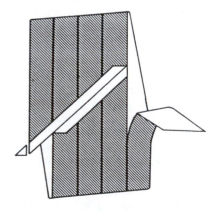

Fig. 16.7   Cutting a continuous bias strip

Cutting Bindings from Knitted Fabric

Strips that would be cut on the bias in woven fabric are cut in the direction of the greatest stretch in knitted fabric. In most knitted fabrics, that would be in the crosswise direction. Strips are cut the width needed and joined, if necessary, along a wale to produce the required length.

Casings

Casings are fabric enclosures that hold a drawstring or elastic. They are of two types: (1) the applied casing and (2) the folded casing. Openings for inserting elastic can be made along the seam where the ends of the casing meet or along one edge of the casing seam line. Openings for inserting a drawstring are made with buttonholes or grommets, which must be made before applying the casing to the garment. (See the section on Casing Openings for Draw Strings.)

Applied Casing

The applied casing makes use of bias strips, either purchased or self-made. Applied casings are found in many areas of the garment: at the lower edge of sleeves, at the waistline of shirts and dresses, and as the waistline finish for some skirts and pants. While it usually is stitched to the inside of the garment, for decorative purposes the applied casing sometimes appears on the outside of the finished garment.

To apply casing to a waistline:

1. The bias strip can be made from fashion fabric or bias binding can be purchased for use as the casing. Its width should equal the width of the elastic to be used plus ¾ inch (1.9 cm), ¼ inch (6 mm) for ease allowance and ½ inch (1.3 cm) for finishing the edges. The length of the strip equals the length of the area on which it is to be placed plus ½ inch (1.3 cm) on each end for finishing purposes.
2. Turn under ¼ inch (6 mm) on both the upper and lower edges of the casing strip (omit this step if purchased bias binding is to be used) and ½ inch (1.3 cm) on each end and press (Fig. 16.8). Machine stitch along the ends of the casing to hold the turned back ends in place (a in 16.9 and a in 16.12).

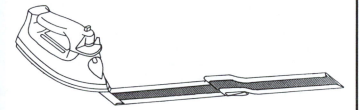

Fig. 16.8   Pressing under sides and ends of casing

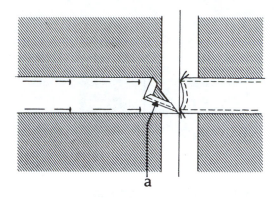

Fig. 16.9   Attaching a casing leaving a vertical opening in the casing

3. Place the casing strip over the area where it is to be stitched and pin in place. An opening can be left on the inside of the casing along the seam joining the ends of the casing (Fig. 16.9) or along one edge of the casing (Fig. 16.10). These openings will be closed by hand or with machine stitching after inserting elastic into the casing.
4. Stitch along both sides of the strip forming the casing.

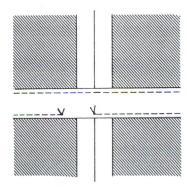

Fig. 16.10   Attaching a casing leaving a horizontal opening along the edge of the casing

To apply casing to an edge:

1. Make the casing strip as described in steps 1 and 2.
2. Mark the hemline on the garment (a in Fig. 16.11) and trim the hem allowance to ¼ inch (6 mm) (b in Fig. 16.11).
3. Unfold one edge of the casing and place it along the lower edge of the garment. Stitch along the crease line in the casing (b in Fig. 16.12).
4. Unfold casing and press flat, then fold up, rolling the seam slightly to the wrong side (Fig. 16.13).
5. Pin the free edge of the casing in place and topstitch close to the edge, tieing thread ends where the stitches meet (Fig. 16.14).

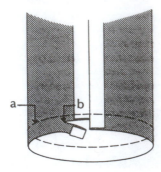

Fig. 16.11   Trimming hem allowance before applying a casing

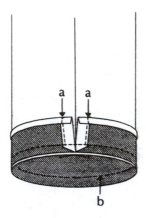

Fig. 16.12   Stitching one edge of casing

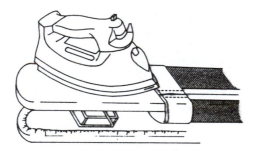

Fig. 16.13   Pressing casing to wrong side

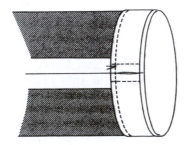

Fig. 16.14   Stitching second edge of casing

Folded Casing

The folded casing (also called the self-faced casing) is created when the edge of a garment is turned under to form the enclosure for the elastic or drawstring. This casing is best suited for a straight edge, but can be used on a slightly curved edge if kept fairly narrow. The amount to be turned under for the casing depends on the width of the elastic to be used. The casing equals the width of the elastic plus ½ inch (1.3 cm).

To make a folded casing:

1. Finish the raw edge of the casing with a method appropriate for the fabric (zigzag, serge, turn under and press, or leave unfinished on most knits).
2. Trim the seam allowance diagonally within the casing to reduce bulk (a in Fig. 16.15). Machine or hand baste or fuse the edges of the seam allowance to the fashion fabric to hold it in place (b in Fig. 16.15).

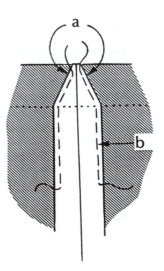

Fig. 16.15   Preparing folded casing

3. Turn the casing to the inside along the casing fold line and press. Machine stitch close to both the upper and lower edges. Leave an opening along the lower edge to allow for inserting the elastic or drawstring (a in Fig. 16.16). The opening will be closed with machine stitching after the elastic has been inserted into the casing. When applying a casing to a very stretchy knitted fabric, the straight machine stitching can be replaced with a narrow zigzag stitch to allow the stitching to stretch with the casing as the garment is being used.

To insert elastic into a casing:

1. Cut the elastic the length needed for the casing plus ½ inch (1.3 cm). The elastic is usually cut 1–2 inches (2.5–5 cm) smaller than the body circumference.

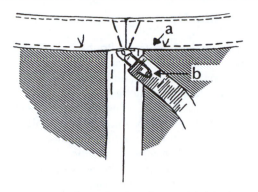

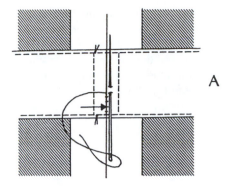

A

Fig. 16.16   Stitching both edges of folded casing
and inserting elastic

2. Insert the elastic through the casing opening using a safety pin, bodkin, or special elastic carrier at one end of the elastic (b in Fig. 16.16). Pin the free end to the garment to keep it from being pulled through the opening.

3. Work the elastic through the opening so that it is not twisted. Pin the ends of the elastic together with a safety pin. Try on the garment and adjust elastic to fit.

4. Overlap elastic ends about ½ inch (1.3 cm) or more and stitch together securely by machine (Fig. 16.17).

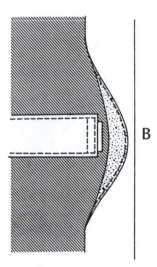

B

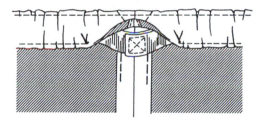

Fig. 16.17   Stitching ends of elastic

Fig. 16.19   Securing casing opening

5. Stitch across the casing opening, tieing thread ends on the inside of the garment. A folded piece of seam tape or fabric can be caught in the stitching to identify the garment back (a in Fig. 16.18). For a vertical opening slip stitch the folded ends of the casing together (A in Fig. 16.19), or the ends can be machine stitched (B in Fig. 16.19) if the casing will be covered by a belt or sash.

6. Distribute the fullness at the waist. Remove the stitching used to hold the seam allowances flat.

7. If the elastic will not remain flat inside the casing, stitch-in-the-ditch through the elastic and the casing at the seams (b in Fig. 16.18).

Casing Openings for Drawstrings

If a drawstring is used inside the casing, an opening must be made on the appropriate side of the casing *before* it is machine stitched to the garment. The opening can be made in three ways: (1) an opening can be left in a vertical seam within the area forming the casing; (2) one or two buttonholes can be put into the appropriate layer of the garment; or (3) grommets may be purchased and applied along the casing. If a vertical opening is left in the seam, the seam stitching above and below the opening should be backstitched to secure the opening. The opening can be reinforced with a bar tack, if desired (A in Fig. 16.20). The seam allowance on the inside can be catch stitched down in the casing area to keep the

b

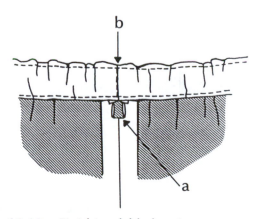

a

Fig. 16.18   Finishing folded casing

drawstring from catching under the edge of the seam allowance (*B* in Fig. 16.20). If buttonholes or grommets are used (Fig. 16.21), they would be applied to the appropriate section of the garment before stitching the casing. The area behind the opening should be interfaced for stability before putting in the buttonholes or grommets.

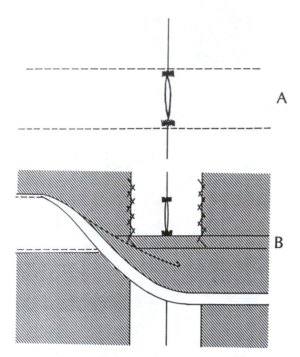

Fig. 16.20   Reinforcing a vertical opening located in a seam

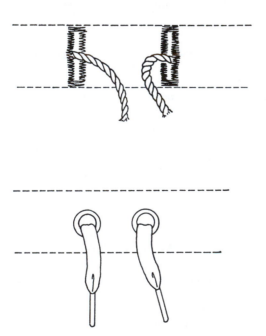

Fig. 16.21   Using buttonholes or grommets as openings for a drawstring

Front Band Openings

Many garments contain a front band opening. These may be extended bands that are cut as one with the garment front but folded and stitched in such a way to form a band, or they may be made from a separate pattern piece. Front bands may extend the full length of the garment (Fig. 16.22) or they may be partial placket openings that end within the garment section (Fig. 16.23). This type of band may be a variation of the continuous lapped placket discussed in Chapter 19. This section will concentrate on full-length band fronts as well as the two-piece placket band that extends only part way into the garment front.

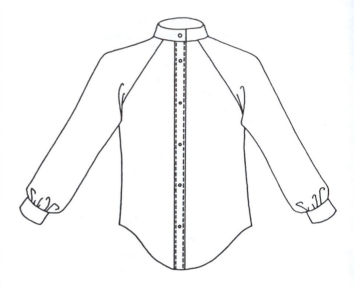

Fig. 16.22   Garment with front band

Fig. 16.23   Partial front placket that ends within the garment

Front Bands

Tailored shirts are often styled with front bands extending the full length of the opening. This section will cover five methods for making the front band: (1) an attached band with narrow facings stitched to the inside; (2) separate band stitched to the outside; (3) separate band turned to the inside and stitched; (4) separate band with a front neck facing; and (5) a simulated band. Both sides of the front may be finished using the same technique, or the overlap side may be finished with one of these methods and the underlap finished with an attached facing turned to the wrong side (a variation of the simulated band). Most patterns can be adapted to use any one of these methods.

Method I—To make an attached
band with narrow facing turned
to the inside and stitched:

With this technique the band and interfacing are cut as an extension of the garment front. It is probably the fastest method for making a front band. The facing and interfacing layers are caught in a tuck at the back edge of the front band. Both edges of the band are topstitched.

1. On the wrong side of the garment mark the fold line for interfacing (a in Fig. 16.24), the fold line for facing (b in Fig. 16.24), the fold line for the tuck at the back of the band (c in Fig. 16.24), and the stitching lines for the tuck (d in Fig. 16.24).
2. Fold the interfacing layer to the wrong side on the interfacing fold line (a in Fig. 16.25) and press.

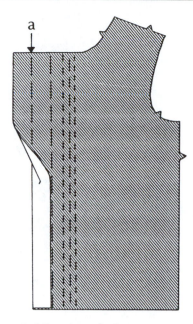

Fig. 16.25   Folding interfacing to wrong side

3. Fold the interfacing and facing layers to the wrong side on the facing fold line (b in Fig. 16.26) and press. The folded edge of the facing should be aligned with the fold line for the tuck (c in Fig. 16.26).
4. Fold all layers one more time on the tuck fold line (c in Fig. 16.27) to position the fabric for stitching the tuck. Pin along the fold (b in Fig. 16.27).
5. Machine topstitch on the stitching line forming the tuck (a in Fig. 16.27). A longer stitch length may be used. Be sure this stitching catches the back edge of the facing. The width of the band is usually 1¼ inches (3.2 cm) and the width of the tuck ¼ inch (6 mm).
6. Open the front band and press flat.
7. Topstitch ¼ inch (6 mm) from the outer edge of the band (a in Fig. 16.28).

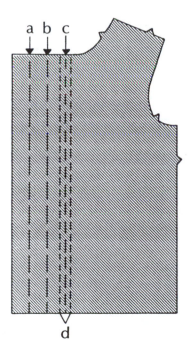

Fig. 16.24   Transferring pattern markings to the fabric

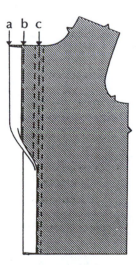

Fig. 16.26   Folding facing and interfacing to wrong side

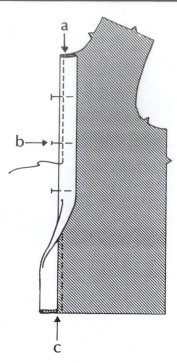

Fig. 16.27 Folding all layers in position to stitch tuck

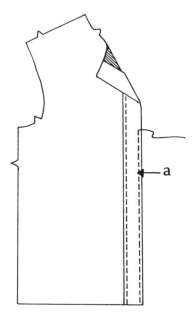

Fig. 16.28 Topstitching edge of band

Method II—To make a separate band stitched to the outside:

With this method a strip of fabric is stitched to the wrong side of the garment front, then turned to the outside and topstitched. The neck edge is left unfinished and will need to be completed with some type of band collar.

1. Interface the unnotched side of the band, placing the interfacing along the band fold line. Machine or hand baste interfacing along both long sides of the interfacing (Fig. 16.29).

2. Place *right* side of band to *wrong* side of garment, matching notches. Stitch seam (Fig. 16.30). Press seam open then press toward the band. Layer seam allowances (a in Fig. 16.30).

3. Open up the front band and press flat. Fold the band to the outside and press along the fold.

Fig. 16.29 Interfacing front band

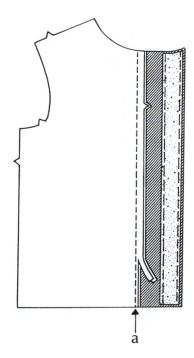

Fig. 16.30 Joining front band to the wrong side of the garment front

4. Measure over from the folded edge the desired width for the band and fold under the seam allowance along the free edge (*a* in Fig. 16.31). Pin or hand baste in place.

5. Topstitch close to each folded edge of the band (Fig. 16.31).

6. Remove basting threads.

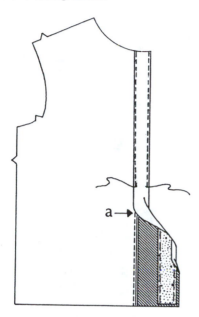

Fig. 16.31   Folding band to the outside and topstitching

Method III—To make a separate band turned to the inside and stitched:

With this method a separate piece is stitched on the outside then turned to the inside and topstitched to form the band. On this example the front band provides a finish to the front edge of a stand-up collar (Fig. 16.32).

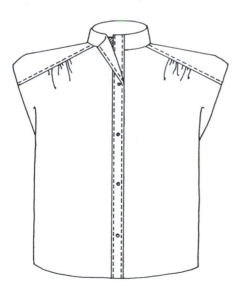

Fig. 16.32   Front band extending to the neck edge

1. If the band is to extend all the way to the finished neckline edge, the remaining portion of the neckline needs to be finished with a stand-up collar (Fig. 16.33).

2. Transfer the fold line marking to the band (*a* in Fig. 16.34).

3. Interface the portion of the band that will form the outer band (notched edge of the band). Hand or machine baste interfacing along both long sides of the interfacing (*b* in Fig. 16.34).

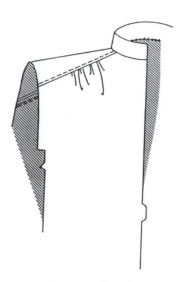

Fig. 16.33   Finishing neck edge except for front band

Fig. 16.34   Attaching interfacing to band

4. With right sides together, pin front band to garment front, matching notches and other markings. The band will extend ⅝ inch (1.6 cm) beyond the upper edge of the collar (a in Fig. 16.35).

5. Stitch band seam. Layer/grade seam allowances and press toward the band (Fig. 16.35).

6. Fold the band along the fold line with *right* sides together (a in Fig. 16.36). Stitch across the upper edge from the seam line to the fold line (b in Fig. 16.36). Layer/grade the seam and trim the corners.

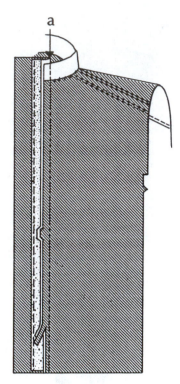

Fig. 16.35 Attaching band to front edge

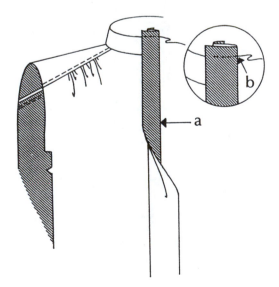

Fig. 16.36 Stitching upper edge of band

7. Turn band right side out, pushing out the corner (a in Fig. 16.37). Press.

8. Turn under the inside edge of the band, bringing the folded edge to the seam line. Pin in place (Fig. 16.37). Stitch the inside edge of the band with a blind or slip stitch.

9. Topstitch each side of the band from the right side.

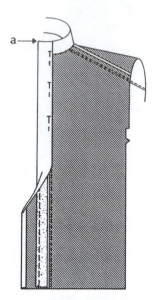

Fig. 16.37 Turning band right side out and finishing inside edge

Method IV–To make a separate band with a front neck facing:

This method for making a front band produces a smooth, neat finish to the inside of the neck edge by using a fitted neck facing to finish the front neck edge in addition to forming a front band. This technique is recommended when the neckline is worn open and a finished appearance is desired (Fig. 16.38).

Fig. 16.38 Smooth facing finish on a neckline worn open

1. Transfer the band front fold line marking to the wrong side of the front facing/band piece.

2. Interface the wrong side of the front facing/band piece, placing one edge of the interfacing along the band front fold line. Machine or hand baste the interfacing along both long sides of the interfacing (a in Fig. 16.39). If the band is not going to be topstitched, catch stitch the interfacing to the fold line.

3. Finish the unnotched edge and shoulder edge with a method appropriate for the fabric (b in Fig. 16.39).

4. With right sides together, pin front facing/band to the garment front, matching notches. Stitch seam (a in Fig. 16.40). Layer/grade the seam (b in Fig. 16.40).

5. Press the front facing/band flat, press the seam open, then press the seam toward the band (Fig. 16.41).

6. On the outside, topstitch the band ¼ inch (6 mm) from the seam (Fig. 16.42).

7. Finish the neck edge by folding the facing over the collar when attaching the collar (see Chapter 15, attaching flat or partial roll collars or full roll collars).

8. Finish the band front by topstitching ¼ inch (6 mm) from the front edge (see Fig. 16.38).

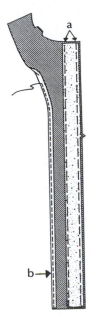

Fig. 16.39   Interfacing wrong side of front facing/band piece

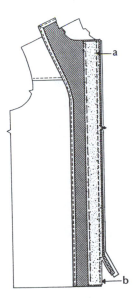

Fig. 16.40   Stitching front facing/band piece to garment front

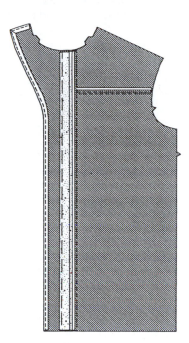

Fig. 16.41   Pressing seam toward band

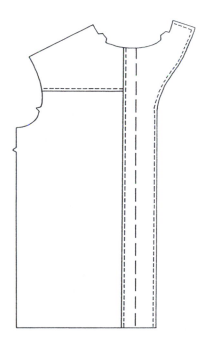

Fig. 16.42   Topstitching band ¼ inch (6 mm) from seam

Method V—To make a simulated band:

This technique can be used on the underlap side of the front opening when the overlap side is completed using one of the above methods, or it can be used on both sides of a front band opening. The band "look" is created by a row of topstitching done from the outside a designated distance from the front edge.

1. Transfer the fold line (a in Fig. 16.43) and center front (b in Fig. 16.43) markings to the wrong side of the garment front. Baste along the center front line to transfer that line to the right side.

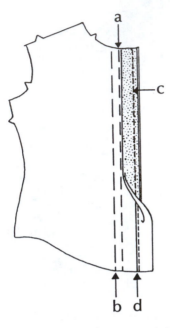

Fig. 16.43   Joining interfacing to right side of facing

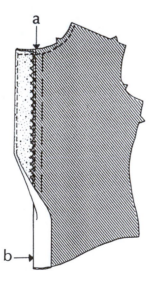

Fig. 16.44   Catch stitching interfacing to fold line and turning facing to wrong side

2. Interface the facing by placing the interfacing on the right side of the facing with one edge along the fold line (a in Fig. 16.43). The interfacing also may be cut all-in-one with the facing.

3. Stitch ¼ inch (6 mm) along the outer edge (c in Fig. 16.43).

4. Understitch along the seam that joins the interfacing to the facing, stitching on the interfacing side (d in Fig. 16.43).

5. Turn the interfacing to the wrong side and press (Fig. 16.44).

6. Catch stitch the interfacing along the fold line (a in Fig. 16.44).

7. Turn the facing to the wrong side along the fold line and press (b in Fig. 16.44). Staystitch the neck edge.

8. Topstitch close to the front edge and again a designated distance from the edge; 1–1¼ inches (2.5–3.2 cm) is the usual width of the front band (Fig. 16.45).

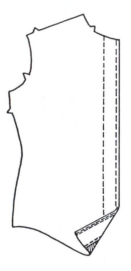

Fig. 16.45   Topstitching front band

Placket Bands

Partial placket bands are done as one-piece or two-piece applications. The one-piece band is applied much the same as described in Chapter 19 for the tailored sleeve placket. Following are directions for a two-piece partial placket band.

Two-piece Placket Opening

The shorter front placket is commonly used for front openings on many styles of blouses, shirts, and dresses (Fig. 16.46). The procedure described here for applying the two-piece placket leaves the neckline unfinished; a traditional collar or a commercial ribbing or single layer collar can be used with this type of application to provide the neckline finish. Other neckline variations would require some change in these directions to accommodate the finishing of the neckline edge.

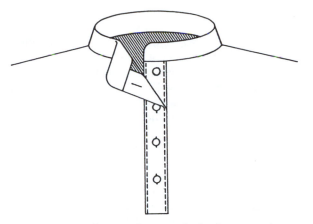

Fig. 16.46   Shirt with partial placket opening

To make a two-piece placket opening:

1. Stitch the marked placket opening on the garment, using a shorter stitch length at the corners for reinforcement (Fig. 16.47). A small piece of fusible interfacing could be applied to the lower corners of the placket opening before stitching. The width between the two vertical rows of stitching must equal the width of the finished placket. Cut down the center of the placket opening and diagonally to the corners (a in Fig. 16.47).

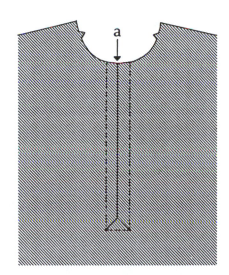

Fig. 16.47   Reinforcing placket opening

2. Transfer pattern markings to the placket bands.
3. Interface each placket band with an interfacing appropriate for the fabric (see Chapter 4). The interfacing is placed so that it will be on the side of the band forming the upper band (Fig. 16.48). If fusible interfacing is used on a knit fabric, interface the entire placket band piece.
4. With *right* sides together, pin the interfaced side of the placket band to the garment opening. Stitch just to the outside of the reinforcement stitching, ending the stitching exactly at the marking on the lower corner of the placket opening (a in Fig. 16.49).

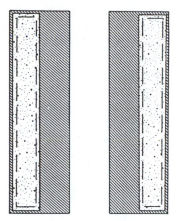

Fig. 16.48   Interfacing placket band

5. Open the band; press the seam open; then press the seam toward the band. Layer/grade the seam.
6. Turn the band to the inside of the garment along the fold line. Turn under the raw edge on the inside of the band and pin in place. Check to be sure that the width of the band on each side is the same and equal to the space designated on the garment for the placket opening. Hand stitch in place (a in Fig. 16.50) Repeat the process for the other side. The band pieces can be topstitched, if desired (b in Fig. 16.50).
7. Lap the band pieces as they will be in the finished garment (Fig. 16.51), traditionally right over left for women's garments and left over right for men's garments. Pin, making sure the band looks even on the outside, and that the top band fully covers the bottom band.

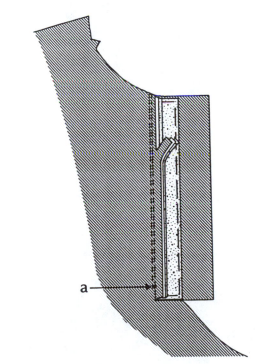

Fig. 16.49   Stitching placket band to placket opening

8. Pin the ends of the lapped bands to the triangle of fabric at the lower edge of the opening. Stitch in place through all thicknesses (Fig. 16.52).

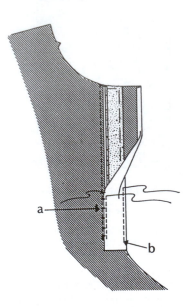

Fig. 16.50   Hand stitching band on inside

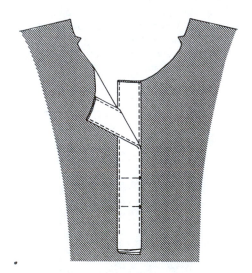

Fig. 16.51   Topstitching band lapped and pinned

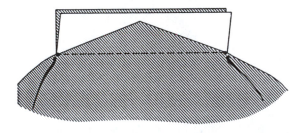

Fig. 16.52   Finishing lower end of placket band

Yokes

Many yokes are lined, either with self-fabric or with a lightweight or medium-weight fabric, so that all seams are enclosed. The yoke is often topstitched along one or both seams. Two methods will be presented: (1) finishing by topstitching the yoke to the garment, and (2) incorporating all the machine stitching between the two yoke layers.

To construct a topstitched yoke:

1. Pin back yoke to garment back section, right sides together, matching center backs and notches. Pin the *right* side of yoke facing to *wrong* side of garment back section.
2. Stitch the seam through all three layers. Layer/grade seams (Fig. 16.53). Press yoke and yoke facing over the seam. Topstitch the seam (a in Fig. 16.53).
3. Pin right sides of yoke facings to wrong sides of garment fronts, matching notches. Stitch and layer/grade seams. Press seams toward the yoke (a in Fig. 16.54).
4. Turn under front yoke seam allowance so that it overlaps the seam line. Press. Pin the folded edge over the yoke facing seams and topstitch through all layers, close to the folded edge (b in Fig. 16.54).
5. Staystitch the neck edge through both layers (Fig. 16.54).

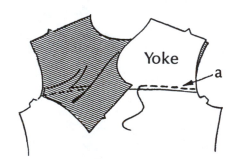

Fig. 16.53   Joining yoke and yoke facing to garment back

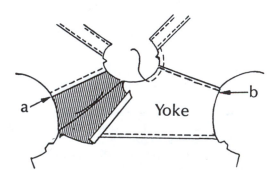

Fig. 16.54   Joining yoke and yoke facing to garment front with topstitching

To construct a yoke with all inside stitching:

1. Attach yoke and yoke facing to the garment back section following steps 1 and 2. After pressing the yoke and yoke facing, trim both layers so they are even along the front yoke seamline.

2. Pin the *right* side of yoke to *right* side of garment front at shoulder seam.

3. Bring the yoke facing up over the garment front, matching the shoulder seam of yoke facing to *wrong* side of garment front, rolling up the garment between the yoke and the yoke facing (Fig. 16.55).

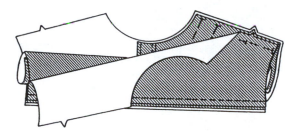

Fig. 16.55   Joining yoke and yoke facing to garment front with an enclosed seam

4. Stitch through all layers along the yoke seam (Fig. 16.55). Layer/grade seam.

5. Turn garment to the right side and press.

6. Repeat for the other yoke seam.

7. The yoke seams may be topstitched, if desired.

17 Zippers

Many decisions need to be made before the zipper is installed in the garment.

—Is the zipper to be a conventional or an invisible zipper?
—Is the application to be lapped, centered, or fly front?
—Will the zipper be applied by hand or by machine?
—Will the application make use of an open or a closed seam?
—Will the zipper be concealed or exposed in the garment?

The five types of zipper plackets commonly used are: (1) the lapped placket, (2) centered or slot seam placket, (3) fly front placket, (4) invisible zipper placket, and (5) exposed zipper placket (Fig. 17.1). Conventional zippers usually have two rows of top stitching on the outside of the garment. Only one row shows on the lapped and fly front applications while two rows are visible with the centered application. The invisible zipper, because of its construction, has no stitching on the outside of the garment. In the exposed zipper, the entire zipper is visible.

The lapped and centered applications can be used almost interchangeably; however, the zipper teeth or coil and pull tab are less likely to show in a lapped application. The centered application often is used for short openings, such as at the wrist of a fitted sleeve and for center front openings where a balanced effect is desired. The lapped application is recommended for garment side and center back openings; less risk of catching the fabric in the zipper teeth or coils exists with a lapped application. Invisible zippers can be used almost anywhere, but they are particularly suited for use on fabrics where topstitching is not desirable, such as on velvets or knits. The exposed zipper is used for neck openings where there is no seam in the garment. It is also used in full-length center front openings, such as on a jacket.

While most zippers are applied by machine, they can be installed by hand, giving a custom appearance to the garment. The hand stitches are less obvious than the machine stitches and the hand application will not damage delicate fabrics.

Most zippers are concealed in the finished garment; they serve a functional purpose, not an aesthetic one. However, in a few cases, an exposed zipper may be desired. On some fabrics, such as sweater knits, an exposed zipper is recommended because the fabric could become tangled in the zipper teeth or coils if a centered or lapped application were used. The exposed zipper also is used, sometimes with a trim, to give a decorative touch to the front of some garments.

Zippers are available in several weights, lengths, widths, with knit or woven tape, and with teeth or coil construction. Zippers should be selected in a weight appropriate to the fashion fabric.

182

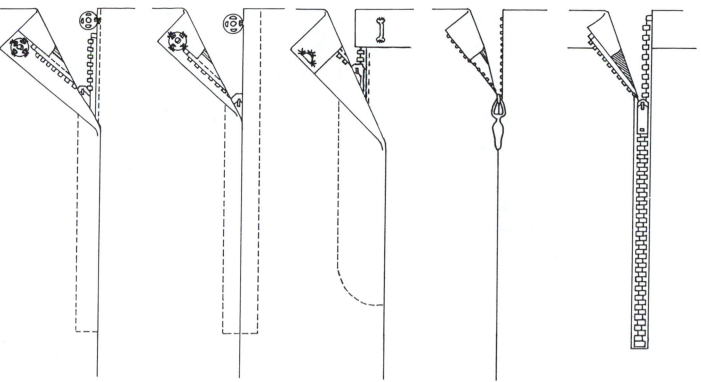

Fig. 17.1   Types of zipper applications: lapped, centered, fly front, invisible, and exposed

Characteristics of a Well-Constructed Zipper Placket

From the outside:

—Zipper is concealed beneath the edge of the overlap from top to bottom.
—Pull tab is well covered.
—Folded edge on the underlap side is edge stitched to the zipper tape close to the zipper teeth.
—Placket opens to the end of the zipper teeth.
—Stitching across the bottom is ⅛ inch (3 mm) beyond the end of the zipper stop.
—Closed placket lies smoothly with neither side appearing stretched or puckered and with both sides the same length.
—Topstitching lines are straight and parallel to the seam line.

From the inside:

—Thread ends for all seams not to be crossed by another row of machine stitching are securely fastened and clipped short so that they will not be caught in the zipper teeth.

Preliminary Procedures

A number of procedures need to be followed before the zipper is installed in the garment.

1. Preshrink the zipper (see Chapter 7).
2. Check the length of the zipper (or placket) opening in the garment and correct, if necessary.

a. On a skirt or pants placket, the opening equals the functional length of the zipper teeth or coils from above the top stop to below the bottom stop, plus one seam allowance, plus about ¼ inch (6 mm) for ease in manipulating the pull tab.

b. On a dress placket (side seam zipper), the opening equals the length of the zipper from the stop at the bottom of the zipper to just above the bar tack on the zipper tape.

c. On a neck placket, the opening equals the functional length of the zipper teeth or coils to below the bottom stop, plus ⅜ inch (1 cm) for a fastener, plus one seam allowance. If the facing or collar has been attached the opening equals the length of the zipper teeth or coils to below the bottom stop plus ⅜ inch (1 cm) for the fastener.

3. Seams that meet at the zipper opening need to match exactly. If they do not, corrections need to be made. The seams need to be trimmed to reduce bulk. If the seam is pressed in one direction, it should be pressed open for about 1 inch (2.5 cm) at the zipper opening and trimmed (Fig. 17.2).

4. Placket seam allowances need to be at least ⅝ inch (1.6 cm) wide for centered/slot zipper applications.

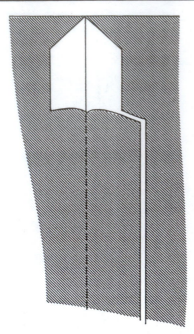

Fig. 17.2   Reducing bulk in seams that meet at zipper opening

A 1 inch (2.5 cm) seam allowance is recommended for lapped applications and a 1½ inch (3.8 cm) extended facing for the fly front application. If the seam allowance was not widened at the time the garment was cut, it can be extended through the addition of strips of seam tape sewn along the edges of the seams (Fig. 17.3).

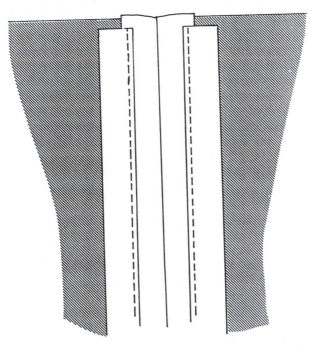

Fig. 17.3   Extending seam allowances in placket opening by adding tape

5. Zippers can be shortened, if they are not the appropriate length for the garment opening, by hand stitching several times across the zipper teeth (Fig. 17.4). The excess zipper is trimmed away to about ¾ inch (1.9 cm) below the stitching.

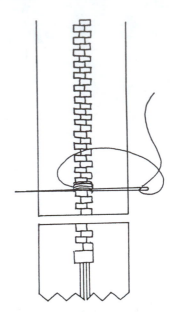

Fig. 17.4   Shortening zippers

6. Finish the seam of the zipper placket in an appropriate way *before* installing the zipper.

7. The zipper is easier to install in a flat piece of fabric; therefore, when possible, the zipper should be applied before that unit is stitched to other units of the garment. For example, the zipper can be applied to the center front of pants before the back is attached.

8. If the zipper will be placed in a bias seam, stay stitch the zipper opening about ⅛ inch (3 mm) from the seam line and within the seam allowance.

9. Attach the appropriate zipper foot to the machine. Adjust the conventional zipper foot to the left or right of the needle so that the toe of the foot is away from the teeth of the zipper and the edge of the foot is directly in line with the needle on the machine. Adjust the invisible zipper foot so that the needle is directly in line with the center of the foot.

10. Decide on the overlap and underlap position for the lapped or fly front style zipper placket.

   a. Side seam placket: the underlap is the garment back, the overlap is garment front. The zipper is typically placed on the left side of the body.

   b. Center front seam placket: the overlap can be either left or right. Typically the overlap is on the left front for menswear, but can be on either side for womenswear.

   c. Center back seam placket: The overlap is on the garment left back and the underlap is on the garment right back.

Lapped Application

Closed Seam Method

In the closed seam method, the placket opening is machine basted closed *before* installing the zipper.

To insert a lapped zipper using the closed seam method:

1. Stitch the portion of the zipper seam below the placket opening using a regular stitch length, backstitching at both ends to secure the seam. Machine *baste* the placket opening (Fig. 17.5). Finish the edges of the seam in an appropriate manner, and press the seam open.

2. Attach the zipper foot to the machine and adjust so that the foot is to the right side of the needle.

3. Turn the garment inside out, and extend only the *underlap* seam allowance.

4. Open zipper and place it face down on the opened seam with the teeth/coils lying close to the basted seam line and the bottom of the zipper stop at the end of the placket opening (Fig. 17.6). Pin or baste the zipper tape to the seam allowance.

5. Machine stitch the zipper tape to the seam allowance, starting at the bottom of the zipper tape and stitching to the top (Fig. 17.7). This stitching should be placed close to the teeth or coils of the zipper.

6. Close the zipper and turn face up. Move the zipper foot to the left side of the needle.

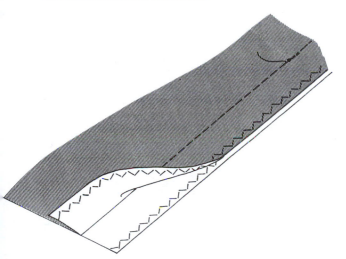

Fig. 17.5 Machine basting the placket seam closed: closed seam method

7. Fold the fabric close to the teeth/coil of the zipper and stitch *close* to the fold (Fig. 17.8). This stitching extends from the lower end of the zipper tape to the upper end, backstitching at both ends.

8. Spread the garment so that the placket area is flat. Turn the zipper tape face down over the free seam allowance (Fig. 17.9), forming a pleat on the *underlap seam allowance* at the lower end of the zipper. The pleat allows the overlap to be positioned such that it covers the stitching on the under-

lap. Turn the zipper pull tab up and pin the zipper tape to the garment at each end.

9. Turn the garment right side up, keeping the zipper against the seam allowances. Smooth the garment away from the basted seam line. Hand or pin baste along what will be the topstitching line for the overlap (Fig. 17.10). The basting line should be about ½ inch (1.3 cm) from the seam line and parallel to it. A strip of ½ inch (1.3 cm) transparent tape can be placed along the seam line and used as a stitching guide if the tape does not mar the fabric surface. The stitching line may be marked with a ruler and chalk or washable marking pen.

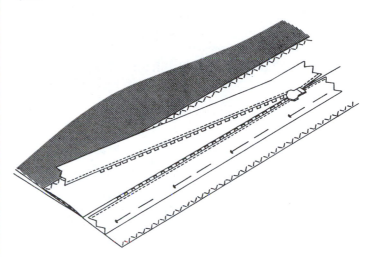

Fig. 17.6 Placement of zipper for stitching underlap: closed seam method

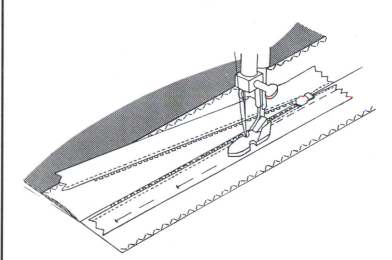

Fig. 17.7 Stitching zipper to underlap: closed seam method

10. Shift the position of the zipper foot to the right side of the needle.

11. Starting at the bottom of the zipper just below the zipper stop, stitch at right angles to the seam line across the end for about ½ inch (1.3 cm). Keeping the needle in the fabric, raise the presser foot and pivot the garment to form a

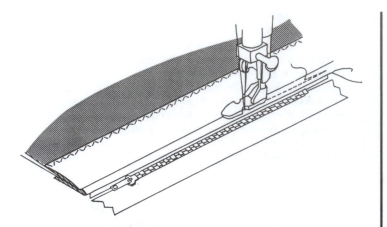

Fig. 17.8 Second stitching on underlap of zipper: closed seam method

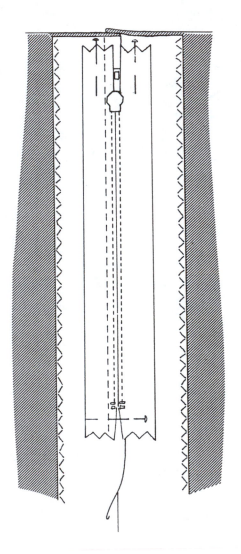

Fig. 17.9 Placement of zipper for overlap: closed seam method

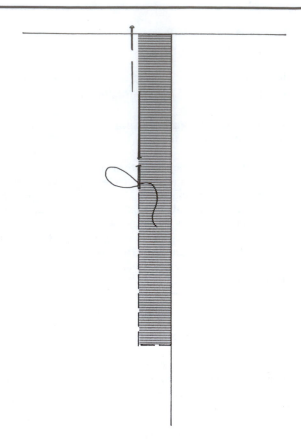

Fig. 17.10 Basting stitching line for overlap: closed seam method

square corner. Stitch parallel to the seam line to within 2 inches (5 cm) of the top. Stop with the needle in the fabric. Lift the presser foot and slide the pull tab down for about 3 inches (7.5 cm). Be sure there is a pin holding the top of the zipper tape in place. Lower the presser foot and stitch to the top of the zipper tape, backstitching to secure the threads. The threads at the lower end should be pulled to the inside and tied. Backstitching is not appropriate on the lower end of the zipper where the stitching would show in the finished garment.

12. The stitching for the overlap must be straight; it is the only stitching on this zipper application that shows on the outside of the finished garment.

13. Remove the machine basting from step 1 and carefully press the zipper area. A press cloth will be necessary when pressing on the right side or when pressing over the zipper coils. The coils often are made of a synthetic material that melts at a relatively low temperature.

Open Seam Method

In the open seam method, the placket opening is not stitched prior to installing the zipper. This method can be used for any lapped zipper application, but it is recommended when applying a lapped zipper to an opening that has been finished with a fitted facing prior to putting in the zipper (see Facings, Chapter 15).

To insert a lapped zipper using the open seam method:

1. Stitch the portion of the zipper seam below the placket opening, using a regular stitch length, backstitching at both ends to secure the seam. Press the seam open and finish the seam edges in an appropriate manner.

2. Turn under the seam allowance on the *overlap* side on the *seam line* and pin or baste in place (a in Fig. 17.11).

3. Turn under the seam allowance on the *underlap* side *⅛ inch (3 mm) into the seam allowance from the seam line,* forming a tuck at the bottom of the placket opening that extends for 1 inch (2.5 cm) past the bottom of the placket opening (b in Fig. 17.11). Pin or baste in place. The ⅛ inch (3 mm) extension on the underlap is needed so that the stitching and the zipper will be hidden under the overlap.

4. Press both sides, removing pins while pressing to avoid pressing in pin marks.

5. Place the tape of the closed zipper right side up beneath the underlap fold of the garment and adjust so that the fold is exactly 1/16 inch (1.5 mm) from the zipper teeth and the zipper stop is at the end of the placket opening (Fig. 17.12). Pin or baste in place.

6. If a fitted facing has been attached to the garment upper edge, curve the ends of the zipper tape away from the opening so that they will be covered by the facing when it is folded down over the completed zipper (see Fig. 15.18). Trim any tape that extends beyond the garment edge.

7. Attach the zipper foot and adjust the foot to the right of the needle.

8. Starting at the top of the zipper, stitch the entire length of the zipper tape, close to the fold; backstitch at both ends (Fig. 17.13).

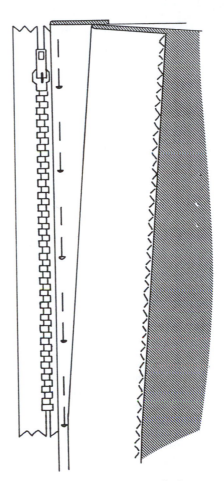

Fig. 17.12 Pinning zipper to underlap: open seam method

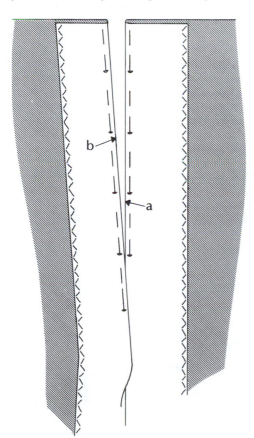

Fig. 17.11 Turning under seam allowances for lapped zipper: open seam method

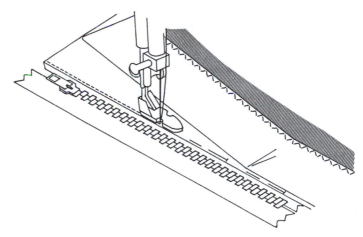

Fig. 17.13 Stitching underlap: open seam method

9. Position the garment right side up.

10. Starting at the upper end of the zipper, pin the overlap placket fold to the underlap side. The fold should extend about ⅛ inch (3 mm) beyond the zipper, covering the zipper and the machine stitching of the underlap. Place pins parallel to the folded edge (Fig. 17.14).

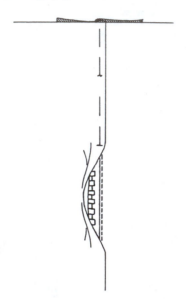

Fig. 17.14   Pinning overlap: open seam method

11. To mark the machine stitching line and to hold the fabric in position, pin or hand baste just below the zipper stop across the end of the placket and parallel to the seam line the full length of the placket. Remove the pins along the placket fold. Open the zipper.

12. Adjust the zipper foot to the left side of the needle.

13. Using the ½ inch (1.3 cm) marking on the throat plate as a guide, machine stitch from the top of the zipper to within 1 inch (2.5 cm) of the bottom of the placket opening (Fig. 17.15). Leaving the needle in the fabric, lift the presser foot

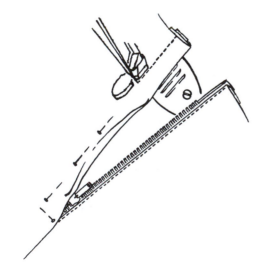

Fig. 17.15   Stitching the overlap: open seam method

and close the zipper for about 2 inches (5 cm). Lower the presser foot and stitch to a point even with the end of the placket opening. Leave the needle in the fabric; raise the presser foot; pivot garment to form a square corner and stitch across the placket lap to the seam line. Pull the threads at the end of the zipper to the inside and fasten securely.

14. Carefully press the zipper area. A press cloth will be necessary when pressing on the right side or when pressing over the zipper coils, because the coils often are made of a synthetic material which melts at a relatively low temperature.

Centered or Slot Seam Application

On the centered/slot seam zipper placket, two rows of topstitching are visible on the outside of the garment and the zipper is centered beneath the seam. This method is used when a balanced or symmetrical opening is desired. The two rows of stitching are placed about ¼ inch (6 mm) from the seam line and must be parallel to the seam. It is often difficult to keep the zipper teeth and pull tab concealed when using this method.

Closed Seam Method

To insert a centered/slot seam zipper
using the closed seam method:

1. Stitch the seam below the placket opening, using a regular stitch length, backstitching at both ends. Machine baste the placket opening closed. Finish the seam edges in an appropriate way and press the seam open.

2. Attach the zipper foot to the machine and adjust to the right of the needle.

3. Turn the garment inside out, and extend only the right hand seam allowance.

4. With the garment wrong side up, open the zipper and place it face down on the opened seam with the teeth/coils lying along the basted seam line and the bottom of the zipper stop at the end of the placket opening (Fig. 17.16). Pin or baste the zipper tape to the seam allowance.

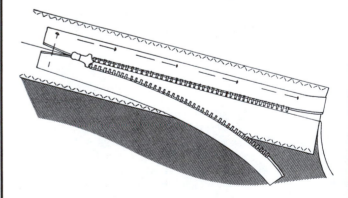

Fig. 17.16   Placement of zipper to right seam allowance: centered zipper

5. Machine stitch the zipper to the seam allowance, starting at the bottom of the zipper tape and stitching to the top (Fig. 17.17). This stitching should follow the stitching guide on the zipper, which is about in the center of the tape.

6. Spread the garment so that the placket area lies flat. Turn the zipper face down over the other seam allowance. Turn the zipper tab up and pin at each end (Fig. 17.18).

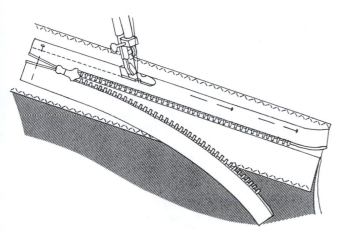

Fig. 17.17   Stitching zipper to right seam allowance: centered zipper

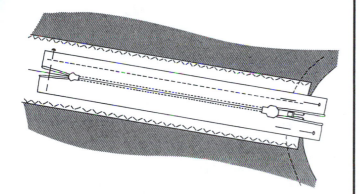

Fig. 17.18   Pinning zipper for final stitching: centered zipper

7. Turn the garment right side up, keeping the face of the zipper against the seam allowances. Smooth the garment in the placket area. Starting at the lower end of the zipper and at the center seam, hand baste the zipper to the garment through the seam allowance in preparation for the final stitching (Fig. 17.19). Both sides of the zipper are hand basted in this way. A strip of ½ inch (1.3 cm) wide transparent tape can be centered over the seam line and used as a stitching guide if the tape does not mar the fabric surface.

8. The final stitching can be done in either of two ways:
    a. The stitching can start at the seam line at the lower end of the zipper and proceed across the end and then up one side; the stitching for the second side also starts at the seam line at the lower end of the zipper and proceeds up the other side (Fig. 17.20). The rows of stitching are about ¼ inch (6

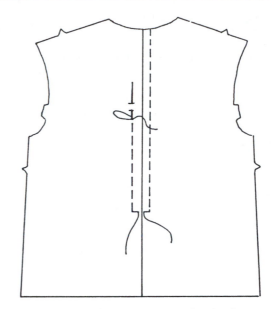

Fig. 17.19   Hand basting zipper for final stitching: centered zipper

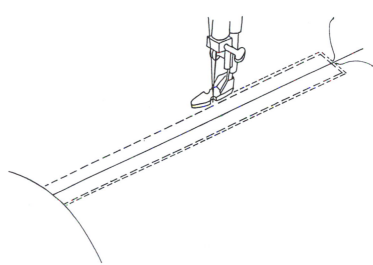

Fig. 17.20   Stitching zipper, beginning at center seam: centered zipper

mm) from the seam line. The threads at the beginning of each row of stitching would need to be pulled to the back and tied.
    b. The stitching can start at the top of the zipper, with the stitching line being continuous to the top of the zipper on the other side. This stitching method has a tendency to push the fabric in front of the presser foot, resulting in a rippled appearance to the placket.

9. Remove all basting. Carefully press the zipper area. A press cloth will be necessary when pressing on the right side or when pressing over the zipper coils, because the coils often are made of a synthetic material that melts at a relatively low temperature.

Open Seam Method

To insert the centered/slot seam zipper using the open seam method:

1. Stitch the seam below the placket opening using a regular stitch length, backstitching at both ends. Finish the seam edges in an appropriate way and press the seam open. Turn under and press the seam allowances on both sides of the placket on the stitching line.

2. Place the opened zipper under the garment opening, with the coils or teeth on each side just covered by the folds of the seam allowances.

3. Hand baste the zipper in this position.

4. Close the zipper to be sure that the folds of the seam come together and cover the zipper without overlapping.

5. Stitch the zipper (Fig. 17.21) using either of the methods described previously.

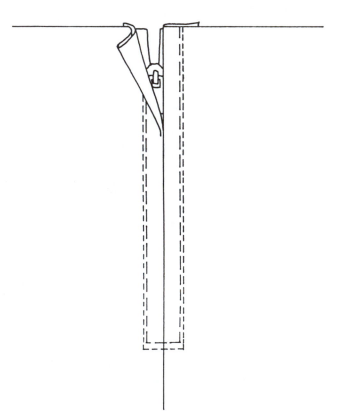

Fig. 17.21   Stitching zipper, open seam method: centered zipper

Fly Front Zipper

The fly front zipper placket is designed with the facing as a part of the garment or with separate facings finishing the placket edges. If facings are cut in one piece with the garment, zipper insertion into the fly front placket is simpler and less bulky than when placket facings are cut separately. A placket with separate facings can be changed to a placket with an extended facing by placing the fly facing piece on the center front of the garment pattern matching the *stitching lines* (Fig. 17.22). The facing is cut in one piece with the garment, eliminating the placket facing seam allowance.

The fly, as illustrated here, has the lap on the left side of the garment; in some designs, the lap is on the right. Reversing the directions will accommodate that type of fly front zipper. These directions are written for pants. Adapt as needed for a skirt.

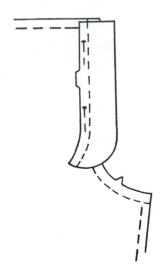

Fig. 17.22   Changing pattern for an attached facing

A special trouser zipper sometimes is used with the fly front application. If it is not appropriate, a conventional zipper can be used. As the fly front often is shorter than other zipper plackets, the zipper may need to be shortened. The shortening occurs at the *top* of the zipper and will be demonstrated as a part of the instructions for constructing this type of zipper.

To insert a fly front zipper:

1. Mark the fold and stitching lines for the fly front zipper on the inside of the appropriate garment pieces (a in Fig. 17.23). Using hand basting, transfer the topstitching line to the outside of the garment on the side with the lap.

2. Interface the fly facing to the fold line if additional body is desired. A fusible interfacing works well for this purpose.

3. Finish the outer edge of the facings in a manner appropriate for the fabric.

4. Pin the front crotch seam with right sides together.

5. Machine stitch front crotch seam to the dot marking the bottom of the zipper placket, starting the stitching 1½ inches (3.8 cm) from the inseam (b in Fig. 17.23). Double stitch this seam for reinforcement (c in Fig. 17.23). On a skirt stitch the entire seam below the zipper placket using a regular stitch length, backstitching at both ends.

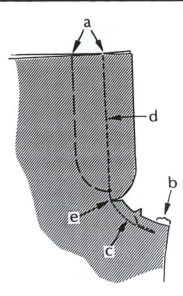

Fig. 17.23   Preparing fly front zipper placket
opening

6. Close the zipper opening with machine basting following the center front seam markings (d in Fig. 17.23).

7. Clip through the seam allowances to the stitching at the bottom of the facing (e in Fig. 17.23). Press the seam open above the clip. On a skirt press the seam open below the zipper placket.

8. Lay the garment wrong side up so that only the *underlap facing* is extended. Place the closed zipper face down on the extended facing and pin so that the *left* edge of the *zipper tape* is along the center front seam and the bottom of the zipper stop is at the bottom of the placket opening (Fig. 17.24). Pin in place.

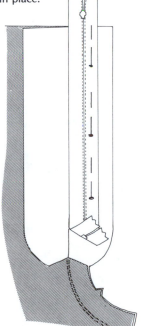

Fig. 17.24   Positioning zipper to facing for
underlap: fly front zipper

9. Attach the zipper foot and adjust to the right of the needle.

10. Stitch the zipper to the facing, stitching one line close to the zipper teeth and a second line close to the edge of the zipper tape (Fig. 17.25). The stitching goes from top to bottom.

11. Refold the garment so that only the overlap facing is extended. Pull the zipper onto the facing as far as it will go and still remain flat. The free edge of the zipper tape will be on the left facing and a pleat will form at the bottom of the placket (a in Fig. 17.26).

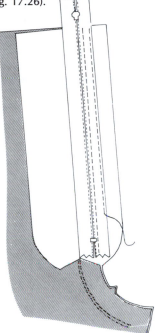

Fig. 17.25   Stitching zipper to underlap facing:
fly front zipper

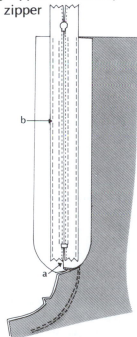

Fig. 17.26   Stitching zipper to overlap facing:
fly front zipper

12. Adjust the zipper foot to the left of the needle.

13. Stitch the zipper to the facing as in step 10 (*b* in Fig. 17.26).

14. Press the placket lightly from the right side, using a press cloth.

15. Topstitch the overlap from the outside, following the marked stitching lines from the pattern (Fig. 17.27). This

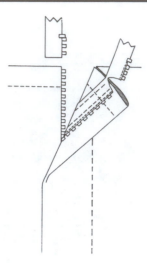

Fig. 17.28 Shortening zipper to match garment edge

Fly Shield

The fly shield sometimes is attached to the underlap side of a fly front zipper to provide a finish on the inside of the garment. The fly shield usually is cut from the fashion fabric; the fly shield facing can be cut from the fashion fabric or a lining-weight fabric, depending on the weight of the fashion fabric.

To make and attach a fly shield:

1. With right sides together stitch the fly shield to its facing along the curved edge. Layer/grade the seam, notch the curve, and understitch (Fig. 17.29). Turn the shield right side out and press.

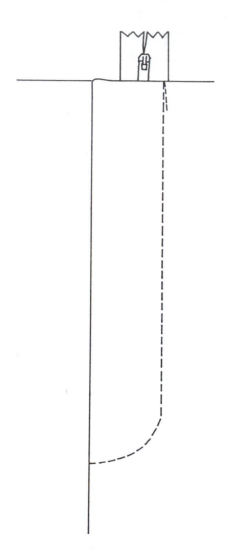

Fig. 17.27 Final stitching for fly front zipper

stitching may not go through the zipper tape but must go through the overlap facing. The threads at the lower end of the zipper are pulled to the inside and tied; the threads at the top of the zipper can be backstitched.

16. Remove the machine basting holding the placket closed and open the zipper.

17. Stitch the zipper tape to the waistline seam on both sides to prevent the pull tab from coming off. Trim the zipper even with the upper edge of the garment (Fig. 17.28). To bar tack at the bottom of the zipper, see step 5 under Fly Shield.

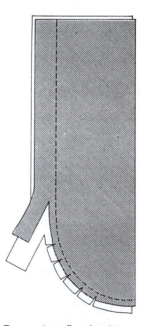

Fig. 17.29 Preparing fly shield

2. Finish the raw edge of the shield in a manner appropriate for the fabric.

3. Place the shield right side up beneath the underlap of the zipper.

4. Stitch through all thicknesses close to the fold of the underlap using the zipper foot (a in Fig. 17.30).

5. Close the zipper. With the fly shield in position underneath, bar tack at the lower end of the fly opening for additional reinforcement (b in Fig. 17.30).

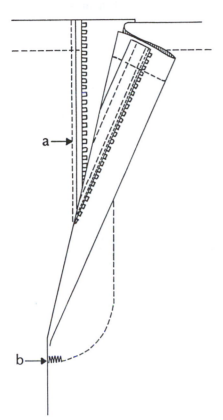

Fig. 17.30   Stitching fly shield to garment with bar tack at end of placket opening

Hand Application of a Zipper

A zipper may be totally or partially hand stitched into the placket. Generally, the hand stitching is used as a substitute only for that machine stitching that would show on the outside of the finished garment when the zipper is closed. The zipper tape may be machine stitched to the seam allowance if additional reinforcement is desired. For some delicate and fragile fabrics, all the sewing is done by hand. The pick stitch, a half backstitch, is used when installing a zipper by hand. When using regular sewing thread, a double thread is usually used; when using a heavier topstitching thread, a single thread is appropriate. Running the thread through beeswax before sewing will keep the thread from becoming knotted and tangled during construction.

To make the pick stitch:

1. Secure the thread to the underside of the zipper tape just below the bottom stop.

2. Bring the thread to the right side one or two yarns from the seam line at the lower end of the zipper.

3. Take a small stitch back toward the starting point, catching all layers of fabric and the zipper tape (Fig. 17.31). Bring the needle to the right side about ⅜ inch (1 cm) away from where it went into the fabric in preparation for the next stitch.

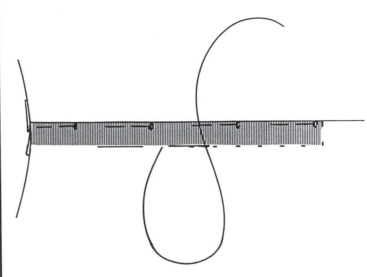

Fig. 17.31   Using the pick stitch to attach a lapped zipper

4. Place stitches about ⅜ inch (1 cm) apart. Pull thread securely at each stitch, but not so tight that they pucker the fabric.

5. Tape or hand basting can be used as a guide for straight stitching.

6. Repeat the stitch the entire length of the placket and fasten threads securely.

Exposed Zipper

The exposed zipper uses either a conventional zipper or a heavier, more decorative zipper, and is installed in an area where there is no seam or as a separating zipper in the center front of a garment. While it can be used in woven fabrics, it is found most often in knits. If the exposed zipper extends into a neck band or collar, those garment edges are finished before the zipper is installed (Fig. 17.32).

To insert an exposed zipper:

1. Mark the zipper opening on the outside of the garment, with a line of basting or other appropriate marking, the length of the zipper from the top to the bottom stop (a in Fig. 17.33).

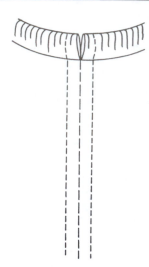

Fig. 17.32   Neckline edge finished before installing an exposed zipper

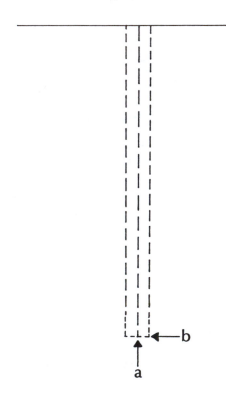

Fig. 17.33   Marking opening for exposed zipper

2. The lower end of the opening can be stabilized by applying a small piece of fusible interfacing to the wrong side of the fabric. In some fabrics it is desirable to stabilize the entire length of the opening with a lightweight, nonfusible, nonwoven interfacing.

3. Staystitch the zipper opening; shortening the stitches at the bottom for reinforcement (b in Fig. 17.33). The opening is usually ¼–⅜ inch (6–10 cm) wide, but may vary with the size of zipper teeth and personal preference as to the amount of zipper tape to be exposed.

4. Attach the zipper foot and adjust to the right of the needle.

5. Place the zipper face down on the right side of the fabric with the bottom stop centered *below* the base of the staystitching. Stitch across the zipper tape the width of the staystitching, using a shorter than average stitch length (Fig. 17.34). Stitch the area two or three times for reinforcement.

6. Turn the garment wrong side up and cut between the staystitching from the top to within ¼ inch (6 mm) of the bottom and then diagonally to the corners (Fig. 17.35).

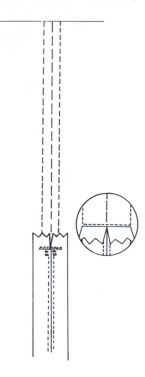

Fig. 17.34   Stitching zipper to lower end of opening: exposed zippers

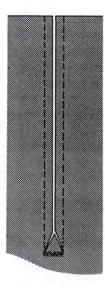

Fig. 17.35   Cutting opening: exposed zipper

7. Bring the top of the zipper to the garment edge. Pin the right side of the fabric to the right side of the zipper tape, placing the staystitching along the edge of the zipper teeth/coils. Place pins parallel to and directly on the staystitching so the right side of the placket can be checked for stitching accuracy (Fig. 17.36).

8. Stitch the fabric to the tape (from the bottom to the top) a uniform distance from the zipper teeth or coils (Fig. 17.37). Both sides are stitched in the same manner.

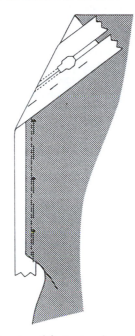

Fig. 17.36   Pinning fabric to zipper tape: exposed zipper

Fig. 17.37   Stitching garment to zipper tape: exposed zipper

9. Turn under the top of the zipper tape and secure by hand. Press.

10. The zipper placket may be topstitched, if desired.

An exposed zipper opening can be faced before the zipper is applied. This method is recommended for fabrics where extra reinforcement is needed to keep the opening from stretching or raveling.

To face an opening for an exposed zipper:

1. Cut a strip of firmly woven lightweight fabric 3 inches (7.5 cm) wide and 2 inches (5 cm) longer than the zipper opening.

2. Place the facing on the garment right sides together and over the marked zipper opening.

3. Stitch the facing to the garment following the marked lines from the garment and using a shorter-than-average stitch length at the bottom for reinforcement when cutting into the corners (Fig. 17.38).

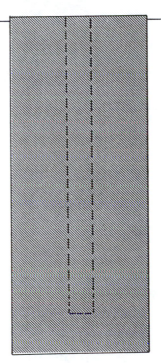

Fig. 17.38   Joining facing to garment: exposed zipper

4. Cut the opening to within ¼ inch (6 mm) of the bottom and then diagonally to the corners (Fig. 17.39). The seam can be understitched to help in rolling the seam toward the facing.

5. Press the facing to the wrong side.

6. Place the zipper under the opening with the folded edges next to the teeth or coils of the zipper.

7. Topstitch the garment close to the folded edge to hold the zipper in place (Fig. 17.40). If topstitching is not desired, the zipper could be slip stitched by hand or machine stitched by folding back the fashion fabric and stitching close to the seam joining the facing.

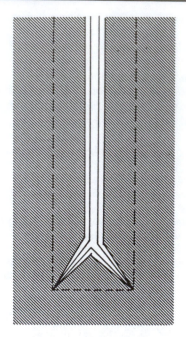

Fig. 17.39   Cutting facing: exposed zipper

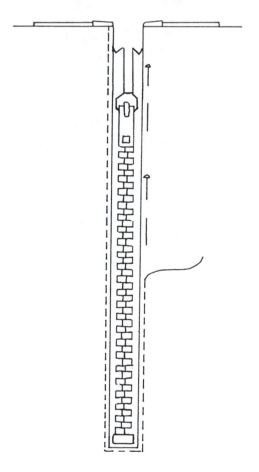

Fig. 17.40   Topstitching zipper to opening: exposed zipper

Invisible Zipper

Invisible zippers are a special type of zipper inserted in a garment in a way so that no stitching is visible on the outside. When installed, the zipper looks like a plain seam; only the pull tab is visible. A special zipper foot is required to install the invisible zipper, and the entire seam in which the zipper is located is left open until after the zipper is inserted.

To insert an invisible zipper:

1. Press the fold of the zipper coil flat with fingers or with the iron so that only the tape is visible.

2. Leave the complete length of the garment seam open until after the zipper is inserted. Finish the edges of the seam in an appropriate manner.

3. Open the zipper and place face down on the right side of the fabric. The *right* zipper tape is placed to the *right* garment section, *right* sides together. Place the top of the zipper stop 1 inch (2.5 cm) from the raw edge. This placement provides space for a fastener above the zipper pull tab. Place the teeth (or coil) on the seam line with the tape into the seam allowance. Pin in place with the pins close to the edge of the zipper tape (Fig. 17.41).

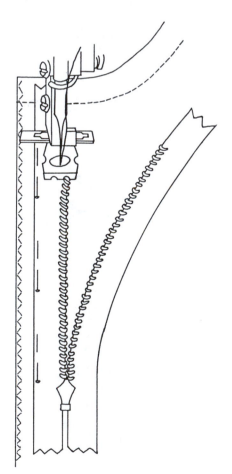

Fig. 17.41   Placement of zipper for first row of stitching: invisible zipper

4. Align the special zipper foot over the zipper. The machine needle should be centered in the hole of the zipper foot and the coil of the zipper should run through the groove to the right of the needle (Fig. 17.41).

5. Stitch the zipper from the top of the zipper tape to the pull tab, securing threads on both ends with backstitching. This stitching will not extend to the bottom of the zipper tape.

6. Close the zipper. Pin the zipper tape to the second seam allowance so that the zipper is the same distance from the upper edge as on the previous right side.

7. Open the zipper; stitch the second side using the left groove in the zipper foot (Fig. 17.42).

8. Close the zipper. Pin the seam below the zipper, placing the top pin directly below the stitching used to secure the zipper. Check the placement of the pin on both sides so that the seam lines up directly below the zipper. Also check the pin placement from the right side to be sure that the seam is smooth and in proper alignment.

9. Adjust the zipper foot to the left of the needle and use like a traditional zipper or cording foot. Pull the tail of the zipper away from the seam and stitch the seam, starting the first stitch exactly at the same point as the stitching at the bottom of the zipper (Fig. 17.43). Do not backstitch. Stitch to the bottom of the garment. Tie threads at the base of the zipper. Press the seam open below the zipper.

10. Tack the lower ends of the zipper tape to the *seam allowance* by hand or by machine (Fig. 17.44).

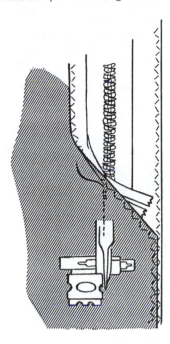

Fig. 17.43 Stitching garment seam below invisible zipper

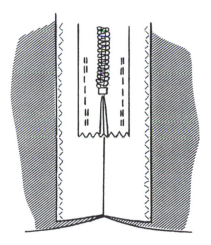

Fig. 17.44 Stitching lower ends of zipper tape to seam allowances

Fitted Facing for the Invisible Zipper

If the top of an invisible zipper is finished with a fitted facing, certain procedures can be followed to reduce the bulk that can be created at the garment edge.

To finish a garment edge with a facing after inserting an invisible zipper:

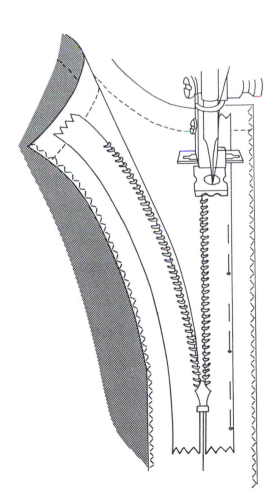

Fig. 17.42 Stitching second side of invisible zipper

1. Stitch garment and facing shoulder seams. Press seams open. Trim the *facing* seam allowances to 1/4 inch (6 mm).

2. Finish the outer edge of the facing with an appropriate method.

3. Trim ⅝ inch (1.6 cm) from the end seam allowances at the *center back edges* of the facing.

4. Pin the right sides of the facing and the garment together at the center or *zipper edges only*. Do not try to align neck edges or shoulder seams at this time. Stitch ½ inch (1.3 cm) from the pinned edge through the facing, zipper tape, and the garment seam allowances (a in Fig. 17.45).

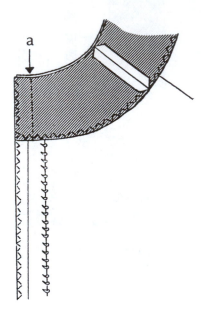

Fig. 17.45   Stitching end of facing to garment at opening for invisible zipper

5. With right sides together pin the neck edges of the facing and the garment together, matching shoulder seams and notches. The zipper seam allowance should fold to the outside forming a fold along the zipper stitching line. Stitch the facing to the garment at the upper edge (Fig. 17.46).

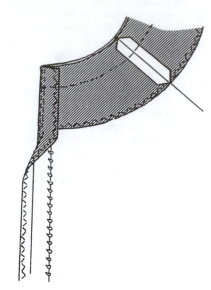

Fig. 17.46   Facing stitched to garment at neck edge

6. Trim corners. Layer/grade, clip, and understitch the seam allowances. Turn facing to the wrong side and press.

7. Fasten facing to the shoulder seams.

8. Attach an extended snap or hook and eye above the zipper to hold the center back edges together (see Chapter 18).

18 Buttonholes and Other Closures

Buttons and buttonholes serve both a practical and a decorative function. Before making buttonholes, a number of questions need to be asked.

—Are machine-made buttonholes the best choice, or should hand-stitched or bound buttonholes be considered?

—Are the buttonholes as marked on the pattern in the appropriate position for the wearer and for the design of the garment?

—What length do the buttonholes need to be?

—When in the construction of the garment should the buttonholes be made?

Buttonholes

Preliminary Preparation

The *machine-made buttonhole* (Fig. 18.1) is the most commonly used. It requires the use of a machine with a built-in buttonhole stitch or an attachment that can be placed on the machine for this purpose. Machine-made buttonholes are appropriate for most all fabrics except those that might be damaged by the zigzag motion of the buttonhole stitch on the machine. It is a durable buttonhole and works well in many different types of garments.

The *hand-stitched buttonhole* (Fig. 18.2) is reserved for use on fine fabrics and for tailored suits or coats. It is made over a slit of fabric using the buttonhole stitch. In

Fig. 18.1 Machine-made buttonholes: square end, round end, and keyhole

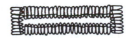

Fig. 18.2 Hand-stitched buttonhole

some cases, the hand-stitched buttonhole is made over a machine-made buttonhole for greater durability.

Bound buttonholes (Fig. 18.3) (also called fabric buttonholes) have strips of fabric forming the welts for the buttonhole. While the fabric used most often to make the welts for the buttonholes is self-fabric, sometimes a contrasting fabric is used for decorative or functional purposes. For example, in fabrics such as fake furs, leather or a leatherlike fabric often is used to form the welts of the bound buttonhole. Bound buttonholes are used for finely tailored garments; they are not recommended for use on sheer and lightweight fabrics nor for very small buttons. As a general rule, bound buttonholes are not used for buttons smaller than ½ inch (1.3 cm).

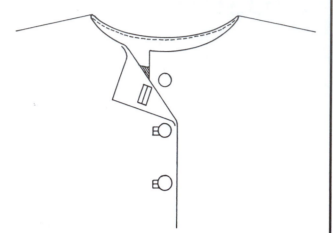

Fig. 18.3   Bound buttonholes

Bound buttonholes are made early in the assembly process; machine-made or hand-stitched buttonholes are among the last details to be completed unless the garment style has a concealed button opening, in which case the buttonholes are made very early in the assembly process. Both types of buttonholes require the use of interfacing to stabilize the area where the buttonhole will be placed. When making a bound buttonhole, the interfacing needs to be placed on the garment piece where the buttonhole will be made. For machine-made or hand-stitched buttonholes, the interfacing is usually placed on the facing, but can be on either the garment section or the facing.

Buttonholes can be placed in a horizontal, vertical, or diagonal direction on the fabric. Horizontal and vertical buttonholes, because they are on the straight grain of the fabric, are used more often than diagonal. Horizontal buttonholes are recommended in areas of strain because the button pulls against the end of the buttonhole and is more likely to stay closed than the vertical buttonhole, which pulls the button against the side of the buttonhole and has a tendency to pop open under strain.

Buttonholes that are related to structural lines of the garment need to be placed in the same direction as the structural line. For example, buttonholes in front bands would be made vertical to follow the vertical lines of the band (a in Fig. 18.4); whereas, a buttonhole in a neckband collar is made in the horizontal direction to follow the horizontal line of the neckband (b in Fig. 18.4). Buttonholes for a front opening are placed on the right side

for women's garments and on the left for men's. In the back, generally buttonholes on women's garments are on the left.

For center front openings, horizontal buttonholes are 1/8 inch (3 mm) into the overlap or extension from the center front line, with most of the length of the buttonhole extending into the body of the garment (Fig. 18.5). Buttonholes are positioned in this way to allow for the thickness of the shank, so that buttons will be aligned exactly on center front when buttoned. Vertical buttonholes are placed directly on the center front line with the top of the buttonholes beginning 1/8 inch (3 mm) above the center of the button (Fig. 18.6).

Buttonholes need to be placed far enough from the edge so that, when the button is in position, all of the button lies within the garment piece. As a minimum, the center of the button should be located a distance equal to the diameter of the button from the edge (a in Fig. 18.7). This applies to buttons and garment edges regard-

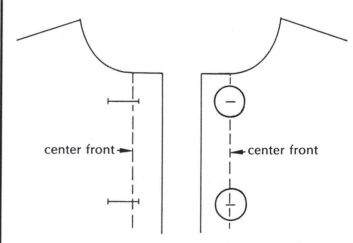

Fig. 18.4   Buttonhole placement related to structural lines of the garment

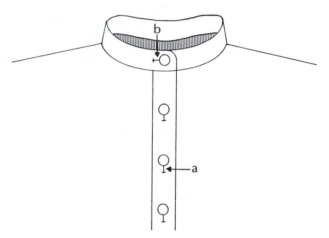

Fig. 18.5   Horizontal buttonhole location in relation to center front

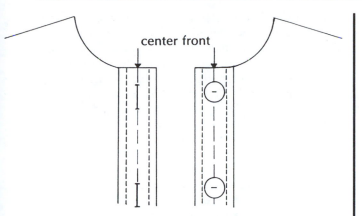

Fig. 18.6   Vertical buttonhole location in relation to center front

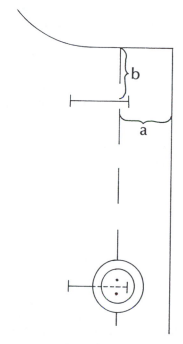

Fig. 18.7   Position of button and buttonhole in relation to finished garment edges

less of their location—center front or center back openings, cuffs, and waistbands. When using a commercial pattern, the position of the buttonholes cannot be shifted to the left or right without affecting the circumference of the garment. It is best to buy the size button recommended on the pattern. If a larger button has been selected and more overlap or extension is needed, the adjustment should be made at the seam for the opening or along the fold line of the garment edge.

The top buttonhole of a front opening needs to be placed far enough from the neckline edge, too, so that all of the button lies within the garment when the garment is closed. Again, as a minimum, the center of the top button should be located a distance equal to the

diameter of the button from the finished neckline edge (*b* in Fig. 18.7).

If the button opening is intersected by a waistline seam with a belt, the buttonholes need to be spaced so that they are an equal distance on either side of the belt (Fig. 18.8). The distance between the belt and the button usually is equal to the distance between buttons.

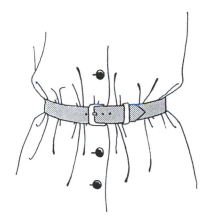

Fig. 18.8   Placement of buttonholes in relation to belt

Buttonholes need to be placed to absorb the strain in a garment. Women should position a buttonhole at the fullest part of the bust, especially for fitted garments, to insure that the garment does not gap open at that spot. This may require placing the buttonholes in a different location on the garment than that recommended on the pattern. If the placement of one buttonhole is changed, the distance between all buttonholes will probably be changed so that the buttonholes remain evenly spaced on the garment.

Since buttonholes need to be adjusted to the wearer, buttonhole placements from the pattern should be used only as a guide; actual placement comes by putting the garment on the wearer and determining the most appropriate location. If the length of a garment piece containing buttonholes has been changed, the location of the buttonholes from the pattern cannot be used.

Some styles of shirts, blouses, or tops that tuck into pants or skirts contain buttons and buttonholes. Sometimes, the buttons and buttonholes do not go all the way to the bottom of the shirt; in other cases they do and a flat button may be used below waist level even though a thicker, more decorative button is used elsewhere.

Sometimes, too, buttonholes are made but not cut, and the button is stitched on top. A patch of hook-and-loop tape is placed under the buttonhole and serves as the closing for the garment (Fig. 18.9). This technique is used especially on garments worn by people with limited finger dexterity, where manipulation of buttons and buttonholes, especially small ones, would be a challenge.

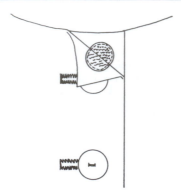

Fig. 18.9   Hook-and-loop tape used to secure a garment opening

The bottom button generally is placed above the hem in a garment. Rarely, if ever, is a buttonhole placed in the hem. For shirts, blouses, or shirtwaist dresses, the bottom button should be the same distance (or a greater distance) from the hemline as the space between buttons. Proportion looks strange if this space is shorter than the space between other buttons.

Buttonholes can be corded for a raised effect. For machine-made or hand-stitched buttonholes, the buttonholes are made over a cord, such as a piece of buttonhole twist thread. Some machines have an attachment or small hole on the buttonhole foot to hold the cording in place as the machine makes the buttonhole stitch over it. Cording can be added to the welts of a bound buttonhole; commercial cording or several strands of yarn can be used for this purpose.

Marking Buttonhole Location

The placement of the buttonholes needs to be determined and marked on the outside of the garment. This can be done with pins, hand basting, or a washable marking pen.

The length of the buttonhole opening equals the length of the button plus its thickness. Thickness or height is of little importance for flat buttons but is a major consideration for rounded ones, such as ball buttons.

Regardless of the type of buttonhole being made, a trial buttonhole should be constructed through the same number of layers of fashion fabric plus the interfacing to check for size and technique. Buttonholes are made only after the appropriate buttons have been purchased and are on hand to use when determining size of buttonhole.

Machine-made Buttonholes

Machine-made buttonholes are made by an adjustment of the zigzag setting on the machine as specified in the instruction manual or by the use of a buttonhole attachment placed on the machine. More automated machines make buttonholes by using the built-in zigzag function and do not require the pivoting of the garment at one end of the buttonhole. Buttonholes made on less automated machines require manually adjusting the zigzag setting and turning the fabric at the desired end for each buttonhole. The ends of the buttonhole have a square "bar tack." The zigzag setting has the advantage of being able to make the buttonhole any length, not just those available with the buttonhole attachment. When making the sample buttonhole, the width of the stitch, the closeness of the stitches, the sewing machine thread tension, and the space between the rows of stitches need to be checked. Computerized sewing machines can be programmed to make a series of buttonholes of the exact same length without the use of an attachment. Attachments have the advantage of guiding the fabric while the buttonhole is being made and of making each buttonhole a uniform size. With the attachment the ends are rounded. Keyhole buttonholes or thread eyelets can also be made with the attachment.

After *all* the buttonholes have been made and checked for accuracy, the buttonholes are cut carefully using the sharp points of shears or scissors. Generally, buttonholes are cut from the center out; a pin across each end will guard against cutting through the end. The frayed threads from the center of the cut buttonhole need to be trimmed close to the machine stitching.

If the stitching for a buttonhole needs to be removed after being placed in the garment, a large needle or a seam ripper can be used and the stitches carefully taken out from the wrong side. This process must occur *before* the buttonhole is cut.

Hand-stitched Buttonholes

Hand-stitched buttonholes are used on fine fabrics, on tailored garments, and often with small buttons; they are not recommended for fabrics that fray readily. They are made late in the construction process and go through the outer fabric, the interfacing, and the facing. Often, they are made with a fan shape or keyhole at the end, closest to the garment opening, and a bar tack on the other end.

The thread used for making hand-stitched buttonholes depends on the fabric. A single thread is easier to handle than a double thread. A heavy-duty thread such as buttonhole twist or topstitching thread is appropriate; two or three strands of regular sewing thread can be used but require careful handling. Running the thread through beeswax before sewing helps to prevent tangling and knotting.

The buttonhole stitch has many uses besides making hand-stitched buttonholes, such as securing fasteners such as snaps or hooks and eyes. Occasionally, it is worked over the edge of a garment for decoration, when the stitch is called the blanket stitch. These stitches are often farther apart than the true buttonhole stitch.

To make a hand-stitched buttonhole:

1. After the garment is completed and the buttonhole locations have been determined, mark the buttonhole location on the outside of the garment, using a basting stitch or a washable marking pen (a in Fig. 18.10).

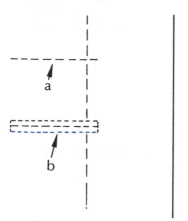

Fig. 18.10   Stitching a rectangle around marked buttonhole

2. Machine stitch a narrow rectangle ⅛ inch (3 mm) wide around the marked line, using a shorter-than-average stitch length (b in Fig. 18.10). Count the stitches at each end so that the width at the ends is the same. This stitching serves as a guide for the depth of the buttonhole stitches.

3. Cut the buttonhole exactly on grain with sharply pointed shears or scissors. If a series of buttonholes is being made, this cutting should occur for each at the time the actual hand stitches are to be done.

4. Use a single thread of buttonhole twist or topstitching thread (or two or three strands of regular sewing thread) long enough to complete the entire buttonhole, usually 36 inches (91.5 cm) is long enough for most buttonholes. Secure by inserting the needle into the upper side of the buttonhole between the machine stitches and the slash and take three or four running stitches toward the farthest end from the garment edge (Fig. 18.11). Backstitch at the end to fasten the thread securely.

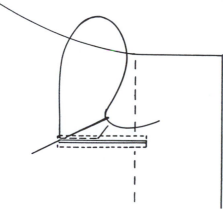

Fig. 18.11   Securing thread end to begin buttonhole stitch

5. For right-handed sewers, begin work on the buttonhole at the upper corner farthest from center front as illustrated. Work clockwise around the buttonhole. For left-handed sewers, begin work on the lower corner and work counterclockwise around the buttonhole.

6. Turn the garment upside down. Insert the needle into the slash and bring the point up through the fabric just outside the machine stitching line (Fig. 18.12).

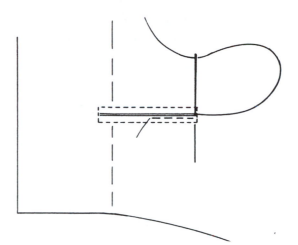

Fig. 18.12   Garment turned upside down for first stitch for hand-stitched buttonhole

7. Slip the thread under the eye end of the needle, circling the thread *counterclockwise*, and pass under the point of the needle (Fig. 18.13). For left-handed sewers the thread will circle the needle in a clockwise direction. Push the needle through the fabric and pull the thread away from the buttonhole at a right angle to the slash until a knot forms at the cut edge of the slash (Fig. 18.14). Pull the thread firmly but not tightly enough to cause puckering or drawing.

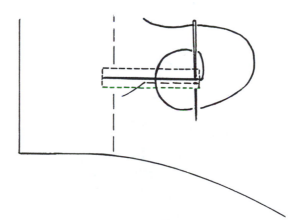

Fig. 18.13   Thread circling counterclockwise under needle for forming the buttonhole stitch

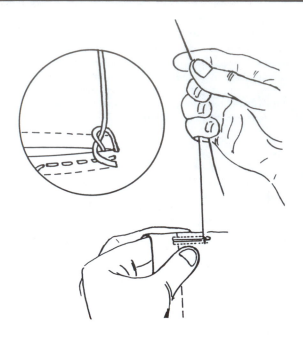

Fig. 18.14   Pulling knot into position against slash

8. For the second stitch, again insert the needle into the slash and bring the point through exactly in line with the first stitch. Leave enough distance between the stitches so that they lie parallel to each other in orderly rows and knots touch like beads along the edge of the slash (Fig. 18.15).

9. Working from right to left, make buttonhole stitches to the end of the slash nearest the overlap edge. Left-handed sewers will work left to right. At the end closest to the garment edge the stitches are spread farther apart to form a fan-shaped pattern (or keyhole, if desired). The stitches need to be kept the same depth as those along the edge. The knots will crowd a little, thus reinforcing the end of the buttonhole for the shank (Fig. 18.16). Turn the garment while proceeding around the end so that the needle will point down as it is inserted in the slash.

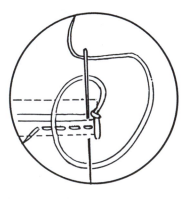

Fig. 18.15   Placing second stitch parallel to the first

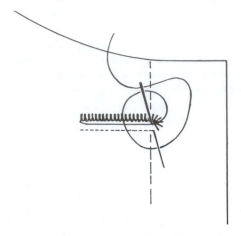

Fig. 18.16   Forming fan on end of buttonhole nearest fold

10. Continue along the other side of the buttonhole toward the bar end. The last stitch will end exactly opposite the first one.

11. Make the bar tack by taking two long stitches across the end in exactly the same position. The bar stitches start and stop in line with the buttonhole stitches and lie parallel to the stitches (Fig. 18.17).

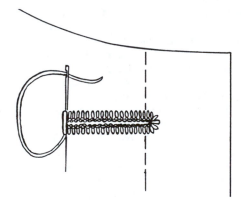

Fig. 18.17   Forming the bar tack

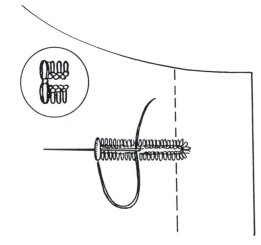

Fig. 18.18   Securing the bar tack

12. To secure the bar tack, take several stitches in the same place in the center of the stitching (Fig. 18.18).

13. Fasten the threads on the wrong side by running the needle under the completed stitches for ½ inch (1.3 cm). Backstitch to secure the thread.

Bound or Fabric Buttonholes

Bound buttonholes are made before the unit containing them is joined to other units. The area is interfaced before the buttonholes are made. When making bound buttonholes, the interfacing needs to be applied to the garment piece in which the buttonholes will be placed, not the facing.

Many methods are appropriate for making a bound buttonhole; the one chosen depends on the fabric and the skill of the sewer. Two methods are included in this chapter: (1) the five-line method and (2) the window opening method. The directions are given for horizontal buttonholes.

Making Bound Buttonholes

A separate piece of fabric is used to form the welts of the bound buttonhole. The fabric used for this purpose generally is cut on straight grain and from matching fabric. For interest and to avoid matching of designs, the fabric for the welts may be cut on the bias or on the crosswise grain. A different fabric can be used to avoid bulk and for interest. Accurately constructed fabric buttonholes have the following characteristics.

Right side of finished buttonhole:

- The buttonholes are in proper alignment.
- The buttonholes are all the same measured length.
- The finished width is in proportion to the length and is related to the fabric thickness.
- Both folds are the same width (one-half the total width of the buttonhole).
- The folds meet exactly at the center along the entire length of the buttonhole.
- The folds are exactly on a crosswise yarn matching the grain of the garment.
- The corners are square and held in place firmly.
- The buttonholes are the right length for the buttons.
- The buttonholes are well placed for a pleasing appearance.

Wrong side of buttonhole (to be checked before garment is faced):

- The buttonhole piece has been trimmed to within ½ inch (1.3 cm) of the opening.
- The triangular ends are machine stitched securely to the buttonhole piece.

Wrong side of finished buttonhole:

—The facing has been cut on the grainline, turned under, and neatly stitched around the buttonhole with no raw edges showing.
—The facing lies smoothly between buttonholes.
—The facing lies smoothly between the end of the buttonhole and the edge of the garment.
—The facing is not visible from the right side of the garment.

To mark horizontal buttonhole locations:

1. Hand or machine baste interfacing and garment layers together on the exact center line marking for the buttonhole (a in Fig. 18.19). This is the cutting line.

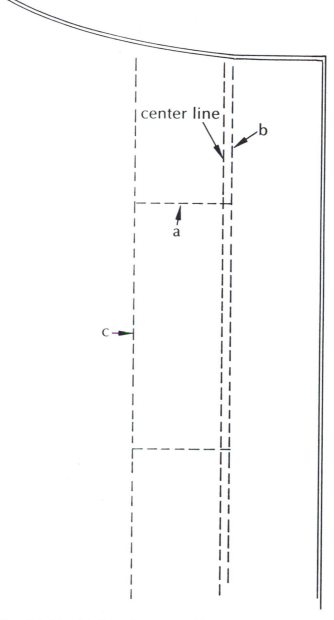

Fig. 18.19 Marking location of buttonholes on garment and interfacing

2. Baste two continuous vertical lines parallel to the center line on lengthwise grain to indicate the exact length of the buttonhole (*b* and *c* in Fig. 18.19). The line closest to the front edge should be about ⅛ inch (3 mm) beyond the center line. Machine basting can be used if needle holes do not permanently mark the fabric.

When making a series of buttonholes, it may be more efficient and more accurate to complete each step on all buttonholes than to complete each buttonhole before starting the next one.

To make a bound buttonhole using the five-line method:

1. Cut the fabric piece that will form the welts of the buttonhole 1½ inches (3.8 cm) longer than the buttonhole length and 2 inches (5 cm) wider than the buttonhole width. The rectangle should be grain perfect and generally matches the grain of the garment, but it can be cut on crosswise grain or on the bias for special effects.

2. Mark the basting and stitching lines on the interfacing side of the garment section.

a. Draw basting lines (*a* in Fig. 18.20), one on each side of the cutting line, ¼ inch (6 mm) away from and parallel to the cutting line. Extend the lines at each end about ½ inch (1.3 cm) beyond the vertical lines.

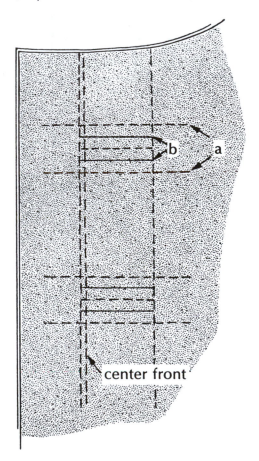

Fig. 18.20   Basting and stitching lines for buttonholes

b. Draw the stitching lines halfway between the basting line and the cutting line (*b* in Fig. 18.20). These lines begin and end on the vertical lines marking the ends of the buttonhole. The buttonhole markings now consist of five lines, each ⅛ (3 mm) apart.

3. With *right* sides together, place the center of the buttonhole piece over the center of the buttonhole marking. Match grainlines carefully and pin in place.

4. With the interfacing side up, machine baste through all layers directly on the basting lines or the lines farthest from the center buttonhole marking. Extend the stitching the full length of the marked line. Check each buttonhole on the right side to see that these stitching lines follow the grain in the fabric and are parallel to each other. Repeat for all buttonholes.

5. On the right side, fold one side of the buttonhole piece over the machine basting toward the center of the buttonhole (Fig. 18.21). Press the fold with an iron or the fingers and pin in place close to the outer edge of the piece.

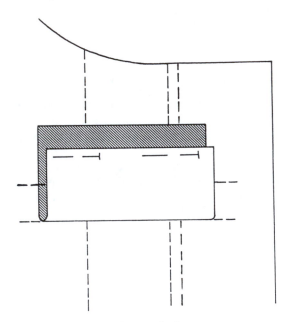

Fig. 18.21   Folding buttonhole piece over basting

6. From the *interfacing side,* stitch the buttonhole on one of the marked stitching lines, using a shorter-than-average stitch length. This is the line midway between the basting line and the cutting line or center of the buttonhole. (If a narrow toe presser foot is available, it can be used as a guide for stitching on the midway line, stitching from the garment right side instead of the wrong side. The edge of the narrow toe would be placed along the fold of the buttonhole piece.)

7. Unpin the buttonhole piece and repeat this folding and stitching process on the other fold. Use the same amount of tension when pinning and folding in place in order to make welts of equal width. Backstitching is not recommended, as it could cause the lines to become uneven in length. Leave thread ends to be tied later.

8. Check that the folds forming the welts are equal in width (Fig. 18.22).

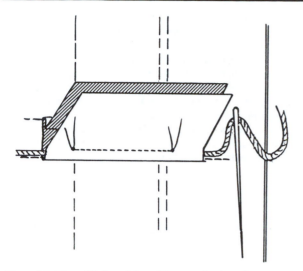

Fig. 18.22 Right side of buttonhole after stitching

9. Repeat these steps for all buttonholes.

10. Check all buttonholes from the wrong side to be sure that the stitching lines are the same length and each two rows are ¼ inch (6 mm) apart and parallel to each other.

11. Pull thread ends through to the right side (buttonhole piece) and tie, leaving ½ inch (1.3 cm) of thread (Fig. 18.22).

12. For corded buttonholes, thread a piece of yarn or cord through the welts. Pull through the fold and cut off the excess yarn (Fig. 18.22).

13. Remove all horizontal basting threads from the buttonhole area.

14. Working from the *right* side and using scissors with sharp points, cut *only* the buttonhole piece midway between the stitched lines, separating the buttonhole piece into two strips (Fig. 18.23).

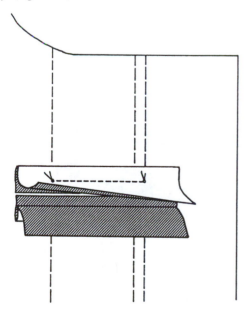

Fig. 18.23 Cutting buttonhole piece into two strips

15. Working from the *wrong* side of the buttonhole, slash through the *interfacing and garment fabric layers*. Start at the middle of the buttonhole area and cut each direction to within ¼ inch (6 mm) from each end. Clip diagonally *to but not through* the stitching at the corners (Fig. 18.24). The buttonhole area can be painted with seam sealant before cutting to prevent raveling of the triangles.

16. Turn the buttonhole strips to the inside of the garment and adjust to form square corners (Fig. 18.25).

17. Bring the folded welts of the buttonhole together and baste with a diagonal stitch (Fig. 18.26).

18. Fold the garment and interfacing back on itself at one end of the buttonhole (Fig. 18.27).

19. Starting at the base of the triangle, stitch the triangle to the buttonhole strips, keeping the stitching along the triangle base as close as possible to the fold (Fig. 18.27). This stitching must not go through to the right side of the fabric. The stitch-

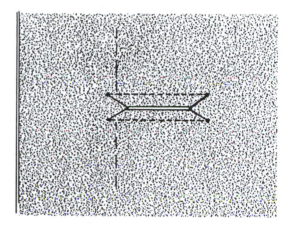

Fig. 18.24 Cutting interfacing and garment fabric from wrong side

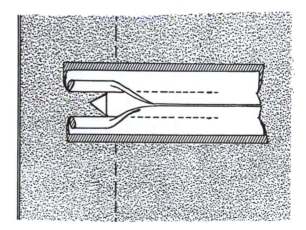

Fig. 18.25 Turning buttonhole piece to the wrong side of the garment

ing forms the vertical ends of the buttonhole. The triangle can be stitched several times to hold it securely in place. The procedure is repeated on the other end of the buttonhole.

20. Press carefully, using a press cloth when pressing from the right side. The basting that holds the edges of the welts together should be left in place until the garment is finished.

21. Trim the excess fabric for each buttonhole to within ½ inch (1.3 cm) of the stitching line.

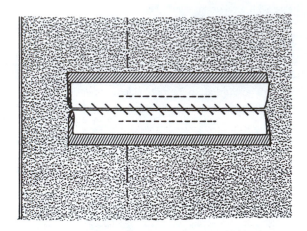

Fig. 18.26   Basting folded edges of buttonhole together

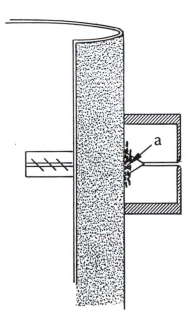

Fig. 18.27   Stitching triangle to buttonhole piece

To make a bound buttonhole using the window opening method:

1. Mark the guidelines for the buttonholes on the garment as illustrated in Figure 18.19.

2. Prepare a cardboard pattern to serve as a guide when stitching the window opening. Draw a lengthwise line through the center of the pattern measuring 1½ inches (3.8 cm) by 3 inches (7.5 cm) (a in Fig. 18.28). Draw a rectangle the length of the finished buttonhole and ¼ inch (6 mm) wide over the lengthwise line (b in Fig. 18.28).

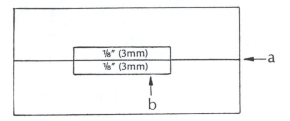

Fig. 18.28   Cardboard pattern for stitching window opening of buttonhole

3. Cut out the rectangle carefully. This opening becomes the stitching guide for forming the window opening of the buttonhole.

4. Cut a piece of lightweight, firm fabric about 2 inches (5 cm) wide and 1½ inches (3.8 cm) longer than the buttonhole marking. This will be used to face the window opening.

5. With right sides together, center the fabric strip over the buttonhole marking on the garment and pin in place (Fig. 18.29).

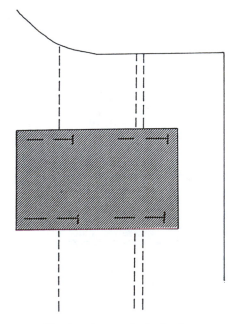

Fig. 18.29   Placing buttonhole facing on garment

6. Turn the garment piece to the wrong side, and place the stitching guide over the buttonhole marking with the length line of the cardboard pattern matched to the buttonhole marking. Tape the pattern in place.

7. Stitch along the inside edges of the rectangle using a shorter-than-average stitch length (Fig. 18.30). Overlap the stitching on one of the long sides.

8. When all the window openings have been stitched, cut the buttonhole as indicated in (Figure 18.31). Turn to the inside and adjust; press to form the window (Fig. 18.32).

9. The welts of each buttonhole are formed from two pieces of self-fabric cut 2 inches (5 cm) wide and 1½ inches (3.8 cm) longer than the buttonhole marking.

10. With right sides together, machine baste the two pieces together along the center (Fig. 18.33).

11. Fold the fabric wrong sides together and press the seam open.

12. Place the buttonhole piece behind the window opening with the seam in the center of the opening and pin in place (Fig. 18.34).

13. With the right side of the garment up, fold the garment away from the buttonhole, exposing the seam of the window opening. Stitch the welts to the garment following the previous stitching lines (Fig. 18.35). Each side and the two ends are stitched separately. The buttonhole needs to be checked after each stitching to make sure that the sides and ends are even and the welts are uniform in width.

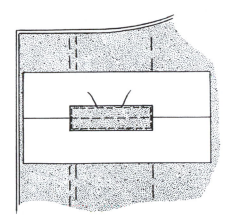

Fig. 18.30   Stitching window opening

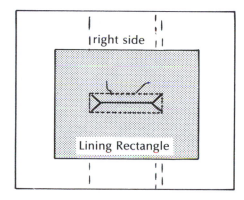

Fig. 18.31   Cutting window opening

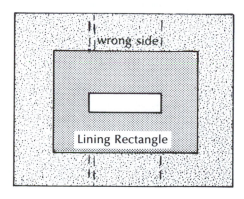

Fig. 18.32   Window opening with facing turned to the inside

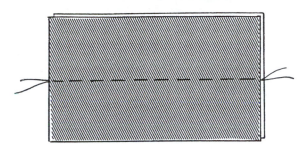

Fig. 18.33   Forming buttonhole welts

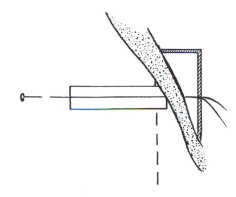

Fig. 18.34   Placing buttonhole piece behind window opening

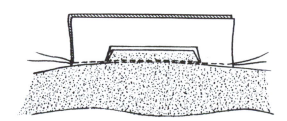

Fig. 18.35   Stitching garment to buttonhole piece

14. Trim excess fabric for each buttonhole to within ½ inch (1.3 cm) of the stitching line. The basting in the center of the buttonhole is left in place until the garment is completed.

15. Press carefully, using a press cloth when pressing on the right side.

Opening the Back of Bound Buttonholes through the Facing

When the garment assembly is completed, the buttonholes need to be opened through the facing to be functional. The three methods described here are: (1) the slash method, (2) the window opening method, and (3) stitch-in-the-ditch.

Method I – To make a slashed opening with an oval finish:

1. Baste the facing to the garment around each of the buttonholes to hold the two securely in place, matching the grain in the facing to the grain in the garment.

2. Working from the right side, push pins through each end in the center of the buttonhole opening (Fig. 18.36).

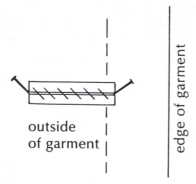

Fig. 18.36 Transferring button location from garment side to facing

3. Turn the garment with the facing side up and the pins pointing up (*A* in Fig. 18.37). Slash the facing along the buttonhole line between the pins, using the points of shears or scissors. At the center of the slash, clip ⅛ inch (3 mm) in each direction away from the slashed line (*B* in Fig. 18.37).

4. Fold under the cut edges and hand stitch to the garment so that the stitches do not show on the right side (*C* in Fig. 18.37).

Method I – To make a slashed opening with a square finish:

Buttonholes may be made to appear the same on the facing side as the right side by slashing the facing to form a square.

1. Baste the facing to the garment around each of the buttonholes to hold the two securely in place, matching the grain in the facing to the grain in the garment.

2. Place pins in all four corners of the buttonhole (*A* in Fig. 18.38).

3. Slash the facing through the center and diagonally to the corners (*B* in Fig. 18.38).

4. Fold under the cut edges and hand stitch to the garment so that the stitches do not show on the right side (*C* in Fig. 18.38).

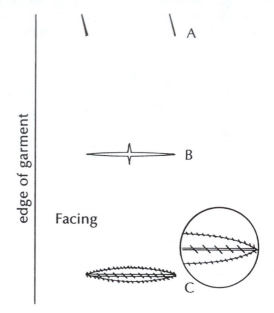

Fig. 18.37 Cutting and finishing buttonhole in facing

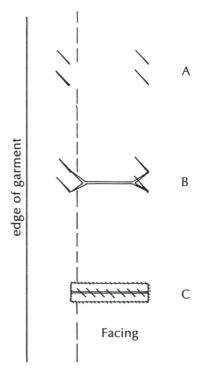

Fig. 18.38 Finishing buttonhole with square opening in facing

Method II—To open a bound buttonhole using the window opening method:

For this method, the backs of the buttonholes would need to be finished in the facing before the neckline is finished if there is a buttonhole close to the neck edge. A faced window opening is made in the facing before the facing is attached to the back of the buttonhole made in the garment.

1. Cut a rectangle of lightweight lining fabric to serve as the facing for the window opening in the facing. With right sides together, place the lining fabric on the facing, centering it behind the buttonhole area. Pin or baste in place.
2. Pin the facing to the garment buttonhole, matching the grain in the facing to the grain in the garment.
3. Mark the location of the buttonhole in the facing and lining rectangle by placing pins in all four corners of the buttonhole (A in Fig. 18.38). Mark the rectangle on the lining fabric.
4. Remove the pins holding the facing to the garment. Using a shortened stitch length, stitch the rectangle through the facing and lining to outline the buttonhole opening.
5. Slash the opening (B of Fig. 18.38).
6. Turn the lining to the wrong side and press to form a window opening.
7. Finish the neckline.
8. Position the window opening in the facing exactly under each buttonhole. Pin. Hand stitch the facing to the garment so that the stitches do not show on the right side.

Method III—To open a bound buttonhole using the stitch-in-the-ditch method:

This technique works only for those fabrics that will not ravel. It has the advantage of being quick and easy and less bulky since the edges of the buttonhole opening in the facing are not turned under.

1. Baste the facing firmly in place around each of the buttonholes, matching the grain in the facing to the grain in the garment.
2. From the right side of the garment, stitch-in-the-ditch around each buttonhole seam, using a shorter stitch length (a in Fig. 18.39). Overlap the stitches.

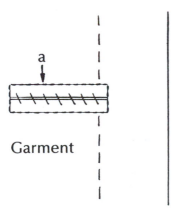

Fig. 18.39　Finishing buttonhole with stitch-in-the-ditch technique

3. On the facing side, trim away the fabric behind each buttonhole close to the machine stitching (a in Fig. 18.40).

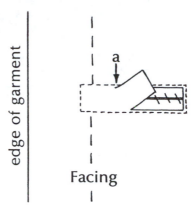

Fig. 18.40　Trimming fabric behind buttonhole

Button Loops

Button loops made from fabric tubing or commercial cording may replace buttonholes as a garment closure. The ends of the loops are stitched into the seam line where the facing is attached to the opening. Loops cannot be used with an extended facing, as they need to be sewn into a seam. An extended facing can be changed into a fitted facing by cutting along the facing fold line and adjusting the pattern.

The side of the garment that contains the loops has no extension or overlap; the loops are placed in a seam that is directly on center front or center back. An extension does exist on the underlap to accommodate the placement of the buttons.

While button loops are appropriate for many kinds of buttons, they are used most often with ball buttons that fit well through the loops.

To make self-filled fabric tubing:

1. Cut bias strips of fabric 1–1⅛ inches (2.5–2.8 cm) wide and the length needed for the total number of loops.
2. Fold the strip in half lengthwise with right sides together.
3. Stitch the strip ⅛–¼ inch (3–6 mm) from the folded edge. If the fabric is not trimmed, the seam allowance forms a soft filling for the fabric loops. If this becomes too bulky, the seam allowance can be trimmed.
4. Turn the fabric strip right side out, using a loop turner or a bodkin. Turning also can be accomplished by inserting a threaded needle backwards through the tube and gently pulling on the thread (Fig. 18.41).

To make corded tubing:

1. Cut a bias strip of fabric to cover the cording. The length of fabric equals that needed to make all of the button

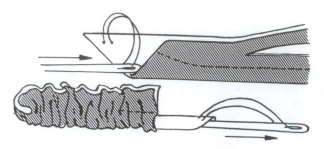

Fig. 18.41   Turning self-filled fabric loop

loops. The width of the fabric equals the diameter of the cording plus 1 inch (2.5 cm).

2. Cut the piece of cording twice as long as the piece of fabric cut to cover it.

3. Fold the fabric around one-half the length of the cording, with *right* sides together. Use a zipper foot to stitch across the end of the bias at the center of the cording and then down the long edge, keeping the stitching close to the cording (Fig. 18.42). Trim the seam allowances to reduce bulk.

4. To turn the fabric to the right side, draw the fabric across the cording onto the other half (Fig. 18.43). The excess cording is cut off at the stitched end.

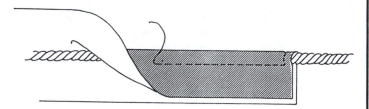

Fig. 18.42   Sewing fabric to cording

Fig. 18.43   Turning fabric over cording

To attach loops to the garment:

1. Determine the length needed for each loop by placing the cording around the button. Add seam allowances. Cut the cord into equal lengths.

2. Mark the position of each loop on lined paper (graph paper is ideal), and pin the loops in position on the paper.

3. Stitch the ends of the loops to the paper (Fig. 18.44).

4. Place the paper and loops on the garment in the proper location and stitch; tear away the paper.

5. Attach the facing to the garment following directions in Chapter 15. Layer seam allowances. Understitch. Turn the facing to the inside and press (Fig. 18.45).

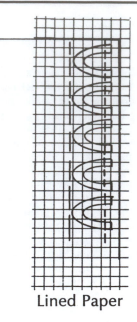

Lined Paper

Fig. 18.44   Stitching loops to lined paper

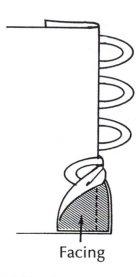

Facing

Fig. 18.45   Finishing button loop closure

Other Closures

Buttons

The location of the buttons needs to be marked in relation to the buttonholes. For center front or center back openings, the garment is lapped with the centers and the top and bottom edges of the garment matched. Buttons under horizontal buttonholes are placed directly on garment centers; the pin placed through the buttonhole to mark the button location enters the buttonhole ⅛ inch (3 mm) from the end closest to the overlap edge of the garment (*A* in Fig. 18.46). Buttons under vertical buttonholes are placed on garment centers; the pin marking the button location enters the buttonhole ⅛ inch (3 mm) from the top of the buttonhole (*B* in Fig. 18.46). Buttons located close to the top of vertical buttonholes stay buttoned better than those located in the center of the buttonhole.

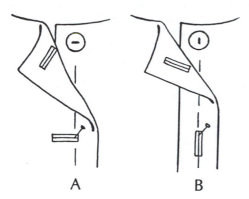

A   B

Fig. 18.46   Marking location of buttons for vertical and horizontal buttonholes

To be functional, buttons need a shank, the loop on the back of the button that adds height and allows the button to rest smoothly on top of the buttonhole. Some buttons are made with a metal or plastic shank; others need to have a thread shank made for them. The length of the shank is determined by the thickness of the buttonhole; the thicker the buttonhole, the longer the thread shank needs to be. The shank needs to be long enough for the button to go through the buttonhole and fit against the garment without pulling or puckering. Shanks are not required on strictly decorative buttons.

Buttons are usually sewn using a double thread. The thread used should match the button in color, unless a decorative effect is desired with the thread on a sew-through button. Heavy-duty thread is recommended for coat buttons.

To attach buttons with a built-in shank:

1. If the button shank is sufficiently long for the thickness of the fabric, stitch the button directly to the fabric (Fig. 18.47).

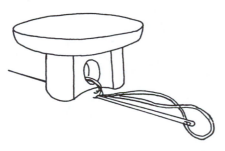

Fig. 18.47   Attaching button with built-in shank

2. If additional length is needed for the shank, make a thread shank by placing the shank button on top of a device such as a matchstick or toothpick and sew the button in place. After the button is securely attached to the garment, remove the matchstick or toothpick, and pull the button firmly away from the fabric. Tightly wrap the thread around the extra thread between the button and the fabric, forming a wrapped shank (Fig. 18.48).

Fig. 18.48   Shank button with additional thread shank

To attach sew-through buttons:

A thread shank needs to be formed as the sew-through button is attached to the garment. The length of the shank is dependent upon the thickness of the buttonhole.

1. Fasten the thread for sewing on the button on the right side of the garment at the location where the button is to be attached. Make one stitch through the holes in the button.

2. Place an object such as a matchstick or toothpick on top of the button to serve as a guide for the size of the shank (Fig. 18.49).

Fig. 18.49   Attaching a sew-through button

3. Sew on the button with each stitch passing over the object. If the sew-through button has more than two holes, it can be stitched in place using any one of a variety of patterns for a decorative effect (Fig. 18.50).

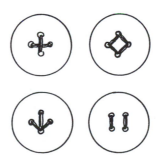

Fig. 18.50   Stitching patterns for attaching sew-through buttons

4. After the button is firmly attached, remove the object. Tightly wrap the shank between the button and the garment with thread to form the thread shank and to make it more durable (Fig. 18.51).

5. Bring the needle to the wrong side of the garment and fasten thread securely with several small stitches that do not go through to the right side.

Fig. 18.51   Thread shank in sew-through button

Snaps

Snaps are used for closures on areas of the garment that receive little strain during wear. The ball portion of the snap is placed on the top layer, the socket portion on the bottom layer (Fig. 18.52).

Generally, the ball portion of the snap is stitched in place first; the socket is aligned with it to be even and in the appropriate location. The blanket stitch gives a neat and a durable finish when attaching snaps to the garment.

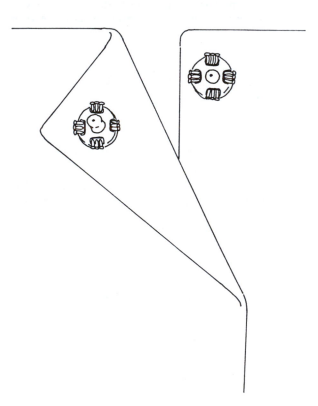

Fig. 18.52   Placement of snaps on edges that overlap

To attach snaps on a garment:

1. Take several small stitches in the fabric at the point where the snap is to be attached to the garment.

2. Place the snap on the garment and attach using a double thread. Several stitches are taken in each hole, carrying the thread under the snap or top layer of fabric between holes. If the blanket stitch is used, each stitch is made with the needle inserted first from the *outside* of the snap and coming up through each hole (A in Fig. 18.53). Then insert the needle back through the loop to complete the stitch (B in Fig. 18.53). The blanket stitch is a neat and durable stitch recommended for snaps and hooks and eyes. Be sure that none of the stitches shows on the right side of the finished garment.

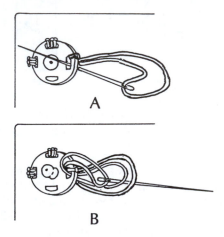

Fig. 18.53   Attaching snap with blanket stitch

3. Fasten the thread securely by taking several small stitches that do not go through to the outside.

4. Press down the ball to mark the location of the center of the corresponding socket half of the snap. Mark the location with pin or chalk.

5. Place the socket of the snap so that the hole will lie exactly on the depression made by the ball and sew it securely to the garment as previously described.

To attach an extended snap:

The extended snap works well where two edges that receive little strain need to come together and match or overlap just slightly (Fig. 18.54).

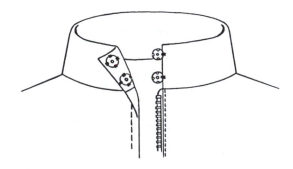

Fig. 18.54   Extended snaps

1. Place the ball portion of the snap against the edge of one garment section. The back side of the ball portion is smooth and will feel more comfortable placed against the body than would the socket half.

2. Sew to the edge of the garment, securing one or two of the holes with the blanket or overcast stitch.

3. Position the socket portion of the snap under the other edge of the garment so that the edges of the garment come together or lap as designed.

4. Stitch the socket through all holes making sure no stitches show on the right side.

Hooks and Eyes

Hooks and eyes are used in areas of the garment where there is strain. The eyes can be straight or round; the straight eyes are recommended for openings that *overlap*, the round eyes for edges that *meet*. Thread eyes are less noticeable and sometimes are used in place of the metal eyes (Fig. 18.55). Large, flat hooks and eyes, commonly called trouser hooks, are made for use on waistbands in pants and skirts (Fig. 18.56).

Fig. 18.55   Hook, straight eye, round eye, thread eye

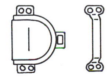

Fig. 18.56   Trouser hook and eye

Hooks usually are placed on the *overlap side* of the garment and on the underside of that overlap. They need to be far enough from the edge of the opening so that they are invisible when the garment is worn, yet not so far back that the edge gaps or does not remain flat.

The eye is placed on the underlap in the position needed for the hook and eye to close and the edges to overlap as designed. Generally, the eye is sewn on the garment after the hook is in place. The correct placement of hooks and eyes is illustrated in Figures 18.57 and 18.58. The curved eye would be used on garment edges that just meet, with both hook and eye being placed on the inside of the garment.

Fig. 18.57   Hook and straight eye attached on edges that overlap

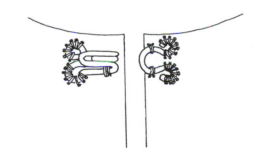

Fig. 18.58   Hook and round eye attached on edges that just meet

To sew hooks and eyes on a garment:

1. Place the hook on the underside of the overlap.

2. Position hook about ¼ inch (6 mm) back from the edge of the opening so that it will not be visible. Use a sufficient number of hooks to prevent gaping.

3. Use a sufficient number of hooks to prevent gaping.

4. Stitch around the curved end of the hook to keep it flat against the fabric (Fig. 18.59). This step would be omitted when attaching trouser hooks.

5. Secure each of the holes of the hook with a blanket stitch (*A* and *B* in Fig. 18.60) or overcast stitch, taking care that no stitches show on the right side. The blanket stitch is a neat and durable stitch recommended for attaching hooks and eyes. Slide the needle under the fabric when going between each of the holes. When attaching a hook to a waistband, try to catch the interfacing inside the waistband with a few of the

stitches to give the hook added stability, but *do not* allow any of the stitches to show on the right side of the garment.

6. Sew the eye to the underlap exactly opposite the hook. Stitch the eye through *all* layers of the garment to give it added stability. Fasten threads securely.

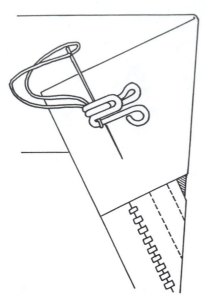

Fig. 18.59   Stitching curved end of hook

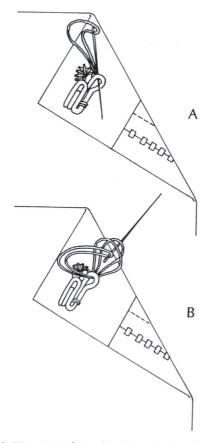

Fig. 18.60   Attaching hook with blanket stitch

Thread Eye

The thread eye can be used in place of the metal eye. Since it is not as strong, it would not be appropriate for areas of strain. The shape of the eye can be straight or curved. The thread eye can be made from a single strand of buttonhole twist or topstitching thread or two strands of regular sewing thread. The technique used for making a thread eye can also be used for belt carriers.

To make a thread eye:

1. Secure the end of the thread to the garment and make the foundation stitch the desired length of the eye.
2. Repeat the stitch three or four times in the same place to make a firm base for the thread eye (*a* in Fig. 18.61).
3. Cover the foundation stitch by making a series of blanket stitches on top of it (*b* in Fig. 18.61).
4. Fasten securely the threads on both ends of the thread eye to keep the eye from pulling out.

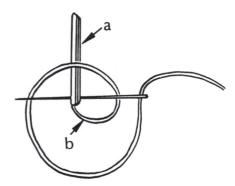

Fig. 18.61   Making thread eye

Hook-and-Loop Tape

Hook-and-loop tape provides a self-gripping fastener that can be used in place of other closures. It consists of two tapes, one covered with tiny, finely woven hooks and the other with looped pile. The tapes fasten securely when pressed together and separate by pulling apart. Hook-and-loop tape is available as a tape in a variety of widths or as precut dots and squares.

To attach hook-and-loop tape:

1. Cut the fastener the desired length and shape, or select a precut dot or square of the appropriate size.
2. Position the looped tape on the overlap of the garment far enough away from the edge so it will not show from the outside.
3. Place the hook side so that it faces away from the skin (garment underlap) opposite the looped tape.
4. Use a bit of glue or pins to hold the tape in place.

5. Machine or hand stitch securely around all edges of the tape. On the overlap side sew only to the facing so that the stitching is not visible on the outside of the finished garment (Fig. 18.62).

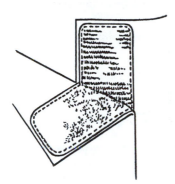

Fig. 18.62   Attaching hook-and-loop tape

19 Sleeves and Sleeve Plackets

Most sleeves can be categorized as set-in, raglan, or kimono (Fig. 19.1). The set-in sleeve, which includes both the regular set-in and the shirt-style sleeve, is the one most commonly found in apparel. This chapter includes discussion of the three types of sleeves as well as sections on the sleeve placket and cuffs.

Set-in Sleeve

The regular set-in sleeve differs from the shirt-style sleeve in the shape of the top of the sleeve. The regular set-in sleeve is much more curved and the sleeve cap is higher (A in Fig. 19.2) than in the shirt-style sleeve (B in Fig. 19.2). The techniques used to insert the sleeve into the armhole also differ; the regular set-in sleeve is inserted by the closed construction techniques; the shirt-style sleeve is inserted by the open construction techniques. The lower edge of the regular set-in sleeve usually is finished completely before the sleeve is sewn to the armhole; finishing of the lower edge of the sleeve and sewing of the underarm seam of the shirt-style sleeve comes after the sleeve is put into the armhole.

The amount of ease in a sleeve can be calculated by measuring the sleeve cap stitching line and the garment armhole stitching line above the notches. If working

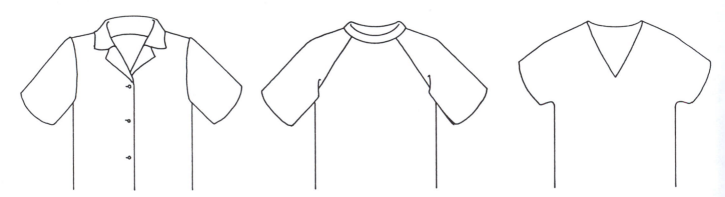

Fig. 19.1   Set-in, raglan, and kimono sleeves

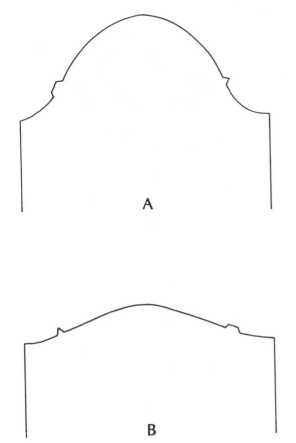

Fig. 19.2 Shape of regular set-in sleeve and shirt-style sleeve

with a difficult-to-ease fabric, the amount of ease can be decreased to minimize the puckering effect that could result when the sleeve is installed in the garment. The amount of ease is decreased by taking a small tuck across the sleeve pattern (Fig. 19.3) or by reducing the

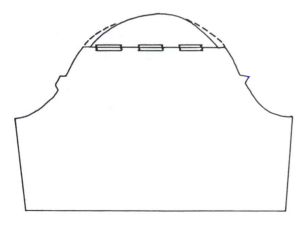

Fig. 19.3 Reducing sleeve cap length with tuck across cap

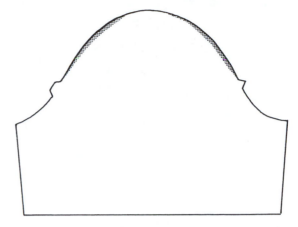

Fig. 19.4 Reducing sleeve cap length by reducing shape of cap

amount of the curve between the notches and the top of the sleeve (Fig. 19.4).

Sleeves can have a smooth cap or they can be gathered, tucked, or pleated. The directions given here are for a smooth cap; the procedures are the same for the other types, except that the fullness needs to be distributed evenly. Chapter 14 contains discussion that should be reviewed when working with gathers and tucks. A well-made set-in sleeve has these characteristics:

– Smooth, rounded cap with no pleats or gathers unless these are fashion features.
– Ease evenly distributed.
– Good armhole line resulting from straight, even stitching and well-matched seam lines.
– Crosswise grain parallel to the floor, lengthwise grain perpendicular to the floor, and no diagonal wrinkles.
– Seam finish appropriate for the fabric.

The sleeves should be carefully fitted to check the location of the elbow darts and the sleeve length. After the sleeves are fitted, they may be completely finished at the lower edge before they are permanently stitched into the armhole. Because the set-in sleeve is larger than the armhole into which it will be placed, the sleeve needs to be eased to the armhole.

To prepare a regular set-in sleeve:

1. Place a row of ease stitching ⅝ inch (1.6 cm) from the edge of the seam around the cap of the sleeve between the notches (Fig. 19.5). The weight of the fabric will determine the length of the machine stitch (see Chapter 14). If a second row of stitching is needed, it is placed in the seam allowance about ¼ (6 mm) from the first row of stitching.

2. Stitch the underarm seam of the sleeve; finish the seam edges; and press open.

3. Complete the lower edge of the sleeve according to pattern instructions.

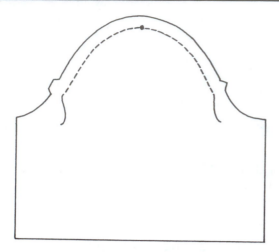

Fig. 19.5   Placement of ease stitching on set-in sleeve

Attaching Regular Set-in Sleeve

Two methods can be used to adjust the sleeve cap to fit into the armhole. In one, the sleeve is pinned to the armhole and the ease thread is pulled up. In the other, the ease thread is pulled up on the sleeve before it is pinned to the garment, and the sleeve is placed over a pressing cushion where the ease is shrunk out of the seam allowance by the use of steam. The latter works best on those fabrics that can be shrunk with steam, such as wool and wool blends.

Try on the garment to check the armhole location for setting in the sleeve. Note the location for the seam line and mark with pins or washable fabric pen. A smooth set-in sleeve will be positioned at the end of the shoulder and the seam line will fall in a smooth straight line down the front of the armhole. A set-in sleeve with gathers or tucks is positioned about ½–1 inch (1.3–2.5 cm) in from the end of the shoulder seam.

To set sleeve into armhole
using ease stitching:

1. Pull up the ease thread from both sides to shape the sleeve cap. Hold the sleeve cap over your fingers and note its shape and position of grain. Adjust the ease so that it is distributed evenly and smoothly.

2. With right sides together, fit the sleeve into the armhole. Attach the sleeve to the garment with four pins: at the top of the sleeve to the shoulder line marking, the underarm seam, and the notches (Fig. 19.6). The notches must match for the sleeve to be in the correct armhole; usually the single notches appear in the sleeve front and the double in the sleeve back. *Place all pins on the sleeve side directly on and parallel to the seam line.*

3. Adjust the ease so that the sleeve fits smoothly over the garment armhole, with most of the ease located 3 inches (7.5 cm) in front and in back of the shoulder seam. Very little ease is located at the top of the sleeve cap. Working over the

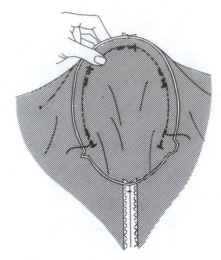

Fig. 19.6   Pinning regular set-in sleeve to armhole

hand sometimes helps to facilitate distributing the ease. There may be a small amount of ease in the underarm area of the sleeve, which can be distributed by careful pinning. It should not be allowed to shift into the upper armhole by mis-matching the notches. Do not pull up the ease stitching too much as the measurement of the sleeve capline seam could become shorter than the armhole seam.

4. Pin baste the entire sleeve, placing pins on the sleeve side directly on and parallel to the seam line.

5. Put the garment on to check the position of the armhole seam and placement of the grain of the sleeve. Make any necessary adjustments and try it on again until the proper fit is achieved.

6. With the sleeve side facing up, stitch the armhole seam. Starting at one of the notches, stitch the underarm and around the cap to the starting place. To strengthen the seam, continue stitching to make a double row of stitches through the underarm between the notches (Fig. 19.7). Check the position of the stitching line on the garment side to be sure it is a smooth curve and is not puckered. Remove the stitching and restitch, if necessary.

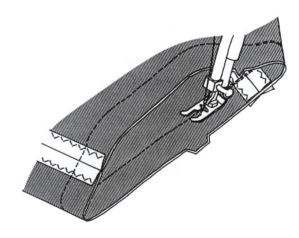

Fig. 19.7   Stitching and reinforcing sleeve seam

7. Trim the underarm curve to ⅜ inch (1 cm) between the notches. *Do not clip the armhole curve.*

8. The upper portion of the sleeve cap may be trimmed to ⅜ inch (1 cm) or left as is.

9. Finish the armhole seam allowance by overcasting or zigzagging the edges together, stitching from the *garment* side.

10. Turn the seam allowance of the cap portion into the sleeve, but do not press.

Shoulder Pads

Shoulder pads are used in garments to provide more shape to the shoulder area. Shoulder pads can be purchased at fabric stores or can be made a variety of shapes and thicknesses. Shoulder pads that are more squared off at the end are suitable for regular set-in sleeves, while others that are more shaped and extend over the end of the shoulder are used for shirt-style sleeves, raglan, and kimono sleeves. Graduated layers of polyester fleece can be hand stitched together to make shoulder pads the desired thickness. A commercial pattern can be purchased or shoulder pads can be made following these instructions.

To make shoulder pads:

1. Overlap shoulder seams of the garment front and back patterns, matching the stitching line. Pin darts or seams that extend into the shoulder or armhole seam lines (a in Fig. 19.8).

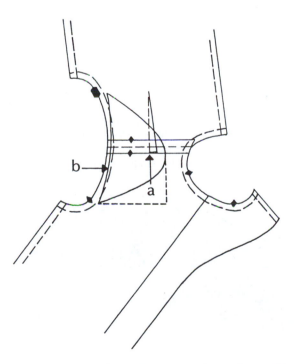

Fig. 19.8   Positioning pattern pieces for making shoulder pads

2. Draw the shape of the pad as desired. Shoulder pads usually extend ¼ inch (6 mm) beyond the armhole seam line at the end of the shoulder (*b* in Fig. 19.8). The front and back may be curved or the front may have an extended lower edge (Fig. 19.8).

3. Use this pattern to cut several graduated layers from polyester fleece; all layers should match along the armhole edge. For a firmer pad, the largest layer could be cut from a piece of heavyweight, nonwoven interfacing. This layer would be the top layer and be placed against the wrong side of the garment.

4. Curve the layers for the shoulder pads over the hand to match the shape of the shoulder; pin together with the largest layer on top (Fig. 19.9).

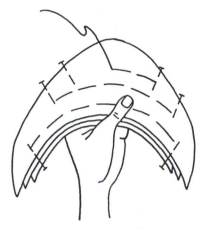

Fig. 19.9   Shaping shoulder pad and hand stitching layers together

5. Loosely hand stitch all layers together with a long running stitch or a padding stitch (Fig. 19.9).

6. Cover the shoulder pads with fashion fabric, if desired.

To attach shoulder pads:

1. Try on the garment to determine the shoulder pad placement. Pin pad to the garment (Fig. 19.10). On a regular

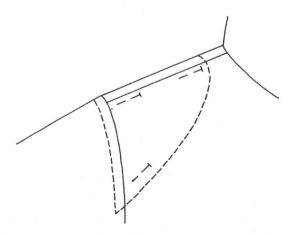

Fig. 19.10   Positioning shoulder pad in garment with set-in sleeve

set-in sleeve, the shoulder pads usually extend about ¼ inch (6 mm) beyond the armhole seam line. On garments with extended shoulder seams, the shoulder pad needs to be positioned with the garment on for correct placement. For this type of garment a shaped shoulder pad that curves over the end of the shoulder often is used.

2. Fasten shoulder pads in place by hand stitching between the shoulder pad and the shoulder seam (A in Fig. 19.11). Loosely stitch the shoulder pad to the armhole seam. If removable shoulder pads are desired, they can be attached with hook-and-loop tape fastener dots or strips in place of the permanent hand stitching (B in Fig. 19.11).

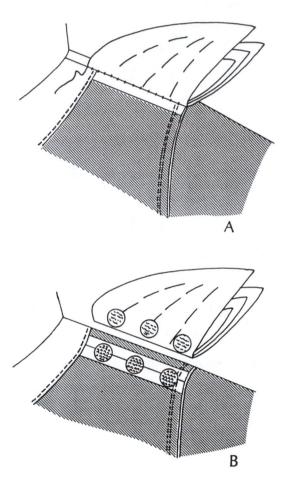

Fig. 19.11   Fastening shoulder pad to shoulder seam of garment

Shirt-style Sleeves

The shirt-style sleeve cap seam line, because it is flatter than the traditional set-in sleeve, can be sewn as a plain seam, a flat-fell seam, or topstitched to look like a flat-fell seam. While the lower edge cannot be finished until after the sleeve has been stitched to the armhole, the sleeve placket, if one is present, can be completed before setting in the sleeve. Sewing in the sleeve placket

on the flat sleeve is easier than sewing it after the sleeve is in the garment.

A shirt-style sleeve has less ease over the cap of the sleeve than the regular set-in sleeve and usually can be attached to the garment without an ease stitch. The small amount of ease present can be worked to fit the garment by manipulating the sleeve over the hand as it is being pinned.

To set in a shirt-style sleeve
with no ease stitch:

1. Pin the sleeve to the garment, right sides together, matching notches and other pattern markings.
2. From the wrong side roll the sleeve over the hand and pin, placing the pins parallel to and directly on the seam line (Fig. 19.12). The small amount of ease should be placed within about 3 inches (7.5 cm) on either side of the top of the sleeve.

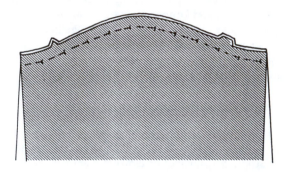

Fig. 19.12   Pinning shirt-style sleeve to armhole

3. Stitch the armhole seam (a in Fig. 19.13). If a plain seam is used, trim the seam allowance to ⅜ inch (1 cm) and finish with a method appropriate for the fabric (b in Fig. 19.13). If the armhole seam is to be topstitched, trim the seam allowance to the appropriate width and finish the edges before topstitching.
4. Stitch the underarm seam of the sleeve and garment, finish, and press before finishing the lower edge of the sleeve (Fig. 19.14). This seam is often trimmed to ¼ inch (6 mm) and the edges finished together. Press the seam toward the back.

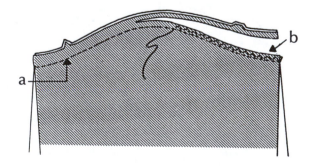

Fig. 19.13   Finishing armhole seam of shirt-style sleeve

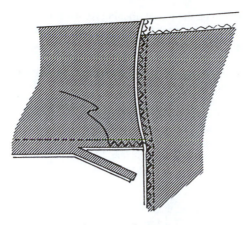

Fig. 19.14   Stitching underarm seam

Kimono Sleeves

Kimono sleeves (see Fig. 19.1) are cut in one with the garment front and garment back. The underarm curve of a kimono sleeve may be finished in several ways. On medium- to lightweight fabric, the seam may be double stitched, trimmed, and the seam edges finished together. This method is desirable as the curved seam does not need to be clipped, which weakens the seam. If the seam needs to be pressed open, the curved area needs to be reinforced and clipped for the seam to lie flat. Another option is to add a gusset to the underarm curve to reduce strain on the sleeve. Each of these methods will be discussed.

**To make a kimono sleeve finished
with a narrow seam:**

1. Machine stitch the underarm seam of the garment, using a shorter stitch length through the underarm curve.
2. Trim the seam allowance to ⅜ inch (1 cm).
3. Finish the edges of the seam allowance using a method appropriate for the fabric (Fig. 19.15).

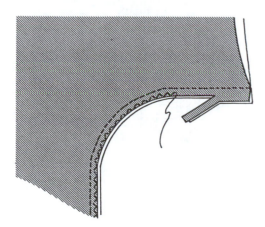

Fig. 19.15   Finishing kimono sleeve with a
narrow seam

4. Press the seam allowances to one side.

**To make a kimono sleeve reinforced
with an underarm stay:**

1. Stitch the underarm seam of the kimono sleeve, using a shorter stitch length in the underarm area. Finish the seam edges separately, clip the curved area as needed to straighten the seam line, and press the seam open (Fig. 19.16).

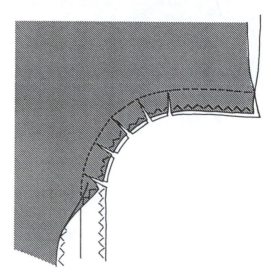

Fig. 19.16   Stitching and clipping a kimono
sleeve seam to be pressed open

2. Bias seam tape can be applied in two ways to provide additional reinforcement to the underarm area of kimono sleeves.
   a. Sew in a piece of tape as the seam is being stitched (Fig. 19.17). Do not clip the tape when clipping the seam allowance.

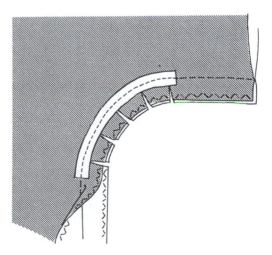

Fig. 19.17   Sewing reinforcement tape into
kimono sleeve seam

b. Place a piece of tape on the pressed open seam and pin in place (Fig. 19.18). Topstitch in place (Fig. 19.19). Because the stitching is only in the underarm area and is placed close to the original stitching line, it is not noticeable from the outside of the finished garment.

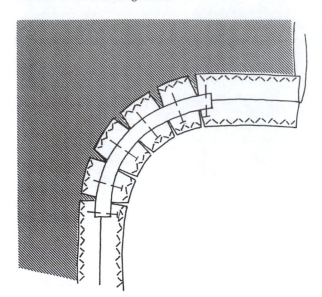

Fig. 19.18 Pinning reinforcement tape to open seam allowance

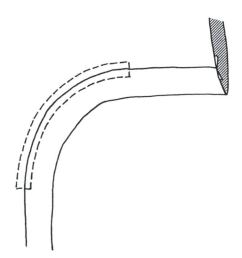

Fig. 19.19 Completed reinforcement stitching to open seam allowance

To make a kimono sleeve with a gusset:

A *gusset* is a bias piece of garment fabric placed in a slash at the underarm area of a kimono sleeve to provide for ease of movement. The typical gusset is a diamond-shaped inset and may be one piece or two; these directions are for a two-piece gusset.

1. Mark the location of the stitching lines for the gusset on the wrong side of the fabric.

2. Reinforce the gusset opening on the garment with a 2 inch (5 cm) bias square of firmly woven, lightweight fabric. With right sides together, place this square of fabric over the point of the gusset and pin or baste (Fig. 19.20).

3. Stitch the square to the garment on the marked stitching line (a in Fig. 19.21) using a shorter stitch length. Take one stitch across the point (b in Fig. 19.21). Double stitch at the point exactly on the first line of stitching.

4. Slash the garment and reinforcing square *to but not through* the point, and turn the reinforcing piece to the wrong side of the garment and press (Fig. 19.22).

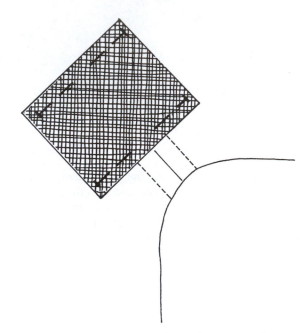

Fig. 19.20 Placement of reinforcement for gusset

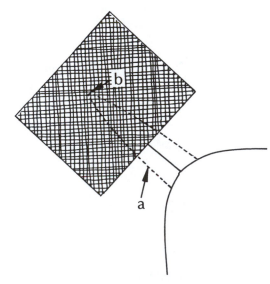

Fig. 19.21 Stitching reinforcement in place

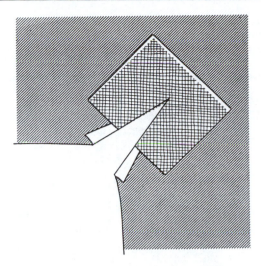

Fig. 19.22   Turning and pressing reinforcing piece

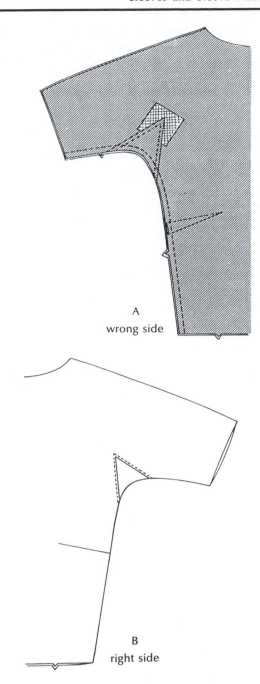

5. Position the faced slash of the garment along the stitching line of the gusset and topstitch ¹⁄₁₆ inch (1.5 mm) from the edge (Fig. 19.23). An optional method for stitching would be to stitch the gusset on the inside following the marked stitching lines.

6. Repeat steps 1–5 on the other bodice piece.

7. Join the front to the back at the underarm seam, matching notches, seam edges, and gusset seam lines. Machine stitch on the seam line (A in Fig. 19.24).

8. Finish the underarm seam using one of the methods described above. Press (B in Fig. 19.24).

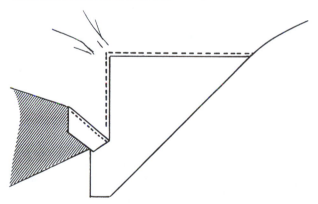

Fig. 19.23   Topstitching garment to gusset

Fig. 19.24   Joining bodice front and back at underarm seam

Raglan Sleeves

Raglan sleeves have a seam that extends diagonally from the underarm to the neckline on both bodice front and back (see Fig. 19.1). Often, a dart extends from the neckline to the end of the shoulder along what would be the original or typical shoulder seam line to provide fitting in that area of the raglan sleeve. A two-piece raglan sleeve has a seam extending from the neckline, across the top of the shoulder, and through the sleeve area to the hemline. The sleeve can be attached using either the open or closed construction technique. The open or flat construction technique makes it easier to manipulate the garment under the machine, and it is used extensively in mass production. The raglan seam line is either trimmed narrow and the edges finished together or clipped in the curved area and pressed open. An advantage of the closed construction technique is that the underarm curve does not need to be clipped; therefore the seam is stronger than when the seam is clipped. Both methods will be described.

To make a raglan sleeve—open construction:

1. Stitch the shoulder seam or dart in the sleeve. Finish seam edges in an appropriate manner and press.
2. With right sides together, stitch the raglan sleeve to the garment front and back.
3. Finish the seam in one of the following ways:
   a. Trim the seam allowance to ¼ inch (6 mm) and finish the seam edges together. Press the seam in one direction, usually toward the sleeve (Fig. 19.25).

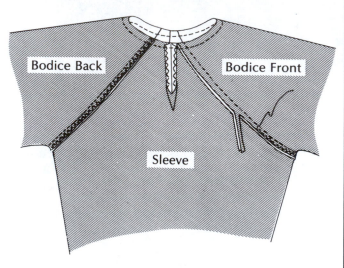

Fig. 19.25   Joining raglan sleeve to garment; seam trimmed and finished together

   b. Reinforce the curve with a second row of machine stitching directly on top of the first (a in Fig. 19.26). Finish the seam edges in an appropriate manner. Clip the curved area, as necessary, and press the seam open (a in Fig. 19.26).

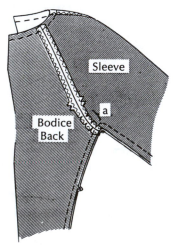

Fig. 19.26   Joining raglan sleeve to garment; seam reinforced and pressed open

4. Stitch the underarm seam of the sleeve and bodice in one continuous seam, matching the raglan seams in the underarm area.
5. Trim the seam allowance to ⅜ inch (1 cm) and finish the seam edges together (Fig. 19.27). Press in one direction.

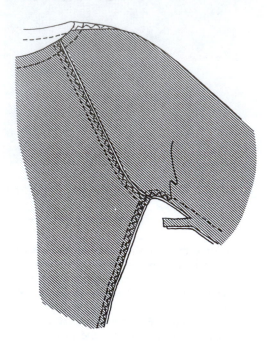

Fig. 19.27   Finishing underarm seam of raglan sleeve

To make a raglan sleeve—closed construction:

1. Stitch the shoulder seam or dart in the sleeve (a in Fig. 19.28). Finish seam edges in an appropriate manner and press.
2. Stitch the underarm seam of the sleeve (b in Fig. 19.28) and the side seam of the garment (c in Fig. 19.28). Finish seams and press.

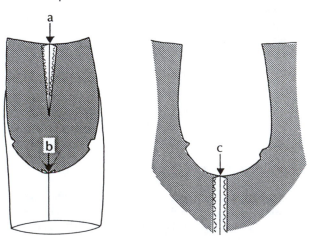

Fig. 19.28   Raglan sleeve — closed construction: stitching bodice and sleeve seams

3. With right sides together, join the sleeve to the garment in one continuous seam, matching seams and notches (Fig. 19.29).

4. Place a second row of straight or machine zigzag stitching between the notches at the underarm about ¼ inch (6 mm) from the original stitching for reinforcement. Trim the seam close to this stitching and finish the seam edges together (Fig. 19.30).

5. Press the seam allowance open above this point.

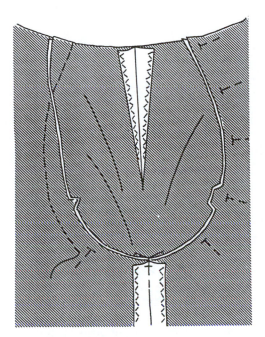

Fig. 19.29   Raglan sleeve — closed construction: stitching armhole seam

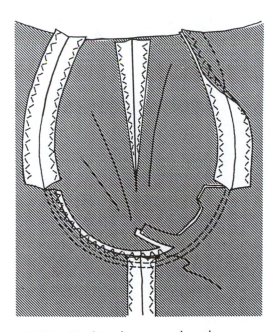

Fig. 19.30   Raglan sleeve — closed construction: finishing armhole seam

Sleeve Placket Openings

Several styles of sleeve placket openings are used on garments. Four different types are presented in this chapter: (1) the continuous lapped placket, (2) the faced placket, (3) the dart placket, and (4) the tailored placket.

Continuous Lapped Placket

The continuous lapped placket (Fig. 19.31) generally is applied to a slashed opening in the garment. The sleeve placket technique can be used for plackets located in other areas on a garment, such as on necklines of shirts or blouses. The strip of fabric used to bind the opening can be cut on straight grain or on the bias.

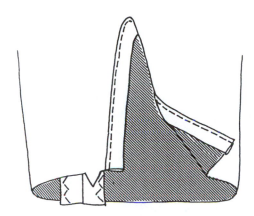

Fig. 19.31   Continuous lapped placket

To make a continuous lapped placket:

1. Mark the slash line for the continuous lapped placket on the fabric.

2. Cut the strip of fashion fabric used for the continuous lapped placket twice the length of the opening plus two seam allowances. It should be 1 inch (2.5 cm) wide plus the needed ¼ inch (6 mm) seam allowances. If the strip is cut on a selvage edge, one of the seam allowances may be omitted.

3. Using a shortened stitch length, reinforce the placket by stitching parallel to the slash line and not more than ¼ inch (6 mm) from the line. When within ½ inch (1.3 cm) of the termination point, taper toward the end to make a narrow curve. Raise and lower the presser foot as needed to make one stitch across the end of the slash. Continue stitching along the other side of the slash line (Fig. 19.32).

4. Cut the garment along the slash line *to but not through* the point.

5. With right sides together, pin the placket strip to the slashed opening following the reinforcement stitching line on the garment. Keep the stitched reinforcing line ¼ inch (6 mm) from the raw edge of the strip. The seam allowance along the garment slash will not be even. Sew the placket strip to the garment stitching just to the outside of the reinforcement line (Fig. 19.33).

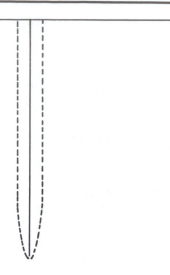

Fig. 19.32   Reinforcing placket slash line

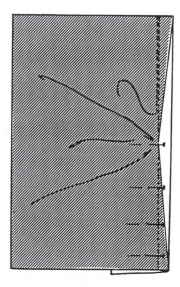

Fig. 19.33   Stitching continuous placket strip to slashed opening

6. Press the seam allowances toward the placket strip.

7. Turn under the inside edge of the placket strip ¼ inch (6 mm) and press. If the continuous placket piece was cut on the selvage, omit this step. If the selvage edge cannot be used, a zigzag or overlock edge finish can be used to finish the edge of the strip for fabrics that are too bulky to turn under.

8. Place the finished edge of the strip along the seam line of the placket, covering the seam allowances. Stitch the edges of the strip to the garment by hand or machine (Fig. 19.34). If stitching by hand, the finished edge of the strip must not overlap the stitching line. When using the machine, either stitching-in-the-ditch or topstitching are appropriate. If stitching-in-the-ditch is used, the edge of the strip needs to be placed far enough over the seam of the placket so that it is caught in the stitching.

9. Press the placket.

10. From the wrong side, stitch diagonally across the folded end of the placket (a in Fig. 19.35) to keep it flat and smooth and to prevent undue strain at the bottom. This stitching also helps to keep the placket to the inside of the garment.

11. Fold the upper placket lap (overlap) to the inside of the garment and machine baste on the seam line to hold it in place. The placket underlap (the side of the placket closest to the underarm seam) is left extended on most plackets of this type.

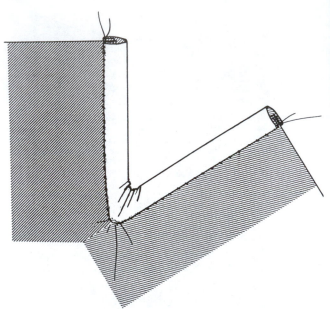

Fig. 19.34   Finishing continuous lapped placket

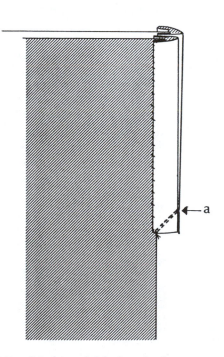

Fig. 19.35   Stitching folded end of continuous placket

Faced Plackets

The faced placket can be used in place of the continuous lapped placket and works well on fabrics that ravel. Two types of faced plackets will be discussed: (1) the faced placket for a vertical slashed opening and (2) the faced placket for a pleated sleeve closure.

**To make a faced placket for
a vertical slashed opening:**

1. Mark the slashed opening on the garment.
2. If a facing is not provided with the pattern, cut one to match the area to be faced. It should be 2½ inches (6.3 cm) wide and 1 inch (2.5 cm) longer than the slashed opening.
3. Finish the edges of the facing in an appropriate way (Fig. 19.36).

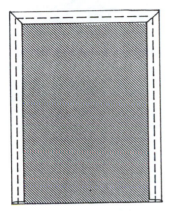

Fig. 19.36   Facing for faced placket

4. Center the facing over the marked opening, right sides together and stitch from the sleeve side using a shortened stitch length at the point of the slash, taking one stitch across the point (Fig. 19.37).
5. Slash the opening *to but not through* the point. Understitch on the facing side of the seam.
6. Turn the facing to the wrong side of the garment and press, rolling the edges slightly to the inside (Fig. 19.38).

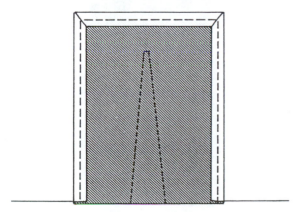

Fig. 19.37   Stitching facing to sleeve

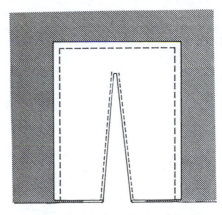

Fig. 19.38   Turning under stitched facing to the inside

7. Topstitch the opening, or use a hemming stitch to hold it in place on the inside edge. If the facing stays in place without the stitching, this step can be omitted.

**To make a faced placket for
a pleated sleeve closure:**

1. Mark two points 1 inch (2.5 cm) apart on the seam line of the lower sleeve edge directly below the elbow area. This marking may be on the pattern.
2. Cut two straight-grain facing pieces, each 1½ inches (3.8 cm) wide and 2½ inches (6.3 cm) long.
3. Center the facing over the markings on the sleeve, right sides together and lower edges even.
4. Stitch as illustrated in Figure 19.39. Trim seam allowances of the opening to ¼ inch (6 mm) and clip to the corners.
5. Press the facing to the inside. Finish the outer edges with a method appropriate for the fabric and hand stitch in place (Fig. 19.40).

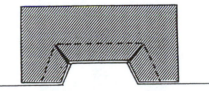

Fig. 19.39   Preparation of pleated sleeve placket

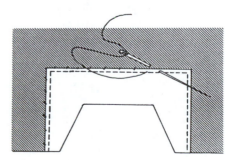

Fig. 19.40   Hand stitching placket to sleeve

6. Apply the interfaced cuff to the sleeve so that the cuff ends match the finished corners of the faced opening (Fig. 19.41).

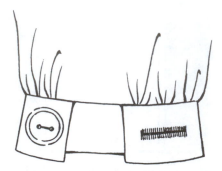

Fig. 19.41   Cuff attached to sleeve with pleated sleeve placket

Dart Placket

The dart placket creates an opening in the sleeve without adding any extra bulk to the sleeve placket area (Fig. 19.42). It is especially suited for very lightweight fabrics or fabrics that ravel easily (for which a continuous lapped or faced placket may not be suited) as well as heavier fabrics where bulk in the placket area may be a problem.

To make a dart placket:

1. Mark the stitching lines for the dart placket on the wrong side of the sleeve directly below the elbow area. If there are no markings on the pattern, the slash line (a in Fig. 19.43) would be about 6½ inches (16.5 cm) long and the

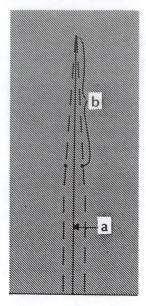

Fig. 19.43   Marking for dart placket

stitching lines would be drawn ¼ inch (6 mm) on either side and parallel to the slash line, gradually tapering to a point at the end of the dart. Place a dot about 3 inches (7.5 cm) down from the point to mark the termination point for the machine stitching (b in Fig. 19.43).

2. To stitch the placket, fold the dart right sides together, matching the stitching lines. Place pins directly on and parallel to the stitching lines.

3. Stitch the dart from the marking in the center of the placket to the point, securing threads at both ends of the stitching (from a to b in Fig. 19.44).

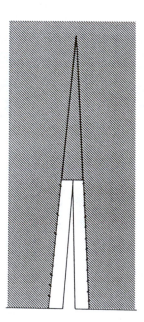

Fig. 19.42   Dart placket

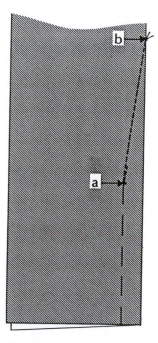

Fig. 19.44   Stitching dart placket

4. Cut the dart along the slash line beginning at the lower edge of the sleeve and extending to a point ¼ inch (6 mm) beyond where the stitching began.

5. Fold back ¼ inch (6 mm) on each side of the slash line and press. Press the top half of the dart flat (Fig. 19.45).

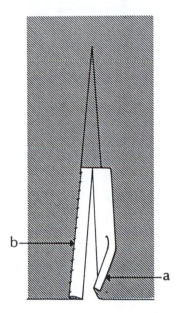

Fig. 19.45   Cutting and pressing dart placket

6. Finish each side of the slashed opening in one of the following ways:

a. For lightweight fabrics, turn under ⅛ inch (3 mm) along the cut edge and press (a in Fig. 19.45). Hand stitch along the folded edge using an appropriate hemming stitch (b in Fig. 19.45).

b. For heavier fabrics, finish the cut edge with hand overcasting or a machine zigzag or overlock stitch. Hand stitch along the finished edge using an appropriate hemming stitch.

c. For knit fabrics, leave the edge unfinished and hand stitch using an appropriate hemming stitch.

Tailored Placket

The tailored placket (Fig.19.46) is often used on men's shirts. The placket is visible on the outside of the sleeve and is finished with machine topstitching. It is best suited for medium- to lightweight fabrics, as there are many layers of material in the placket area. Accuracy in marking and stitching is critical to the success of the finished appearance.

To make a tailored placket:

1. Transfer the stitching line markings to both the placket and the sleeve.

2. Press under the seam allowance on the two sides and the pointed edges of the placket. Baste close to the edges. Trim seam allowance to ¼ inch (6 mm) (Fig. 19.47).

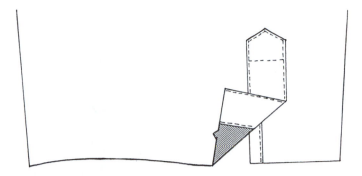

Fig. 19.46   Tailored placket

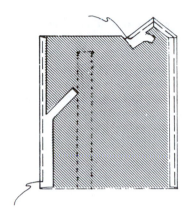

Fig. 19.47   Turning under and basting placket edges

3. Pin *right* side of the placket to the *wrong* side of the sleeve, matching stitching lines. Stitch along the dotted stitching lines, using a shortened stitch length at the corners (Fig. 19.48).

4. Cut along the solid line and diagonally to the corners (Fig. 19.48).

5. Turn the placket to the *outside*. Press the triangular end at the top *upward* and the long seam allowances *toward the placket* (Fig. 19.49).

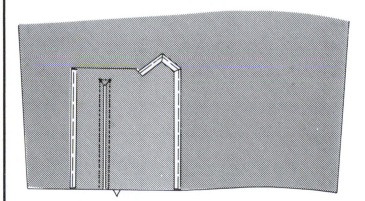

Fig. 19.48   Stitching and cutting placket opening

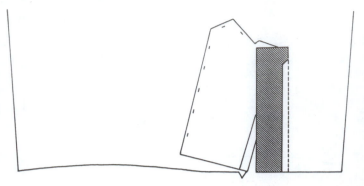

Fig. 19.49   Pressing placket

6. Fold the narrow side of the placket on the fold line, with *wrong sides together.* Stitch the pressed-under edge *over the seam,* stitching very close to the edge (Fig. 19.50).

7. Fold the wider side of the placket on the fold line, *wrong sides together,* placing basted edge over the seam. Stitch close to both long edges from the lower edge to the dotted line, *keeping the narrow edge of the placket free.* Tie thread ends instead of backstitching at the upper end of the seam line (Fig. 19.51).

Fig. 19.50   Stitching narrow side of placket

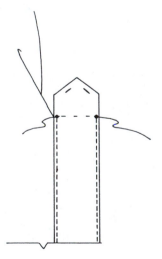

Fig. 19.51   Stitching both edges of wide side of placket

8. Pin the pointed edges of the placket to the sleeve. Stitch close to the outer edge and along the dotted line, through all thicknesses. Be sure that both sides of the finished placket are symmetrical in shape. Tie threads on the wrong side (Fig. 19.52).

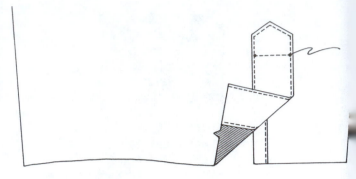

Fig. 19.52   Stitching pointed end of placket through all layers

Cuffs

Two kinds of cuffs are the lapped cuff and the shirt cuff. The lapped cuff (Fig. 19.53) is used with the continuous lapped placket, the faced placket, and the dart placket, and has the underlap of the cuff extended beyond the finished edge of the sleeve placket. The edge of the overlap on the cuff is aligned with the overlap on the garment. The shirt cuff (Fig. 19.54) is stitched with both ends of the cuff aligned with the finished edges of the placket.

Cuffs may be one piece or two; the procedures to follow when attaching the cuffs to the garment are the same. Making the two-piece cuff is similar to constructing a pointed collar. Cuffs usually are interfaced, with the

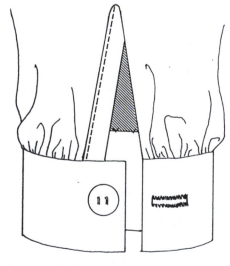

Fig. 19.53   Lapped cuff

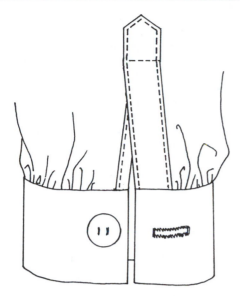

Fig. 19.54   Shirt cuff

interfacing most often placed on the upper cuff. On some styles a cuff will be joined to a sleeve with no placket opening, as is the case with short or three-quarter length sleeves. This style cuff can be attached most efficiently using the open construction technique.

To make a one-piece cuff:

1. Press the cuff in half to determine the fold line.
2. Place the interfacing on the wrong side of the upper cuff (notched edge) with one edge of the interfacing along the fold line. Catch stitch the interfacing to the cuff keeping the stitches into the fabric small and toward the under cuff (Fig. 19.55).

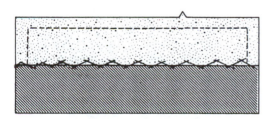

Fig. 19.55   Applying interfacing to one-piece cuff

3. Machine stitch the interfacing to the remaining three edges of the cuff.

To make a two-piece cuff:

1. Place the interfacing to the wrong side of the upper cuff. Machine stitch ⅛ inch (3 mm) into the seam allowance from the seam line on the outer edges (a in Fig. 19.56).

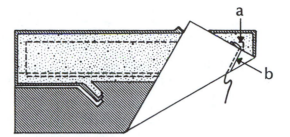

Fig. 19.56   Applying interfacing to two-piece cuff

2. With right sides together, pin the upper and under cuff pieces together along outer (unnotched) edge.
3. Stitch outer seam. Layer/grade the seam allowance and understitch (b in Fig. 19.56).
4. If the cuff has curved rather than square corners, assemble the cuff in the same manner as for making a round collar (see Chapter 15).

To attach cuff to sleeve with a placket opening:

1. If a continuous lapped placket is being used, turn under the bound edge on the overlap side and baste to hold in place; the bound edge of the underlap side is left extended.
2. With right sides together, pin the sleeve and the upper cuff (the interfaced side) edges together, matching notches and other pattern markings. If gathers or tucks are a part of the design of the garment, Chapter 14 should be reviewed.
3. On sleeves with a continuous lapped, faced, or dart placket, there may be a ½–¾ inch (1.3–1.9 cm) extension in addition to the ⅝ inch (1.6 cm) seam allowance on the underside of the sleeve (a in Fig. 19.57). On the overlap side of the sleeve the cuff should extend only the ⅝ inch (1.6 cm) seam allowance beyond the edge of the sleeve placket (b in Fig. 19.57).

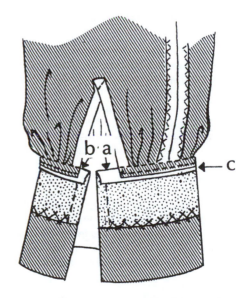

Fig. 19.57   Stitching upper cuff edge to sleeve

4. On sleeves with a tailored placket and the pleated sleeve closure, the cuff extends only the ⅝ inch (1.6 cm) seam allowance beyond the sleeve placket on both ends of the cuff.

5. Stitch the cuff to the sleeve.

6. If the sleeve is gathered, stitch this seam a second time ¼ inch (6 mm) into the seam allowance from the first row of stitching.

7. Layer/grade the seam allowance (c in Fig. 19.57).

8. Turn the seam toward the cuff and carefully press. If the sleeve is gathered, place the seam on a seam roll when pressing and press the seam line, but avoid pressing over the gathered area.

9. Fold the one-piece cuff in half along the fold line, right sides together, or fold the two-piece cuff in half along the seam line, right sides together. Be sure the *outer seam is folded toward the under cuff.*

10. At the seam joining the cuff to the sleeve, turn the *upper cuff seam allowance* toward the cuff (a in Fig. 19.58); the under cuff seam allowance is left extended (b in Fig. 19.58).

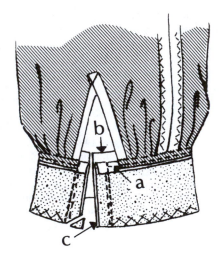

Fig. 19.58   Stitching ends of cuff

11. Pin the ends, *extending the under cuff ⅛ inch (3 mm) beyond the upper cuff,* making the upper cuff slightly larger than the under cuff (c in Fig. 19.58). Stitch the ends, following the seam line on the upper cuff.

12. Trim the corners; press the seam open using a point presser. Layer/grade the seam allowances.

13. Turn cuff to the outside, carefully pushing out the corner.

14. Press the cuff, rolling the end seams slightly to the wrong side.

15. Turn the raw edge of the under cuff to the inside and pin along the seam line (Fig. 19.59). Secure the inside edge by hand or topstitch by machine. To reduce bulk, the inside edge can be cut on a selvage or finished with a machine zigzag or overlock stitch and secured in place by stitching-in-the-ditch.

To attach cuff to a sleeve with no placket opening:

1. Interface the cuff as previously described.

2. With right sides together pin the cuff to the sleeve; stitch and layer/grade the seam allowance. Press the seam toward the sleeve.

3. Pin the underarm seam of the sleeve and the cuff, matching the seam joining the cuff to the sleeve. Try on the garment to determine the correct circumference for the cuff.

4. Stitch the underarm seam of the sleeve and cuff in a continuous seam (a to b in Fig. 19.60). Press the seam open.

5. Trim the cuff facing seam allowances to the fold line (c in Fig. 19.60).

6. Fold the cuff to the inside along the fold line. Secure the inside edge by hand or machine.

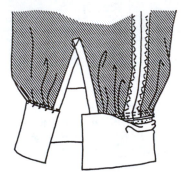

Fig. 19.59   Finishing inside of cuff

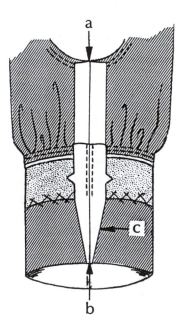

Fig. 19.60   Attaching cuff to sleeve with no placket opening

20 Pockets

Pockets may be on the outside of the garment and serve both a functional and a decorative purpose, or they may be inside the garment and be primarily functional. The inclusion of pockets on most garments is optional; they may or may not be used. Large patch pockets might be eliminated if they call unwanted attention to an area of the body. An inside pocket that could show through on lightweight or light-colored fabrics and create an unattractive appearance also might be omitted from a garment.

Many types of pockets are accented by flaps at the upper edge. The flaps are attached above the pockets after the pockets have been stitched to the garment.

There are many different pockets that can be included in the design of a garment. This chapter will discuss four: (1) patch pockets, (2) in-seam pockets, (3) in-set pockets, and (4) welt pockets. The chapter will focus both on preparing the pockets and on attaching them to the garment.

Patch Pockets

Patch pockets, because they are on the outside of the garment, generally are made from the fashion fabric. Sometimes, for emphasis, a contrasting fabric is used, or the fashion fabric may be cut on a different grain. Special details, such as tucks or pleats, may be a part of the patch pocket to give it a special touch. Sometimes, cov-ered cording is used to outline a patch pocket. Patch pockets can be almost any shape and size; they also can be lined or unlined. They are stitched to the outside of the garment in the desired location by topstitching or by invisible hand or machine stitching.

Round, Unlined Patch Pocket

To make a round, unlined patch pocket:

1. Mark the fold line for the hem of the pocket on the fabric (a in Fig. 20.1). Interface the hem allowance, if necessary, to provide additional support. A strip of fusible interfacing can be pressed to the pocket hem allowance, (b in Fig. 20.1) or a piece of sew-in interfacing can be attached by hand along the pocket hem fold line. The entire pocket area can be interfaced in some knit fabrics for added stability.

2. Finish the hem edge of the pocket in a manner appropriate for the fabric, (c in Fig. 20.1) (see Chapter 12).

3. Fold the pocket on the hemline, right sides together, and stitch from the fold to the lower edge of the hem (Fig. 20.2). Continue stitching around the pocket just *outside* the seam line, or ½ inch (1.3 cm) from the outer edge (a in Fig. 20.2). In addition to sewing the hem ends, this stitching serves as a guide line for turning the patch pocket.

4. Trim diagonally across the corner of the pocket hem; layer/grade the seam allowance to reduce bulk (Fig. 20.3).

5. Press the seam in the pocket hem open using a point presser. Turn the hem right side out, push out the corner, and press, rolling the seam slightly toward the wrong pocket.

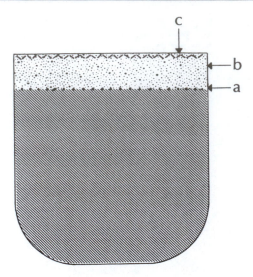

Fig. 20.1 Interfacing pocket hem and finishing hem edge

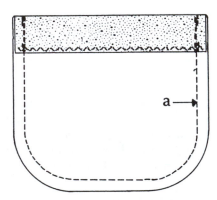

Fig. 20.2 Stitching hem ends and guide line for turning patch pocket

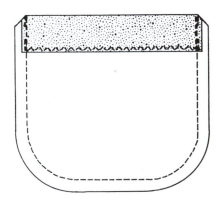

Fig. 20.3 Trimming corners and layering/ grading seam allowances in pocket hem

6. Press under the remainder of the seam allowance of the pocket, using the stitching line as a guide. A cardboard pattern cut the size of the *finished* pocket (without hem and seam allowances) can be placed inside the pocket when pressing (a in Fig. 20.4). This pattern helps to make the pocket symmetrical in shape and keeps the seam allowances from producing a ridge on the outside of the pocket.

7. Notch the curves to reduce bulk. Make small notches and place them close together in the curved area (b in Fig. 20.4).

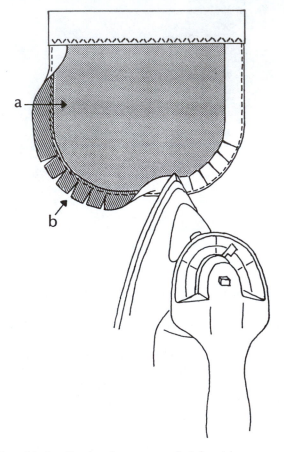

Fig. 20.4 Pocket hem turned right side out; pressing pocket seam allowance over a cardboard pattern

Square, Unlined Patch Pocket

To make a square, unlined patch pocket:

1. Finish the hem of the square, unlined pocket as previously described. Cut a cardboard pattern the size of the finished pocket and place inside the pocket when pressing to insure accuracy when forming the square corners.

2. Miter the lower corners on square pockets to produce a sharp corner with reduced bulk. Most of the steps in mitering a corner can be done while pressing as folding, trimming, and pressing need to occur simultaneously.

a. Fold under the seam allowances along all sides of the pocket and press (A in Fig. 20.5).

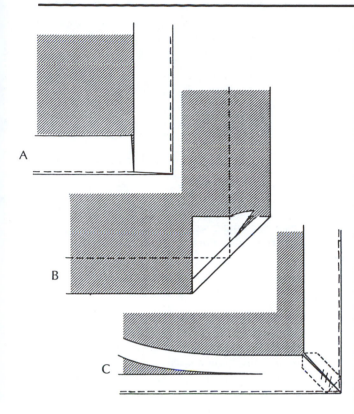

Fig. 20.5   Mitering a corner: *(A)* pressing under
seam allowance; *(B)* mitering corner;
(C) stitching mitered corner

b. Unfold the seam allowances; press a diagonal fold exactly across the point of the corner (*B* in Fig. 20.5).

c. Trim the seam allowance of the folded corner to ⅜ inch (1 cm). The seam must not be trimmed too close, or it may be hard to hold in place for the final steps.

d. Fold under the seam allowances on the sides of the pocket so that the folded edges meet on a diagonal in the corner (*C* in Fig. 20.5). Stitch the folded edges together by hand to hold them securely in place.

e. If the fabric is bulky, trim the seam allowances of the pocket to ⅜ inch (1 cm). Trimming would not be appropriate if the seam allowance is needed under the topstitching.

Lined Patch Pocket

To make a lined patch pocket:

1. Interface the pocket hem, if necessary.

2. If no pocket lining pattern is provided, cut one by folding the top edge of the pocket pattern along the fold line and cutting the lining from this pattern.

3. Press under the top edge of the lining ½ inch (1.3 cm) to the wrong side of the fabric (Fig. 20.6).

4. Pin the lining to the pocket with right sides together. Extend the lining ⅛ inch (3 mm) beyond the fashion fabric to make the lining slightly smaller than the pocket (Fig. 20.7).

5. Fold the pocket hem on the fold line, right sides together, and pin on top of the lining (Fig. 20.8). Stitch the hem and the lining to the pocket along outer edges. Layer/grade and notch, if needed (Fig. 20.9). Trim the corners of the hem diagonally to reduce bulk.

Fig. 20.6   Pressing hem in pocket lining

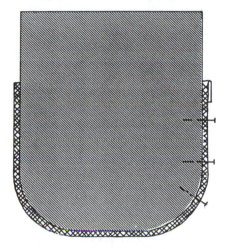

Fig. 20.7   Extending lining when joining to
pocket

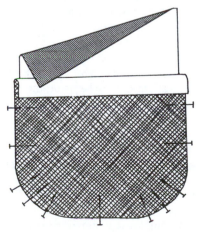

Fig. 20.8   Folding pocket hem over lining

6. Turn the pocket right side out and work the corners out carefully. Press, rolling the outer seam slightly to the underside. Hand basting the outer edge may be helpful in pressing.

7. Attach the pocket lining by hand to the pocket hem (Fig. 20.10).

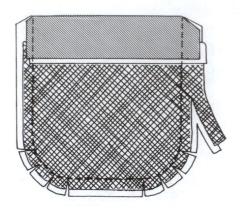

Fig. 20.9   Stitching pocket and lining

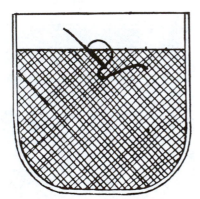

Fig. 20.10   Hand stitching lining to pocket hem

Attaching Patch Pockets

The location of patch pockets needs to be marked on the outside of the garment with pins or hand basting. After the pockets have been prepared, they are placed on the garment for sewing. Pinning, hand basting, or a glue stick all are appropriate methods for holding the pocket to the garment for sewing.

One of the rows of stitching that holds the pocket to the garment needs to be near the outer edge of the pocket, especially if the pocket is unlined. Often, a second row of stitching is used for reinforcement or for decoration. The stitch length used to attach the pocket should be the same as that used to topstitch other parts of the garment, or a longer stitch can be used for a more decorative effect. All threads should be pulled to the back and tied; backstitching is not appropriate on the outside of the garment.

The tops of the pockets need to be reinforced to keep them from pulling loose when the pocket is used. Figure 20.11 (a, b, c, or d) shows four ways that the corners of a

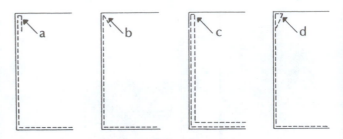

Fig. 20.11   Methods of reinforcing top corners of patch pocket

patch pocket can be reinforced. Pockets can be applied by hand as well as machine; however, the hand-stitched pocket may not be as durable as the machine-stitched pocket.

Pocket Flaps

Many pockets are accented by flaps attached to the upper edge after the pockets are stitched to the garment. The upper flap should be interfaced; a light- to medium-weight fusible interfacing usually works well. The pocket facing or under pocket piece can be cut from a lining fabric to reduce bulk. The pocket flap should be ⅛–¼ inch (3–6 mm) wider than the patch pocket to cover it appropriately, or about ¹⁄₁₆ inch (1.5 mm) narrower than the pocket opening if it is inserted into a welt opening.

To attach pocket flaps:

1. Prepare the pocket flap similar to methods for assembling a collar (see Chapter 15). Layer/grade, clip, and/or notch the seam inside the flap to reduce bulk. Make the under layer smaller than the top layer so that the seam edge will not show from the right side of the flap. This is done by extending the under layer about ⅛ inch (3 mm) when the seams of the flap are pinned together. Press the flap and topstitch, if desired.

2. Fold the pocket flap near the upper seam line to establish a roll line. Pin the flap close to the fold, and trim all layers of the flap to match that of the upper flap. This procedure allows the flap to lie flat against the garment because the upper flap is slightly larger than the under flap.

3. Hand baste the edges together, and remove the pins (Fig. 20.12).

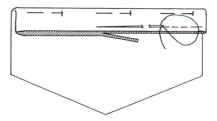

Fig. 20.12   Folding pocket flap to make upper flap larger than under flap

4. Place the flap on the garment in the position designated on the pattern, right sides together. Stitch through all thicknesses along the seam line (Fig. 20.13).

5. Trim seam allowance to ¼ inch (6 mm) and turn under the corners (Fig. 20.14). Place a second line of stitching ⅛–¼ (3–6 mm) from the first. The second row of stitching may be a machine zigzag stitch to finish the raw edge (Fig. 20.15).

6. Press the flap down against the garment. Topstitch through all thicknesses at the top of the flap (Fig. 20.16). Press. Hand stitching may replace topstitching by catching the under flap to the garment (Fig. 20.17). Hand stitches should not catch through to the outside of the flap.

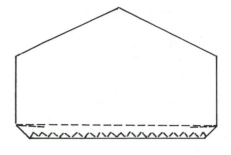

Fig. 20.15   Finishing seam of pocket flap with second stitching

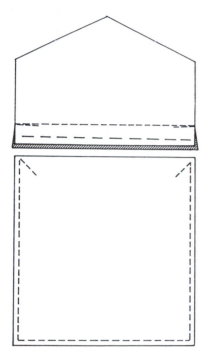

Fig. 20.13   Stitching lower edge of pocket flap to garment

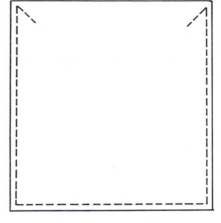

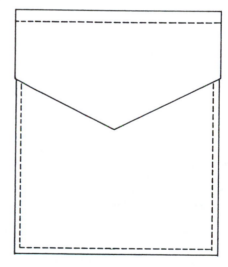

Fig. 20.16   Topstitching pocket flap

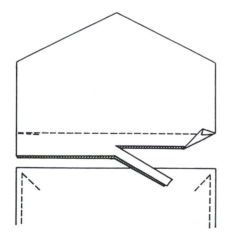

Fig. 20.14   Trimming pocket flap seam allowance and turning under corners

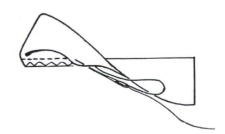

Fig. 20.17   Hand stitching pocket flap

Invisibly Stitched, Lined Patch Pocket

The invisibly stitched, lined patch pocket is a technique that attaches the pocket by machine from the inside of the pocket so no topstitching is visible on the outside of the garment. This pocket is most often used on tailored suits and coats. The lining can be eliminated, if desired. This procedure is best suited for a round patch pocket, and would require some modification if applied to a square pocket.

To make an invisibly stitched,
lined patch pocket:

1. Accurately mark the location of the pocket on the right side of the garment with hand basting (a in Fig. 20.18).

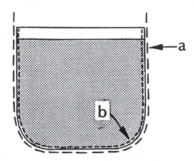

Fig. 20.18   Stitching pocket lining to garment

2. Cut the pocket lining from a lightweight, knitted fabric ⅛ inch (3 mm) *smaller than the size of the finished pocket.* Fold a ½ inch (1.3 cm) hem to the *wrong* side of the pocket lining and press.

3. Place the lining inside the pocket markings on the garment, with right sides together, and stitch close to the cut edge of the lining (b in Fig. 20.18).

4. Interface the hem of the fashion fabric pocket, if needed. The entire pocket may also be interfaced if more stability is needed, such as on a pocket for a tailored jacket. Fusible interfacing works well for this purpose.

5. Staystitch the pocket just outside the stitching line, within the seam allowance. Press the pocket over a cardboard pattern, that is cut the size of the finished pocket. Notch the curves, as needed, to reduce bulk (similar to Fig. 20.4 with the hem not stitched).

6. Press under the hem of the fashion fabric pocket on the marked line. Unfold.

7. Pin the pocket in position on the garment just inside the placement markings on the garment; the pocket will appear slightly full for the area. Baste in place, using a long, narrow zigzag stitch that just barely catches the edge of the pocket (a in Fig. 20.19). Slip basting can be used in place of the zigzag stitching if the latter is unavailable or inappropriate.

8. Pull the pocket open from the top with the hem extended. Machine stitch around the inside of the pocket using a straight machine stitch (a in Fig. 20.20). Begin the stitching at the fold line of the pocket hem and follow the line of stitching created by the machine zigzag basting used in step

7. Continue stitching to the fold line of the pocket hem on the other side. Fasten threads securely.

9. Remove the basting stitch.

10. Trim seam allowances at the ends of the pocket hem to reduce bulk. The seam allowance around the inside of the pocket can be trimmed, if desired. Fold the hem to the inside. Bring the lining over the pocket hem and slip stitch in place (a in Fig. 20.21).

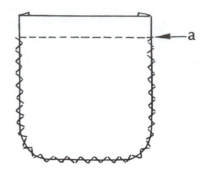

Fig. 20.19   Basting pocket to garment with zigzag stitching

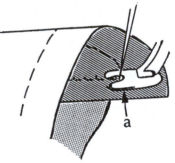

Fig. 20.20   Machine stitching inside of pocket to garment

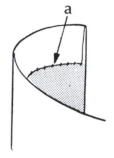

Fig. 20.21   Hand stitching lining to hem

In-seam Pockets

In-seam pockets are an extension of the side seam of the garment and are not seen from the outside of the finished garment. They are not appropriate in very lightweight or light-colored garments or in garments that fit snugly, as they will tend to leave an unattractive ridge on the outside of the finished garment.

There are two types of in-seam pockets: (1) those that are cut in one with the garment piece (*A* in Fig. 20.22) and (2) those that have a separate pattern piece. Those with a separate pocket piece can be made of lining weight fabric that is stitched directly on the seam line (*B* in Fig. 20.22), or they may be stitched to an extension (*C* in Fig. 20.22).

When the pocket is cut in one with the garment piece, the pocket will be from the fashion fabric. If this is not desirable because of the weight of the fashion fabric, the pattern can be cut to create a pattern with a separate pocket that could be cut from a lining-weight fabric. The patterns having a separate pocket piece also can be adjusted so that the pocket is cut in one with the garment. Such would be appropriate for fabrics of a weight suitable for both the fashion fabric and the pocket.

Since the pocket opening generally is not on straight grain, it may have a tendency to stretch and become distorted. Therefore, reinforcing the pocket opening may be necessary. A piece of straight seam binding can be cut the length of the pocket opening plus 2 inches (5 cm) and stitched to the opening. The stay tape goes on the wrong side of the pocket *front* and is placed so that its edge rests along the fold line of the pocket (Fig. 20.23). The stay tape is stitched in place before the pocket sections are joined to other parts of the garment.

To make an in-seam pocket cut in one with the garment:

1. Transfer the dots indicating the top and bottom of the pocket opening to the fabric.

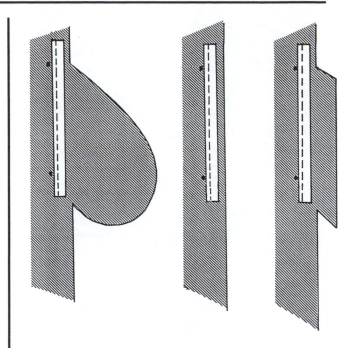

Fig. 20.23   Applying tape to reinforce pocket opening

2. After the stay tape is applied, if one is needed, join the two sections containing the pocket, right sides together, matching notches, dots, and other pattern symbols.

3. Hand baste the pocket opening closed between the dots (Fig. 20.24) so that it will not become stretched during construction.

4. Stitch the seam and pocket as one continuous seam; reinforce the corners of the pocket with a shorter stitch length for about 1 inch (2.5 cm) on each side of the corner (Fig. 20.25).

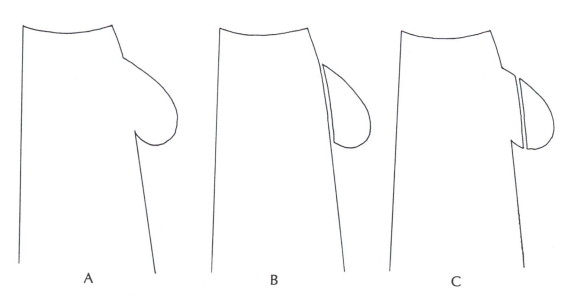

A   B   C

Fig. 20.22   Types of in-seam pockets

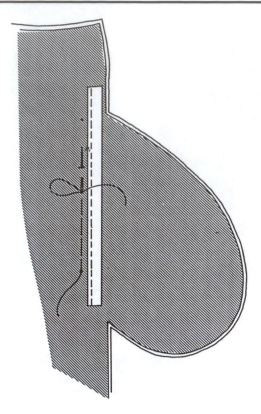

Fig. 20.24   Basting pocket opening closed

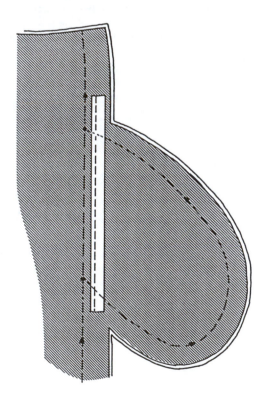

Fig. 20.25   Sewing the pocket and seam

5. Clip the seam allowance of the *back section* of the garment at a point below the lower corner of the pocket so that the seam can be pressed open (a in Fig. 20.26). The seam above the pocket opening usually is pressed toward the front (b in Fig. 20.26).

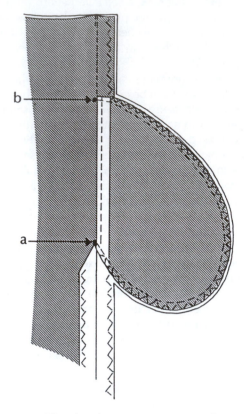

Fig. 20.26   Clipping lower corner, pressing, and finishing seams

6. Finish the edges of the pocket seam together in a manner appropriate for the fabric. To help hold the pocket in place, the front seam allowance should be caught in with the edge finish at the top and bottom of the pocket. The seam edges above and below the pocket also need to be finished (Fig. 20.26).

7. Carefully press the pocket, using some form of protection (e.g., strips of paper) between the pocket seam allowances and the fashion fabric. The basting along the pocket opening can be removed now or left until all construction on the garment is completed.

To make an in-seam pocket cut as a separate piece:

The procedure for attaching a two-piece, in-seam pocket follows exactly that of the one just described after the pocket piece has been joined to the extension.

1. Join the pocket to the extension on garment front and back, right sides together. Finish seam allowances of the pocket and the extension together (Fig. 20.27). Press toward the pocket.

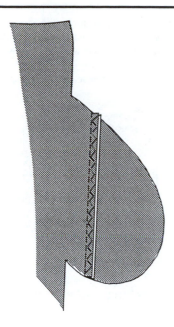

Fig. 20.27   Joining pocket to pocket extension

2. Stitch, reinforce, finish, and press the pocket and seams as previously described.

To make an in-seam pocket without an extension:

When no extension is present, the pocket is joined at the seam line.

1. Pin the pocket section to the garment right sides together (Fig. 20.28).

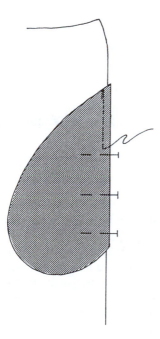

Fig. 20.28   Joining pocket to garment for pocket
             without extension

2. Stitch the seam, using a very narrow seam allowance, and finish the seam edges; turn the seam toward the pocket and understitch (Fig. 20.29).

3. Stitch, reinforce, finish, and press the pocket and seams as previously described.

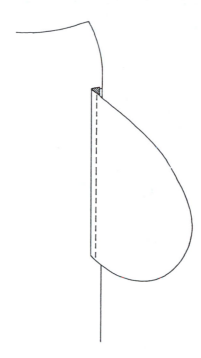

Fig. 20.29   Understitching pocket

Inset Pocket

The inset pocket (Fig. 20.30) is seen on pants, shorts, and skirts. The facing piece for the front edge can be cut from a lining-weight fabric to reduce bulk; the pocket would be cut from fashion fabric since it is a visible part of the garment or it can be cut from lining fabric, to reduce bulk. The upper portion of this piece, which would be visible from the outside, would be covered with a layer of fashion fabric.

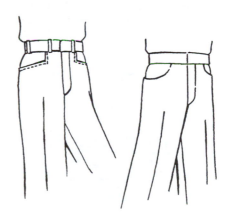

Fig. 20.30   Inset pocket

To make an inset pocket:

1. The edge of the garment forming the front of the pocket may need to be interfaced if the fashion fabric has a tendency to stretch and become distorted. If an interfacing is desired, cut one the shape of the pocket area and about 2 inches (5 cm) wide.

2. Pin the pocket facing (usually cut from a lining-weight fabric) to the garment front, right sides together, matching notches and other pattern symbols. Stitch along the seam line.

3. Layer/grade, clip, and understitch the seam (a in Fig. 20.31).

4. Turn the pocket facing to the inside and press, rolling the facing seam slightly to the wrong side. Topstitch the pocket edge if desired (Fig. 20.32).

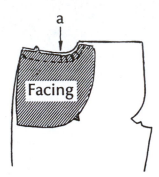

Fig. 20.31   Attaching pocket facing to garment

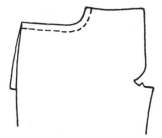

Fig. 20.32   Topstitching pocket edge

5. If the back pocket section consists of two pieces, pin the wrong side of the pocket yoke (cut of fashion fabric) to the right side of the back pocket piece. Stitch the upper edges together ½ inch (1.3 cm) from the edge. The lower edge can be zigzagged to the pocket, stitching over the cut edge (Fig. 20.33).

Fig. 20.33   Attaching yoke to back pocket piece

6. Pin the back pocket section to the garment front/pocket facing, matching notches and markings. Stitch the outer seam of the pocket together. Place a second line of straight or zigzag stitching ¼ inch (6 mm) from the first to reinforce the pocket seam and to finish the seam, if necessary (Fig. 20.34).

Fig. 20.34   Stitching pocket to pocket facing

7. Pin the upper and side edges of the pocket in position against the garment, matching markings. Baste edges together (a in Fig. 20.35).

8. Side edge of the pocket will be caught in the stitching of the side seams and the upper edge in the waistband.

9. After the garment is completed, reinforce the pocket end with a bar tacking, if desired.

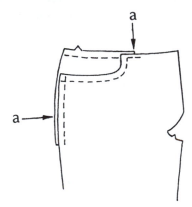

Fig. 20.35   Basting pocket edges to garment

Welt Pocket

Welt pockets can be made with either a single or double welt. Back pockets are often designed with a single welt (Fig. 20.36) at the opening. The pocket is one piece, usually cut from a firm pocket fabric, with a welt at the opening and a facing that covers the pocket fabric behind the welt opening, cut from the fashion fabric. The following directions are for a single welt pocket.

Adjust the size of the pocket opening if necessary to allow the hand to slide comfortably inside. Especially check the pocket size on boys' and teen-boys' patterns.

Fig. 20.36   Single welt back pockets

To make a single welt pocket:

1. Transfer pocket markings to the wrong side of the garment. Reinforce the pocket opening by machine stitching along the marked lines.

2. Interface the welt piece. Fusible interfacing usually works well for this purpose. Fold the welt in half lengthwise, *wrong* sides together. Press.

3. On the outside of the garment, position the stitching line for the welt over the bottom stitching line of the pocket opening. The fold of the welt is at the lower edge. Baste in place (Fig. 20.37).

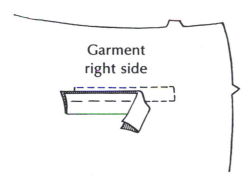

Fig. 20.37   Basting welt in place over pocket marking

4. Place the wrong side of the back pocket facing to the right side of the pocket. Position the facing edge about 2½–3 inches (6.5–7.5 cm) from the top edge of the pocket piece. Zigzag the edges of the facing to the pocket (Fig. 20.38).

5. Baste unfaced end of the pocket over the welt and marked pocket lines on the garment, right sides together.

6. Stitch along the stitching lines (a in Fig. 20.39). Stitch from the wrong side of the garment following the machine stitching lines made in step 1. *Do not stitch the ends.* Fasten threads securely.

7. Slash the pocket through all layers lengthwise through the center, between the stitching lines, and diagonally to the corners (b in Fig. 20.39).

8. Turn the pocket to the inside of the pants through the opening.

9. Stitch clipped corners and welt ends to the pocket piece inside the garment (Fig. 20.40). Press the opening.

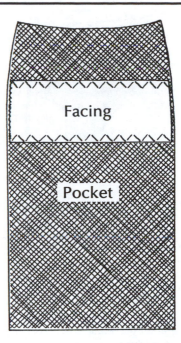

Fig. 20.38   Attaching facing to pocket piece

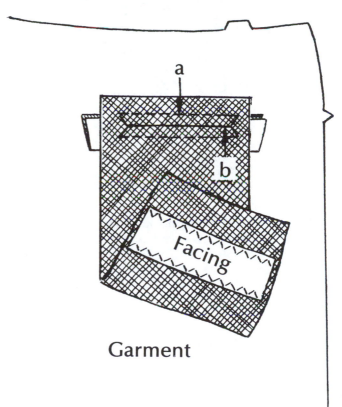

Fig. 20.39   Stitching pocket to garment

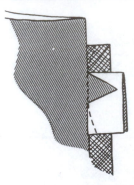

Fig. 20.40 Stitching pocket ends

10. Fold the pocket along the fold line and with right sides together pin the edges. The raw edge of the pocket piece should extend to the waistline edge.

11. Stitch the pocket edges, catching in the V-shaped ends of the opening. Place a second line of straight or zigzag stitching ¼ inch (6 mm) from the first line to reinforce the pocket seam and to finish the seam, if necessary (Fig. 20.41). Trim edges close to stitching.

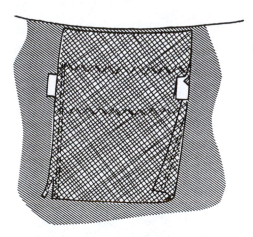

Fig. 20.41 Stitching pocket edges

12. Lay garment right side out. Turn upper edge down, exposing slashed edges of the pocket opening. Pin slashed edges to the back pocket piece. Stitch through all thicknesses (a in Fig. 20.42).

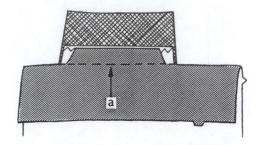

Fig. 20.42 Stitching upper edge of welt seam to pocket

13. Fold the garment waistline up and baste the upper edge of the pocket to the waistline so the pocket edge will be caught with the waistband stitching (Fig. 20.42).

14. Reinforce the pocket ends with bar tacking, if desired (Fig. 20.43).

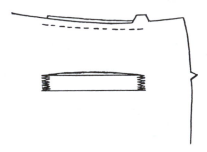

Fig. 20.43 Reinforcing pocket ends

21 Waistline Treatments and Belts

Waistlines in garments may consist of a waistline seam joining a garment top and a bottom or a waistband as is found on pants and skirts. Because these are areas in the garment that fit closely to the body, they usually are reinforced with interfacing or tape.

The correct fit of the waistline of a dress, skirt, or pants contributes much to the comfort and appearance of the garment. Before stitching the waistline seam, the garment should be fitted with the waistband or bodice temporarily in place to determine the right length of the bodice, the correct position of the waistline seam, and the correct waistline circumference. The waistline of the garment should be approximately ½–1 inch (1.3–2.5 cm) larger than the actual body measurement to allow for movement and for variation in size.

Waistbands

Waistbands of pants and skirts may be straight or contoured, wide or narrow. The shape and width of the waistband determines, to a great extent, the type of interfacing that can be used with it. Many of the special interfacing products work only with bands that are cut straight. Straight waistbands usually have a fold at the top edge unless a seam is needed for a special purpose, like attaching belt loops.

Cutting the Waistband

The waistband pattern can be used, or a band can be cut to the person's body measurements. Any adjustments made in the waistline of the garment pattern would also need to be made in the waistband pattern before it is cut.

Straight waistbands can be cut on lengthwise or crosswise grain, though usually they are cut with the lengthwise grain going around the body. A basic waistband is cut the length of the waist measurement plus 3 inches (7.5 cm) and twice the desired width plus two seam allowances. If the inside edge of the waistband is cut on the selvage or is finished with a flat finish such as a zigzag or overlock stitch, one seam allowance can be omitted. Using the selvage edge or a flat finish helps to reduce bulk since this edge is not visible from the outside and does not have to be turned under for finishing.

Interfacing the Waistband

In addition to sew-in and fusible interfacings, special products such as monofilament tape are available to provide support for waistbands. The monofilament tape is quite firm and is appropriate for use only with straight waistbands. This interfacing is more satisfactory on bands of narrow to medium width.

Sew-in Interfacings

Sew-in interfacings, which are medium- to heavyweight, usually are cut the width of the finished waistband and placed on the front half of the band to help hide the seam line. The interfacing can be placed against the fold line of the waistband and held in place with a catch stitch (Fig. 21.1), or the interfacing can be placed across the fold line of the waistband by ⅜ inch (1 cm) and held in place with a row of machine stitching (Fig. 21.2). The machine stitching must be placed on the back of the waistband in such a position that it will not show from the outside of the finished garment.

If placed on the back half of the waistband, the interfacing can be machine stitched (Fig. 21.3) to hold it securely in place.

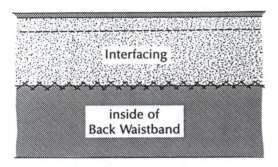

Fig. 21.1   Interfacing held to waistband with a catch stitch

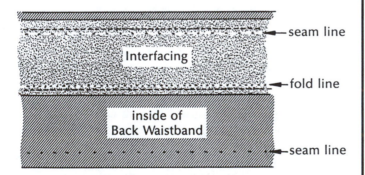

Fig. 21.2   Interfacing held to waistband with machine stitching on back side near fold line

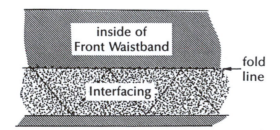

Fig. 21.3   Interfacing stitched to back side of waistband

Fusible Interfacings

Fusible interfacings usually are placed across the entire waistband; ½ inch (1.3 cm) can be trimmed from the seam allowances before the interfacing is fused to the fashion fabric to reduce bulk, if desired (Fig. 21.4). Special fusible interfacings for waistbands are available; directions on the package need to be followed when applying the interfacing to the fashion fabric.

Fig. 21.4   Fusible interfacing attached to entire waistband

Interfacing Tapes

Monofilament nylon waistband interfacings are available by the yard or in packages; widths range from 1 to 2½ inches (2.5 to 6.5 cm). They are light in weight, will not shrink or stretch, and do not roll. The amount of interfacing tape needed to interface a waistband equals the length of the finished waistband plus 1½ inches (3.8 cm) for the overlap/underlap. Monofilament tapes are applied after attaching the waistband to the garment (see page 250).

Applying the Waistband

After the band has been cut, markings can be made on the band for center front, center back, and the side seam position (Fig. 21.5). Determine these markings by fitting the waistband around the waist, first marking with pins where the band comes together. An extension should be left on one end of the waistband for the underlap. Remove the band and fold in half to determine the halfway point. If the waist section to be attached to the band is gathered, fold the waistband in half again to determine the quarter point markings. Since the pant or skirt is usually slightly larger than the waistband, it is eased to the waistband while pinning. In the following method, the band is first sewn to the outside of the garment, turned to the inside on the fold line, and then stitched again by hand or by machine.

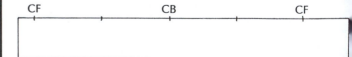

Fig. 21.5   Marking waistband to fit

To apply waistbands with sew-in or fusible interfacing:

1. Apply the waistband interfacing in an appropriate manner.

2. Pin the waistband to the garment, right sides together, matching the waistband markings to those on the garment. If the waistband has been cut from the pattern, match the notches and other pattern markings. If the waistband has been cut from body measurements, use the pin markings on the band to indicate matching points. If the garment has gathers along the waistline, several matching points need to be determined and used to guarantee even distribution of gathers. Place the pins *parallel to and directly on the seam line* so that the garment can be fitted before stitching (Fig. 21.6).

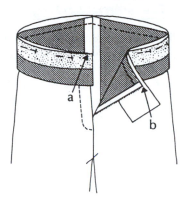

Fig. 21.6   Pinning waistband to garment for fitting

3. For proper alignment a basic waistband should extend just one seam allowance beyond the edge of the garment on the overlap side opening (a in Fig. 21.6) and at least 1½ inches (3.8 cm) beyond the edge of the garment on the underlap opening (b in Fig. 21.6). This allows for an underlap of ¾– 1 inch (1.9–2.5 cm) (Fig. 21.7). If the garment has a fly front zipper, there is sufficient underlap as a part of the zipper application so that the additional extension on the band may not be needed.

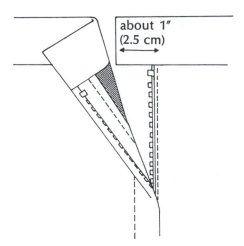

Fig. 21.7   Underlap for waistband

4. Try on the garment. Fold the waistband in half and pin the waistband in its proper position. Check for fit. Readjust, if necessary.

5. Stitch the waistband seam, making sure that the horizontal stitching lines match on each side of the zipper when the zipper is closed. Add a second row of stitching ¼ inch (6 mm) into the seam allowance if gathers are a part of the seam.

6. Layer/grade the seam to reduce bulk.

7. Press the seam toward the band. Place the seam on the edge of a seam roll or near the edge of the ironing board to avoid pressing beyond the seam line.

8. To close the ends of the waistband, fold the band in half along the fold line, right sides together. To make the underside of the band a little shorter so that it won't show from the outside of the finished garment, extend the underside ⅛ inch (3 mm) when pinning the ends together (a in Fig. 21.8). The waistline seam joining the band to the garment is folded toward the band; the lower seam on the back of the band is left extended (b in Fig. 21.8). If a selvage edge (or zigzagged edge) is used to finish the back of the band, the lower edge of the back side will be even with the seam allowance joining the waistband to the garment.

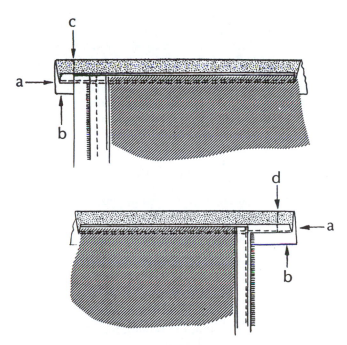

Fig. 21.8   Closing ends of waistband

9. Stitch the ends of the band. On the overlap side of the zipper, the band is stitched even with the overlap (c in Fig. 21.8). On the underlap, the band is stitched about ¾–1 inch (1.9–2.5 cm) from the edge to form an underlap (d in Fig. 21.8).

10. Trim diagonally across the corners to reduce bulk. Press end seams open using a point presser. Layer/grade the seam allowances.

11. Turn the band right side out, carefully pushing out the corner. Press the band, rolling the end seams slightly to the back side of the band to prevent its showing on the outside of the finished garment.

12. If there is a seam allowance on the back side of the waistband, turn under so that the fold lies just *above* the stitching line. Blind or slip stitch in place. A variation of this is to turn under the seam edge so that the fold lies just *below* the stitching line. Pin. Topstitch or stitch-in-the-ditch by machine stitching from the right side.

13. When a selvage edge or a zigzag edge finish is used for the back side of the band, the finished edge comes just above the stitching line if stitched by hand or will extend to just below the stitching line if finished by machine.

14. Topstitch the waistband, if desired. Attach an appropriate fastener when the band is complete.

To apply waistband with interfacing tape:

Since interfacing tapes are firm and should not fold back on themselves, they are not caught in any of the regular machine stitching when attaching the waistband. The waistband is attached to the garment, then the interfacing tape is stitched into the waistline seam allowance.

1. Apply the waistband to the garment as described in steps 2–6, omitting the interfacing.

2. Cut the interfacing tape ¾ inch (1.9 cm) longer than the waistline measurement plus ease.

3. With the waistband still folded down against the garment, right sides together, place the interfacing tape over the *waistline seam allowance* with one edge of the tape *along the seam line* joining the band to the garment (a in Fig. 21.9 and 21.10). On the overlap side of the waistband, the end of the interfacing is placed *even* with the finished edge of the garment (b in Fig. 21.10); on the underlap, the interfacing ex-

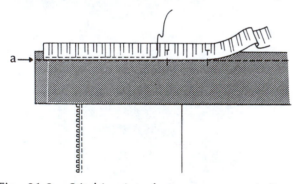

Fig. 21.9   Stitching interfacing tape to waistline seam allowance

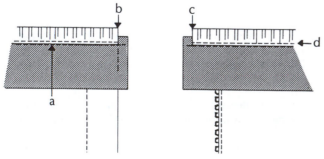

Fig. 21.10   Alignment of interfacing tape at ends of waistband

tends about ¾ inch (1.9 cm) beyond the edge of the garment opening providing the underlap for the waistband (c in Fig. 21.10). The seam allowance at the ends of the waistband extends beyond the interfacing.

4. Stitch the interfacing tape close to the lower edge using a straight or a zigzag stitch (d in Fig. 21.10).

5. Finish the waistband ends and the underside of the waistline seam as described in steps 7–12; the interfacing tape should *not* be caught in the stitching of the ends.

6. When attaching a fastener to the waistband, some of the stitches should be caught into the interfacing tape. Buttonholes do not work well with this type of waistband finish.

Waistbands Backed with Ribbon or Commercial Backing

Grosgrain ribbon or a commercial backing for waistbands can be used for the inside edge of the waistband. The ribbon or backing is applied to the waistband along the upper edge of the front half of the band. The front band would be interfaced in an appropriate manner. The grosgrain ribbon should be preshrunk before using it as a backing for a waistband.

To prepare waistband with backing:

1. Cut a strip of fabric for the band 4 inches (10 cm) longer than the waistline measurement and the width of the finished band plus two seam allowances.

2. Fold the seam allowance at the upper edge of the band to the inside and press. The fold will serve as a guide for attaching the backing.

3. Open flat and place one edge of the backing slightly below the fold of the seam allowance so that it will not show on the right side of the band when it is finished (Fig. 21.11). Stitch the backing to the band, leaving the seam allowances free at both ends.

4. Attach the band to the garment, following directions for a waistband with sew-in interfacing.

To close ends of band made with backing:

1. For lightweight backing and fabric, follow the directions for finishing the ends of the band with sew-in interfacing.

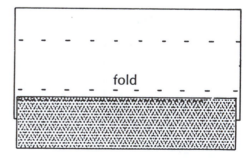

Fig. 21.11   Attaching ribbon or backing to waistband

2. When heavier backing is used:
   a. Trim seam allowance from ends of backing.
   b. Turn in ⅝ inch (1.6 mm) seam allowances on ends of the band and trim out excess bulk at the corners (Fig. 21.12).
   c. Crease or baste the fold.

To finish inside waistband made with backing:

1. Fold backing to the inside of the garment.
2. Pin the backing in place at the ends of the band, center front, center back, side seams, and other points as needed, keeping the edge of the backing just above the waistline seam.
3. Stitch backing along the waistline seam and across the ends by hand (Fig. 21.13).

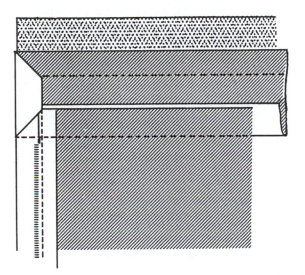

Fig. 21.12   Turning under and trimming ends of waistband

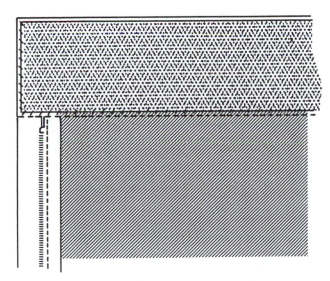

Fig. 21.13   Finishing waistband made with backing

Waistband with Center Back Seam

Some waistbands are cut as two pieces and are attached separately to the right and left half of the garment. This technique is found most often in tailored pants, especially ones for men. The band is attached to each half of the garment before the upper part of the center back seam is stitched (Fig. 21.14). With the waistband extended (a in Fig. 21.15), the back seam of the garment and waistband are stitched (b in Fig. 21.15). The seam is often larger—typically about 1½ inches (3.8 cm) wide—so adjustments for fit can be made. The waistband would be completed as previously described.

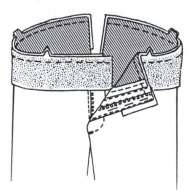

Fig. 21.14   Attaching waistband to each half of pants

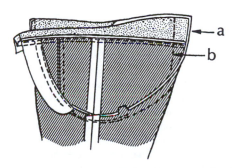

Fig. 21.15   Stitching center back seam of pants and waistband

Belt Loops

Fabric belt loops are used with many garments having waistbands. The loops or carriers are placed at strategic spots on the garment, usually at center back, at the side seams, and 2–3 inches (5–7.5 cm) on either side of center front and center back. The length of the belt loop is equal to the width of the belt plus 1 inch (2.5 cm). Belt loops are usually stitched at the top edge of the waistband and extend below the band to allow the belt to cover the waistline seam. Belt loops can be reinforced by using twill tape or a woven fusible interfacing cut to the width of the finished loop and placed inside the belt loops before they are topstitched.

To apply belt loops:

1. Cut the strip of fabric that will form the belt loops or carriers 3 times the width of the finished carriers and as long as needed for all the loops. One edge of the strip can be cut on a selvage edge, finished with a zigzag or overlock stitch, or an additional ¼ inch (6 mm) can be added to the width and folded under to finish the edge.

2. Interface the strip with a fusible interfacing or with twill tape, if desired. Fold the strip in thirds (a in Fig. 21.16). The inside edge will be a selvage, finished by zigzagging, overlocking, or folding under ¼ inch (6 mm). Topstitch as close as possible to both sides (b in Fig. 21.16). Wider loops may be topstitched twice down each side.

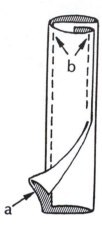

Fig. 21.16   Topstitching belt carriers

3. Cut the strip into equal lengths for the individual belt carriers. Finish the cut ends with zigzag stitching.

4. Pin all loops (except the one at center back on waistbands with a center back seam) in place, right sides together, allowing the cut edge to extend ¼ inch (6 mm) into the waistline seam (a in Fig. 21.17). Machine baste in place along the waistline seam. Machine stitch across the lower fold line of loop several times (b in Fig. 21.17).

5. Attach the waistband to the garment. After the waistband is attached, the belt loops can be completed.

6. Fold loop along lower machine stitching (a in Fig. 21.18).

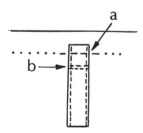

Fig. 21.17   Attaching belt loops to waistline

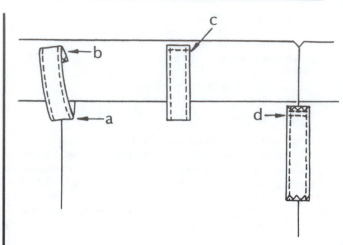

Fig. 21.18   Stitching top of belt loops and securing loop at center back

7. Turn under ⅜ inch (1 cm) (b in Fig. 21.18) and place the folded edge even with the top edge of the waistband (c in Fig. 21.18).

8. Securely machine or hand stitch close to the folded edge (c in Fig. 21.18).

9. Attach the loop over the center back seam as illustrated in Figure 21.18 (d). Fold loop up and finish top as described above.

An alternate procedure can be used to attach the loops to the upper edge of the waistband so that no machine stitching is visible on the outside.

1. Cut the loops about ½ inch (1.3 cm) longer than those which will be attached by machine.

2. Attach the lower end of the loops as described in steps 4–5.

3. Finish the upper edge of the loops with a machine zigzag stitch.

4. Fold the upper edge of each loop over the top and to the back side of the waistband.

5. Attach the end of the loop to the back side of the waistband by stitching around the folded portion by hand (Fig. 21.19).

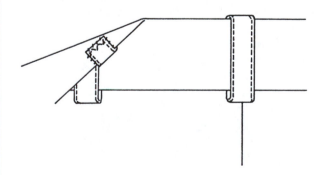

Fig. 21.19   Hand stitching top of belt loop to back side of waistband

Faced Waistline

Skirts and pants without visible waistbands are usually finished with a fabric facing or grosgrain ribbon.

To finish waistline with facing:

1. Make and attach a fitted facing at the waistline, following directions to apply a facing before installing a lapped zipper in Chapter 15. The waistline facing is usually interfaced to prevent stretching.

2. Complete placket opening by inserting a zipper by the open seam method (see Chapter 17).

To finish waistline with ribbon:

1. Use grosgrain ribbon ¾–1 inch (1.9–2.5 cm) wide and waist measurement plus 6 inches (15 cm) long. Preshrink the ribbon before using.

2. Clip the waistline seam to the staystitching.

3. Lap the ribbon to the waist seam line, ⅛ inch (3 mm) beyond the staystitching. Extend the ribbon ½ inch (1.3 cm) beyond the right side of the opening and 1½ inches (3.8 cm) beyond the left side of the opening.

4. Shape the ribbon over the hip area by making two or three ¼ inch (6 mm) tucks near each side seam (a in Fig. 21.20).

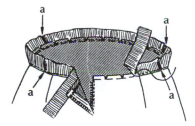

Fig. 21.20   Ribbon stitched to waistline

5. Machine stitch the ribbon to the garment close to the ribbon edge (Fig. 21.20).

6. Fold the ribbon to the inside of the garment and press. Hand tack the ribbon to the garment seams and darts.

7. Turn under the ½ inch (1.3 cm) extension of ribbon on the right side and hand stitch to the zipper tape. On the left side, turn under 1 inch (2.5 cm) of ribbon extension so that the end is between the garment and the grosgrain facing. Allow ½ inch (1.3 cm) of folded ribbon to extend beyond the opening. Hand stitch along the zipper tape.

8. Attach a hook on the left extension and an eye on the right side (Fig. 21.21).

Fig. 21.21   Placement of hook and eye on ribbon

Waistline Seam

The waistline seam joining the top and bottom of a garment can be reinforced with a piece of straight seam binding to hold it in place and to prevent it from stretching. If the fabric stretches easily, or if the skirt is very heavy, a stay is necessary.

The waistline stay can be applied either before or after the waistline seam has been stitched and fitted. The waistline seam is pressed toward the area with the least fit; if each area has approximately the same amount of fit, the waistline seam is pressed toward the top. The stay is applied so that it does not fold against itself when the waistline seam is pressed.

The waistline stay may be stitched to either the bodice or the skirt to help adjust the ease and any additional fullness. It is easier to attach the stay to the section of the garment that is less full. It should be placed on the wrong side of the garment over the seam line so that it will be caught in the waistline stitching. The ends of the stay may be extended so that they fasten with hooks and eyes under the placket of the garment closing to relieve strain and to maintain design lines when the garment is worn.

To attach a waistline stay:

1. Cut the stay several inches (cm) longer than the waist measurement.

2. If the dress has a side placket, measure the length on the stay tape to equal the distance from the placket to the center front and mark with a pin (a in Fig. 21.22).

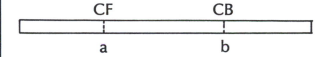

Fig. 21.22   Locating center front and center back on waistline stay

3. From center front, measure one-half the total waist measurement on the stay tape and mark for center back (b in Fig. 21.22).

4. Match center front and center back of the stay tape to the center front and back of the garment (a and b in Fig. 21.23). Pin in place.

5. Distribute ease as needed between center front and center back on the right half of the garment. Retain position of side seam established in fitting. Pin in place (Fig. 21.23).

6. To obtain the same ease distribution for the left half of the garment, fold the unpinned ends of stay tape at center lines and measure the distance to the right side seam. Mark the exact length of stay required for the left front and left back (a to c, and b to d in Fig. 21.23). Pin these points at the left side seam line.

7. Distribute the ease and pin the stay in place.

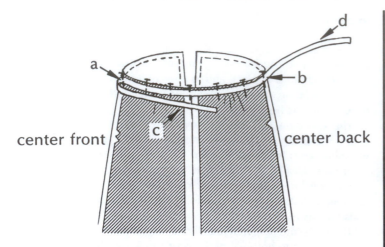

Fig. 21.23   Pinning stay to waistline

8. If the dress has a center front or back placket, divide the stay in half to locate center mark and proceed as previously described.

9. Stitch the stay to the garment close to the waist seam line.

10. Check the fit and ease distribution before cutting off the excess length of the stay.

Belts

Belts may be stiffened or left unstiffened. Stiffened belts have commercial belting, cording, or interfacing added to give shape to the belt. Belting is available in a variety of widths and can be purchased by the yard or in a package that may contain a buckle as well. Nonstiffened belts usually are tie belts, which have a softer look. Tie belts are made by folding a piece of fabric in half and stitching, leaving an opening for turning.

The method described here for covering a belt involves making a fabric tube and inserting the belting into the tube. An alternate method involves pressing under the raw edges of the fashion fabric and topstitching it to the belting.

To cover commercial belting:

1. Cut belting 6 inches (15 cm) longer than the waistline measurement.

2. Trim one end of the belting to form a point or other desired shape.

3. Cut the fashion fabric 1 inch (2.5 cm) longer than the belting and twice the width plus two seam allowances. Always cut the fabric following the grainline. It can be cut on either lengthwise or crosswise grain.

4. With right sides together, fold the fabric in half the entire length.

5. Slip belting between the two layers of fabric, fitting it snugly against the fold. Pin the layers together close to the belting (Fig. 21.24).

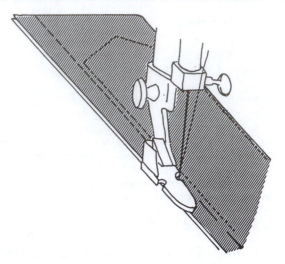

Fig. 21.24   Stitching seam in belt tube

6. Using the zipper foot, stitch through the two layers of fabric close to the belting (Fig. 21.24). Care must be taken not to catch any of the belting in the seam.

7. Remove the belting. Manipulate the seam line to a place slightly off-center of the fabric tube and press open over a point presser or seam roll (Fig. 21.25). Trim the seam to ¼ inch (6 mm) to reduce bulk.

Fig. 21.25   Pressing open seam in belt tube

8. Lay the point of the belting tube ½ inch (1.3 cm) from one end. Following the point of the belting, sew the pointed end of the fabric (Fig. 21.26). Secure thread ends. Layer/grade the seam allowances and trim corners and point.

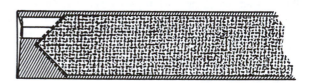

Fig. 21.26   Stitching point end of belt loop

9. Turn the fabric tube right side out, shape point, and press. Insert belting in the tube and work it into the point. If desired, the belt may be topstitched close to the edges. To avoid pulling the fabric off grain, stitch in the same direction along both edges.

10. Turn the unstitched end to the inside and stitch by hand, or the cut edge can be finished with a machine zigzag.

To make a belt with a backing:

1. Cut a strip of belting 6 inches (15 cm) longer than the waist measurement.

2. Shape the point of the belting as directed for the covered belt.

3. Cut a strip of fabric ½ inch (1.3 cm) longer than the belting and twice the width plus ⅛ inch (3 mm).

4. Place the belting in the center of the fabric strip. The fabric should extend ½ inch (1.3 cm) beyond the pointed end of the belting.

5. At the pointed end, fold and press a seam allowance of the fabric over the belting (Fig. 21.27).

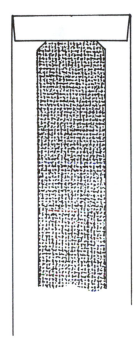

Fig. 21.27   Turning fabric over shaped end of belting

6. Fold and press the sides of the fabric over the belting so that the edges meet in the center (a in Fig. 21.28).

7. Fold the corners of the fabric over the point of the belting (b in Fig. 21.28); press.

8. Slip the belting out of the fabric. Trim excess fabric around the point. Trim to within about ¼ inch (6 mm) of the fold (a in Fig. 21.29). A few small stitches at the point will

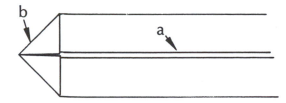

Fig. 21.28   Turning sides and ends of fabric over belting

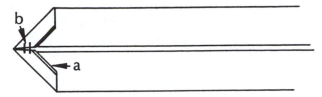

Fig. 21.29   Trimming and securing fabric at point end

hold two folded edges together (b in Fig. 21.29) and assure a sharp smooth point on the finished belt.

9. Place the wrong side of the belting over the wrong side of the folded and shaped belt. Hand baste together, if necessary, and topstitch along the edge of the belting, catching both the fabric and belting (Fig. 21.30). To avoid pulling fabric off grain, stitch both sides of the belt in the same direction.

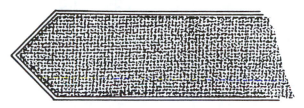

Fig. 21.30   Stitching backing to folded edges of fabric

To finish the belt:

1. If the buckle has a prong, mark the location for three or more eyelets on the finished end of the belt, beginning 1½–2 inches (3.8–5 cm) from the end and spacing them about 1 inch (2.5 cm) apart. Punch eyelets and finish with a buttonhole stitch (Fig. 21.31) or with metal eyelets.

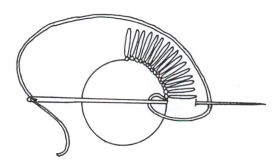

Fig. 21.31   Making an eyelet by hand using a buttonhole stitch

2. Fit the belt to the waistline over the garment and mark the location for the buckle prong. Machine stitch around the prong location and cut out between the rows of stitching (Fig. 21.32). The cut edge may be finished with a buttonhole stitch or machine zigzag stitch, if needed.

3. Place the buckle and prong on the end of the belt. Stitch in place by hand or by machine (Fig. 21.33).

4. A fabric belt guide, similar to a belt loop, can be placed on the belt, if desired (Fig. 21.34).

Fig. 21.32   Stitching opening for belt prong

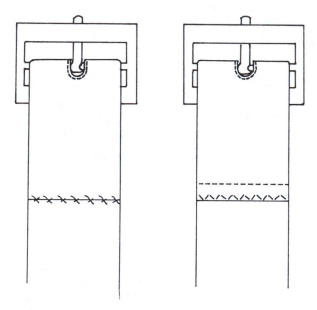

Fig. 21.33   Stitching end of belt

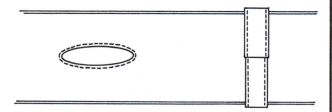

Fig. 21.34   Stitching belt guide to belt

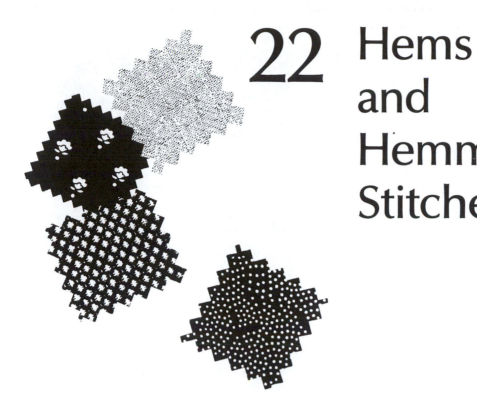

22 Hems and Hemming Stitches

Hems are used as a finish for edges in garments. They may include the turned-up hem, the faced hem, or the bound hem. Facings and bindings are discussed in other chapters of this book; this chapter will concentrate on turned-up hems. A well-made hem will have the following characteristics:

—Hem is inconspicuous on the right side except when the hem becomes part of the design, such as in sheer fabrics.

—Hemline is an appropriate distance from and parallel to the floor.

—Hem width is even and the appropriate depth for the style and the fabric.

—Bulk is removed from garment seams that fall within the hem.

—Fullness is eased in and evenly distributed for a flat, smooth finish.

—Edge finish must not create unnecessary bulk.

—Hemming stitches are evenly spaced.

—The type of hemming stitch used is appropriate for the fabric.

Marking the Hemline

Hemlines in skirts, dresses, or pants are marked with the garment on the wearer. The garment should be completed except for the hem when the marking is done.

This means that, if the garment is a skirt or pants, the waistband is finished and the fasteners are attached. If the garment is to be worn with a belt, the belt should be in place when the hemline is marked. Shoes appropriate for the garment should be worn to insure that the correct finished length for the garment is obtained. For flared or bias-cut styles, allow the garment to hang overnight before marking the hemline.

Hem lengths vary according to the type of garment, fashion, and individual preference. A commercial hem marker or a yard/meter stick can be used for marking the hemline on a skirt so that the edge is parallel to the floor. Pants hemlines are marked by folding up the extra fabric at the bottom toward the outside or the inside of the pant leg.

To mark the hemline:

1. Determine the distance from the floor for the hemline according to figure proportions, garment style, and fashion. Adjust the hem marker to the desired length.

2. Move the marker around the person wearing the garment. Insert pins parallel to the edge of the skirt to indicate the hemline (Fig. 22.1). When marking a garment with pleats, the outer and inner edges need to be marked carefully to insure that they are even.

3. The person wearing the garment needs to stand erect with equal weight on each foot while the hem is being marked.

4. Once all pins are in place, a quick check will identify those that are not accurate and that need to be moved.

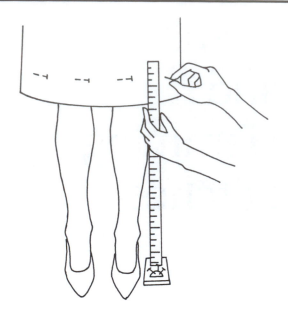

Fig. 22.1   Marking the hemline

Preparing the Hem

When the marking process is completed, the garment should be removed and placed on a flat surface or over an ironing board to prepare the hem. The correct hem width needs to be determined. The appropriate width for a hem is determined primarily by the shape of the hem edge. The more curved the hem, the more narrow the hem width; the straighter the hem, the wider the hem can be; lighter weight fabrics can take a deeper hem than can heavier weight fabrics.

Hem widths on skirts to be finished with a hand hemming stitch range from 1½ inches (3.8 cm) to 3 inches (7.5 cm), with the average being around 2 inches (5 cm). Hem width for pants is usually from 1½ to 2 inches (3.8 to 5 cm), with extra length needed if the pants are to be cuffed.

Hems to be finished with machine topstitching are usually narrower in width, and will range from ¼ inch (6 mm) for a single topstitched hem to 1–1½ inches (2.5–3.8 cm) for a hem with two or more rows of top stitching.

To turn up the hem:

1. Place the garment on a flat surface, and correct the marked line for pins that are not properly aligned.
2. Turn the hem to the inside of the garment along the pinned line; pin the hem in place about 1 inch (2.5 cm) above the fold line (a in Fig. 22.2). Match hem seam lines to garment seam lines (b in Fig. 22.2) and distribute fullness evenly. Remove pins from the hem fold. Add a second row of pins along the upper edge of the hem if necessary to hold the hem allowance in place.

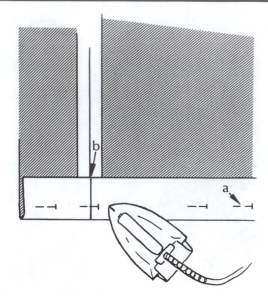

Fig. 22.2   Pinning hem in place

3. Try the garment on to check the length and evenness of the line. Adjust if necessary.
4. Remove garment and press along the fold, removing pins just before pressing. (To avoid pin marking the fabric and scratching the iron, do not press over pins.)
5. For skirts with pleats, fold the pleats in place to check the length of the underlay in relation to the skirt hemline.

When the hemline is determined to be the appropriate length and is even around the garment, the hem allowance needs to be trimmed to an appropriate and even depth.

To mark hem depth:

1. Determine the appropriate hem depth, considering the style of the garment, the weight of the fabric, and the type of hem to be used.
2. Spread garment wrong side out on a table or an ironing board. Unfold the hem. On the hem allowance, measure and mark the desired hem depth from the fold line using pins or chalk (Fig. 22.3).

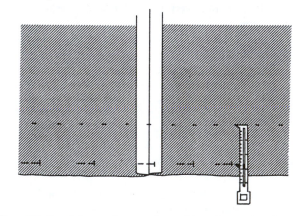

Fig. 22.3   Measuring and marking hem depth

3. Trim excess fabric from the hem allowance so that the cut edge will be parallel to the fold line.

4. Trim excess fabric from the vertical seams within the hem allowance by cutting the seam diagonally from the hem edge to the hem fold line (*a* in Fig. 22.4).

5. For seams located at the fold of a pleat, use one of the following methods to achieve a sharp fold on the finished pleat:

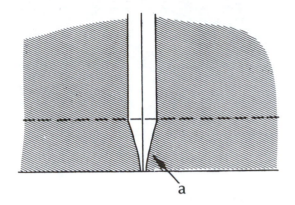

Fig. 22.4   Trimming seams from hem fold line to hem edge

Method I:

a. If bulk is not a problem, slash both seam allowances almost to the seam line just *above* the top of the hem (*a* in Fig. 22.5). Press open the seam inside the hem. Layer seam allowances from the hem edge to the fold line. Do not press open the pleat seam above the top of the hem.

b. Press the pleat through the hem area on the pleat fold line and the vertical seam line (Fig. 22.6).

c. On the inside of the garment, topstitch the pleat fold through the hem area to keep the pleat sharp (*a* in Fig. 22.6).

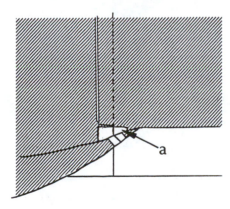

Fig. 22.5   Clipping, layering/grading, and pressing pleat seam in hem—Method I

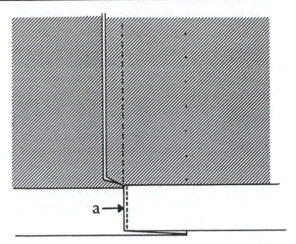

Fig. 22.6   Finishing pleat in hem—Method I

Method II:

a. When fabric is bulky or not easily pressed, leave the seam open about 8 inches (20.5 cm) from the lower raw edge.

b. Complete the garment assembly, including the hem. Be sure that both sides of the hemline are even at the bottom of the open seam.

c. Stitch the open section of the seam through the finished hem (*a* in Fig. 22.7).

d. Miter the seam corners by turning in the ends on medium- or lightweight fabric, or trimming diagonally on heavy fabrics. Overcast edges together (*b* in Fig. 22.7).

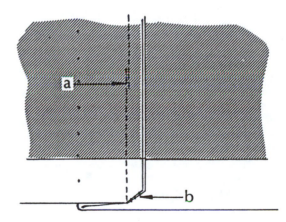

Fig. 22.7   Stitching pleat through hem—Method II

Shaping the Hem

Hem edges in flared garment styles will be larger than the area of the garment to which they are attached; therefore, the hem must be eased or shaped to fit. Fabrics such as woolens that will shrink with heat and moisture can be shaped while pressing; other fabrics will need to be eased using an easing thread. Shaping of the hem occurs *after* the hem has been trimmed to an even depth but *before* the edge finish is applied. If there is too much fabric to be eased in, the depth of the hem may need to be reduced.

To ease a hem:

1. Using a slightly longer stitch, machine stitch ⅛–¼ inch (3–6 mm) from the cut edge.
2. Draw up the ease thread and distribute fullness so that the hem fits the garment without distorting the hemline and the vertical seams are aligned (Fig. 22.8). Use a needle or pin and draw up the fullness by pulling up on the easing thread from the wrong side of the hem at regular intervals. Work with the garment over the ironing board to facilitate this process.

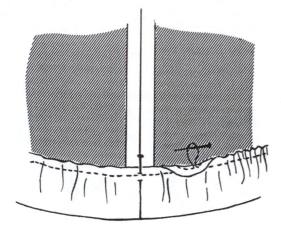

Fig. 22.8   Shaping the hem with an easing thread

3. Press the hem. Place a strip of paper between the hem allowance and the garment to prevent press marks on the right side of the garment.
4. Apply the appropriate edge finish to the hem edge. To keep the easing in place, seam binding or stretch lace can be used to finish the hem edge.

Finishing Hem Edges

The raw edge of the hem needs to be finished in a manner appropriate for the fabric and the shape of the hem (see Chapter 12). Hem edges are often finished in the same manner as other garment edges like seams and facings. The finish chosen depends on the extent to which the fabric will ravel, the weight of the fabric, the shape of the hem, the end use of the garment, and whether the hem is exposed in the finished garment. If the edge is not finished correctly, the type of finish used may cause the hem to show on the right side of the garment. Generally the more a hem edge is stitched or

manipulated, the greater the likelihood that the hem will show on the outside of the garment.

The *edge stitched hem edge* (Fig. 22.9) that is left plain or pinked is a flat finish that is effective for fabrics that do not ravel, especially worsted wool. It is used, too, for hems that are covered by a lining.

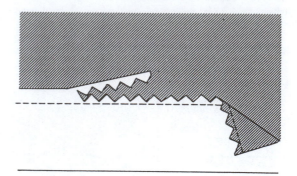

Fig. 22.9   Hem edge pinked and stitched

To edge stitch a hem:

1. Using a regular machine stitch, stitch ¼ inch (6 mm) from the hem edge.
2. Trim the edge with pinking shears.

The *overcast hem edge* (Fig. 22.10) provides a flat finish that is recommended for medium- to heavyweight fabrics. The regular zigzag (A in Fig. 22.10) or multiple zigzag stitch (B) on the conventional machine or the overlock stitch (C) on the overlock machine may be used. The hand overcast stitch (D) may be substituted for machine stitching on very delicate fabrics. This finish is very versatile and provides an effective finish without adding any unnecessary bulk.

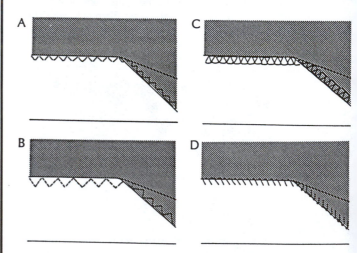

Fig. 22.10   Overcast hem finish: (A) regular machine zigzag; (B) multiple stitch zigzag; (C) overlock stitch; (D) hand overcasting

To overcast a hem edge:

1. Using the appropriate machine or hand overcast stitch, stitch along the hem edge, enclosing the edge in the stitching.
2. Trim away any loose threads along the edge.

The *turned and stitched edge finish* (Fig. 22.11) is appropriate for lightweight fabrics and provides a durable finish especially for washable garments.

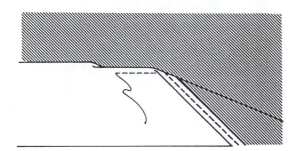

Fig. 22.11   Turned and edge stitched hem finish

To turn and edge stitch the hem edge:

1. Turn under the hem edge ¼ inch (6 mm) and pin.
2. Machine edge stitch ⅛ inch (3 mm) from the fold.

Seam binding (Fig. 22.12) is a straight piece of tape that is placed over the hem edge and stitched in place with a straight or a zigzag stitch. Since it covers the raw edge, it provides a neat appearance to the inside of the garment. It is often used on a hem edge that has been eased with an easing stitch. The tape is applied *after* the hem has been shaped and pressed. Care must be taken not to pull the tape too tight, as this will cause the hem to show on the outside of the garment.

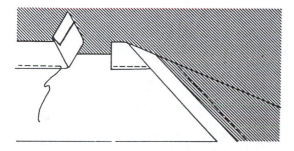

Fig. 22.12   Seam binding hem finish

Stretch lace (Fig. 22.13) is a form of seam binding that has built-in flexibility. Because of this characteristic, stretch lace molds well to curved hems. It is placed over the seam edge as is seam binding and stitched in place. Care must be taken not to stretch the lace during application.

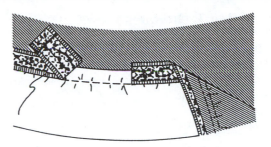

Fig. 22.13   Stretch lace hem finish

To finish the hem edge with seam binding or lace:

1. Lay one edge of the seam binding or stretch lace ¼ inch (6 mm) over the cut edge on the right side of the garment hem and pin in place.
   a. If the edge is curved, ease the hem to fit the garment before applying the binding or lace. Place the binding or lace so it covers the raw edge of the fabric and one edge of the binding is on the ease stitching line.
   b. If the hem edge is straight, allow a small amount of ease in the binding or lace to provide some give along the hemline. Binding or lace that is applied too tight will cause the hemline to show from the outside of the garment.
2. Fold under ¼ inch (6 mm) on the cut end of the binding or lace and overlap the first end about ¼ inch (6 mm).
3. Machine stitch the seam binding or lace to the hem edge, stitching close to the edge.

Bias tape (Fig. 22.14), either commercially prepared or self-made, can be placed over the edge of the hem and stitched in place. Because the bias will mold to the fabric, this finish is suitable for hems in medium- and heavier weight fabrics where a curved edge is present. Several weights, widths, and types of bias tape are available commercially.

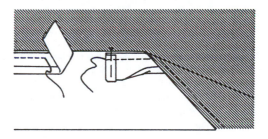

Fig. 22.14   Bias tape hem finish

To finish the hem edge with bias tape:

1. Open up one folded edge of the tape and place the raw edge along the hem edge. Pin in place.
2. Fold back the end of the tape ¼ inch (6 mm) and pin.
3. Overlap the opposite cut end about ¼ inch (6 mm).
4. Machine stitch along the fold line.
5. Fold the bias tape up against the stitching and press.

Hemming Techniques

The hem can be secured to the garment by hand stitching, machine stitching, or fusing. The choice depends on the style of garment, type of fabric, and end use of the garment.

Hand-stitched Hems

Several procedures are important to follow when doing a hand hemming stitch to insure that the finished hem is invisible on the outside of the garment.

1. Use a single thread of matching color for hemming. Running the thread across beeswax before hemming will keep the thread from tangling and knotting during the hemming process.
2. Place stitches ½–¾ inch (1.3–1.9 cm) apart and keep them loose. Catch only one thread of the fashion fabric when sewing the hem.
3. Hemming between the hem and the outer layer produces a more durable and less obvious hem than hemming directly on or over the edge.

Several kinds of stitches are suitable for hems. When used for hemming, the stitches are kept loose and spaced further apart. When used to secure the inside edges of cuffs and waistbands, the stitches are shorter and pulled up tighter.

The *blind or slip stitch* is usually done on an edge or through a fabric fold. It is often used on turned and stitched edges or when seam binding or stretch lace has been used to finish the hem edge. As very little thread is exposed in this stitch, it is considered a very durable stitch. Since the stitch is usually done on the edge, it is more suited to finishing the back side of cuffs, waistbands, and collars, and less desirable as a hemming stitch.

To make a blind or slip stitch:

1. Fasten the thread securely under the edge of the hem. Take a small stitch into the fashion fabric directly *below* the stitch in the hem (*A* in Fig. 22.15).
2. Directly above this stitch insert the needle into the fold at the hem and slide it through the fold for ½–¾ inch (1.3–1.9 cm) (*B* in Fig. 22.15).
3. Bring the needle out of the fold and again pick up one yarn of fashion fabric directly below and return the needle to slide through the fold in the hem edge. These stitches are very nearly at right angles to the hem edge.
4. If the hem edge is not a fold, slide the needle under the hem edge between each stitch taken in the fashion fabric. When done this way the stitch is called a blind stitch (Fig. 22.16).
5. Continue in this manner for the entire hem.

The *catch stitch* can be done either over an edge or under an edge between the hem and the outer garment

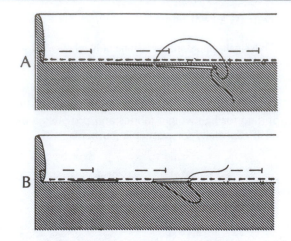

Fig. 22.15   Making a slip stitch through a folded edge

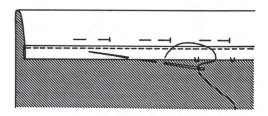

Fig. 22.16   Making a blind stitch under the edge of seam binding

layer. When stitched over the edge it is often used to attach the interfacing to fold lines on facings, collars, and cuffs (see Chapter 14). If used as a hemming stitch it must be done between the two layers to prevent a ridge from showing on the right side of the garment. The catch stitch is sewn from left to right, for right-handed sewers, and right to left for left-handed sewers. When completed, it looks like a cross-stitch.

To make a catch stitch:
(described for a right handed sewer)

1. Fasten thread securely under the hem edge.
2. Fold the hem edge back ¼ inch (6 mm). The rolled edge of the hem is held in place with the thumb as the stitching progresses.
3. Move the needle to the right ¼–½ inch (6–13 cm) and take a stitch in the garment, parallel to the edge, with the needle pointing back toward the left.
4. Again move to the right ¼–½ inch (6–13 cm) and take a similar stitch in the hem (Fig. 22.17).
5. Alternate catch stitches between the hem edge and the garment.

The *lock stitch* is a type of blanket stitch done between the hem and the outer fabric. It is suitable mainly for hems. If done on the edge, all of the thread is ex-

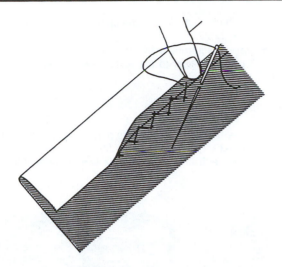

Fig. 22.17   Using the catch stitch for a hem

posed, making the hem subject to snagging and excessive wearing. Since there is a twist of the thread at each stitch, the lock stitch is quite durable making it a desirable hemming stitch. Stretch can be built into the stitch when working with knit fabrics.

To make the lock stitch:

1. Fold the hem edge back ¼ inch (6 mm). Fasten hemming thread under the hem edge.

2. The *folded hem edge and the thread* are held in place with the thumb. Take a small stitch in the garment and then in the folded edge of the hem (Fig. 22.18). The thread loop should be *under* the needle as each stitch is taken.

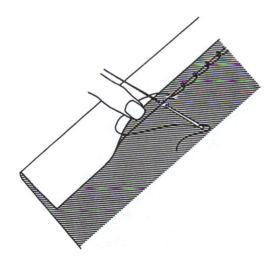

Fig. 22.18   Using the lock stitch for a hem

3. Pull the thread up, leaving the stitch slightly loose. If stitches are pulled too tight, a ridge will show on the right side of the garment.

4. Continue around the garment, spacing stitches ½–¾ inch (1.3–1.9 cm) apart.

Machine-stitched Hems

Hems can be machine topstitched or machine blind stitched. Topstitching can be done through a single or a double fold in the fabric and is recommended for garments with a great deal of flare, on shirts and blouses, and for ones constructed from single-knit fabric with a tendency to curl. It may be done with one or more rows of topstitching and with a single or double needle. Narrow hems usually are turned twice before stitching to give a neat appearance to the lower edge of the shirt or garment; however, if working with heavier fabric, the lower edge may be finished with a zigzag or overlock stitch and turned up once and stitched.

Topstitching on hems often coordinates with other topstitching done on the garment. For a decorative effect, a longer stitch length is used and can be done with a double thread through the needle or with the use of the heavier top stitching thread. Decorative stitches or zigzag stitches on conventional sewing machines also can be used for hemming of garments (Fig. 22.19) as can the narrow rolled hemming stitch on an overlock machine (Fig. 22.20). All threads should be tied on the wrong side. Refer to Chapter 10 for topstitching procedures.

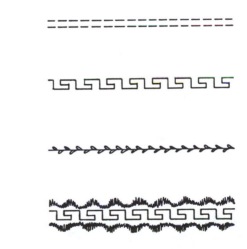

Fig. 22.19   Using decorative stitch for topstitched hem

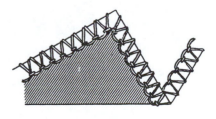

Fig. 22.20   Using an overlock machine for a narrow rolled hem

To topstitch a narrow hem:

1. For a curved hem, machine stitch about ⅛ (3 mm) from the hem edge in the curved area (a in Fig. 22.21). Place a second row of stitching ¼ inch (6 mm) from the first in the same curved area (b in Fig. 22.21). Use the two rows of stitching as guides for turning and easing the hem when preparing the hem for stitching.

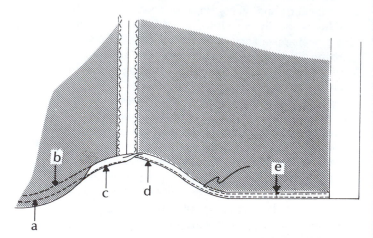

Fig. 22.21 Double-folded narrow machine-stitched hem

2. Fold under and press, if desired, ¼ inch (6 mm), close to the first row of stitching (c in Fig. 22.21). Fold again another ¼ inch (6 mm) for a double fold hem (d in Fig. 22.21).

3. In the curved areas, use a pin to pull on the guide stitching to ease in the fullness in the areas where there is a convex curve.

4. For fabrics too bulky for a double folded hem, zigzag or overlock the hem edge and fold the hem up ¼ inch (6 mm). One row of machine stitching near the fold line will aid in turning in the curved areas (a in Fig. 22.22).

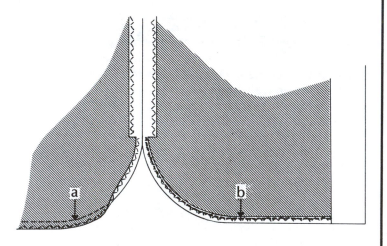

Fig. 22.22 Single-folded narrow machine-stitched hem

5. Machine stitch close to the upper edge (e in Fig. 22.21 or b in Fig. 22.22).

6. If there is a front facing, it should be finished over the hem, if possible. Refer to the section on Hemming a Faced Opening.

To topstitch a wide hem:

1. Press under the desired amount for the hem, 1–1½ inches (2.5–3.8 cm) is a typical width.

2. Layer vertical seams inside the hem to the fold line (a in Fig. 22.23).

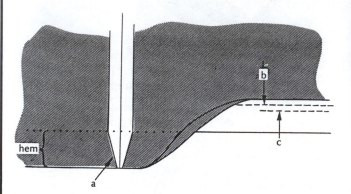

Fig. 22.23 Making a wider machine-stitched hem

3. Finish the hem edge, if necessary.

4. Machine topstitch from the wrong side ⅛–¼ inch (3–6 mm) from the upper edge of the hem (b in Fig. 22.23).

5. Place a second row of stitching ⅛–¼ inch (3–6 mm) below the first, if desired (c in Fig. 22.23). A double machine needle may also be used, to make two parallel rows of machine stitching. If a double needle is used, the stitching must be done from the *right* side of the garment.

Machine blind hemming is durable but has a tendency to show on solid color, smooth textured fabrics. It works well on patterned fabrics and fabrics with surface interest, such as corduroys, where the stitch is hidden under the nap.

To machine blind stitch:

1. Set the sewing machine for the blind hemming stitch.

2. Finish the raw edge of the hem with one of the methods described above.

3. Fold the hem back against the garment, exposing about ¼ inch (6 mm) of the hem edge.

4. Guide the hem into the machine so that the straight stitching is along the hem edge. Every fourth or fifth stitch is a lateral zigzag, which catches the fold of the outer fabric (Fig. 22.24). Some practice may be necessary to avoid catching too much of the fashion fabric in this lateral stitch and creating a hemming stitch that is conspicuous on the outside of the finished garment. Some adjustment in the stitch width may also be necessary to accommodate the thickness of the fabric.

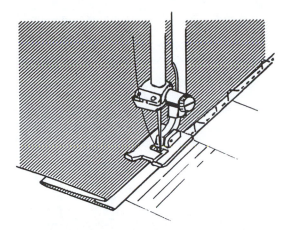

Fig. 22.24   Machine blind hemming stitch

Fused Hems

A hem can be attached to the fashion fabric with a strip of fusible web, which can be purchased in prepackaged strips or by the yard. The fused hem is recommended for use on knit fabrics that are difficult to hem by hand, and where a machine topstitched hem would not be appropriate, such as on interlocks or soft jersey knits. It is especially suited for hems on flared skirts. If properly done, the fused hem should remain secure through normal wear and laundering. The hem depth on a garment with a fused hem is generally no wider than 1½–2 inches (3.8–5 cm).

To make a fused hem:

1. Prepare the hem as previously described. Press the edge being careful not to stretch the fabric.
2. Cut the fusible web ¼ inch (6 mm) narrower than the width of the finished hem.
3. Place the web between the hem and the garment, with one edge against the fold (Fig. 22.25). The upper edge of the web should be placed about ¼ inch (6 mm) down from the upper edge of the hem.

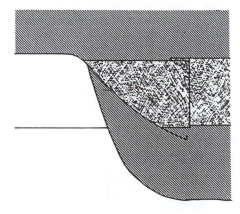

Fig. 22.25   Placing a strip of fusible web between hem and outer fabric

4. Fuse baste in place by lightly pressing down with the iron over the hem (Fig. 22.26). Do not slide the iron while pressing. Be careful not to place the iron directly on the fusible web.
5. Cover the hem with a damp press cloth and press with the iron for 10 seconds on each area of the hem (Fig. 22.27).
6. Dampen the press cloth, as necessary, to complete the hem.
7. Allow fabric to cool before handling.

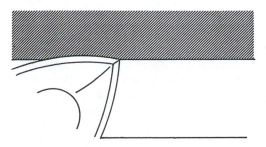

Fig. 22.26   Fuse basting hem to the fusible web

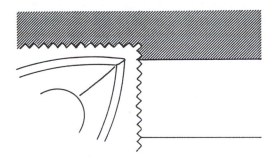

Fig. 22.27   Completing the fused hem by pressing with a damp press cloth

Other Hemming Techniques

Some hems may require a facing (see Chapter 15); others may have an exposed bias binding around the edge (see Chapter 16). In a few exceptional cases, no hem finish is used at all (e.g., some garments made from fabrics such as knits, felt, suedes, and leathers). Fringing the edges of open weave fabrics is yet another hemming alternative for some garments when the hem is parallel to the grainline.

Special Hemming Techniques
Lined and Underlined Garments

When hemming a garment with an underlining, all hemming stitches are taken through the underlining layer only. This insures that the hem will be invisible on the outside of the finished garment.

Garments with a lining can be hemmed either separately or together. If the hemming stitches would show and if the garment style is appropriate, the lining can be placed inside the hem and the garment hemmed as with an underlining. If the lining is hemmed separately from the fashion fabric, generally the lining is made ½ inch (1.3 cm) shorter than the garment. The lining hem is turned toward the fashion fabric so that the inside of the garment has a finished look. A machine topstitched hem often is used for the lining to avoid unnecessary bulk and to speed up the process of hemming.

Hemming a Faced Opening

When hemming a faced opening, the facing is folded so that it is on top of the hem (Fig. 22.28). This finish gives a smoother, less conspicuous look to the open edge of the garment and is less bulky than when folding the hem up over the facing. If the front of the garment is to be topstitched or if it has a topstitched band or placket, the hem would need to be completed before the garment is topstitched. To reduce some of the bulk in the hem area, the hem may be layered/graded behind the facing. This hemming procedure is recommended for the lower corners of full-length faced openings on shirts, blouses, jackets, and coats, and also for openings like slits in vertical seams.

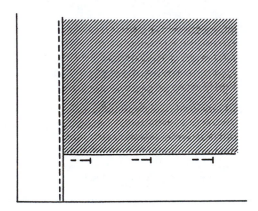

Fig. 22.28   Hem of a faced opening

To finish a hem with a faced opening:

1. Fold up the hem on the garment and facing and press to identify the hem fold line.
2. Turn down the hem and fold the facing to the outside and against the garment with right side of the facing against the right side of the garment.
3. Match and pin the creased hem lines of the facing and garment.
4. Machine stitch on the creased line (a in Fig. 22.29).
5. Trim out excess fabric at the corner and layer/grade the hem allowance (b in Fig. 22.29).
6. Turn the facing to the wrong side pushing out the corner; press.
7. Turn up the garment hem and pin in position. Finish with a suitable hem finish.

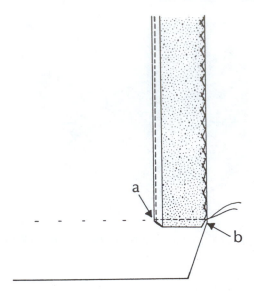

Fig. 22.29   Stitching and layering/grading the faced opening

Pants Hems

The length of pants varies with the style of the pants and with fashion. Tapered styles are usually shorter than tubular styles. Flared styles can be longer. The hemline at the back of pants can be ½ inch (1.3 cm) longer than the front, if desired. Before establishing the hem, allow pants to hang from the waist overnight, so that fabrics tending to stretch will hang correctly. To mark the hem, put pants on with belt, if desired. Wear shoes of appropriate height. Determine the correct length by folding up the excess fabric to the outside or to the inside of the pants leg. Pin close to the fold.

To make pants hem:

1. Mark hem fold line with pins or hand basting (a in Fig. 22.30).
2. Fold excess fabric to the inside along fold line.
3. Try on the garment to check length and evenness of the hemline. Adjust, if necessary.

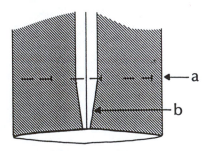

Fig. 22.30   Preparing a regular pants hem

4. Spread hem area flat and measure down from the fold line markings the desired width for the hem, 1½ inches (3.8 cm) is usually adequate.

5. Trim away excess fabric.

6. Layer seams inside hem to reduce bulk (*b* in Fig. 22.30).

7. Finish the cut edge with a method appropriate for the fabric (zigzag, edge stitch, or overlock).

8. Stitch hem with a durable hand stitch or by machine. The lock stitch is recommended.

Folded Cuffs

To make folded cuffs:

1. Mark the desired hem length on the pants or sleeve.

2. Spread the hem area flat, and measure down the amount needed for the cuff and the hem. The cuff requires twice the width desired for the finished cuff plus the hem allowance. For a 1½ inch (3.8 cm) cuff, this amount would equal 4–4½ inches (10 to 11.5 cm) (Fig. 22.31).

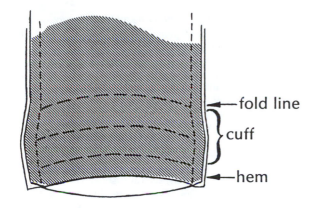

Fig. 22.31   Markings for folded cuff

3. Turn the fabric under along the *hem fold line for the cuff* (the middle marked line on Fig. 22.31) and press lightly.

4. Turn up the cuff and try on garment to check for length and evenness of hem. Adjust if necessary.

5. Trim away excess fabric.

6. Layer vertical seams.

7. Finish cut edges of cuff (zigzag, edge stitch, or overlock).

8. Stitch hem in place with a durable hem stitch or a machine blind stitch. Hemming with a regular machine stitch is also possible as it will be covered by the cuff.

9. Form the cuff by folding along the hemline.

10. Press. A damp press cloth will help to give sharp folds and creases.

11. Secure the cuff along the seams with a hand stitch between the cuff and the pants (Fig. 22.32), or by stitching-in-the-ditch.

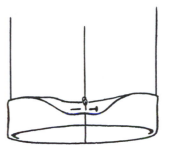

Fig. 22.32   Securing folded cuff at seam

GLOSSARY

AGAINST THE GRAIN—Working with the garment bias edge in the direction that forces the yarn ends to ravel out from the fabric and the cut edge to stretch.

ALL-BIAS INTERFACINGS—A nonwoven interfacing that stretches in all directions.

ALTER—To change a pattern so that it corresponds to body measurements plus appropriate ease allowances. To change a portion of a garment so that it fits the body.

ALTERATION LINE—Horizontal double lines, printed on commercial patterns, indicating the location for making certain pattern alterations.

ALTERNATE CLIPPING—Clipping each layer of a concave seam allowance separately so that the layers spread in different places.

APPLIED CASING—See CASING.

ARMHOLE—The opening in a garment for insertion of the arm. Also called *armscye*.

ARMSCYE—See ARMHOLE.

BACKING—A second layer of fabric used to reinforce the underside of a garment piece, a waistband, or a belt.

BACKSTITCH—To machine stitch two or three stitches back on the same line to secure the end of a seam line. Sometimes used instead of tying a knot at the end of stitching.

BALANCED PLAID—See EVEN PLAID.

BALLPOINT NEEDLES—Hand and sewing machine needles with slightly rounded points that are recommended for use when sewing on knitted fabrics. The needle point pushes between fabric yarns instead of piercing them.

BAR TACK—A series of hand or machine zigzag stitches forming a bar to reinforce points of strain, such as the ends of hand-stitched or machine-stitched buttonholes and other garment openings.

BASTE—To make a long, loose, temporary stitch by machine, hand, or with pins (1) to mark portions of a garment, such as a center front, pocket placement, pleats; (2) to hold two pieces of fabric together until permanently stitched. The length of stitches depends on the purpose of the basting and its placement.

BEESWAX—Used to reduce the tendency of thread to tangle and knot during hand sewing. To apply wax, slide thread through the wax several times to coat the thread.

BELTING—A heavy woven material, available in various widths and weights, used to reinforce garment fabric when making belts or waistbands.

BELT LOOPS—Belt carriers, made in various widths and shapes, applied to the waistline for keeping a belt in place. May be made from strips of fabric or from several threads covered to make a heavy chain.

BIAS—Any direction on a fabric that does not exactly follow a lengthwise or crosswise yarn.

Garment bias—Any angle between the lengthwise or crosswise grain and true bias.

True bias—A 45 degree angle between the lengthwise and crosswise grain. It has the greatest stretch and ravels less than any other cut edge.

BIAS BINDING or TAPE—Single or double folded strips of fabric, available in a variety of widths, used to finish a garment edge, make a casing, or add a decorative trim.

BIAS FACING—See FACING.

BIAS STRIP—A narrow strip of fabric cut on the bias and used as a facing or a binding to finish a garment edge.

BINDING—A bias or straight strip of fabric stitched to a garment edge and folded so that it covers the edge and shows on both the right and wrong sides. On a curved edge the strip must have give (cut on true bias on woven fabrics); on a straight edge it may be cut on either straight grain or true bias.

BLANKET STITCH—A decorative hand stitch used to cover fabric edges or to attach fasteners, such as snaps and hooks and eyes.

BLEND—A fabric made from two or more different fibers of different composition, length, diameter, or color spun together into a yarn.

BLIND or SLIP STITCH—A hand stitch that is almost invisible from either the right or wrong side of the garment. The thread is concealed by slipping the needle through a fold in the cloth, through layers of a seam allowance, or under the edge of a garment piece, such as a waistband or hem.

BLISTER—Excess fabric that pushes up in front of the presser foot during sewing.

BODICE—The part of a garment above the waistline. It may or may not be joined to a skirt or pant.

BONDED FABRIC—Two fabric joined together by an adhesive for added body and durability.

BOUND EDGE FINISH—See EDGE FINISH.

BOX PLEAT—See PLEAT.

BUTTONHOLE—A finished slash in a garment used with a button as a fastener on a garment.

Bound or *fabric*—Buttonhole opening finished with a fold of fabric, called a welt, on each side of the slash.

Hand-stitched—Buttonhole edge finished with buttonhole stitches made by hand.

Machine-made—A buttonhole made with zigzag stitches made by a sewing machine attachment or by special settings on a conventional sewing machine.

BUTTONHOLE STITCH—A knotted hand stitch used to make hand-stitched buttonholes. It also may be used to attach fasteners or as a trim.

BUTTONHOLE TWIST—A heavy thread used for making hand-stitched buttonholes and for hand or machine topstitching.

BUTTONHOLE WELTS—Folds of fabric forming the inside edges of the bound or fabric buttonhole.

BUTTON LOOP—Loop of cording or fabric serving as a buttonhole.

BUTTON SHANK—The protruding portion on the underside of a button to hold it up from the fabric. It may be part of the button or made of thread while sewing on the button. Used so that the fabric does not pucker under the button when the garment is buttoned. The length of the shank is related to the thickness of the buttonhole.

CARBON PAPER—*See* DRESSMAKER'S CARBON PAPER.

CASING—A tunnel through which elastic or cording is threaded.

Applied casing—Formed by sewing a separate strip of fabric to either the right or wrong side of the garment area to be drawn up. The fabric strip may be cut from self fabric or from a lightweight knit or woven fabric.

Folded casing—Formed by turning an extension along a garment edge to the inside. The fold of fabric is usually stitched close to the folded edge and again a specified distance from the edge to form the tunnel.

CATCH STITCH—A cross-stitch formed by short backstitches taken alternately along two layers of fabric.

CENTERED or SLOT ZIPPER—*See* ZIPPER.

CENTER FRONT/BACK—The position on a pattern or garment that is the exact center line.

CLEAR PLASTIC RULER—A gridded flexible ruler useful when making pattern alterations and drawing straight lines. Allows pattern markings to show through the ruler during use.

CLIP—A short cut made with the point of the shears into the seam allowance, to but not through the stitching line. Used on concave curved seams, such as a neckline, to allow them to lie flat when turned.

CLOSED CONSTRUCTION—A method of garment assembly whereby as much construction as possible is finished on individual units before combining to form larger units. Also called *unit construction*.

COLLAR—That part of the garment joined to the neckline by a seam.

Convertible—A collar with a convex curved neck edge, usually worn open. The upper collar layer usually provides the finish for the neck edge at center back.

Flat or *partial roll*—A collar with a concave curved neckline, that lies nearly flat at the neckline of the garment. The neckline edge is usually finished with a facing or bias strip.

Full roll—A collar with a straight neck edge, worn either open or closed. The upper collar layer usually provides the finish for the neck edge at center back.

Mandarin—A narrow, stand-up collar fitting closely to the neck.

Neckband—A collar with an attached or separate band that forms the stand of the collar.

Shawl—A collar cut in one with the bodice or garment front.

COLLAR FALL—The portion of the collar that shows on the outside and covers the collar stand.

COLLAR STAND—The portion of the collar that rises above the neck edge at center back. The stand is covered by the fall of the collar.

COLLAR STAY—Plastic strips with one pointed end used to provide support to the front of a collar and to prevent the collar point from curling upward.

COMBINED FACING—*See* FACING.

COMFORT EASE—*See* EASE.

CONCAVE CURVE—An inward curve, such as a neckline curve.

CONTINUOUS LAPPED PLACKET—*See* PLACKET.

CONTINUOUS STITCHING—Sewing a series of seams, especially short ones, in one continuous operation, by placing the second seam under the presser foot without cutting the thread from the first stitching. The beginning and end of each seam would be backstitched to secure the thread ends, if necessary.

CONTINUOUS THREAD DART—The stitching of a dart using the bobbin thread threaded up into the needle and upper portion of the machine; eliminates the necessity of securing the thread ends at the point of the dart using a knot. An appropriate technique for stitching darts in sheer fabric.

CONVENTIONAL SEWING MACHINE—*See* SEWING MACHINE.

CONVERTIBLE COLLAR—*See* COLLAR.

CONVEX CURVE—Outward curve, such as on the outer edge of a round collar or round pocket.

CORDED SEAM—*See* SEAM.

CORDING—A strip of bias-cut fabric, wrong sides folded over a cord and stitched close to the cord, used to make corded seams. Commercial cording can be purchased in a variety of colors.

COURSE—Crosswise row of stitches in knitted fabric. Corresponds to crosswise grain in woven fabric.

CREASE—A sharp edge or line made by folding the fabric and pressing along the fold.

CREWEL NEEDLE—Sewing needle of medium length with a long, oval-shaped eye. Also called *embroidery needle*.

CROSSWISE GRAIN—Yarns running across the fabric, perpendicular to lengthwise grain or to the selvage edges.

CROTCH SEAM—Curved seam formed by joining legs of a garment.

CUFF—A band resembling a turned-back hem, finishing the lower edge of sleeves or pants.

CURVED STICK—*See* HIP CURVE.

CUTTING LINE—The long, unbroken line that forms the perimeter of each pattern piece and indicates the location for cutting.

DART—A fold of fabric stitched at a specified width and tapering to nothing at one or both ends, shaping the fabric to a curved surface.

DART LINE—Markings for the dart; also the stitching line of the dart.

DART PLACKET—*See* PLACKET.

DART TUCK—Released tucks used to control fullness that is released at a desired point. The stitching, which may be on the inside or outside of the garment, covers only a short distance of the dart.

DECORATIVE FACING—*See* FACING.

DECORATIVE TUCK—Tucks stitched on the outside to provide a focal point of the design of the garment.

DESIGN EASE—*See* EASE.

DIRECTIONAL FABRIC—Fabric with an "up" and "down" effect requiring a with nap layout. Includes uneven stripes and plaids, napped fabrics, knits, and prints in which all of the designs are going in one direction.

DIRECTIONAL STITCHING—Stitching "with the grain" of the fabric to prevent distortion of fabric edges. Especially important on curved areas or garment bias seams.

DOUBLE KNIT—Fabric knit with two sets of needles, giving double thickness and more body to the fabric.

DOUBLE-STITCHED SEAM—*See* SEAM.

DRESSMAKER'S CARBON PAPER—A type of tracing paper, available in a variety of colors, designed especially for marking cloth.

EASE, GARMENT—Difference between body measurements and garment measurements at a given point.

Comfort or *wearing*—A minimum amount of ease provided in a pattern to allow for movement.

Design or *style*—Additional ease beyond what is needed for comfort provided by the designer for special fashion effects.

EASE STITCH—A slightly lengthened stitch, 8 to 10 stitches per inch (2.5 cm) or a setting of 3 on the metric dial, used for easing slight fullness at seam lines or at the hem edge.

EASING—Fitting two seam lines of uneven length together without gathers or puckers.

EDGE FINISH—Treatment of raw edges, especially on seams and hems, such as:

Bound—Narrow, straight, or bias tape stitched to encase a raw edge.

Edge stitched—Raw edge machine stitched 1/8 inch (3 mm) or less from the edge.

Hong Kong—A bias piece of fabric used to bind a garment edge using a two-step stitching process.

Machine zigzag—A machine serpentine stitch placed along the very edge of the seam.

Overcast—A hand-applied stitch, carrying the thread over the raw edge as the needle is inserted from the underside.

Pinked—An edge trimmed with pinking or scalloping shears. Also used with edge stitching.

Turned and stitched edge—Raw edge turned under and stitched 1/16 to 1/8 inch (1.5 to 3 mm) from the folded edge. Also called *clean finish.*

EDGE STITCHED—*See* EDGE FINISH.

ENCLOSED SEAM—A seam that is incased between two layers of fabric, such as inside a collar or cuff, and is not seen on the inside of the finished garment.

EVEN PLAID—Plaid with a symmetrical arrangement of lengthwise and crosswise lines; the repeat of color patterns is identical right and left of a center line and up and down.

EXPOSED SEAM—Seams that are visible on the inside of the finished garment and usually require an edge finish on woven fabrics.

EXPOSED ZIPPER—*See* ZIPPER.

EXTENDED FACING—*See* FACING.

EXTENDED SNAP—*See* SNAP.

FABRIC—Cloth; material of which a garment is made.

FABRIC MANIPULATION—Handling of fabric during cutting, sewing, and pressing.

FABRIC MARKING PEN—Pens that come in a variety of colors and are used to transfer pattern markings and to mark topstitching lines and other details for sewing. Some ink is air-erasable and will fade in 48 hours; others will disappear with water. They should not be used on fabric that water spots.

FACED PLACKET—*See* Placket.

FACING—A piece of fabric stitched to a raw edge on a garment for the purpose of finishing it. It is turned to the right or wrong side of the garment and lies flat.

Bias—A narrow strip of true bias stitched to the edge of the garment and turned so that it lies flat. The free edge of the bias strip is usually secured with hand or machine stitching.

Combined—A single garment piece that combines the finish for both the armhole and the neckline edges.

Decorative—A fitted facing turned over to the right side of the garment and lying flat. It may be contrasting in color or texture.

Extended—Facings cut in one with the area to be faced; possible only where the fold line of the facing follows a straight line.

Shaped—A facing cut the same shape of the area of the garment to which it is stitched and usually turned to the wrong side of the garment.

FASTENER—A device, such as a snap, hook and eye, button, zipper, or self-gripping tape, that provides for the opening and closing of a garment.

FIGURE TYPE—A classification of body shapes for men's, women's, and children's patterns based on differences in body proportions.

FILLING YARNS—The crosswise yarns in a fabric. They usually have more stretch than lengthwise yarns.

FITTED FACING—*See* FACING, shaped.

FLAT COLLAR—*See* COLLAR.

FLAT-FELL SEAM—*See* SEAM.

FLATLOCK STITCH—A decorative seam, with stitching visible on the right side of a garment, made on a two- or three-thread overlock machine.

FLEXIBLE RULER—*See* CLEAR PLASTIC RULER.

FLY ZIPPER—*See* ZIPPER.

FOLDED CASING—*See* CASING.

FRAY—Ravel. Yarn ends that work out along a cut edge during handling or wearing.

FRENCH CURVE—A pattern-making tool useful when redrawing curved lines on patterns, such as armholes and necklines.

FRENCH SEAM—*See* SEAM.

FRENCH TACK—A thread chain used to link two separate garment sections, such as a lining to a garment.

FULL ROLL COLLAR—*See* COLLAR.

FUSE BASTE—Using the iron to temporarily hold a fusible interfacing to the wrong side of the garment piece to be interfaced, until permanently fused.

FUSIBLE INTERFACING—A woven, nonwoven, or knitted fabric treated with a heat-sealable adhesive on one side that will adhere to fashion fabric with heat, moisture, and pressure.

FUSIBLE WEB—A sheer weblike bonding material that, when melted between two layers of fabric, will join them together. Used to hold a hem, facing, or trim to a garment with no hand sewing. Not recommended to be used as an interfacing.

GARMENT BIAS—*See* BIAS.

GATHERING STITCH—Two or three parallel rows of slightly lengthened machine stitching, 8 to 10 stitches per inch (2.5 cm) or a 3 setting on a metric dial, or short, even, running hand stitches used to work in fullness at a seam line.

GATHERS—Fabric drawn together by two or three rows of gathering stitches.

GAUGE—Denotes the number of stitches per inch (cm) on knitted fabric; the higher the number, the finer the fabric.

GLUE STICK—A washable glue that can be used on paper, cardboard, and all fabrics. Used to temporarily hold two layers together.

GRADE—*See* LAYER.

GRAIN—The lengthwise and crosswise direction of yarns in a fabric. Also called *grainline.*

GRAINLINE PATTERN MARKING—A heavy arrow on the pattern marking the lengthwise direction.

GRAIN PERFECT—Garment cut and constructed with the grain of the garment pieces corresponding exactly to the grainline on the pattern.

GROSGRAIN RIBBON—A heavy ribbon having crosswise ribs.

GUIDESHEET—*See* PATTERN GUIDE.

GUSSET—A square, diamond, or triangular piece of garment fabric cut on the bias and inserted in a slash at the underarm curve of a kimono sleeve to provide freedom of movement without tearing the garment.

HEM—To turn under a raw edge, such as the lower edge of a skirt, pant, sleeve, or blouse, and to hold in place with hand or machine stitching or with a fusible web.

HEMLINE—The line that indicates where the hem will be turned.

HEM MARKER—An adjustable device used to measure the distance of the hem from the floor.

HEMMING STITCH—Any stitch suitable for sewing a hem to a garment, such as a blind or slip stitch, lockstitch, or machine blind stitch.

HIP CURVE—A metal stick, shaped similar to the body hip curve, used to perfect gradually curved seam lines.

HONG KONG FINISH—See EDGE FINISH.

HOOK AND EYE—A metal fastener with a curved end that hooks over a straight or curved piece.

HOOK-AND-LOOP TAPE—A self-gripping fastener that consists of two tapes, one covered with tiny, finely woven hooks and the other with looped pile. The tapes fasten securely when pressed together and separate by pulling apart.

INSEAM—Inside leg seam of pants and shorts.

IN-SEAM POCKET—See POCKET.

INSET POCKET—See POCKET.

INSET CORNER—A corner created when an "inside" corner is joined to an "outside" corner, such as in a "V" yoke.

INSIDE CURVE—See CONCAVE CURVE.

INTERFACING—Fabric, placed between two layers of fashion fabric, used to give support and body to garment areas, such as buttons and buttonholes, collar, cuffs, and waistband.

INTERLINING—Fabric applied to the inside of a jacket or coat, between the lining and outer garment, to provide warmth.

INTERLOCK KNIT—A firm double-filling knit that looks the same on both sides of the fabric. Interlock knits tend to run, especially those made from filament yarns, and should be cut out so that the runs would go from the lower part of the garment upward, since there is less strain in that part of the garment.

INTERSECTING SEAMS—Seams that cross each other.

INVERTED PLEAT—See PLEAT.

INVISIBLE ZIPPER—See ZIPPER.

IRONING—A sliding motion of the iron used to smooth and dry a stable fabric.

KEYHOLE BUTTONHOLE—A buttonhole with an eyelet-shaped oval on the end of the buttonhole closest to the garment opening; used mainly on tailored garments.

KICK PLEAT—See PLEAT.

KIMONO SLEEVE—Sleeve cut as one piece with the bodice front and bodice back.

KNIFE PLEAT—See PLEAT.

KNITTED FABRIC—Material made from a series of interlocking loops that result in more flexibility or stretch than in most woven fabrics.

LAPPED SEAM—See SEAM.

LAPPED ZIPPER—See ZIPPER.

LAYER—To trim seam allowances to different widths to reduce bulk within the seam allowance. Also called grade, stagger, or bevel.

LAYOUT—Diagram on the pattern guide sheet showing how to place pattern pieces on the fabric.

LENGTHWISE GRAIN—Yarns running up and down the fabric, parallel to the selvage.

LETTUCE LEAF EDGE—A "leafy" edge finish on knitted fabric created by using the narrow rolled hemming stitch on an overlock machine or the satin stitch on a conventional lock stitch machine, stretching the edge while stitching.

LINING—Support fabric cut and assembled like the garment sections to be lined; attached to the garment at the waistline, placket, neckline, and sleeve hem or armholes.

LOCKSTITCH—A type of blanket stitch, used mainly as a hemming stitch, placed between the hem and outer fabric. Stitches are spaced about ½ to ¾ inch (1.3 to 1.9 cm) apart.

LOOPERS—Part of the stitch-forming mechanism on the overlock sewing machine; instead of bobbins, threads go through one or two loopers that interlock with one or more needle threads to form the stitch.

LOOP TURNER—Tool used to turn bias tubing inside out to make bias cording.

L-SQUARE—A measuring tool shaped like an "L"; useful when locating crosswise grainlines and squaring off edges.

MACHINE BLIND STITCH—Straight stitches alternating with a narrow zigzag stitch every 4 to 5 stitches producing an almost invisible hem on the right side of the garment.

MACHINE TENSION—The looseness and/or tightness of the thread in machine stitching.

MANDARIN COLLAR—See COLLAR.

MAN-MADE FIBER—Fiber manufactured from natural or synthetic fiber-forming substances.

MARKING PENCIL—Chalk pencil available in a variety of colors; used in transferring pattern markings.

MATCHING POINTS—Symbols, such as dots, squares, or triangles printed on the pattern pieces, used to ensure accurate joining of garment sections during garment assembly.

MERCERIZED—Treatment of thread by an alkali to make it stronger, more lustrous, and more absorbent.

METRIC SYSTEM—A decimal system of weights and measures: millimeters, centimeters, meters, etc.

MITER—To remove excess fabric from the corner of a seam allowance so that the edges will meet in a diagonal line.

MULTIPLE ZIGZAG STITCHING—A three- or four-step zigzag stitch available on most conventional sewing machines; also called a serpentine stitch. Useful for finishing garment edges on fabrics that tend to curl when stitched with a regular zigzag stitch.

MULTIPURPOSE SEWING MACHINE NEEDLE—A type of sewing machine needle, with a slightly rounded point, designed to be used when sewing either woven and knit fabrics.

MULTI-SIZED PATTERN—A commercial pattern that includes several sizes on one pattern.

NAP—A fuzzy surface on fabrics made by brushing fiber ends out from the yarn after the fabric is woven, as on flannel.

NATURAL FIBERS—Fibers made from raw materials found in nature (cotton, flax, silk, and wool) then woven or knitted into cloth.

NECKBAND COLLAR—See COLLAR.

NEEDLE BOARD—A board covered with fine short wires used for pressing pile fabrics, such as velvet or corduroy.

NONWOVEN FABRIC—Fabric that is formed by matting together fibers through pressure and the use of heat or chemicals. These fabrics have no grain and usually can be cut in any direction. Some nonwoven interfacings may have some stretch in one direction, or they may stretch in all directions and are called "all-bias."

NOTCH—A V-shaped marking on the edge of pattern pieces to indicate matching locations along a seam line. When cutting garments, notches are usually cut out from the cutting edge away from the seam line.

NOTCHING—Cutting V-shaped wedges from a seam allowance on a convex (outside) curve or corner to reduce bulk.

OFF-GRAIN FABRIC—Fabric finished with the crosswise yarns not at right angles to the lengthwise yarns.

OFF-GRAIN PRINTING—Fabric printed with the design not perfectly aligned on the crosswise yarns.

ON-GRAIN FABRIC—Fabric finished with the crosswise yarns at right angles to the lengthwise yarns.

OPEN CONSTRUCTION—A construction procedure that keeps the garment or garment section flat as long as possible.

OPEN-END DART—A dart stitched only partially, leaving the pointed end open.

OUTSEAM—The outside leg seam on pants or shorts.

OUTSIDE CURVE—See CONVEX CURVE.

OVERCAST STITCH—See EDGE FINISH.

OVERLOCK SEWING MACHINE—A sewing machine that sews a seam, cuts off the excess fabric, and overcasts the raw edges in one operation. Overlock machines are classified according to the number of threads used to make the stitch, varying from two to five threads. Instead of a bobbin, the overlock machines have one or two loopers that interlock with one or more needle threads to form the stitch.

OVERLOCK STITCH—The stitch formed by threads that go through one or two loopers, which interlock with one or more needle threads.

PARTIAL ROLL COLLAR—See COLLAR.

PATCH POCKET—See POCKET.

PATTERN—Usually one-half of a garment printed on lightweight paper to be used as a guide for cutting the garment from fabric.

PATTERN GUIDE—A sheet of directions enclosed with the pattern for cutting and constructing a garment.

PATTERN LAYOUT—See LAYOUT.

PATTERN MARKINGS—Symbols printed on commercial patterns used to identify pattern markings, such as darts, seam lines, grainlines, etc.; used at every stage of construction: pattern alteration, layout, cutting, marking, joining sections, and fitting.

PERMANENT PRESS FABRIC—A finish applied to fabric that aids in shedding wrinkles from normal wear; requires little or no ironing after washing and drying according to care instructions.

PICK STITCH—A small, durable hand stitch used in place of machine stitching for inserting zippers. Also called *half backstitch* or *prick stitch.*

PILE—Ends of yarns extending above the surface of the fabric, such as in corduroy, velvet, and velveteen. Pile fabrics always have an "up" and "down" and must be cut using a with-nap layout.

PINKED—See EDGE FINISH.

PINKING SHEARS—Shears with serrated blades used for cutting zigzag edges on fabric. Should not be used to cut out a pattern.

PIN TUCK—Very narrow folds of fabric stitched close to the fold; forms tucks that may be decorative, functional, or both.

PIVOT—To turn a corner by leaving the needle in the fabric at the exact corner, lifting the presser foot, turning the fabric being stitched in another direction, then lowering the presser foot and continuing the stitching.

PLACE ON FOLD—A bracketed grainline marking located on the edge of pattern pieces that must be placed even with the folded fabric edge during layout.

PLACKET—A finished opening in a garment, made for convenience in putting on the garment.

Continuous Lapped—A placket finished with one continuous strip of fabric that folds back under one edge and extends along the other edge of the placket.

Dart—A slashed placket opening with the upper end stitched as a dart.

Faced—A slashed placket opening with the slashed edges finished with a facing that is turned to the inside of the garment.

Pleated—An opening that forms a pleat when the finished placket is in position.

Tailored—A placket found on tailored shirts and jackets. The fabric forming the placket is turned to the outside and provides a decorative feature to the garment.

Zipper—Placket closed with a zipper or slide fastener.

PLAID—A fabric with a woven or printed pattern with lengthwise and crosswise bars or stripes forming a geometric pattern. See EVEN and UNEVEN PLAID.

PLAIN SEAM—See SEAM.

PLEAT—A fold of fabric over fabric, usually of equal width from top to bottom. It provides controlled fullness in the garment.

Box—Two identical mirror folds that meet on the inside of the garment.

Inverted—Two identical mirror folds that come together on the right side of the garment. Also called *inverted box pleat.*

Kick—One fold pressed against the fabric and secured at the top. May be a single pleat or a series of pleats. Also called *knife pleat.*

Knife—Narrow folds of fabric turned in one direction.

PLEATED PLACKET—See PLACKET.

POCKET—One or two layers of fabric cut in the desired shape and applied to the right side of a garment or set into a garment opening or seam forming an enclosed bag.

In-seam—Two pocket sections set into an opening in a seam.

Inset—A pocket set into a garment with one or two edges stitched in a seam.

Patch—A single layer of fabric applied to the right side of the garment, hemmed and secured to the garment with a finish suitable to the fabric. Pocket may be lined or unlined.

Welt—Inserted pocket with edges finished as for a bound buttonhole.

POINT PRESSER—A pressing board, ¾ to 1½ inches (1.9 to 3.8 cm) wide and pointed at one end, on which enclosed seams, such as collar seams and points, may be pressed open before turning the garment section to the right side.

PRESHRINK—See SHRINK.

PRESSER FOOT—The attached part of a sewing machine that holds fabric firmly on the feed dogs at the point it is being stitched.

PRESSING—Up and down motion of the iron, with or without moisture, to open up seams, attach fusible interfacing, and to smooth fabrics during garment assembly.

PRESSING CLOTH—A piece of fabric that is placed over the garment section when pressing; usually produces a sharper, smoother press if dampened.

PRESSING CUSHION—A shaped pad, such as tailor's ham or pressing mitt, used to press darts and curved seams to retain the curved surface in the garment.

PRESSURE—The force the presser foot exerts on the fabric during machine stitching; can be regulated on some machines to suit the weight of the fabric being stitched.

PUCKER—To draw up into folds or wrinkles; usually undesirable.

PURL OR TWIST—The knot formed when making the buttonhole stitch.

RAGLAN SLEEVE—Sleeve cut separately from the bodice with a diagonal seam extending from the neckline to the underarm; often shaped to fit the shoulder by a large curved dart extending from the neck to the end of the shoulder.

RAVELING—Yarns pulling away from the fabric along a cut edge.

RECOVERY—Ability of a knit fabric to return to its original shape after being stretched.

REINFORCE—To strengthen an area that will be subject to strain with an extra layer or patch of fabric or with a row of machine stitching.

REINFORCEMENT STITCHING—Short machine stitches, placed close to or on the stitching line, reinforcing corners or points that will be clipped into or closely trimmed.

RESIDUAL SHRINKAGE—The amount of shrinkage remaining in a finished fabric.

RESIN-TREATED FABRICS—Fabrics treated with chemical substances to produce special finishes, such as crease resistance, soil release, or shrinkage control.

RIBBING—A stretchy knit fabric used to finish garment edges. May be cut from self-fabric, if it has appropriate stretch and recovery, or purchased as yardage.

ROTARY CUTTING WHEEL—A circular device used with a cutting mat to cut suede, leather, and multiple layers of fabric.

SAFETY STITCH—A chain stitch, located a specified distance from the cut edge on a serged seam, used with a two- or three-overlock stitch to form a durable seam resembling that found in ready-to-wear.

SCALLOPING SHEARS—Shears that work much like pinking shears; produce rounded edges rather than zigzag edges.

SCISSORS—A cutting tool with blades under 6 inches (15 cm) in length and with identical handles. They are smaller than shears.

SEAM—The stitching that joins two or more edges of fabric to form a garment.

Corded—A seam with a cording placed between the two layers of fabric. The final stitching is positioned close to the cording so none of the stitching forming the cording is visible from the right side.

Double-stitched—A second row of stitching in the seam allowance close to the seam line to give strength to seams under strain, such as armholes or crotch seams. Seams are often trimmed close to the second row of stitching.

Flat-fell—Seam allowances trimmed, turned, and stitched flat to the garment with no raw edges showing and with two rows of stitching on one side and one row of stitching on the other.

French—A narrow, self-enclosed seam in which all seam allowances are contained within the finished seam; a seam within a seam. Appropriate for visible seams on sheer or lightweight fabrics.

Lapped—One edge turned under and lapped to the seam line of the other edge, with stitching close to the folded edge.

Plain—Two layers of fabric placed right sides together and held in place with one row of stitching positioned on the seam line. The seam allowance on exposed seams is usually pressed open.

Welt—A plain seam with both seam allowances turned to one side and held in place with a row of topstitching.

SEAM ALLOWANCE—The space between the cut edge of the pattern or fabric and the stitching line. Most seam allowances are ⅝ inch (1.5 cm) wide, unless designated differently on the pattern piece.

SEAM BINDING—A narrow, selvage-edged ribbon used to finish the raw edge of hems, seams, or to reinforce seams on knits.

SEAM EDGE—The cut edge of a seam.

SEAM FINISH—See EDGE FINISH.

SEAM GAUGE—A 4- or 6-inch (10 or 15 cm) metal or plastic ruler with an adjustable tab that may be set at a desired point and used to mark accurately the width of buttonholes, hems, etc.

SEAM GUIDE—A machine attachment that may be adjusted to guide stitching for seams of various widths.

SEAM LINE—Long, broken lines, usually placed parallel to the cutting line, designating the stitching lines.

SEAM RIPPER—A small tool with a sharp point and cutting blade; used to slip under threads to aid in taking out unwanted stitches.

SEAM ROLL—A hard roll used in pressing open seams.

SEAM SEALANT—A colorless liquid that can be applied to seam edges or thread ends to prevent further raveling.

SELF-GRIPPING TAPE—See HOOK-AND-LOOP TAPE.

SELVAGE—The finished lengthwise edge of woven fabric running parallel to warp or lengthwise yarns. Knits and felt fabrics do not have a selvage.

SERGER—See OVERLOCK SEWING MACHINE.

SET-IN SLEEVE—A sleeve cut as a separate piece from the bodice and stitched into the armhole of the garment. A regular set-in sleeve with a high sleeve cap is usually set in using the closed-seam method of construction. *See also* SHIRT-STYLE SLEEVE.

SHARPS—Sewing needles of medium length with small eyes.

SHAWL COLLAR—See COLLAR.

SHEARS—A cutting tool with a long cutting blade and one handle larger than the other. Larger than scissors.

SHIRT-STYLE SLEEVE—A set-in sleeve with a low curve to the sleeve cap, usually installed by the open-seam method of construction.

SHOULDER PADS—Triangular-shaped pads, usually made of several layers of polyester fill and curved to fit the shape of the shoulder, used to build up the shoulder area of a garment.

SHRINK—To relax or contract fabric so that the size of a garment will not be altered appreciably after washing or dry cleaning. Also called *preshrinking*.

SILK PINS—Fine, medium-length, rustproof pins with sharp, tapering points.

SILKY WOVEN FABRIC—Lightweight fabric with a soft, smooth hand; difficult to handle because of its smooth, slippery surface.

SINGLE KNIT—Fabrics knit with one needle. They are usually lightweight and have a definite right and wrong side.

SIZING—A substance added to fabric to improve its appearance and add body to the fabric. It may be temporary or permanent.

SLASH—To cut, as through the center fold of a dart.

SLEEVE—See KIMONO, RAGLAN, SET-IN, SHIRT-STYLE SLEEVE.

SLEEVE BOARD—A small, padded ironing board, shaped like a full-sized board, used to press seams, especially those inside sleeves or pant legs.

SLEEVE CAP—The upper curved portion of a set-in or shirt-style sleeve.

SLEEVE CAP SEAM LINE—The curved seam line following the upper edge of the sleeve cap.

SLEEVE PLACKET—See PLACKET.

SLEEVE ROLL—See SEAM ROLL.

SLIP BASTING—Basting together two layers of fabric by stitching back and forth between the two layers.

SLIP STITCH—See BLIND STITCH.

SLOT ZIPPER—See ZIPPER.

SNAP—A metal fastener consisting of two parts, one with a depression and the other with a ballpoint prong. It is used to hold two sections of a garment together.

Extended snap—A snap with one part attached along the edge of the garment through one or two holes with most of the snap extending out away from the garment, and the second half set back on the other side of the garment so that, when closed, none of the fastener is visible. It is often used in place of a hook and eye when edges meet or slightly overlap.

STABILIZED FABRIC—A specially constructed knit fabric or a woven fabric treated with a finish to add durability and to prevent shrinkage, stretch, and wrinkling.

STAY—A small piece of fabric that is attached, either by fusing or by sewing, to an area of the garment for reinforcement; often used at the point of a slash.

STAY BUTTON—A small button used on the facing or underside of a garment directly under the top button to prevent the fabric from tearing or pulling out in the button area. The top button and stay button are sewn on at the same time, with the garment fabric between the buttons.

STAYSTITCHING—Stitching through a single thickness of fabric in the seam allowance 1/16 to 1/8 inch (1.5 to 3 mm) from the seam line to prevent the stretching of garment bias edges. It holds the grain in its correct position during construction of the garment.

STAY TAPE—Narrow, straight-grain tape or ribbon, or a length of selvage from lightweight, firmly woven fabric, used along a seam line to prevent stretching.

STITCH FINGER—See STITCH FORMER.

STITCH FORMER—An extended prong, located on either the throat plate or presser foot of an overlock machine, around which the overlock stitch is formed; also called the *stitch finger*. The width of the stitch former determines the width of the stitch.

STITCH-IN-THE-DITCH—A type of inconspicuous topstitching done in the crevice of a previously stitched seam. It is used for tacking facings in place, attaching waistbands, etc.

STRAIGHT GRAIN—The grainline marking on the pattern piece, usually indicating lengthwise grain.

STYLE—The distinctive lines and characteristics of a garment design, such as in an A-line skirt.

STYLE EASE—See EASE.

SUPPORT FABRIC—Fabric used to give body, add strength to garment areas under strain, or to prevent stretch of the garment during normal wear. This includes interfacings, linings, and underlinings.

SURFACE TEXTURE—Characteristics of the fabric surface, such as smooth, soft, nubby, etc.

SYNTHETIC FIBER—See MAN-MADE FIBER.

TACK—To attach one section of a garment to another with a few small hand stitches taken in one place.

TAILORED PLACKET—See PLACKET.

TAILOR'S CHALK—Special chalk used for marking fabric.

TAILOR'S HAM—See PRESSING CUSHION.

TAILOR'S KNOT—A knot made by forming a loop with two threads and inserting the thread ends through the loop and pulling taut, with the knot lying next to the fabric.

TAILOR'S TACKS—A loop of thread made by taking two small stitches at a single location on a garment, leaving a 1 inch (2.5 cm) loop; used to transfer construction markings from the pattern pieces to the garment pieces.

TAPE MEASURE—A narrow flexible measuring device with measurements on both sides used for taking body measurements.

TAPER—To decrease width or thickness gradually, usually narrowing toward a point.

TENSION—See MACHINE TENSION.

TERMINATION POINT—End of a construction line.

THIMBLE—A form of cap or cover used to protect the middle finger when pushing the needle while hand sewing.

THREAD EYE—A type of eye fastener made of thread; used with a hook fastener in place of a metal eye.

THREAD SHANK—See BUTTON SHANK.

THROAT PLATE—A flat metal plate with a hole through which the needle passes as it stitches; located under the presser foot on a sewing machine. Throat plates usually have guidelines etched on them to aid in sewing a straight seam.

TOP FEED FOOT—A special attachment for the conventional sewing machine that grasps the top layer of fabric to assist in the even feeding of fabric under the presser foot.

TOPSTITCHING—To stitch on the top an even distance from a seam, garment edge, or fold; often done with a lengthened machine stitch and heavier thread. Stitching shows on the right side of the garment.

TOPSTITCHING THREAD—Heavier thread used to provide more decorative topstitching; may be applied by hand or by machine stitching.

TRACING PAPER—See DRESSMAKER'S CARBON PAPER.

TRACING WHEEL—A serrated or smooth circular wheel used with or without dressmaker's carbon paper to transfer pattern markings to the fashion fabric.

TRIM—To cut off ragged edges or part of a seam allowance to reduce bulk.

TROUSER HOOK AND EYE—Large, extra sturdy hooks and eyes suitable for securing ends of waistbands.

TRUE BIAS—See BIAS.

TUBULAR KNIT—Knit fabrics constructed on a circular knitting machine resulting in a tubular fabric with no cut edges. Tubular knits are often cut open along a lengthwise wale in order to open up flat before laying out the pattern.

TUCK—A stitched fold in the fabric. Also, a fold in the pattern used to decrease the size.

TURN AND EDGE STITCH—See EDGE FINISH.

TWILL TAPE—A strong woven tape in a twill weave often used to reinforce seams, especially in garments made of knit fabrics.

UNDERARM STAY—Bias strip of firmly woven, lightweight fabric stitched to underarm curve of kimono sleeve to prevent the garment from tearing.

UNDER COLLAR—The garment pieces forming the underside or facing side of the collar.

UNDERLINING—Lining fabric cut exactly like the garment or garment section and stitched to the outer edges of the garment pieces before construction begins.

UNDERSTITCHING—To stitch both seam allowances to the under section, such as the under collar or the garment facing, to keep the seam edge from showing on the right side of the garment.

UNEVEN PLAID—Plaids without a symmetrical arrangement of lines. The design may differ in the number, size, or color of lengthwise or crosswise lines.

UNIT CONSTRUCTION—See CLOSED CONSTRUCTION.

UNLIKE CURVE—A curved seam, such as a curved yoke seam, formed by joining two unlike curves: a concave curve and a convex curve. Before joining the unlike curves, the concave curve must be staystitched and clipped in order to fit the shape of the convex curve.

VENT—A lapped opening or finished slit often located in the hem of a straight skirt, jacket, or tailored sleeve.

WAISTBAND—A band encircling the waistline at the top of a skirt or pant.

WAISTBAND HOOK AND EYE—See TROUSER HOOK AND EYE.

WAISTLINE—The smallest part of the body between the shoulders and hip; located by bending sideways.

WALE—The loops (ribs) running lengthwise in knitted fabric; corresponds to lengthwise grain in woven fabric.

WARP—Lengthwise yarns in woven fabric, usually stronger, with less stretch than crosswise yarns.

WASHABLE FABRIC MARKING PEN—See FABRIC MARKING PEN.

WEARING EASE—See EASE.

WEDGE-POINT NEEDLE—A sewing machine needle with a wedge-shaped point designed for use on leather and vinyl; not to be used on ultrasuede. The needle easily pierces these fabrics to make a hole that closes back upon itself.

WEFT INSERTION—Interfacing constructed with yarns laid in the crosswise direction of a warp knit.

WEIGHTS—Several heavy objects placed strategically around a pattern to hold it in place for cutting.

WELT POCKET—See POCKET.

WELT SEAM—See SEAM.

WHIPSTITCH—Stitching over the edge of a fold with stitches made very small and close together.

"WINDOW OPENING"—A faced rectangular opening made in the facing behind a bound buttonhole or in the garment front in preparation of a "window opening" bound buttonhole.

WITH NAP—Indicates fabric that must be cut with the top of all pattern pieces placed in the same direction due to differences in light reflection; this includes napped fabrics, pile fabrics, and one-way designs (uneven plaid or stripe, knits, or directional prints).

WITHOUT NAP—Term used in pattern layout where the top of all pattern pieces may be placed in either direction on fabrics that do not have a nap or a one-way design.

WITH THE GRAIN—To sew or press along garment bias edges in the direction that reduces the amount of raveling or stretching of that edge. This means working from the wider to the narrower part of the garment section, such as from the hem to the waistline in a skirt, or from the higher to the lower section, such as from the neck to the armhole along a shoulder seam.

WOVEN FABRIC—Term used for fabric produced on a loom by interlacing warp and filling yarns.

YOKE—A shaped part of a bodice, blouse, shirt, or skirt, usually the upper part.

ZIGZAG STITCHING—A stitching pattern on the conventional sewing machine that forms a zigzag pattern, with all stitches having the same width. The stitch width and length can be adjusted to be compatible with the weight of the fabric as well as the effect desired.

ZIPPER—A fastener made with metal teeth or synthetic coils that mesh together when the tab is pulled.

Centered or *slot*—A zipper application, using a conventional zipper, where there are two parallel rows of stitching equal distance from the center of the placket opening; a symmetrical application appropriate where a balanced closure is desired on the center front or center back of a garment. This technique may not conceal the zipper as well as the lapped or fly zipper application methods.

Exposed—A zipper application technique where the two edges of the zipper opening come just to the coils or teeth of the zipper, leaving the zipper exposed. This technique is most suited in garments where there is no seam at the location where the zipper is inserted or when using a separating zipper in the center front.

Fly—A type of lapped zipper application, using a conventional zipper, with the lap usually 1 to 1½ inches (2.5 to 3.8 cm) in width. This technique is appropriate for center front openings on skirts, pants, or shorts.

Invisible—A type of zipper that is detected only by a pull tab at the top of the zipper; no other stitching is visible from the outside of the garment when the zipper is properly inserted. Requires the use of a special type of zipper and zipper foot. This technique can be substituted for lapped or centered zippers.

Lapped—A type of zipper application where one side of the zipper opening forms a lap that covers the zipper and the machine stitching on the underlap side; only one row of machine stitching, located about ½ inch (1.3 cm) from the seam, is visible on the completed zipper.

ZIPPER FOOT—An attachment for the conventional sewing machine used in place of the presser foot to facilitate stitching close to raised edges, such as zippers and cording.

ZIPPER PLACKET—See PLACKET.

INDEX